On the Date,
Sources and Design
of Shakespeare's *The Tempest*

On the Date, Sources and Design of Shakespeare's *The Tempest*

ROGER A. STRITMATTER *and*
LYNNE KOSITSKY

Foreword by WILLIAM S. NIEDERKORN

McFarland & Company, Inc., Publishers
Jefferson, North Carolina, and London

LIBRARY OF CONGRESS CATALOGUING-IN-PUBLICATION DATA

Stritmatter, Roger A., 1958– author.
    On the date, sources and design of Shakespeare's The tempest /
Roger A. Stritmatter and Lynne Kositsky ; foreword by William S.
Niederkorn.
       p.   cm.
    Includes bibliographical references and index.

    ISBN 978-0-7864-7104-1
    softcover : acid free paper ∞

    1. Shakespeare, William, 1564–1616 Tempest—Sources.
I. Kositsky, Lynne, 1947– author. II. Title.
PR2833.S76 2013
822.3'3—dc23   2013019264

BRITISH LIBRARY CATALOGUING DATA ARE AVAILABLE

Front cover: Alonso, King of Naples, shipwrecked with his court
(Photos.com/Thinkstock); border (iStockphoto/Thinkstock)

Manufactured in the United States of America

McFarland & Company, Inc., Publishers
  Box 611, Jefferson, North Carolina 28640
   www.mcfarlandpub.com

In memory of
K.C. Ligon and R. Thomas Hunter

It is really quite amazing by what margins competent but conservative scientists and engineers can miss the mark, when they start with the preconceived idea that what they are investigating is impossible. When this happens, the most well informed men become blinded by their prejudice and are unable to see what lies directly ahead of them.

—Arthur C. Clarke,
Profiles from the Future, 1963

Table of Contents

Acknowledgments

Many have contributed substantially toward the development of this work. David Lindley's 2002 Cambridge *Tempest* edition was among the first studies to confirm our suspicion of how paper-thin the Strachey argument is. Two distinguished Shakespeare colleagues, Andrew Gurr, editor of the forthcoming Variorum edition of *The Tempest*, and the late Douglas Brooks, editor of *The Shakespeare Yearbook*, had the independent vision to read and encourage our work. Penny McCarthy's impressive 2005 *Shakespeare Yearbook* article, "Some Quises and a Quem," further emboldened us to "think outside the box" about the topic of *Tempest* chronology.

During the earliest phases of our research, the late Peter Moore offered invaluable suggestions, especially with reference to the history of storm description conventions in early-modern travel narratives. Richard Malim's argument identifying *The Tempest* with "The Tragedy of the Spanish Maze," a play performed at Shrovetide in 1605, excited our curiosity and eventually provoked the two chapters of the book devoted to illustrating the play's numerous and compelling Shrovetide connections. Without the suggestion of Hank Whittemore we would never have discovered the importance of *Orlando Furioso* as a *Tempest* source and influence. Tom Veal and Terry Ross also kindly read and gave useful criticism on early drafts of some of the chapters.

Professor Bill Leahy did much to support the development of a more rational discourse of Shakespearean studies by supporting the publication of our 2009 *Critical Studies* article, "Brave New World: *The Tempest* and *De Orbe Novo*." Daniel Wright, Director of Concordia University's Shakespeare Authorship Studies Centre, not only gave us a venue for presenting our work but sponsored a highly educational 2006 debate between Lynne Kositsky and Professor Bill Rubinstein, and recognized our work with a 2012 Conference award. One chapter of the book was completed with the generous support of the Coppin State University Faculty Research and Development Committee, to whom we owe a debt of gratitude. We also received valuable feedback from Folger library scholars, and from William Sherman, editor (with Peter Hulme) of *The Tempest and Its Travels* (2000), a book which anticipated our conviction of the importance of Mediterranean geography in *The Tempest*. David Wilson-Okamura gave generously of his time and expertise in helping us to devise a strategy for finding images of Brant's illustrations of Virgil. Tom Reedy worked with Lynne to survey storm episodes in early modern and ancient travel narratives and also to conduct word scarches of *Purchas His Pilgrimes* and Hackluyt's *Principal Navigations* that became the foundation of one of the arguments in Chapter 12. Thanks are especially due to Oxford University Press's *Review of English Studies, Critical Survey, The Shakespeare Yearbook, The Oxfordian,* and *Brief Chronicles,* for permission to reprint materials previously published in serial form. Marty Hyatt supplied logistical support in locating hard to find materials. Linda Theil and Mark Anderson both went out of their way to spread the news of our research on the internet as it developed. Ted Alexander was always ready, sometimes on very short notice, with invaluable technical assistance, and Earl Showerman, aka the "Earl of Ashland," was a constant source of encouragement and good cheer. Without Richard Whalen's skilled networking we would never have gained the invaluable opportunity to exchange ideas with Andrew Gurr.

Margaret Hart generously agreed to represent our book as an agent. Although much of this research was conducted independently, we are appreciative of the assistance of reference librarians at the University of Toronto, Coppin State University, The University of Maryland at College Park, and the Johns Hopkins Sheridan Library, and the online Kraus Collection of Sir Francis Drake at Library of Congress, as well as the various libraries credited elsewhere for their assistance in procuring images.

We must especially thank Alex McNeil, editor of *Shakespeare Matters,* and Charis Wahl for their painstaking and invaluable editorial assistance. Last but not least, Adam and Michael Kositsky endured many challenging discussions and long readings of the manuscript as well as supplying logistical support with infinite patience. To these and all the others who have encouraged us along the path, *gratias tibi.*

Foreword

by William S. Niederkorn

In the field of Shakespeare studies, there are two factors that impede progress. One is credulous allegiance to eroded scholarship. The other is quasi-religious fervor for biographical dogma. These two tendentious impulses have had unfortunate consequences for academic discourse. They are, obviously, the underlying reasons why Roger Stritmatter and Lynne Kositsky, whose initial groundbreaking and illusion-shattering work on the dating and the nature of *The Tempest* was published in the top-tier Oxford journal *The Review of English Studies,* were denied the right to respond to attacks that followed in other academic journals, and why in the same injurious spirit their acceptances as speakers at two major academic conferences were rescinded.

In bringing out this book, these two accomplished scholars deserve appreciation for their fortitude in advancing their inquiries, resisting ingrained suppression, and making their well-reasoned and painstakingly fair responses to the virulent attacks on their work available so that open-minded readers can judge the matters in question for themselves.

The Tempest is far from the longest or the strongest play in the Shakespeare canon, but it has outsize pride of place in the hearts of many Shakespeare scholars. The first play in the first folio, in the three folios that followed, and in many subsequent Shakespeare collections, *The Tempest* also seems to be first in stimulating scholarly imaginations. Take for instance the distinguished professor, man of letters, and Shakespeare editor Arthur Quiller-Couch, popularly known as Q, whose excellent editions of the works of Shakespeare for Cambridge University Press, co-edited with John Dover Wilson, are among the most elegant and erudite ever produced.

In his maturity, after he was awarded the King Edward VII chair at the University of Cambridge but before he started work on the Cambridge series,

Q collected some of his lectures in a little volume titled *Shakespeare's Work-manship*. The book culminates in a triptych on *The Tempest* originally delivered at Cambridge in 1915, in the midst of World War I, and later judged by Q's biographer, Frederick Brittain, as "among the best lectures he ever gave."[1]

In a prelude, Q evokes the national-religion aspect of Shakespeare in the wartime context:

> Here in Cambridge, in a second Michaelmas Term of War, it may seem an idle-ness to be talking about poetry. But I say to you that it is not. I say that an En-glishman who, not having shirked any immediate services within his power, in these days improves and exalts himself by studying such a work of art as *The Tempest*, lets ride his soul, as good ships should, upon a double anchor. There is the lesser anchor of pride, that, happen what may, here is something our enemy can as little take from us as he can imitate it: that the best part of revenge is to be different from our enemy and hopelessly beyond his copying, whatever he may destroy. But there is also the better anchor of confidence, that in a world where men just now seem chiefly to value science for its power to slay, we hold to something as strong as it is benign, and careless of death, because immortal.[2]

The Tempest, emblematic for all of Shakespeare, thus becomes a refuge and source of strength, a talisman of culture, the sacrament of Extreme Unc-tion. Here we see the Shakespeare professor taking on a quasi-religious role, functioning like a priest or minister, preaching the word of Shakespeare to bring his listeners grace and spiritual solace and assuage the troubles of life. Q's first concern with *The Tempest* is its date of composition. Nurturing the faith of his Shakespeare flock, he writes, "I think most of us would like to believe *The Tempest* his last work and to cherish the fancy (originated, I believe, by a poet, Campbell) that when Prospero puts off his mantle, breaks his staff, and drowns his great book 'deeper than did ever plummet sound,' it is Shake-speare himself who in the ritual bids a long farewell to his realm of magic."[3]

Indeed, among the most hallowed legends in Shakespeare lore, and fodder for professorial quizzes, is the identification of Shakespeare with Prospero, whose promise to renounce magic in the play's final scene has long been viewed as representing the playwright's adieu to his art. Q doesn't insist that his students believe the fable, but he invites them to think it possible, and since it is one of the few striking connections to the real world in all of Shake-speare, he can rest assured that it will remain permanently instilled in their minds.

In discussing a performance of *The Tempest* given around the time of the marriage of Elizabeth of Bohemia, daughter of James I, Q is further revealing of his inclinations. Edmond Malone, whose work is primary in modern Shake-speare scholarship, also cited the record of that *Tempest* performance, which took place early in 1613, and editions of Shakespeare works today continue to cite it as well. Q entertains the "fascinating hypothesis ... that this authentic record of *The Tempest*, a court-play acted to adorn the nuptials of Elizabeth of Bohemia, refers in fact to its first performance; that *The Tempest* was written expressly for her bridal."[4]

Shakespearean proclivities, like their religious counterparts, often spring from wishful longing, and Q makes that motivation quite clear. He continues: "I wish I could believe it true. I would give much to be able to believe it true. For a long while I firmly held it to be true.... For who, knowing the story of Elizabeth of Bohemia, would not be fain to think of her and *The Tempest* together? There are a certain few women in history who in life fascinated the souls out of men, for good or evil, and still fascinate the imagination of mankind, though themselves have been dust for centuries."[5] Elizabeth of Bohemia was "wayward, lovely, extravagant, unfortunate, adorable and peerless."[6]

What Q never mentions, in any of his *Tempest* writing — perhaps he didn't need to because every Cambridge lad already knew it, or perhaps it was because of some sensibility more profound — is that due to various quirks of fate, it was through Elizabeth of Bohemia that the Hanoverian kings of England descended. What could be more satisfying to the Edward VII Professor of Cambridge than promoting the idea that the Bard wrote his last play, or at least put it in final form, for the wedding of the Stuart princess who was to generate the monarchical dynasty that reigned over Britain then, reigns today, in all likelihood will reign *in saecula saeculorum*?

"I say it were pleasant to imagine *The Tempest*," Q told the Cambridge students, "written for the bridals of this wonderful woman; to read this immortal play and think of Shakespeare breaking his staff before one who — if the sceptered race and the charm divine guaranteed aught — guaranteed all for the next generation, in whose hope good men live."[7] With *The Tempest* plumbing such depths of the English-speaking world's psyche, it can be surmised why so many knights-errant of scholarship rise up to man the barricades and defend against any perceived incursions into their illusions.

* * *

The space that Shakespeare occupies in the English cultural realm is vast, and no structure in that space is loftier, more ornate, or better fortified than that of academic scholarship. The foundation of this edifice was laid by Edmond Malone, its cornerstone being his first venture into Shakespearean research, *An Attempt to Ascertain the Order in Which the Plays Attributed to Shakspeare Were Written*.

In its first form, this seminal tract was printed following 268 pages of prefatory matter to the second Johnson-Steevens edition of the Shakespeare plays, published in 1778 — matter such as prefaces to earlier editions, Nicholas Rowe's biographical pamphlet, lists of editions of the ancient classics published in Shakespeare's era, lists of quartos, folios, 17th century Shakespeare adaptations, 18th century Shakespeare editions, all of the folio dedicatory letters and poems, etc., all of which taken together seem to back Malone's claim that his "toil of wading through *all such reading as was never read,* has been chearfully endured"[8] (italics original).

The dating of *The Tempest* as a very late Shakespeare play would remain the fulcrum of Malone's chronology throughout his career, reiterated in quite minor adjustments in the list in 1790 and 1821.[9] Regardless of how and why Malone dated it as he did, it became a citadel for the future of Shakespeare scholarship, because in a field where, Malone admitted, "after the most diligent enquiries, very few particulars have been recovered, respecting his private life, or literary history,"[10] the devotees of Shakespeare have only the inherited wisdom of their scholarly forebears to cherish.

While Malone's chronology remains mostly intact to this day in authoritative Shakespeare editions and criticism, Q in his general introduction to the Cambridge edition of *The Tempest*, mythologizes the chronology a bit, perhaps trying to give it a broader base:

> Out of the cumulative labour of nineteenth century students too innumerable to tell — all devoted, all persistent, the most of them with scarcely a critical gift beyond patience and arithmetic ... — arose, among them, as an atoll grows out of the Ocean, by infinite verse countings and other tests, that century's great discovery — of the chronological order in which Shakespeare wrote his plays. Now the one priceless and irrefragable boon of this discovery is the steady light it throws upon Shakespeare's development as an artist: with its pauses, breaks, trybacks, hesitations, advances, explain them how we may.[11]

But didn't the whole thing work the other way around? Q has inverted the order of causation. The fundamental assumption of Malone that has remained axiomatic for Shakespeare scholars is based on his idea of how Shakespeare developed, getting better through the comedies, and better yet through the tragedies, until he just couldn't get any better, and then easing his way out with some late romantic fluff and finally putting the cherry on top with *The Tempest*.

The authorized chronology proceeds from this imaginative view of Shakespeare's life. "By keeping — as with fair ease we can — a mental list of the plays in their right chronological order — we can trace the Poet as he attains mastery through operation," Q says.[12] Or as he proclaims in an encomiastic outburst: "Only one man has progressed from *Love's Labour's Lost*, on to *As You Like It*, to *Twelfth Night*; only one has proceeded from these comedies to *Hamlet, Othello, Lear, Antony and Cleopatra*; only one has filled up the intervals with *Henry IV*, Parts i and ii, with *Julius Caesar*, with *Coriolanus*; only one, in years of physical weakness, has imagined for us an Imogen; only one has closed upon the woven magic of *The Tempest*."[13]

Why would anyone assume that Shakespeare developed like that? Sometimes a major author's first work is a big one. If we didn't know the chronology of Dickens, it's easy to imagine a Malone making the novelist take his final bow with *The Posthumous Papers of the Pickwick Club*. ("Posthumous" would be the clincher.)

Take away the inane idea of Prospero's exit as a reflection of Shakespeare's, and *The Tempest* is a young man's play. As Q noted in 1915, Act III Scene i is "the most beautiful love-scene in Shakespeare: who, by the way (after *Romeo and Juliet*), was instinctively chary of love-scenes save when he could handle them with raillery."[14]

It is not a novel idea that *The Tempest* was an early Shakespeare play. The historian Joseph Hunter wrote in his 1845 work *New Illustrations of the Life, Studies, and Writings of Shakespeare*: "So far from being the work of a late period of the poet's life, it appears to me to be an early work, the growth of what we may call the youth of his dramatic life; and, indeed, that, of all the plays which are wholly his, it is nearly the first in point of time, and it is indisputably among the first in order of merit."[15]

Even Q at one point in his lectures admits, "Granted that *The Tempest* is the better, more accomplished, work of art, it does not follow that it came later in time."[16]

* * *

Toward the end of his life, Malone published a curious pamphlet titled *An Account of the Incidents, from Which the Title and Part of the Story of Shakespeare's* Tempest *Were Derived; and Its True Date Ascertained*. Here Malone again reviewed the reports on the 1609 storm and the voyagers caught in it, in an effort to make apparent why he believed accounts of this particular storm inspired Shakespeare to write *The Tempest*.

The 1609 storm, as Malone described it, lasted three days and took place at sea; it was not a sudden squall that drove the ship onto the island. When land was sighted, the sailors put up their sails and struggled to get ashore. They made landfall, and "all on a sudden the wind lay, and gave place to a calm, and the sea became so peaceable and still, that with the greatest conveniency and ease they unshipped all their goods, victuals, and people, and in their boats, with extreme joy, almost to amazement, arrived in safety without loss of a man, although more than a league from the shore."[17] Once ashore the 150 passengers and crew[18] had all the food they wanted, due to amazingly plentiful fish, fowl, and hogs. This description does not resonate at all with what happens in *The Tempest*, where only a few disembark, the weather continues threatening and the survivors muddle along in uncertainty and confusion, finding no immediate relief.

In an 1809 appendix to this pamphlet, Malone asserts the primacy of his hypothesis of the 1609 storm as Shakespeare's inspiration, against a claim that Edward Capell had it earlier, and reveals that Lewis Theobald had it even earlier than Capell. This defensive addendum has such a strident, petulant tone, it might easily raise a suspicion that Malone's work in this area is complete rubbish. If the idea that Shakespeare took the subject matter for a play from obscure colonial reports like those of the 1609 storm were not sanctioned by tradition and were today proposed for the first time, orthodox scholars would dismiss the notion as absurd.

Thanks to Stritmatter and Kositsky, Malone's *Tempest* conjectures are demolished impartially, systematically, and convincingly on the most considerate scholarly grounds. The reverberations should be seismic for Shakespeare scholars. The evidence that Stritmatter and Kositsky present shows that a far more likely source for Shakespeare's New World inspirations was Richard Eden's 1555 translations of accounts of the first discoverers and navigators of America, just the sort of book that a boy who would be Shakespeare could easily get access to and read.

Eden's popular translations, as Stritmatter and Kositsky show, have *Tempest* markers in far greater abundance than those claimed for the reports on the storm of 1609. It can only be wondered how naive traditional scholars have been in believing the theory that Malone promulgated and that generations of his successors have adhered to, whereby the first play printed in the 1623 folio has been steeped in erroneous assumptions. Stritmatter and Kositsky have now untied a Gordian knot that has inhibited progress in Shakespeare studies for centuries. Whether the vainglory that rules Shakespeare academics today will be mitigated anytime soon is another question.

William S. Niederkorn is a playwright, composer, and artist who works in a variety of media. For over 23 years he was an editor at The New York Times, *where he began covering and critiquing Shakespeare scholarship. Since 2010, he has been writing long-form criticism for* The Brooklyn Rail *and researching his book on the history of Shakespeare studies.*

Introduction

In the early stages of writing this book we contacted the editor of a major Shakespearean journal with new evidence pertaining to the long tradition of the alleged influence of William Strachey's *True Reportory* on *The Tempest*. For several reasons we had come to doubt this tradition, and were step by step reaching a radical conclusion: Aside from widespread belief, there was little reason to conclude that Shakespeare had consulted Strachey before writing *The Tempest,* or that he was even aware of the 1609 Bermuda wreck of the *Sea Venture*. Idioms and images customarily attributed to Strachey were readily available to Shakespeare in multiple earlier well known sources — one in particular being, we suspected, a primary source of overriding importance. Our reasons, now more fully constituted, comprise the substance of this book.

Somewhat to our surprise, this editor encouraged us to abandon the topic because "*Tempest* editors have recently pulled back from making strong claims for Shakespeare's knowledge of the Strachey material in manuscript."[1] Not long after this exchange, we published the first round of our research in *Review of English Studies*, an Oxford University Press journal with a distinguished history of publishing influential scholarship. Our argument, it seemed, would be baptized by fire. Within a year, Alden Vaughan, an editor of the 1999 Arden edition of the play, shot back in the *Shakespeare Quarterly*, not only seeking to re-establish longstanding belief in "Shakespeare's knowledge of the Strachey material in manuscript,"[2] but also questioning our motives for ever doubting it.

Obviously, the editor had now changed her mind. And whatever the *Tempest* scholars to whom she referred might have thought (some of them *have*, as the following pages demonstrate, raised serious doubts about Strachey's alleged influence), it is still widely believed within *Tempest* studies, and within Shakespearean scholarship at large, that *Reportory* is the main source and inspiration for the play. To John Wylie (2000) *The Tempest* is "historically coterminous with English attempts to establish a colony in Virginia," and especially linked to "the Bermudan wreck of the *Sea Venture*."[3] Three years later David Scott Wilson-Okumura still accepts that Strachey's communiqué "stands behind the composition of *The Tempest*."[4] Michael Neil (2008) continues to insist that "no proposed source gives so much emphasis as Strachey's to the terrifying sound of the storm, nor does any other offer so rich a collection of verbal parallels with *The Tempest*,"[5] and Alden Vaughan (2008) believes in the existence of "abundant thematic and verbal parallels between the play and 'Reportory.'"[6] According to Vaughan's literature review, these "parallels" have "persuaded generations of readers that Shakespeare borrowed liberally from Strachey's dramatic narrative in telling his island tale."[7] Finally, as recently as 2010, Tom Reedy[8] agrees with Vaughan that Strachey's influence is so well established as to be beyond doubt.

The contradiction between the claims of our colleague, who serves as editor of one of the most prominent and authoritative of all orthodox Shakespearean journals, and this testimony to the enduring influence of the Strachey myth cannot be explained by recourse to the usual verities and processes of scholarship. On the contrary it is better explained as symptomatic of the essentially ideological role that the hypothesis of Strachey's influence has come to play within 21st century Shakespearean scholarship. At stake beneath this seemingly obscure and inconsequential dispute are a whole host of interconnected questions about when *The Tempest* was written, what its actual sources of New World imagery are, how early playgoers might have experienced its symbolism and themes, and even what the play might tell us about its author. Within this context, the Strachey theory has persisted, notwithstanding its weak foundations and numerous points of implausibility.

This book challenges a longstanding and deeply ingrained belief in Shakespearean studies, namely that *The Tempest*— long supposed to be Shakespeare's last play — was not written until 1611. In the course of investigating this proposition, which has rarely been questioned and has never received the critical inquiry it deserves, a number of subsidiary and closely related interpretative puzzles came sharply into focus. These include the play's sources of new world imagery; its festival symbolism and structure; its relationship to William Strachey's *True Reportory* account of the 1609 Bermuda wreck of the *Sea Venture* (not published until 1625); and ultimately the tangled history of how and why scholars have for so long misunderstood these matters. When preliminary elements of the case were published in leading Shakespearean journals (starting in 2007), the sometimes intemperate responses they received became part of the critical history, and some scholars supposed that we had been answered. Our reply to these criticisms is here told in full for the first time.

Our book hopes to explore new vistas in *Tempest* scholarship. It is divided into two parts. In the first, we set forth our case for the sources and chronology of the play as we have come to know them through our research. Rather than Strachey's *True Reportory*, *The Tempest* derives its New World ambience primarily from Richard Eden's popular and highly influential 1555 translations of Iberian travel narratives originally published (mostly in Latin) during the first decades of the 16th century. Both the play's ancient sources, such as Ovid's *Metamorphoses*, Virgil's *Aeneid*, or The Book of Acts, and its Renaissance ones, such as Erasmus' dialogue "Naufragium" ("The Shipwreck"), Ariosto's *Orlando Furioso*, or Eden, are far too early to provide a plausible composition date based solely on sources, but tracing the history of the play's extensive influence on early modern drama allows us to establish a *terminus ad quem* (a "date before which") during the final years of the Elizabethan period. Originally composed for performance at Shrovetide (the Christian Carnival, immediately preceeding Lent in the early modern liturgical calendar), this comparative evidence shows that *The Tempest* was performed as early as 1603. This first section offers some limited criticisms of traditional *Tempest* scholarship, but does not engage the play's critical history in detail, nor does it respond to critics of our own previously published work. What it does is to supply the reader with a streamlined account of the positive conclusions of our study.

The second part of the book takes up more broadly the relevant history of *Tempest* scholarship and details some of the debates engendered in response to the arguments set forward in the first half of the book. This section is directed more towards the specialist reader who wants to situate the present debate over the origins and chronology of the *Tempest* in a wider historical framework, or to understand the flaws that permeate recent attempts to recuperate the declining orthodox paradigm. The reader may wonder why in this second section there is such extended discussion of Strachey's *True Reportory*, given that the first half already demonstrates for many reasons that *The Tempest* was completed several years before the events recorded Strachey's narrative, which by itself logically rules out Strachey. The answer lies in the peculiar role this document has played in the history of *Tempest* scholarship, up until the present. Although we were confident by 2007 that the theory of Strachey's influence was groundless, *Reportory* was the focus of that first article. Interestingly, it is also the only one of our previously published articles to elicit an extended (and, in some cases, angry) rebuttal. It is clear that whatever other reasons may be adduced for an early *Tempest*, the emotional commitment to Strachey runs deep. Deprogramming it requires the kind of comprehensively detailed study elaborated in the second half of the book.

Conventions and Major Original Sources Used in This Book

In order to make the content more accessible, we have opted to place all sources in modern spelling, unless the point we are making depends upon original spelling. Titles retain their original spellings in their first uses and in footnotes. The reader may benefit from a brief synopsis of commonly used primary texts, which are reproduced here along with the abbreviations used to denote them.

B = Hume, Ivor Noël, "William Strachey's Unrecorded First Draft of His Sea Venture Saga," *Avalon Chronicles*, VI (2001). This 18th century manuscript, Hume argues, was descended from an early draft of Strachey's *True Reportory*.

Declaration = *A True Declaration of the Estate of the Colony in Virginia* (STC S122265). Anonymous compilation produced for the Virginia Council in London, including the wreck and survival of the colonists and the situation in Virginia. Registered November 8, 1610.

De La Warr Dispatch. Official dispatch of the Colony's new Governor Lord De La Warr to the Virginia Company in London, describing the Colony's circumstances in 1610, the return of the survivors from Bermuda, and the prospects for a renewed colony. Also known as Harl. MS 7009, fol. 58, this is reproduced in Major, xxiii–xxxvi.

Discovery = Jourdain, Sylvester, *Discovery of the Barmudas otherwise called the Ile of Divels*. London: J. Windet, sold to R. Barnes, 1610. (Reg. Oct 13, 1610). ESTC # S109240. Short pamphlet with account of the wreck on Bermuda, natural history of the island, and sailing of survivors to Jamestown. Our standard text has been Wright.

Eden = *The Decades of the Newe Worlde or West India*, London, 1555. Richard Eden's 1555 translation of Spanish and Portuguese accounts of the original voyages of exploration, which popularized the idea of the "new world" in England. Eden's work compiles writings originally published in Latin by Peter Martyr, Gonzalo Oviedo, and Antony Pygafetta. Our standard text is the University Microfilms 1966 reprint, modernized for accessibility.

Map = Smith, Captain John, *A Map of Virginia with a Description of the Countrey, The Commodities, People, Government and Religion. Written by Captaine Smith, sometimes Governour of the Countrey*. (Oxford: University Press, 1612). Smith's natural and cultural history of Virginia, which Strachey consulted in writing *Travel* and *Reportory*. The standard work is contained in *The Complete Works of Captain John Smith (1580–1631) in*

Three Volumes (Chapel Hill: University of North Carolina Press, 1986), Philip L. Barbour, ed., I:121–190.

Pilgrims = *Hakluytus Posthumus* or *Purchas his Pilgrimes, contayning a History of the World in Sea Voyages and Lande Travells, by Englishmen and others,* in four voumes (London: printed by William Stansby for Henrie Fetherstone, and are to be sold at his shop in Pauls Church-yard at the signe of the Rose, 1625) (STC S111862). Samuel Purchas' edited volume of unpublished voyager documents, including papers bequeathed to him by Hakluyt in 1616. Also referred to as "Purchas."

Reportory = "A True Reportory of the Wreck and Redemption of Sir Thomas Gates, Knight," 1734–1758 in Purchas. William Strachey's account of the 1609 wreck of the *Sea Venture* in Bermuda and subsequent trip to Jamestown in 1610, not published until Purchas's *Pilgrims,* 1625. Our standard text has been Wright although we have also consulted and make use of the online edition of *Pilgrims* (courtesy Library of Congress' Kraus Collection), as needed.

Travel = Major, R.H., ed. *Historie of Travail into Virginia Britannia.* William Strachey's most extensive work on the new world, completed circa 1612, but not published until the modern period. The standard text, which we have used throughout, is the Hakluyt Society monograph, *The Historie of Travaile into Virginia Britannia, Expressing the Cosmographie and Comodities of the Country, Together with the Manners and Customes of the People* (London: Printed for the Hackluyt Society, 1849).

Willes = Willes, R. *The history of travayle in the West and East Indies. Done into Englyshe by R. Eden. Newly set in order, augmented, and finished by R. Willes.* London: R. Jugge, 1577. A reprint with additions of Eden's 1555 translations, this is often said to be the source of the word "Setebos" by scholars unfamiliar with the earlier edition. ESTC citation # S122069.

Wright = *A Voyage to Virginia in 1609. Two Narratives: William Strachey's "True Reportory" and Jourdain's "Discovery of the Bermudas,"* Louis B. Wright, ed. Charlottesville: University Press of Virginia, 1964. The standard modern text of both Strachey and Jourdain.

Throughout the book we use a slightly modified form of Chicago style documentation for most citations, except for several original documents which are cited numerous times or in tables. These are cited using an in-text MLA style citation system. These include Eden, *The Tempest*— using Vaughan and Vaughan's admirable Arden edition — Major's edition of *Travel,* Barbour's edition of Smith's *Collected Works,* and a few other primary sources cited only in tables.

Timeline of Events Related to William Strachey's *True Reportory* and the Bermuda Wreck of July 1609

1609

2 June	Nine ships of the Third Supply depart from Plymouth for Jamestown.
24–25 July	Storm separates the flagship *Sea Venture* from the rest of the convoy in mid–Atlantic. One other small vessel, towed by the *Sea Venture*, lost at sea.
28 July	Bermuda wreck of the *Sea Venture*.

1610

26 February	Caulking of pinnace[s] for trip to Jamestown.
10 May	Survivors depart for Jamestown with two pinnaces.
21 May	Survivors arrive at Point Comfort.
23–24 May	Survivors arrive at Jamestown.
6 June	Survivors depart for England.
7–8 June	Survivors meet De La Warr, arriving from England, at Point Comfort.
10 June	Combined forces of De La Warr and survivors arrive back at Jamestown.
10 June	Earliest possible date of completion of B (not June 7 as Reedy claims).
12 June	De La Warr appoints new officers.
13 June	Summers proposes return voyage to Bermuda to supply colony.

15 June	Summers commissioned to return to Bermuda for resupply of the Colony.
19 June	Summers and his company depart for Bermuda.
19 June	Conclusion of Jourdain's *Discovery* narrative.
6 July	Near Warrascoyack, downriver from Jamestown, natives seize and kill one of Gates men.
9 July	In reprisal, Gates and his men, including Strachey, sack Kecoughtan four miles from Algernon Fort near Point Comfort.
15 July	Gates fleet of three ships departs Point Comfort for England.
15 July	Internal date of *True Reportory*.
September	Gates arrives in London.
13 October	Date on dedication of Jourdain's *Discovery*.
8 November	Registration of *True Declaration*.
14 December	Richard Martin pens letter to Strachey.

1611

28 March	De La Warr departs Virginia for the West Indies.
20 April	*Hercules* arrives in Virginia with Martin letter.
May	Sir Thomas Dale arrives in Virginia
11 June	De La Warr unexpectedly arrives back in England via the West Indies.

1

A First Draft of William Strachey's *True Reportory*

According to widely accepted traditional belief, Shakespeare's *Tempest* was inspired by an account of a 1609 shipwreck on the Bermudas, written by William Strachey, secretary to the Virginia Colony. Strachey was a passenger on the *Sea Venture*, bound for Virginia, when the ship encountered a hurricane and went down off the reefs of Bermuda. After nine months stranded on the islands, the survivors built small boats — called pinnaces — and made their way to Jamestown. They discovered the grim spectacle of a settlement burnt and looted, with nine-tenths of its colonists dead. While in Jamestown, according to this traditional belief, Strachey wrote a very long letter "to a noble lady," describing his experiences in Bermuda and the condition of the Jamestown Colony. The document went back to England on a return voyage in July 1610, was delivered to the Virginia Company, and from there somehow found its way into Shakespeare's hands. Inspired by this stirring narrative of shipwreck and survival, the bard penned his *Tempest*, which was first produced on 1 November, 1611, a little over a year after Strachey's narrative had arrived in England.

This story is remarkably clear and concise. It also possesses a special romantic appeal for North American readers who like to think that Shakespeare was paying close attention to the earliest attempts to colonize North America. On closer inspection, however, it is also "bound richly up" in imaginative implausibility. In fact, there is no record of Strachey's manuscript until 1625, when Samuel Purchas, stating that he had found it in Richard Hakluyt's papers in 1616 after Hakluyt died, published it as *The True Reportory of the Wrack and Redemption of Sir Thomas Gates, Knight* (*Reportory*).

By 1625 Strachey himself was gone, having died in 1620–21. Even more damning, almost every critical link in the narrative chain leading from Bermuda shipwreck to Shakespeare's play is a product not of documentable fact, but of imaginative reconstruction. Outside of the ambiguous testimony provided by the document itself, there is no evidence that it was completed in Jamestown, that it went back to England on Gates' boat in July 1610, or that it reached Virginia Company authorities in London (it is actually addressed, in Purchas' published text, to an unknown noble lady). Above all, there is no evidence that it ever reached William Shakespeare, likely living in Stratford-upon-Avon in 1610. And — surprising as it may seem in view of the tenacity with which traditional scholars cling to the notion of Strachey's influence — there is no persuasive evidence that Shakespeare ever read the document. The claim that Strachey's influence is detectable from the play itself is, as we shall see, exaggerated.

Based on such doubts, our fall 2007 *Review of English Studies* article, "Shakespeare and the Voyagers Revisited," argued for an alternative scenario: Strachey may have composed a short account of the Bermuda wreck while still in Virginia, but the 24,000-word version published by Purchas in 1625 was not completed until sometime between 1612 and 1615. This would explain why the evidence for its actual influence on *The Tempest* is so paper-thin (see Chapter 19). As our 2007 abstract put the case,

> A two-century critical tradition that the 1609 Bermuda shipwreck literature ... establishes a *terminus a quo* (a date after which) for *The Tempest* is incorrect. Strachey's *Reportory*, the only Bermuda pamphlet now thought to have significantly influenced *The Tempest*, was put into its only extant form too late to be used as the play's source and probably after it had already been produced in 1611. Strachey, a notorious plagiarist even by early-modern standards, borrowed much that his narrative shares with *The Tempest* from earlier sources also accessible to Shakespeare.[1]

Tempest scholarship, we went on to suggest, had ignored a fundamental truth about Strachey's text. Published in 1625 by Samuel Purchas as a chapter in his sprawling compilation of colonial literature, *Purchas His Pilgrimes*, Strachey's *Reportory* is undeniably a composite text, embodying evidence of a complicated and lengthy editorial process that is typically ignored in the haste to associate it with Shakespeare's play. For one thing, *Reportory* incorporates a lengthy concluding passage of about 1700 words, excerpted from *A True Declaration of the Estate of the Colony in Virginia* (*Declaration*), an anonymous Bermuda pamphlet that was not published until fall 1610—*after Reportory's* supposed date of composition.[2] What is more, Strachey's narrative is a highly literary document, which incorporates material from a wide range of historical and literary sources. For example, it duplicates content found in — and not traceable before — John Smith's *Map of Virginia*, a book not published until

1612. Contrary to the impression one might get from the uniform description of it as a "letter," at 24,000 words the Strachey document is not like any other Transatlantic letter of the period, which typically run no longer than 1,500 words, and are never more than 4–6,000.

We were not the first to notice the composite, literary character of Strachey's lengthy narrative. Harold Francis Watson, in his *Sailor in English Fiction and Drama, 1550–1800* (1931), notes the palimpsest nature of *Reportory* and even attributes key elements of Strachey's description of the storm to a "storm formula" derived from the Greek romantic tradition. Watson pictures Strachey composing or revising in circumstances far removed from the gritty realities of survival in Jamestown in June 1610:

> "William Strachey, Esq.," a gentleman of education, after what was probably one of the great events of his life, sat him down to do justice to what Purchas calls "a pathetical and rhetorical description"; that he was writing at ease with attention to literary effect is indicated by his long philosophical commentary on how much worse death appears at sea than on land.[3]

For many reasons, including the literary nature of Strachey's text as described by Watson, and the evidence for use of sources not available until 1612, we doubted that the manuscript published by Purchas in 1625 could have been completed, as is usually assumed, during the difficult days of 1610 between the arrival of the survivors in Jamestown on May 23/24 and the July 15 departure of Sir Thomas Gates to England. On the contrary, it betrays every mark of having been revised, as Watson implies, at leisure, in England during 1612, when the events it described had been well digested and could be carefully moralized by the author. We did, however, speculate that an early draft of the document might have been sent to England with Gates in July 1610.

It never occurred to us that anything, as Mr. Micawber might say, would "turn up." We did not know that a "first draft" of the Strachey letter, corresponding to our hypothesized document, had in fact been discovered and published in 2001. Ivor Noël Hume's *William Strachey's Unrecorded First Draft of His Sea Venture Saga,* based on a manuscript (B) discovered in a Tucker family trunk in Bermuda in 1983, is only 5,800 words (less than a quarter the length of the published *Reportory*). Transcribed in a late eighteenth or early nineteenth century hand, it appears in every respect to be an authentic but primitive version of the document published by Purchas in 1625. As Hume summarizes the implications of the discovery,

> Purchas' version has ever since [1625] remained the only source for Strachey's powerful narrative, and there has been no reason to doubt that it was his sole account of the events that occurred in Bermuda.... Now, however, there is

persuasive evidence that Strachey had written an earlier version whose manuscript, or a copy thereof, was in Bermuda in the early nineteenth century.[4]

Both the scope of the narrative and many semantic and syntactic details seem to identify B as an early version of *Reportory*, as Hume argues. Like *Reportory*, B starts from the 2 June, 1609 launch of the *Sea Venture* from Plymouth.[5] It focuses on the fate of the ship off the reefs of Bermuda in late June, the survivors' experiences there, and their spring 1610 journey to Jamestown. It ends shortly after the arrival of the new governor, Lord De La Warr, in June of that year.[6] This is only four or five weeks before Gates returned to England in mid–July.

Hume assumes that the B manuscript is written by Strachey — to whom Purchas in 1625 will attribute the completed *Reportory*. This assumption, however, lacks definitive proof, and there are a number of grounds for reasonable doubt. The skeptical reader should note that, throughout his career, Strachey appropriated and/or rewrote works originally written by others, passing them off as his own. Against Strachey's authorship are striking divergences in style between the two documents. B is very straightforward and workmanlike, even staccato at times, in contrast to *Reportory*'s flowery inventiveness (Table 1.1).

Certain of Strachey's linguistic quirks, including his frequent repetition of terms such as "true it is" (eight times in *Reportory*) or "albeit" (also eight times in *Reportory*), are nonexistent in B. *Reportory* uses the transitional "likewise" twenty-nine times, B only once. Even more surprisingly, in a number of passages *Reportory* employs quite distinctive rhetorical cues, such as adopting a different narrative point of view from B, shifting from the third to the first person, as Table 1.2 illustrates.

Such textual differences could be the result of the *Reportory* writer revising his own earlier draft, but they could also indicate that he was revising a manuscript written by another. Barring further inquiry, the case for Strachey's revision of his own draft seems plausible, but far from proven. Internal evidence is consistent with Strachey's known experience, but hardly decisive in view of the stylistic discrepancies between the two documents. In a passage similar to one surviving in *Reportory*, the B author declares that he "had been out in storms before on the coast of Barbara, Algiers, and in the Levant and once in greater extremity in a Candian Ship on the Adriatic."[7] Although this statement matches Strachey's known experience,[8] it remains inconclusive and circumstantial, as it is likely that quite a number of sailors or passengers on the *Sea Venture* might have had similar experiences — as, for example, we know John Smith had (though Smith was not aboard the *Sea Venture*).[9]

Table 1.1. Stylistic Differences Between B and *Reportory*

B	Reportory
A dreadful storm commenced from the northeast, which, swelling and roaring as it were by fits, was some hours more violent than at others, and at length seemed to extinguish the light of heaven and leave utter darkness. The blackness of the sky and the howling of the wind were such as to inspire the boldest of our men with fear. (69)	On St. James his day, July 24, being Monday (preparing for no less all the black night before), the clouds gathering thick upon us and the wind singing and whistling most unusually (which made us to cast off our pinnace, towing the same until then astern), a dreadful storm and hideous began to blow from out the northeast, which swelling and roaring it were by fits, some hours with more violence than others, at length did beat all light from Heaven; which, like an hell of darkness, turned black upon us, so much the more fuller of horror, as in such cases horror and fear use to overrun the troubled and overmastered senses of all, which taken up with amazement, the ears lay so sensible to the terrible cries and murmurs of the winds and distraction of our company, as who was most armed and best prepared was not a little shaken. (4)
The culprit earnestly requested that he might be shot as he was a gentleman, which request being granted he was put to death at sun set. (81)	He earnestly desired, being a gentleman, that he might be shot to death, and toward the evening he had his desire, the sun and his life setting together. (49)

Whether the B manuscript was written by Strachey or by someone else, its greatest relevance is that it apparently supplies a historical antecedent to the *Reportory* text obtained by Purchas many years later. In any case, B corresponds in many particulars to the kind of document that we suggested in our *RES* article might have arrived in London in mid–1610:

- At 5,800 words, compared to *Reportory*'s 24,000, B seems a much more reasonable length for a letter sent on Gates' boat, and is similar to the lengths of De La Warr's dispatch of 4000 words and Jourdain's narrative of 3000, which are known to have gone back in July 1610.
- *Reportory* is not merely an enlarged version of the B text; it has been recast in an entirely new rhetorical context, written from a first

Table 1.2. Point of View Shift
from B to *Reportory* (After Hume, 59)

B	Reportory
The governor was then below at the capstan, encouraging the men to labor; the wave struck him from his seat, and three other persons, the whole who were around him, down on their faces. (71)	*Our Governor* was at this time below at the capstan, both by his speech and authority heartening every man unto his labor. It struck him from the place where he sat, and groveled him, and all us about him on our faces. (11)
...Compassion was excited in all *the higher order of our company.* Thus they *repaired to the governor* and besought him to pardon him, the culprit, which after much entreaty he consented to do. (80)	*The better sort of the company* ... went *unto our governor,* whom they besought (as likewise did Captain Newport and myself), and never left him until we had got his pardon. (45)

person perspective, and conceptualized as a "letter" to a "noble lady," who is frequently addressed directly by the writer.

- *Reportory* introduces effects and passages from a large number of literary and historical sources; these include Virgil, the Greek Romance *Clitophon and Leucippe* (Eng. translation f.p. 1598), as well as quotations from Horace — all absent or greatly attenuated in B.
- While the B manuscript briefly introduces one short passage from Richard Eden's *Decades of the New World* (probably from oral recall), the vast majority of material in *Reportory* borrowed from that source, as well as other accounts of the New World such as Acosta's *Natural and Moral History of the East and West Indies* (1604), is not found in B.
- B contains none of the excerpts from other Virginia documents that are so prominent in *Reportory*; these include Lord De La Warr's official dispatch and John Smith's *Map of Virginia* (not published until 1612). B does, however, include some slight parallels to *Declaration*.
- B is also missing large sections from *Reportory* that seem to have been written in response to a December 1610 letter to Strachey by Richard Martin, the secretary of the Virginia Company in London, which would have reached Strachey in Virginia via the Hercules no earlier than Spring 1611.

For these reasons, we believe that Hume's B manuscript is a game changer for the tradition of Strachey's influence on Shakespeare. It confirms the plausibility of our surmise that a more primitive version of the Strachey manuscript — later revised and edited — might have gone back on the Gates voyage. Strachey's own testimony, in the 1612 introduction to *Lawes for the Colony of Virginea Britannia*, corroborates this scenario. Here Strachey directly refers to his work on Bermuda as not only unpublished but incomplete, a manuscript still undergoing an editorial process of revision:

> I have both in the Bermudas, and since in Virginia been a sufferer and an eye witness, and the full story of both in due time shall consecrate unto your views.... Howbeit ... many impediments, as yet must detain such my observations in the shadow of darkness, until I shall be able to deliver them perfect unto your judgements....[10]

Enigmatically, Raphe Hamor, secretary to the colony immediately after Strachey (1611) and also a survivor of the Bermuda wreck, writing in 1614, employs parallel phraseology to promise his own narrative of the experience:

> Excuse me (courteous Reader) if carried beyond my purpose, I declaim passionately in this passive and innocently despised work, which I am sure is so full of goodness, *and have been almost six years a sufferer and eye witness* of this now well-nigh achieved happiness, *the full and unstained reportory of every accident whereof even from his beginning, together with the causes of the backwardness*, in prosperity thus long, touching at the miraculous delivery of the scattered company, *cast upon the Bermudas*, when those fortunate islands like so many fair Nereids which received our wrecked company, with the death of that pure and noble-hearted gentleman Sir George Summers dying there, *my purpose is shortly at large to publish.*[11]

Not only is no such work of Hamor's known to exist, but the similarity of phraseology between Hamor and Strachey, and Hamor's use of the word "reportory," are sufficient to suggest that they may refer to the same document. How this enigma can be explained we do not profess to understand, but it does complicate the traditional view of the genesis and transmission of Strachey's text, which is why these facts are typically ignored.

Traditional scholars have not known what to make of this inconvenient evidence. Either they have ignored Strachey's *Laws* reference to a plan to "consecrate unto your views" the "full story ... in due time" of his experiences as "a sufferer and an eye witness" to the Bermuda wreck, or they have argued implausibly that Strachey is referring to his *History of Travaile in Virginia Britannia*. But *Travaile* does not even mention Bermuda, and even Wright admits that in it Strachey "did not repeat the story he had related in 'Reportory.'"[12] The discovery of the B manuscript on the other hand, providing an antecedent to *Reportory*, is consistent with Strachey's own testimony that *Reportory* was still unfinished in 1612. These findings, along with other arguments, many introduced for the first time in this book, have devastating consequences for the longstanding theory of Strachey's influence on Shakespeare's *Tempest* and, consequently, the play's chronology.

2

"O Brave New World"

In recent years the concept of early-modern "source studies" has undergone a sea change, with profound but underestimated implications for *Tempest* scholarship:

> Where once it was assumed the term [source] could apply only to those texts with demonstrable verbal connection, critics [now insist] ... upon the dialogue that an individual text conducts both with its recognizable sources and analogues, and with the wider culture within which it functioned.[1]

Coincident with this enlarged interest in the circulation of motifs and ideas throughout the wider early-modern culture has been the emergence of a renewed emphasis on the Mediterranean contexts, both literary and historical, that have shaped the imaginative topography of Shakespeare's play. After decades of the dominance of Americanist readings there has recently emerged a renewed appreciation for the topographical complexity of Shakespeare's imaginative landscape and a renewed focus on the play's Mediterranean antecedents, an emphasis on sources and symbolism that connect *The Tempest* as much to the Old World of Aeneas as to the New World of Christopher Columbus.

Despite this emerging focus on the Mediterranean context of *The Tempest*, mainstream scholars have for the most part not questioned the "standard thesis" of Strachey's influence. On the contrary, Shakespearean studies is still dominated by a series of propositions, inflated into "facts" by a previous generation of scholars who established the priority of the Americanist perspective and agreed that Strachey was the only New World *Tempest* source of any consequence. The most influential example of the continued primacy of this way of thinking is David Kathman's 1995 online essay, "Dating the Tempest."[2] Having replied at length to Kathman's case in another context, we here offer only a few examples of his mistaken reasoning.[3] In tracing the evidence for Strachey's alleged influence, Kathman isolates language supposedly diagnostic of a link to Shakespeare from its larger linguistic context, to create impression of linguistic intimacy where none in fact exists. For example, he derives the *Tempest* phrase "play the men" from Strachey's "heartening every man unto his labour":

> Strachey says that "Our Governor was both by his speech and authority heartening every man unto his labour" [10]; as soon as he appears, King Alonso says, "Good boatswain, have care. Where's the Master? Play the men" [1.1.9–10].[4]

However, the idiom "play the men" was not invented by Strachey, nor was that Shakespeare's source; it occurs in the Bible,[5] a highly probable source for Shakespeare. It also occurs in one of the earliest plays of the Shakespearean canon, one even by conservative estimates at least a dozen years before *The Tempest*: "When they shall hear how we have *play'd the men*" (*I Henry the Sixth*, 1.1.17). This illustrates the inconsistency of Kathman's methodology. When words or phrases shared by Strachey and Shakespeare do not occur previously in Shakespeare (or even occur infrequently), Kathman cites this as significant, but when the evidence points in a contrary direction, he ignores it. He asserts, for example, that "bosky" (4.1.81) constitutes "Shakespeare's only use of this word." This is true only if one ignores the variant spelling "busky" (*I Henry VI*, 5.1.1), which the OED lists as the same lexeme.[6] Kathman goes on to claim that "glut" (1.1.60) in the phrase "gape at widest to glut him" is "the only appearance of the word ... in Shakespeare," implying that the usage must be derived from Strachey. Again the claim, although widely reproduced, is erroneous. What justification can possibly be offered for the inference that "glutted" (*I Henry IV*, 3.2.85) is not the same word as "glut"? It is the past tense form of the same verb, and both uses appear in the OED under a single entry.[7] Kathman did not invent this error. Instead he took the idea from R. R. Cawley, who gives credit where credit is due, to Charles Mills Gayley: "Gayley remarks that 'every drop of water ... gape[s] at widest to glut him' ... contains the poet's solitary use of the word *glut*."[8] As we have already seen, it is not true that this is "the poet's solitary use of the word glut." Unfortunately, we have discovered, *Tempest* scholarship all too frequently prefers to repeat old errors to substantiate doubtful conclusions rather than critically re-examine evidence to consider alternative hypotheses before picking the best one.

Kathman's claim that "hoodwink" (4.1.206) is used only three times in the canon contains another error. Actually[9] the contracted past tense "hoodwink'd" occurs another three times. More importantly, Kathman's claim of significance in finding "only" two or three previous uses of the word, even when his numbers are accurate, demonstrates the fallacy of statistical mumbo jumbo.[10] It is illogical to argue that because Shakespeare infrequently used a particular word or phrase that Strachey employs, his subsequent use of it in *The Tempest* establishes that he must have borrowed it from Strachey. A single previous usage is enough to show that Shakespeare knew the word and did not need to derive it from reading Strachey — who, incidentally, does not himself use "hoodwink" in any of his previous work.[11]

Notwithstanding the recent critique of the "Americanist" perspective by those who read a *Tempest* contextualized by Mediterranean topography, studies such as Kathman's confirm that the traditional view of Strachey as a source remains largely unchallenged. Kathman's work continues to be endorsed by leading Shakespearean scholars, publishing in such journals as the *Shakespeare Quarterly* or *Review of English Studies*, and is widely cited as the definitive rebuttal to anyone who questions the established assumptions of *Tempest* scholarship. Emphasis on the play's Mediterranean context, while amply justified by its textual cues, therefore masks an unresolved, and usually unacknowledged, problem. Although the play engages the richly imaginative traditions of Mediterranean topography, scholars agree that it also responds to — and interrogates — the contemporaneous discourses of the New World voyagers. If Shakespeare did not draw his inspiration from William Strachey's narrative of the wreck of the *Sea Venture*, what sources of New World imagery and ideology did inform the play's construction? How did Shakespeare know of Miranda's "Brave New World," peopled with its fantastical creatures?

Richard Eden's *Decades of the Newe Worlde*[12] (Figure 2.1), originally published in London in 1555 and reissued with supplemental material by Richard Willes in 1577 under a new title, *The History of Travayle in the West and East Indies*,[13] is an obvious but often overlooked candidate.

Even the title of the book, the first to popularize in English the phrase "New World," resonates with Shakespeare's play. Yet, although it is frequently acknowledged as a *Tempest* source (usually as a secondary or incidental one), Eden's work has long suffered from critical neglect. Verbal and thematic parallels between the two works abound, but most of them have been overlooked by a scholarly tradition that has continued to insist on Strachey's *Reportory* as the primary source of New World influence on *The Tempest*.

Many of the most striking connections between Eden and *Tempest*—the appropriation and transposition of theme or narrative element, inspiration for character development, and opportunity for ideological dialogue and parody — are not easily documented by the traditional methods of tracing influence through verbal resemblance. Unlike the theory associating Shakespeare's play with the Jacobean literature of the Bermuda shipwreck, however, the connection to Eden has always rested on distinct and unequivocal verbal sign. As early as 1778 Richard Farmer, in correspondent's notes to the Johnson-Steevens edition of *The Tempest*,[14] had observed that the rare word "Setebos," which Caliban twice uses (1.2.374; 5.1.261)[15] to name a divine power,

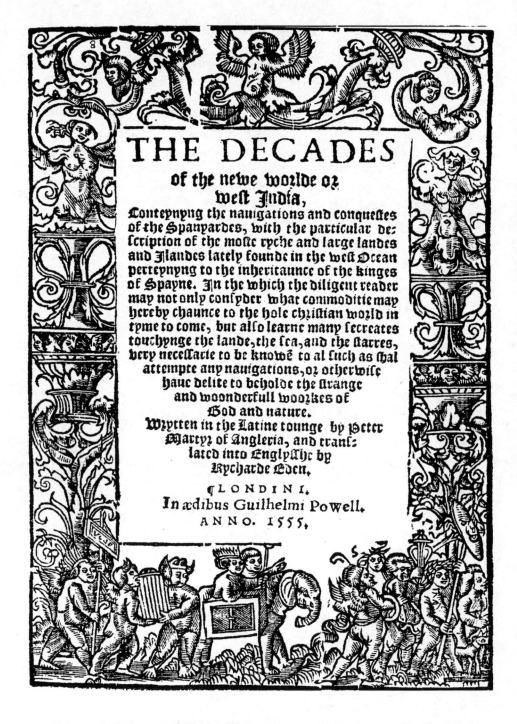

THE DECADES

of the newe worlde or
west India,

Conteynyng the nauigations and conquestes
of the Spanyardes, with the particular description of the moste ryche and large landes
and Islandes lately founde in the west Ocean
perteynyng to the inheritaunce of the kinges
of Spayne. In the which the diligent reader
may not only confyder what commoditie may
hereby chaunce to the hole christian world in
tyme to come, but also learne many secreates
touchynge the lande, the sea, and the starres,
very necessarie to be knowē to al such as shal
attempte any nauigations, or otherwise
haue delite to beholde the strange
and woonderfull woorkes of
God and nature.
Wrytten in the Latine tounge by Peter
Martyr of Angleria, and tranf-
lated into Englyshe by
Rycharde Eden.

¶LONDINI,
In ædibus Guilhelmi Powell,
ANNO. 1555,

Figure 2.1. Title page of Eden's 1555 *Decades* translation (courtesy Readex Microprint Corporation).

is identified as a Patagonian deity in Willes 1577 reissue of Eden's work (as well as in the original 1555 edition).[16] Given the rareness of this word, which appears in only one other known English source, this obviously showed Eden's direct influence on Shakespeare and should have been an invitation to future study. By 1892 it seemed that Eden might even eclipse the Bermuda documents as Shakespeare's source. In his Variorum edition Henry Howard Furness not only repeated Farmer's observation, but went on to remark, with regard to the St. Elmo's Fire motif, that "just before this account ... [in which Setebos occurs] ... there were two separate occasions" on which "the fires called Saint Helen, Saint Nicholas, and Saint Clare appeared upon the mast and cables of the ships."[17]

The rise of the Strachey theory, however, eclipsed critical awareness of Eden's importance as a *Tempest* source. While Frank Kermode's 1954 Arden edition identified a large number of *Tempest* motifs derived from Eden, he continued to endorse the Strachey theory, suggesting that the excerpts from the Bermuda narratives should "justify the assumption that Shakespeare has these documents in mind."[18] Despite this misplaced faith, Kermode deserves credit for emphasizing Eden's critical role as a *Tempest* source. He has done more than anyone since Furness to promote a more balanced and accurate assessment of Eden's role in shaping the ideas and iconography of the play. His list of Eden motifs in *Tempest,* if not exhaustive, is impressive enough to warrant further inquiry:

> the identification of the West Indies with Atlantis, the belief of the natives that the voyagers had descended from heaven; the elaborate description of "the golden world," with land "as common as sun and water," and the natives know-ing no difference between "Mine" and "Thine"; the "horrible roarings of the wild beasts in the woods." But he could also have found here pugnacious and terrible bats, compared to "ravenous harpies"; the Spanish custom of hunting natives with dogs; a Carthage in the New World to remind him of older colonial adventures; and an account of the manner in which natives "were wonderfully astoni[sh]ed at the sweet harmony" of music.[19]

Kermode also influenced other scholars, for example Hallett Smith (1972), to whom it "seem[ed] clear" that Shakespeare had consulted Eden. But without further inquiry Kermode continued to insist that the play "is in part based on some accounts of the shipwreck of Sr. George Summers in Bermuda."[20] Writing a few years later, Charles H. Frey sympathetically summarized Hallett Smith's comprehensive argument as one in which

> Richard Eden's accounts of the explorations by Magellan and others tell of St. Elmo's fires in ship's rigging, Indians who die before their captors can exhibit them in Europe, Caliban-like natives who seek for grace, Utopian, golden world

innocence, strange roaring sounds heard in woods, dogs used to pursue natives, natives interested in music, mutinies suppressed, and so on.[21]

But to Vaughan and Vaughan (1999), even though "commentators since the late eighteenth century have generally agreed" that Eden influenced *The Tempest*, it is still possible to minimize Eden's significance by categorizing it as an "*incidental indebtedness*" to a "highly accessible source...."[22]

Such dismissals are, as we shall see, unwarranted. The evidence for the influence of this "highly accessible source" on Shakespeare's play is much more compelling than even the most optimistic of these extracts might suggest. Unlike Strachey, the Iberian travel narratives, either in their original languages or as translated by Eden, have left an indelible and pervasive imprint on *The Tempest*. When Eden's influence is properly evaluated, the Strachey theory evaporates, melting "into air, into thin air ... leav[ing] not a rack behind."

A striking example is the manner in which Eden, just like *Tempest*, fuses Mediterranean and Colonial frames of reference. Margaret Trudeau-Clayton[23] and David Scott Wilson-Okumura, reviving A.C. Brinton's 1928 studies of 16th century *Aeneid* illustrations, have documented the importance of this syncretism for *Tempest* studies. Brinton observed that woodcuts illustrating *The Aeneid*, originally published in Strasbourg in 1502 but widely reproduced in subsequent editions issued in Lyons and Paris, picture Aeneas' Mediterranean voyages with woodcuts of Spanish caravels.[24] These anachronistic images, which "dominated Vergil illustration for the first half of the sixteenth century,"[25] have been construed as evidence for what Wilson-Okumura calls the Aeneas/Columbus analogy: "as Aeneas colonized Italy, so his descendants were now colonizing the New World."[26] Unfortunately, Wilson-Okumura eventually retreats from applying that analogy to *Tempest* studies on the ground that there is no "corroborating evidence" such as "a reference to the New World in the commentary that accompanied the [Virgil] woodcuts"[27] (Figure 2.2).

Alden Vaughan lists *Reportory*'s reference to Aeneas as one of three chief reasons for favoring it as a *Tempest* source. Such attempts to link Strachey to *Tempest* via the references to Aeneas and Dido ironically overlook the fact that Strachey's "digression"[28] about Aeneas is itself derived — almost verbatim — from Eden. Eden's influential 1555 book, and more specifically his English translation of Peter Martyr's *De Orbe Novo decades cum Legatione Babylonica* (1516),[29] analogizes Aeneas and the Renaissance voyagers more than once.

Educated as a humanist, Martyr was a fluent scholar of rhetoric and letters, as familiar with Ovid, Virgil, and Livy as he was with the momentous navigations and geopolitical controversies of his own age. A leading Lombard

Figure 2.2. Spanish Caravels in a Renaissance edition of Virgil by Brant (courtesy Wikimedia Commons).

intellectual, he was also praised by contemporaries as the best poet among the Italians in Spain[30] and credited with mastering Latin prose as a living language, cultivating a style "vigorous, terse, vitalized." When he lectured on Juvenal's second satire at the University of Salamanca he held four thousand students and faculty "spellbound under the charm of his eloquence."[31]

Shakespeare found the assimilation of the ethos of the New World to the topography and mythology of the Old, so characteristic of *The Tempest*, already present in Eden's translation of Martyr. To illustrate the dispersed sovereignty of New World chieftains, for example, Martyr cites the precedent of Aeneas colonizing Latium: "[the Island] hath many kings, *as when Aeneas arrived in Italy*, he found Latium divided into many kingdoms and provinces"

(2v). Later he recalls how, "As is read in the beginning of the Romans, ... *Aeneas of Troy arrived in the region of Italy called Latium, upon the banks of the river of Tyber*" (124v).[32] But according to Wilson-Okumura, Dido is more central to the Old World literary contexts of *The Tempest* than the more commonplace figure of Aeneas.[33] If so, it would seem that Shakespeare might well have taken his cue from Martyr, who emphasizes that long before Aeneas colonized Tunisia, Dido had already done so:

> The like we read how *the Tirians and Sidonians arrived with their navy in Libya by the fabulous conduction of Dido*. These Matininans, in like manner being banished from their own country, planted their first habitation in that part of the Island of Hispaniola ... [124v].

Martyr's invocation of Aeneas and Dido as typological antecedents of early-modern voyagers and colonizers not only answers the call for further inquiry into the relationship between texts and contexts, but also corroborates Wilson-Okumura's insight. Martyr's *Decades*, a narrative of the voyages of Christopher Columbus and other early Iberian explorers, forms the backbone of Eden's book (folios 1–166), which also reprints English translations containing much of Gonzalo Ferdinando Oviedo's *The History of the West Indies* (173v–214) and Antonio Pygafetta's *Brief Declaration of the Voyage or Navigation Made About the World* (216v–232v).[34] Predating by decades Hakluyt's earliest accounts of English exploration, Eden's translation became a foundational text of the early English colonial imagination. Martyr's tales of a "New World" landscape of metamorphic transformations, tragicomic power struggles between viceroys and cannibals, of water nymphs and Nereids, were the speculative fiction of the age. In England his mention of "another portion of that mainland [beyond the southern Spanish colonies] reaching toward the northeast, thought to be as large as the other, and not yet known but only by the sea coast"[35] did more than any other single work to incite the imagination of a new generation of English explorers. According to Hakluyt editor George Bruner Parks, in England "there were practically no books of oversea interest before 1553"; it was Eden who "broke the long English silence on the New World(s),"[36] and the publication of his *Decades* caused "England [to wake] to the new day"[37] of the age of exploration. Eden, in short, provided the template later employed by Richard Hakluyt and Samuel Purchas in their comprehensive accounts of the English voyagers. Should it be any surprise, then, that it was to Eden, and more specifically his translation of Martyr's "New World," that the leading dramatist of the Elizabethan age turned for his primary source of information about the Americas?

A comprehensive account of Eden's influence on *The Tempest* might begin by noting a structural analogy that has been neglected in the critical literature:

In both texts an Old World narrative of the intrigues of Milanese and Neapolitan dynasts is fused with a New World narrative of shipwreck, colonization, and intercultural conflict. In Eden's New World native and colonizer vie for political dominance, just as Caliban and Prospero contend for power on Shakespeare's island, and like Caliban and Prospero, the struggle for control of the New World imitates — and sometimes parodies — the dynastic conflicts of the Old.

Advocates of the Strachey theory emphasize Shakespeare's supposed dependence on Strachey's anecdotal accounts of conspiracies among the Bermuda adventurers.[38] Textual comparison, however, reveals a significant discrepancy: in Eden, unlike Strachey, the intrigues of Prospero's "New World" island originate in the Old World of Naples and Milan.[39] Given this context, it would seem beyond dispute that Shakespeare drew this dynamic from Martyr's narrative, not from the Bermuda pamphlets, which contain no comparable linkage between Old and New World politics. Dedicated in part to Ascanio Sforza (1455–1505), the youngest of three sons of Francesco, the first Sforza Duke of Milan (who ruled 1450–66),[40] and in part to his kinsman, the Cardinal of Aragon, Martyr's book foregrounds the real-world intrigues of the Sforza and Aragon dynasties.[41] These conspiracies provided Shakespeare with a historical template for the sibling rivalry of Prospero and Antonio. In 1480, after the murder of Ascanio and Ludovico Sforza's elder brother the Duke, Ludovico seized *de facto* power in Milan. He later expelled his young nephew, the *de jure* Duke, together with his nephew's wife, Isabella of Aragon.[42] Before being deposed by the French forces of Louis XII in 1499, Ludovico established a reputation as the archetypal Renaissance prince, ruling a court rife with intrigue and corruption but generous in its patronage of such cultural luminaries as Leonardo da Vinci. With Ludovico in 1499 fell Martyr's patron Ascanio; writing some years later, Martyr compares the power struggles of these Sforza dynasts to violent tempests, much like those literal new world tempests so common in Eden's book:

> In this meantime had fortune overthrown Ascanius (his brother *Lodovike being cast out of Milan* by the Frenchmen) whose authority would not suffer me to be idle, but ever to have my pen in hand.... Fortune did no less withdraw my mind from writing, than disturb Ascanius from power. *As he was tossed with contrary storms* and ceased to persuade me, even so slacked my ferventness to enquire any further until the year of Christ 1500. When the court remained at Granata where you are viceroy: At which time Lodovike the Cardinal of *Aragon,* nephew to king Frederike by his brother's side (being at Granata *the queen* Parthenopea [*of Naples*] the sister of our catholic king) brought me King Frederike's letters, whereby he exhorted me to finish the other books... [47v–48, emphasis ours].

This passage is rich in multiple *Tempest* themes. The coincidence of idea and image includes the metaphor of the storm as an emblem of political instability, the downfall and expulsion of a Milanese duke, and — intriguingly — the idea of writing as a compensation for lost political power. That Shakespeare had in mind these interrelated themes when writing *The Tempest* is confirmed by his adoption of the specific names Alonso and Ferdinand for the father-and-son Neapolitan royals. Both names were traditional among the Aragonese in-laws of the Sforzas, and at least two father/son sets of Aragon kings of Naples were named Al(f)onso and Ferdinand.

The Aragon dynasty engaged in a protracted game of diplomatic chess with its Sforza in-laws for political control of Naples and Milan, and during the late 15th century the two powerful families intermarried across at least two generations. Alfonso II of Naples, before he became king, married the sister of Ascanio and Ludovico Sforza, Ipolita Maria, in 1465. Their daughter Isabella of Aragon, sister to Ferdinand II of Naples, then became the wife of her own Sforza cousin, Gian Galeazzo Sforza, in 1489, just before Gian's uncle Ludovico expelled them. Martyr's description of these diplomatic games, in which that "great Queen Helisabeth with her husband [Ferdinand II]" received the "realm of Castile as her dowry" (80), is reflected in the lover's banter between Miranda and Ferdinand at chess:

> **Mir.** Sweet lord, you play me false.
> **Ferd.** No my dearest love, I would not for the world.
> **Mir.** Yes, for a score of kingdoms you should wrangle... [5.1. 172–4]

Out of this convoluted "Spanish maze" of Aragon/Sforza alliances and intrigues, Shakespeare created his own Alonso and Ferdinand, two Dukes of Milan and their offspring,[43] together with the story of the expulsion of the rightful Duke of Milan and his daughter, and her subsequent marriage to the son of a King of Naples.

The names Ferdinand and Alonso are not the only ones common to Eden and *The Tempest*. Indeed, as Furness, following Malone, noticed,[44] several *Tempest* names owe their apparent genesis to Eden. It must have been this argument by Furness that inspired Gayley, after devoting three and a half pages to the alleged influence of *Reportory* names on *The Tempest*, to conclude, paradoxically, that "whether Shakespeare borrowed names from Strachey or not, to make an argument out of it would be precious and inconsequential. We have already sufficient evidence that he knew his Strachey from first page to last."[45] A list of names common to Eden and *The Tempest*, compared with those found in Strachey (Table 2.1), confirms the centrality of Eden as a *Tempest* source. Of the eleven *Tempest* names found (sometimes in variant form) in Eden's narrative, only four are duplicated in Strachey. Kathman[46] and

Cawley[47] both cite Strachey as the source for the names Gonzalo and Ferdinand, but fail to notice that Strachey is actually copying those names (with attribution) from Eden, who reproduces a portion of Gonzalo Ferdinando Oviedo's *History of the West Indies*.

Table 2.1. Comparative Census of Names in Eden and Strachey

Eden	*Strachey*
Gonzalo	Yes (derived from Eden)
Ferdinand (In Eden but not Strachey, this name refers to Ferdinand II, King of Spain and Naples)	Yes (derived from Eden)
Alonso	No
Duke of Milan	No
Antonio	No
Stephano	Yes. Stephen Hopkins.
Sebastian	No
Ceres	No
Francisco	Yes. Francis Pearepoint.
Caliban (Cannibal)	No

As this list of names might suggest, Martyr's "New World," like Caliban's island, is saturated with Old World magic and mythopoeia. Eden's "fairies or spirits ... called Dryads, Hamadryads, Satyrs, Pans, and Nereids, [who] have the cure and providence of the sea, woods, springs, and fountains" (46) not only recall Ariel, the spritely incarnation of alchemical tradition, but also the "nymphs of the sea" (1.2.302), "water-nymph" (1.2.SD), and *nymphs called naiads of the windring brooks,/*With your sedged crowns and ever-harmless looks..." (4.1.128–129).[48] Eden's female spirit (*zeme*), who "gather<s> together the waters which fall from the high hills to the valleys, that being loosed, they may with force burst out into great floods" (47) prefigures Sycorax' authority to "control the moon, make flows and ebbs" (5.1.270). Eden's "devils incarnate newly broke out of hell" (33v) even anticipate Ferdinand's anguished cry, "Hell is empty, and all the devils are here!" (1.2.214–15). This final comparison illustrates the frequently observable dialogical relationship between Eden and Shakespeare. "Newly broken out of hell," Eden's devils have become, in Ferdinand's outburst, inhabitants of Caliban's island. As this example suggests, not all of Shakespeare's borrowings from Eden are of a serious nature. Some passages appealed to his comic sensibility. Stephano's bawdy jest, "now is the jerkin under the line" (4.1.242), appears drawn from Eden's description, already suggestive of the sexual joke, in which navigators "felt greater heat that day when they were under the Equinoctial line" (218).

Martyr's narrative as translated by Eden draws not only from Virgil but also from the most Shakespearean of all ancient texts, Ovid's *Metamorphoses*.[49] Here we may detect an intriguing triangulation of sources. Martyr's account of the New World transmogrification of natives "turned into a stone ... [or] transformed into myrobalane trees ... [or one who] was turned into a nightingale [who] both in the night with a morning song bewail[s] his misfortune, and call[s] for the help of his master" (43v–44) recalls the arboreal imprisonment, birdlike singing, and plaintive petitions of Prospero's Ariel. Even more strikingly, next to this fantastic description the ethnological humanist Eden attaches a marginal note, observing that New World myths are "Fables much like Ovid his transformations" (43v).

In Eden's Ovidian New World Shakespeare found a copious vocabulary of natural history that is reproduced in *Tempest*. Many details of the natural history of Caliban's Island (Table 3.2)[50] appear to originate in Eden's narrative, among them the leitmotif of woodcutting,[51] the infections from "muddy and stinking marshes,"[52] and Ariel's charge to "do [Prospero] business in the veins of the earth,"[53] as well as numerous specific wildlife references. Eden's New World is one "uninhabitable after the opinion of the old writers ... but now found to be most replenished with people, fair, fruitful and most fortunate, with a thousand Islands crowned with gold and beautifull <p>earls..." (D4v)[54] and equipped, like Stephano's seashore kingdom,[55] with "cellars in the ground, well replenished with wines..." (68v). In the plentiful landscape of this New World are pignuts (2.2.165) and <popin>jays (2.2.166), tortoises (1.2.317), marmosets (2.2.167) and seamews (2.2.169)[56] inhabit "desert woods, craggy mountains, & muddy marshes full of ... quagmires ... (99v)."[57]

And in Eden Shakespeare also found "images ... placed in ... *solemn* halls, *palaces*, or *temples*, with certain verses made to the commendation of them whom the images represented," followed by mention of "*the beginning of the world*" (diii: emphasis supplied), a passage anticipating Prospero's nostalgic Act 4 farewell to the masquers:

> The cloud-capp'd towers, the gorgeous *palaces*,
> The *solemn temples, the great globe itself*,
> Yea, all which it inherit, shall dissolve
> And, like this insubstantial pageant faded,
> Leave not a rack behind [IV.1.152–156]

3

Caliban's Island

It is difficult to overestimate the profound and pervasive influence that Peter Martyr's New World narratives (and those of several other writers such as Gonzalo Ferdinando Oviedo and Antonio Pygafetta compiled in Eden's 1555 translation) exercised over *The Tempest*. Martyr's New World conspiracies set an especially distinctive mark on Shakespeare's play. A number of these, including a plot of "privy conspiracies [by natives] ... to have killed [Columbus'] men" like Alonso's, "*in their sleep...*" (123; our emphasis),[1] involve both native and voyager. In Martyr's narrative, native chiefs, like Caliban, "conspired with desperate minds to rebel" (24v) against colonizers, who sought "freely to possess the full dominion of the Island" (20). In the double-edged power struggle described by Martyr, these conquered chiefs were obliged to pay homage to the Spaniards to survive, but at the same time the unstable colonial government was subject to the mutinous impulses of the conquistadors themselves, some of whom — like Trinculo and Stephano — separated from their former leaders to establish rogue colonies (Table 3.1).

To Tristan Marshall the *Tempest* portrait of Caliban as a rebellious savage enslaved by Prospero's magic is anachronistic from a Jacobean perspective. To promote settlement, Virginia Company policy strove to avoid negative images of New World natives and preferred to portray them as a noble race. Such reports typically attributed conflict not to the aggression of natives, but to the bad practices of the English: "the poor Indians by wrongs and injuries were made our enemies," writes Robert Johnson in the second part of *Nova Britannia* (1612). Only before 1591 and after 1622 was the popular English conception of the New World native dominated by negative sentiment.[2] There are some dissonant notes during the intervening years: *Declaration* refers to Powhatan as a "greedy Vulture" who, "boiling with desire of revenge ... invited Captain Ratclife, and about thirty others to trade for Corn, and under the colour of fairest friendship ... brought them within the compass of his ambush,

Table 3.1. Martyr's New World Conspiracies

Eden

The genesis of the conspiracies

The kings of the islands which had hitherto lived quietly and content with their little which they thought abundant, whereas they now perceived that our men began to fasten foot within their regions and to bear rule among them, *took the matter so grievously, that they thought nothing else but by what means they might utterly destroy them...* (18v)

Here this filthy sink of rebels thus conspired, played their wages and lived with loose bridles in all kinds of mischief robbing the people, spoiling the county, and ravishing both wives and virgins... (28)

The Indies have rebelled sayeth another ... with such other false and licentious talk devised by *unquiet brains in whose heads the hammers of sedition* cease not to forge ingens (?) of iniquity... (biiv)

Incipient mutiny

Then the Spaniards which were accompanied with him, began first to murmur secretly among themselves: and shortly after with words of reproach spoke evil of Columbus their governor, and *consulted with themselves, either to rid him out of the way, or else to cast him into the sea...* (2)

Thus Caunaboa on the one side and the other, being troubled as it were on a rock in the sea ... *having excogitated this deceit, to have slain the Admiral and his company under the color of friendship if opportunity would so have served.* (19)

Tempest

Ant. Th'occasion speaks thee, and/ My strong imagination sees a crown dropping Upon thy head. (2.1.207–9)

Cal. I say, by sorcery he got this isle... If thy greatness will Revenge it on him... Thou shalt be Lord of it... (3.2.50–5)

Cal. As I told thee before, I am subject to a tyrant, /A sorcerer, that by his cunning hath cheated me of the island (3.2.37–38)

Ant. If he were that which now he's like (that's dead) Whom I with this obedient steel — three inches of it — Can lay to bed forever... (2.1.283–5)

Table 3.1. (cont.)

Plots discovered

Hoieda with many fair words and promises, brought [Caunaboa] to the Admiral: At whose commandment, he was immediately taken and put in prison. (19)

But when the Christian men had knowledge hereof, they compelled the poor wretches to confess their intent, and punished the chief authors of the devil. (123)

Sebastian and Antonio's plot to kill Alonso is discovered and interrupted before they do the deed, as is Stephano, Trinculo, and Caliban's plot to kill Prospero.

---

whereby they were cruelly murdered, and massacred."[3] Nevertheless, there is no doubt that such representations were generally discouraged by the Virginia Company during the Jacobean period. In the theatre, particularly, the image of the noble native, so conducive to the purposes of the Company, was especially prominent.

Shakespeare's Caliban, in the contrasting portrait of Marshall, recalls instead earlier "Spanish printed accounts of their exploits in South America."[4] Unsurprisingly, *De Orbe Novo*—by far the most influential of these accounts — contains numerous incidents of interaction between enslaved natives and enslaving voyagers that had little place in the English colonial experience until the second half of the 17th century. As Marshall implies, Eden's book furnishes aspects of Caliban's character not reproduced in the Bermuda pamphlets or any other literature of English voyagers. In Eden's translation of Martyr's neo–Platonic narrative, the physical "deformities" of a "wild and mischievous people called Can[n]ibals" (3) reflect an inward spiritual depravity. The native king Pancra, recalling a Caliban who, as "his body uglier grows,/So his mind cankers" (4.1.191–92), is described as a "monstrous and deformed creature ... worse than a brute beast, with manners according to the lineaments of his body" (97). In both cases the outward deformity signifies a dissolute morality expressed in part through sexual violence. Prospero rebukes Caliban for attempted rape: "Filth as thou art ... [I] lodged thee in my own cell, till thou did didst seek to violate the honor of my child" (1.2. 346–49), while Eden's monstrous king "abused with most abominable lechery the daughters of four kings of his brothers from whom he had taken them by violence" (97).

As transcribed by Eden, Martyr's New World, just like Caliban's island,

Table 3.2.

Eden, 1555	Tempest
Caliban the "mooncalf" monster, with four legs, later likened to a "tortoise."	**Steph.** This is some *monster* of the isle with *four legs*, who hath got, as I take it, an ague... I will give him some relief, if it be but for that: if I can recover him and keep him *tame* and get to Naples with him... *Four legs* and two voices; *a most delicate monster!* (2.2.64–89)
Into his nets chanced a young *fish* of the kind of those huge *monsters* of the sea which the habitors call manatee... This *fish is four footed*, and in shape like unto a *tortoise* ... and her head utterly like the head of *an ox. She liveth both in the water and on the land:* she is slow of moving: of condition meek, gentle, sociable and loving to mankind. And of a marvellous sense or memory as are the elephant and the dolphin... A *monster* of the sea *fed with man's hand.* (130v–131)	
Manatee is very brutish and vile... (202)	
Natives show the sources of fresh water	**Cal.** I lov"d thee And show"d thee all the qualities o" th" Isle, *The fresh springs, brine-pits,* barren place and fertile. (1.2.337–339)
As [the chief] drew near toward our men, he seemed friendly *to admonish them to take none of the water of that river, affirming it to be unwholesome for men: And showed them that not far from thence, there was a river of good water.* (60v)	I'll show thee *the best springs...* (2.2.157)
Numerous references to *springs* occur in Eden (as above and in 84, etc.); to *pools* (standing pools, 79v,. etc.), and *salt water* ("certain springs whose water is *more sharp and salt then the water of the sea*") (39–39v, etc.)	
Natives learn the language of the Old World	**Cal.** *You taught me language,* and my profit on"t
Being demanded what words [the natives] cried upon the Virgin Mary when they assailed their enemies, they answered that *they had learned no other words of the mariners' doctrine but Sancta Maria adiuva nos, Sancta Maria adiuva nos...* (74)	Is *I know how to curse.* The red plague rid you For learning me your language! (1.2.364–366)

is a realm of miracles and magic. The colonizing Spaniards bewilder the native population with superior technology that imitates the destructive force of nature or the terrible power of invisible divinities. Foreshadowing Prospero's power over the storm, the Spanish gunshot, smelling like "brimstone and fire," is mistaken for "thunderbolts and lightnings [that] had been sent from god..." (150v)[5]:

> At length [the Spaniards] were enforced to shoot off their biggest pieces of ordnance.... At the slaughter and terrible noise whereof the barbarians being sore discomfited and shaken with fear, *thinking the same to be thunder and lightning*, turned their backs and fled amain [114v; emphasis added].
>
> But when [the natives] heard the thunder of the guns, saw the smoke, and smelled the savour of brimstone and fire, *they supposed that thunderbolts and lightnings had been sent from god* [150v; emphasis added].

Many further elements of the fantastic *Tempest* landscape are furnished directly from Eden's translation in which the author promises that "You shall now therefore understand the illusions wherewith the people of the Island have been seduced..." (43), and depicts natives astonished by many wonders, including the musical raptures of the colonizers (Table 3.3).

Table 3.3. The Exotic and Fantastic in Eden Echoed in Shakespeare

Eden	Tempest
Miraculous creation of islands	
This Iaia, grievously taking *the death of his son*, after a few months, came again to *the gourd: the which when he had opened, there issued forth many great whales and other monsters of the sea:* where upon he declared to such as dwelt about him, that *the sea was enclosed in that gourd.* ...The which when they had taken in their hands ... suddenly let the gourd fall out of their hands: which being broken in the fall the sea forthwith broke out at the rifts thereof, and so filled the valleys, and overflowed the plains, that *only the mountains were uncovered, which now contain the islands* which are seen in those coasts. And this is	**Ant.** What impossible matter will he make easy next? **Seb.** I think he will *carry this island home in his pocket,* and give it *his son* for an apple. **Ant.** And, sowing the kernels of it in the sea, *bring forth more islands!* (2.1.89–94)

Table 3.3. (cont.)

the opinion of their wise men as concerning the original of the sea. (44v–45)

Roaring animals

Our men lodging in their houses, heard in the *night season horrible noises and roarings of wild beasts in the woods* which are full of exceeding great and high trees of sundry kinds. But the beasts of these woods are not noisome to men. (37v)

Seb. Whiles we stood here securing your repose,
Even now, we heard a hollow burst **of** *bellowing*
Like bulls, or rather lions...

Ant. O! 'twas a din to fright a monster's ear, / To make an earthquake: *sure it was the roar / Of a whole herd of lions.* (2.1.311–317)

Music in the wilderness

And when [the natives] yet drew nearer to the ship, and heard *the noise of the flutes, shawms, and drums,* they were wonderfully *astonished* at the *sweet harmony* thereof. (26v–27)[6]

Ariel *sings...*

Fer. Where should this *music* be? I' th' air, or th' earth? It sounds no more;— and sure, it waits upon Some god o' th' island. (1.2.388–90)

Alon. What *harmony* is this? My good friends, hark!

Gonz. Marvellous *sweet music!* (3.3.18–19)

At 3.2.124 Ariel plays the tune on *a tabor and pipe. [drum and flute]* and Caliban shouts "that's not the tune!"

Europeans as gods with supernatural powers

In so much that they *take [the Spaniards] for gods...* (135)

Shortly after a great multitude of them came running to the shore to behold this new nation, *whom they thought to have descended from heaven.* (2v)

Cal. ...I prithee *be my god.* (2.2.146)

Table 3.3. (cont.)

Spirit Dogs used to attack revellers

The Spaniards use the help of *dogs* in their wars against the naked people whom they *invade as fiercely and raveningly as if they were wild boars or harts.* (90)	A noise of hunters heard. Enter divers Spirits, in shape of *dogs and hounds,* and *hunt them about,* Prospero and Ariel setting them on. (4.1.SD)

Tall tales of travelers

Gonz. *If in Naples*

For who will believe that men are found with only one leg. Or with such such <fe>ete (illegible) whose shadow covereth their bodies? Or men of a cubit height, and other such like, being rather *monsters* than men? (216)	*I should report this now, would they believe me?* If I should say, I saw such islanders— For, certes, these are people of the island— Who, though they are of *monstrous shape,* yet, note, Their manners are more gentle-kind than of Our human generation you shall find Many, nay, almost any.[7] (3.3.27–34)

Eden's translation of the Iberian travel narratives is not only a linguistic foreground for Shakespeare's work, but also the demonstrable source of conceptions that *The Tempest* subverts through parody. The traditional source for Gonzalo's idealistic "golden world" primitivism (2.1.148–168) is a well-known passage in Montaigne's "De Cannibales" (1580, Eng. trans. f.p. 1603). Comparison with Eden, however, illustrates another vector of influence: Montaigne's own source is apparently Oviedo,[8] and while Montaigne's influence is more direct and conspicuous, Shakespeare seems to recall both texts when praising the "golden world" of the Americas, reproduced as Table 3.4.

In this passage Shakespeare is generally closer to Montaigne than to Oviedo; but in other instances Oviedo's influence is direct and unambiguous. Indeed, Shakespeare's Gonzalo parodies the verbose idealism of his namesake, *Gonzalo* Oviedo,[9] as reproduced in Eden's 1555 translation. The resemblance in linguistic pattern between Gonzalo's effusive panegyric to the fertility of the island (2.1.37–159) and Oviedo's confidence that "nature of her self bringeth forth such abundance" is unmistakable in the passages reproduced in Table 3.5.[10]

Ironically, the passage in Oviedo occurs in a text that has long been deprecated by mainstream Shakespearean scholarship as "incidental" and largely

Table 3.4. "Golden World" of the Americas, from Eden, Montaigne, and *The Tempest*

Eden: New World as a "Golden Age"	*Montaigne:* De Cannibales *(Borrowing from Eden)*	*Tempest: New World as a "Golden Age"*
They seem to live in *that golden world* of the which old writers speak so much. (8)	It is a nation, would I answer Plato, that *hath no kind of traffic, no knowledge of letters, no intelligence of numbers, no name of magistrate,* nor of politic superiorities; no use of service, of riches, or of poverty; *no contracts, no successions, no partitions, no occupation but idle*; no respect of kindred, but *common*, no apparel but natural, *no manuring of lands*, no use of wine, corn, or metal. The very words that import lying, falsehood, dissimulation, covetousness, envy, detraction, and pardon were never heard of amongst them.	**Gonz.** And were I king on"t, what would I do?...
A few things content them ... a *few clothes serve the naked: weights and measures are not needful* to such as can not skill of craft and deceit and *have not the use of pestiferous money,* the seed of innumerable mischiefs. So that if we shall not be ashamed to confess the truth, they seem to live in *that golden world* of the which old writers speak so much: wherein men *lived simply and innocently without enforcement of laws, without quarrelling Judges* and libels, content only to satisfy nature... (8)		I' the commonwealth I would by contraries Execute all things; *for no kind of traffic Would I admit; no name of magistrate; Letters should not be known; riches, poverty, And use of service, none; contract, succession,* Bourn, bound of land, *tilth,* vineyard, none; No use of metal, corn, or wine, or oil; *No occupation; all men idle, all:* And women too, but innocent and pure; No sovereignty,—... *All things in common* nature should produce *Without sweat* or endeavour; Treason, felony, Sword, pike, knife, gun, or need of any engine, Would I not have; but nature should bring forth, Of it own kind, *all foison, all abundance,* To feed my *innocent people...* I would with such perfection govern, sir,
For it is certain, that among them, *the land is as common* as the sun and water: And that Mine and Thine (the seeds of all mischief) have no place with them. They are content with so little, that in so large a country, they *have rather superfluity then scarceness.* So that (as we have said before) they seem to live in *the*		

Table 3.4. (cont.)

golden world, without toil living in open gardens, not entrenched with dykes, divided with hedges, or defended with walls. They deal truly one with another, *without laws, without books, and without judges.* (17v)

To excel the golden age. (2.1.146–168)

---

irrelevant to Shakespeare's creative process. Shakespeare's parody of Gonzalo Oviedo, which supplies far more persuasive evidence "from sign" of his knowledge of a particular text than anything proffered by advocates of the Strachey theory, is a striking proof of the mistaken character of this view.

Table 3.5. Gonzalo's Golden Age Parodies of Gonzalo Oviedo's Idealism

Eden

If any one prince had no more signiores than only this island, it should in short time be such as not to give place either to Sicily or England: whereas even at this present there is nothing wherefore it should malice their prosperity not being inferior to them in any felicity that in manner the heavens can grant to any land.... In this island, *nature of herself bringeth forth such abundance* of cotton that if it were wrought and maintained there should be more and *better than in any part of the world....* Cassia ... *increaseth so much* that it is a marvelous thing to consider ... and such seeds, sets, or plants, as are brought out of Spain and planted in this island become much better, bigger, and *of greater increase* then they are in any part of our Europe... (Oviedo in Eden 210v)

Tempest

Gonz. *Had I plantation of this isle, my lord* ... I' the commonwealth I would by contraries Execute all things ... but *nature should bring forth of its own kind, all foison, all abundance...* (2.1.144–164)

Seb. Yet *he would be king on't.* (2.1.157)

To reread *The Tempest* through the lens of Eden's 1555 translation of the Iberian Travel narratives is to confirm the relevance of the New World zeitgeist as a factor shaping the play's conception and imagery. Eden allows us to rediscover a play that is not only rooted in a Mediterranean setting rich in literary and historical precedent (see Chapter 8), but also engaged in the contemporary early-modern discourse of exploration and colonialism. Contrary to popular belief, this zeitgeist did not originate in the Jacobean Bermuda pamphlets — it arose decades earlier, largely as a product of Eden's 1555 translation and works such as those of Hakluyt and the early Virginia explorers that were published before the end of the reign of Elizabeth I.

Many clear parallels between Shakespeare and Eden cannot be duplicated in *Reportory* or the other Bermuda pamphlets. This suggests that Shakespeare read Eden rather than Strachey. Indeed, both Eden's ethos and his language irradiate the Shakespearean canon, leaving a detectable imprint on several plays[11] and an indelible one on *The Tempest*. Given the historical significance of Martyr's work, this is hardly surprising. *De Orbe Novo* was not merely the first of many books of voyager narratives. It was also the first to coin and popularize Miranda's phrase "New World," the first to publicize the voyages and discoveries of Christopher Columbus, and the first to evoke the "golden age" utopianism of America's native cultures (as well as the horrific rumors of cannibalism) for a European readership avid for tales of New World discovery. As Francis Augustus MacNutt has noted, in words that apply also to the uses to which Shakespeare puts Eden, this was one of those rare works that captures the spirit of a historical moment of profound and enduring consequence:

> Where others beheld but a novel and exciting incident in the history of navigation, with all but prophetic forecast [Martyr] divined an event of unique and far-reaching importance.[12]

Like Eden, Shakespeare brings Mediterranean Europe with him in writing about America, revealing a "brave new world" that replicates not only literal but moral topography, one that retains the sins and redemptions of the old one. In this regard, he was a more perceptive student of human nature than either the apologists for New World slavery, who regarded the natives as subhuman, or others, like Montaigne, who idealized them. Indeed, as Charles Frey has noted, *Tempest*'s ironic detachment from colonizing values invites "representatives of the Old World" to see themselves through "New World eyes."[13] There can be no doubt that Martyr's narrative contains — as does Montaigne — the seeds of Shakespeare's skepticism, and shares with *Tempest* an ethnological aesthetic that is absent in the Bermuda tracts of 1610–25.

In the wake of the postmodern interrogation of the colonial enterprise,

Martyr's work has sometimes been condemned for its concealed assumptions about an indigenous people who are "present but almost invisible, simply ornamenting a landscape"[14]; however, a close reading reveals many pages devoted, often with great sympathy, to the varieties of New World custom, mythology, religious practice, law, and social organization. Much that is vital to the ethos he records can be detected in Shakespeare's play: the fear or amazement of natives confronted by the wondrous "magical" technologies of the colonizers; the colonial enslavement of native populations under Spanish dominion, and their impulse for freedom; the conundrums of language difference and the search for shared meaning; the colonizers' quest for "scarce" resources to take from the land and their recurrent schismatic and conspiratorial intrigues. Shakespeare's play emphasizes the shrewd humanistic perception that the "new" world was, after all, kindred to the "old," because human nature is universal.

That Shakespeare apparently consulted not only Eden's influential translations (and possibly the original Latin versions), but also other voyager literature, might be concluded from a final conceptual parallel that is too striking to exclude. In Ferdinand Columbus' account of his father's voyages, first published in Italian in 1571, is a passage that not only recalls Prospero's influence over the storm, but even anticipates the precise rationale for the exercise of his art, and with such fidelity that it seems impossible that Shakespeare did not know it: "[Columbus'] enemies might well blame him, by saying that he had *raised this storm by magic art to be revenged* on Bovadilla and the rest of his enemies...."[15]

But Shakespeare apparently found the antidote to Prospero's stormy rage in Eden, in the moral articulated by Peter Martyr's native sage, speaking to Columbus:

> I have been advertised (most mighty prince) that you have of late with great power subdued many lands and Regions hitherto unknown to you: and have brought no little fear upon all the people and inhabitants of the same. The which your good fortune, you shall bear with less insolence, if you remember that the souls of men have two journeys after they are departed from this body. The one foul and dark, prepared for such as are injurious and cruel to mankind: The other pleasant and delectable, ordained for the which in their lifetime, loved peace and quietness. *If therefore you acknowledge yourself to be mortal,* and consider that every man shall receive condign reward or punishment for such things as he hath done in this life, *you will wrongfully hurt no man* [17; emphasis supplied].

Shakespeare's use of this passage is representative of his powers of humanism at their best. He discovered in the words of Martyr's New World sage a reflection of Old World morality, an echo of the Sermon on the Mount[16] that held the conquistadors to the letter of their own sacred texts. His audience would not have believed the speech in Caliban's mouth. But they (and we) do when it is given to Ariel. To borrow the analysis of Tristan Marshall, although he is writing of Shakespeare's use of a different passage from Eden, the transference of the chief's lines to the sprightly Ariel "invest[s] them with a sublimity and pathos"[17] appropriate to their universality.

It seems that Shakespeare read in these lines Martyr's own ironic answer to Spain's perplexity in the "great debate" at Valladolid[18] over whether the natives of the New World should be considered "human." Ariel's climactic challenge to Prospero's "colonial" authority not only supplies an antidote to the bard's "often farcical versions of the first encounter topos,"[19] but reveals Shakespeare's subtle engagement with the momentous question of Valladolid. At the dramatic turning point of the drama he has Ariel recall the words of Martyr's native sage:

> **Ar.** Your charm so strongly works 'em
> That if you now beheld them your affections
> Would become tender.
> **Pros.** Dost thou think so, spirit?
> **Ar.** Mine would, sir, *were I human*
> [5.1.17–19: emphasis supplied].

4

Amazing Storms

Despite much evidence to the contrary, traditional *Tempest* scholars would have us believe that Shakespeare required the inspiration of the 1609 *Sea Venture* shipwreck in order to conceive particular details of the *Tempest* storm. As recently as 2008, for example, Michael Neil asserts that "no other account of the storm and shipwreck seems as close to Shakespeare's as Strachey's."[1] To Vaughan, likewise, the storm scene is a test case for alternative scenarios of influence. He admits that in composing *The Tempest* Shakespeare "borrowed widely and eclectically" from "English and Continental literature," and that a thorough search "might uncover earlier sources for many, if not most, of the *Tempest*'s similarities to 'True Reportory.'"[2] Nevertheless, he finds that "the argument that Shakespeare could have gotten every detail of the storm, and every similarity of word and phrase from [sources other than Strachey] stretches credulity to the limits."[3]

One must ask whether advocates of the Strachey theory have demonstrated that no other account is as similar to the *Tempest* storm as Strachey's, let alone that Shakespeare is indebted to Strachey for "every detail" of that storm. We argue instead that there is no credible basis for imputing to Strachey, in the B or *Reportory* version, *any* influence on the *Tempest* storm scene, let alone the transcendent influence attributed to it by Vaughan and many others.

The reason may seem surprising. In their search for external sources, defenders of the Strachey theory routinely neglect to consider Shakespeare's own earlier writing. Yet often words or themes they would derive from later sources are demonstrably present in those earlier works. Consider, for example, the following precedent for the *Tempest* storm:

> Great lords, wise men ne'er sit and wail their loss,
> But cheerly seek how to redress their harms.
> What though *the mast be now blown over-board,*
> *The cable broke, the holding anchor lost,*
> *And half our sailors swallow'd in the flood?*

Yet lives our pilot still: is't meet that he
Should leave the helm and like a fearful lad
With tearful eyes add water to the sea,
And give more strength to that which hath too much;
Whiles in his moan *the ship splits on the rock,*
Which industry and courage might have sav'd?
Ah! what a shame! ah, what a fault were this.
Say, Warwick was our anchor; what of that?
And Montague *our top-mast*; what of him?
Our slaughter'd friends *the tackles*; what of these?
Why, is not Oxford here another *anchor*?
And Somerset, another *goodly mast*?
The friends of France our *shrouds and tacklings*?
And, though unskillful, why not Ned and I
For once allow'd the skilful pilot's charge?
We will not from the helm, to sit and weep,
But keep our course, though the rough wind say no,
From shelves and *rocks that threaten us with wrack.*
As good to chide the waves as speak them fair.
And what is Edward but a *ruthless sea*?
What Clarence but a quicksand of deceit?
And Richard but *a ragged fatal rock*?
All those the enemies to *our poor bark.*
Say you can swim; alas! 'tis but a while:
tread on the sand; why, there you quickly *sink*:
Bestride the rock; *the tide will wash you off,*
Or else you famish; that's a threefold death.
This speak I, lords, to let you understand,
In case some one of you would fly from us,
That there's no hop'd-for mercy with the brothers
More than with *ruthless waves, with sands and rocks.*
Why, courage, then! what cannot be avoided
'Twere childish weakness to lament or fear.

This metaphorical storm scene (5.4.1–38) occurs in a speech of Queen Margaret's in *3 Henry VI*, a play usually dated to the early 1590s, about twenty years before the ostensible date of both Strachey's reports and *The Tempest*. Yet it contains many significant parallels to the *Tempest* storm scene that Vaughan, Kathman and others categorically derive from Strachey: Margaret's ship "splits on the rock," her "mast [is] blown over-board," the survivors left to the "mercy" of "ruthless waves, with sands and rocks," and "sailors swallowed in the flood." The closeness of the passage to the *Tempest* wreck is amplified when we realize that Margaret's storm is not literal, but a metaphorical description of a political process (the corresponding *Tempest* scene is, of course, *both* metaphorical and literal); long before conceiving *The Tempest*,

Shakespeare was already exploring *storm* and *shipwreck* as metaphors of political life.

By the time of *Titus Andronicus*, another early play, Shakespeare was already able to prefigure his *Tempest* storm, describing a vision in which "the sea wax[es] mad, threatening the welkin with his big-swoln-face" (3.1.225–26), and going on to characterize this tumult as a "coil" (3.1.227). The passage is far closer to Miranda and Prospero's 1.2 description of the tempest, where the word "coil" occurs with the same association to the storm, than anything in Strachey:

> **Mir.** The sky, it seems, would pour down stinking pitch,
> But that the sea, mounting to the welkin's cheek,
> Dashes the fire out [1.2.3–5].
>
> **
>
> **Pros.** My brave spirit!
> Who was so firm, so constant, that this coil
> Would not infect his reason? [1.2.206–08]

Clearly, Shakespeare had no need to take lessons from Strachey on how to write a storm scene (See Appendix A for further details). The sources of Shakespeare's imagery seem more likely to be the same ones that informed Strachey's own narrative — such Renaissance shipwreck commonplaces as those found in Erasmus, Tomson and De Ulloa in Hakluyt, Ariosto, and Eden, all available no later than 1600. Or perhaps, as has sometimes been suggested,[4] such passages reflect the author's own experiences at sea. In any event, as already shown in our 2005 online rebuttal to David Kathman, three years prior to Alden Vaughan's *Shakespeare Quarterly* article, these earlier documents provide much more impressive and plausible source material for *The Tempest* than Strachey does. That article showed that, with the possible exception of the St. Elmo's fire detail, every storm motif Kathman (or any of Vaughan's other authorities) would derive from Strachey is found in Shakespearean storm scenes and imagery long predating both *Tempest* and *Reportory*.

Of these alternative sources the two most significant appear to have been Erasmus' "Naufragium" or "Shipwreck," and Ariosto's *Orlando Furioso*, both among the most widely available works of early-modern literature. The influence of *Orlando Furioso* on *The Tempest* is further discussed in Chapter 8, but here it may be worthwhile, before proceeding with our discussion of Eden's influence on Shakespeare's storms, to review the use Shakespeare put to Erasmus' dramatic dialogue. "Naufragium" contains the most widely influential of all renaissance storm descriptions, with many elements of what has been variously termed the "storm formula" or "storm set-piece": waves which reach to the sky, praying sailors, St. Elmo's fire, the splitting or overturning of the ship, provisions and baggage thrown overboard, the cutting or blowing down of the mainmast, and a helmsman pale with fear. At several points the dialogue seems to have influenced Shakespeare, having in common with *The Tempest* storm elements not found in Strachey.

Among these is the motif of the pale pilot (Table 4.1).

Table 4.1. The Pale Shipmaster in "Naufragium" and Tempest. Emphasis supplied.

"Naufragium"	Tempest
Adolph. At length the master of the ship came unto us *very pale.* **Anto.** That paleness doth presage some great evil (Gr)	**Gonz.** I have great comfort from this fellow. Methinks he hath no drowning mark upon him. His *complexion is perfect gallows.* (1.1.28–30)

Still more impressive is the manner in which Erasmus seems to have suggested to Shakespeare the dramatic potential of shipwreck passengers trying to bargain their way out of impending death by drowning (Table 4.2).

Table 4.2. Bargaining for Salvation in "Naufragium" and *Tempest*

Ado. Some did nothing but vomit and some made vows. There was a certain Englishman who promised golden mountains to his lady of Walsingham if ever he came safe to land. Others promised many things to a wooden cross that stood at such a place and others to another that stood in another place. The like vows were made to the Virgin Mary, which reigneth in many places, and they think their vow of no effect, unless they name the place. I will make no covenant with Saints, for what is it else but a formal contract, or bargain? I will give you this, if you will do that for me: I will give you a Candle, if I may swim to land. (G3r-v)	**Gonz.** Now would I give a thousand furlongs of sea for an acre of barren ground, long heath, brown furze, any thing. The wills above be done! but I would fain die a dry death. (1.1.65–68)

Eden, too, is filled with references to storms and shipwrecks, several of which show definite traces of linguistic influence on *Tempest*: "so fierce a tempest" that "two [caravels] were drowned even before their eyes" (42v), ships that "leaked and took water" (Eden 232v) or "ran upon a blind rock covered with water, and *clove in sunder*" (2v; emphasis ours), and sailors caught in "so great a tempest ... that they were enforced to cast into the sea, all the household stuff..." (67v).

Perhaps the most striking Eden shipwreck imagery that has left a distinct imprint on *The Tempest* is the example already cited in which ships, confused by St. Elmo's fire, "so wandered out of their course and *were dispersed in sunder*, that they in manner despaired *to meet again*... But as God willed, the seas and tempest being quieted, they came safely to their determined course..." (217v). In this case there is no doubt of direct influence. The latter passage so closely anticipates Ariel's description of his scattering of Alonso's fleet as to put the matter beyond reasonable doubt: "And for the rest o' th' fleet (*Which I dispers'd*), *they have all met again,*/And are.... Bound sadly home for Naples" (1.2.232–35).

As the only *Tempest* storm element that is arguably without Shakespearean precedent, the St. Elmo's fire motif provides an apt illustration of the uncritical reasoning on which the Strachey theory all-too-often depends. Vaughan insists that *Reportory* was probably *The Tempest*'s "immediate inspiration"[5] for the motif. Vaughan's source Cawley, who gives an impressive résumé of the numerous ancient and Renaissance sources on this popular topic, provides an antidote to Vaughan's "probably":

> Douce (*Illustrations of Shakespeare*, London, 1839, p. 3) cites [St. Elmo's Fire] in Pliny, Seneca, Erasmus, Schotti, Eden, and Batman. It is mentioned also by Hakluyt, Purchas, Thevet, Le Loyer, and as illustration in prose or verse it was used by Chapman, Phineas Fletcher, Gomersall, Bacon, Fulke Greville, Drayton, Thomas Watson, Drummond, Lodge, and Thomas Heywood. I am inclined to believe, *therefore since the idea was obviously so current, that Gayley has slightly overestimated Shakspere's indebtedness to this particular version.* That Strachey recalled it to his mind I have no doubt. *But the features mentioned are common in the other versions.* Le Loyer (*Treatise of Specters*, London, 1605, fol. 67v), for instance, speaks of men who "see the fire ... to fly upon their ship, and to alight upon the top of the mast." And Hakluyt, as Luce remarks (Arden ed., p. 163), has "beak" and "it would be in two or three places at once."[6]

Cawley, anticipating Vaughan's robust conviction, entertains "no doubt" that Strachey was responsible for calling the motif to Shakespeare's mind. But all the evidence of his passage suggests a contrary conclusion. Except for two sources, Le Loyer and Hakluyt, Cawley cannot plausibly connect any wording directly to *The Tempest*. And far from supporting Strachey's direct influence on Shakespeare; he even admits that "the features mentioned [by Gayley] are common to the other versions."[7]

Gayley, Cawley, Kathman, and Vaughan have all failed to notice that certain apparently unique characteristics of Antonio Pygafetta's account of St. Elmo's fire, as reproduced in Eden,[8] clearly influenced the *Tempest* version. The account of St. Elmo's fire in Eden's translation of Pygafetta's narrative describes "certeyne *flames* of fire burning very clear ... upon the masts of the ships ... which *some ignorant folks think to be spirits or such other fantasies*" (217v emphasis supplied).[9] From this Shakespeare apparently took inspiration for Ariel's first person account of his bewitching performance as St. Elmo's fire:

> Now in the waist, the deck, in every cabin,
> I flam'd amazement. Sometimes, I'ld divide,
> And burn in many places; on the topmast,
> The yards and boresprit, would I flame distinctly [1.2.196–200].

Although Shakespeare seems to have been familiar with more than one account of St. Elmo's fire,[10] only from Eden could he have taken inspiration for the idea that the phenomenon is caused by "spirits."[11] Shakespeare has also apparently reconfigured Gonzalo's notion of the "drowning mark" (1.1.28)[12] from the same passage of Eden's text, in which St. Elmo's fire is described as "*a token of drowning*" (217v; emphasis supplied).

Gayley,[13] Cawley,[14] Kathman,[15] and Mowat[16] all attempt to trace Ariel's phrase "flamed amazement" to Strachey's observation that St. Elmo's fire "might have strucken amazement"[17] in the sailors. Indeed, Mowat, after acknowledging that "most of the details that ... persuade us that *The Tempest* echoes Strachey's manuscript ... are also to be found in Virgil" and other sources, singles out Ariel's phrase as a unique connection between Shakespeare's play and Strachey, arguing that it "echoes only Strachey" among the play's recognized sources. Though Mowat's treatment of Strachey as a Shakespearean source is more nuanced and thoughtful than that of many other critics, she still favors the link to Strachey, despite mounting evidence to the contrary. She relegates to a footnote her admission that "Strachey's discussion of the corposant [St. Elmo's] echoes Eden" and it is therefore "just possible ... that Ariel's description ... quotes Eden rather than Strachey."[18]

"Amazement," although merely a lexical flourish in Strachey, permeates *The Tempest* thematically.[19] It is so conceptually over-determined, given *The Tempest*'s New World zeitgeist, as to confound any attempt to isolate its inspiration to Strachey. As a commonplace in the contemporaneous discourse of the Americas, the word expresses what A. Pagden has termed the "vertiginous experience of being in a 'new' world"[20] and Stephen Greenblatt describes as "*the* decisive emotional and intellectual experience in the presence of radical difference"[21] on both sides of the historic encounter between New and Old Worlds.[22] Eden's text, a seminal work in this discourse of the exotic, often records the reciprocal "amazement" of explorer and native when confronted by radical otherness:

- The enemies being *amazed* by reason of *this great miracle* (74V)
- [they showed him things that] had further delighted his mind with the harmony of their musical instruments ... they dismissed him *half amazed with too much admiration* (122 v)
- *Whereat the king was greatly amazed* (223V)
- *He was greatly amazed* and made signs holding up his hand to heaven, signifying thereby that our men came from thence (218v–219)[23]

The Tempest reflects the *maze*-like confusion of shipwrecked voyagers treading a "New World" labyrinth of magical signs. The "torment, trouble, wonder, and *amaze*ment" (5.1.104–05) of the court party, wending its way through an island maze, serve to dramatize the "archetypal desires, states, and actions common to the experience of the Christian pilgrims"[24] or Lenten penitents treading a maze (see Chapter 6). Perhaps Richard Eden's prominent mention in the 1555 preface to his *Decades,* of "the Mazes called Labyrinthi ... of knots inexplicable ... and diverse other such portentous inventions..." instilled the idea on which Shakespeare's play depends. The wilderness of the New World was a natural maze, a bewildering macrocosm of which the Old World ritual devices of Cretan legend or Chartres Cathedral were merely artificial derivatives.

5

A Spanish Maze

If *The Tempest* did not depend on William Strachey's *Reportory* as a source, and instead draws its New World ambience from materials that had been widely available since the middle of the 16th century, when was it written? In 2004, independent scholar Richard Malim[1] offered the intriguing suggestion that a 1605 performance record of an ostensibly lost play, *A Tragidye of the Spanishe Maz*, actually referred to an early performance of Shakespeare's *Tempest* under an alternative title. Mainstream scholarship has ignored Malim's idea, but we felt it was worth investigating and testing. The present chapter interrogates Malim's theory to consider whether it must be discarded as a historical red herring or can, on the contrary, be substantiated with further evidence.

The Spanish Maze is known only from a Revels Office document[2] transcribed in 1842 by Peter Cunningham and reprinted by E.K. Chambers,[3] which lists thirteen plays and two masques performed between Hallowmas and Shrove Tuesday 1604/05, all but two produced during the winter festival season between St. Stephen's Night (December 26) and Shrove Tuesday in February. Plays by Chapman, Heywood, Jonson and "Shaxberd" appear on the list, but seven of the thirteen are indisputably by Shakespeare.[4] While it has sometimes been suspected as a forgery, almost all scholars now regard the manuscript, known as Malone ms. 29, as authentic. The final entry reads as follows:

On Shrovsunday A play of
the Marchant of Venis   Shaxberd
On Shrovmonday A *Tragidye* of
the Spanishe Maz:
On Shrovtuesday A play cauled
The Marchant of Venis againe
comaunded by the Kings Majestie.   Shaxberd

Several inferences may be drawn from this listing: First, the Shrove Monday performance of *Spanish Maze*[5] had been intended as the concluding play of the revels season and the Tuesday restaging of *Merchant of Venice* was an unscheduled command performance. This will be significant for evaluating the relationship between *The Tempest* and *Spanish Maze*. Second, of the seven definitely Shakespearean plays on the list, three are identified as by "Shaxberd," but four more list no author:

- *The Moor of Venis*
- *Merry Wives of Winsor*
- *Loves Labours Lost*
- *Henry the fift*

Of the twelve named plays,[6] only one, the *Spanish Maze,* is apparently not extant. Can this anomaly be explained, as Malim has proposed, on the hypothesis that it is an early title of *The Tempest?* There are many known examples of variant play titles in the surviving records. Malone ms. 29 itself lists *Othello* as *The Moor of Venis* and *Comedy of Errors* as *The Plaie of Errors.*[7]

The two earliest documented performances of *The Tempest* (1 November 1611 and 20 May 1613), took place at Whitehall.[8] Scholarly opinion diverges on the question of whether the play was written originally for performance at Whitehall or Blackfriars. At least two recent editions[9] follow Andrew Gurr's (1989) argument for an original performance at Blackfriars. But the two venues had in common a stage apparatus appropriate to the play's elaborate scenic effects. It may therefore be pertinent that the 1604/05 Shrove Monday performance of *Spanish Maze* was by all appearances staged at Whitehall.[10] It is also worth noting that the *Spanish Maze* was performed "By his Majesty's Players" and the paymaster was none other than "Shakespeare's" faithful friend and comrade, John Heminges.[11] These facts do not by themselves prove that *The Spanish Maze* is *The Tempest,* but they do suggest that we should ask whether the premise of an original Shrovetide production might illuminate the *Tempest's* symbolism, imagery, and structure. As we shall see (Chapters 6–7), the answer is a definitive "yes."

Let us start from the title: is *Tragedy of the Spanish Maze* a plausible alternative title for the play we know today as *The Tempest?* As we shall see in detail (Chapter 6), *The Tempest* is a fundamentally about a "maze." Throughout the play the characters wander, in the mode of the Christian pilgrim, through a disorienting labyrinth which induces in them the various altered states of consciousness characteristic of the contemplative penitent treading a maze.

Less obvious, especially to the modern reader, is that *The Tempest* (among other things) is a play about Spain and dynastic Spanish politics. Even though we think of Milan and Naples as Italian cities, the early-modern theatre patron would have readily associated Shakespeare's characters with the Italo-Spanish aristocracy of those two cities, which during the 15th and 16th centuries were "in the undisputed possession of Spain."[12] This dominance was the long-term result of repeated attempts by Spain to extend its influence over the two city states, a process consolidated before Phillip II became King in 1556. During the 1590s many plays were published in London concerning Spain and Spanish politics, including *Spanish Tragedy* (1592, 1594, 1602), and culminating around the time of the death of Phillip II in 1598 with *Mucedorus* (1598)[13] and *Alphonsus* (1599).[14] A second wave, including *Othello* (Q 1621)[15] and Massinger's *The Duke of Millaine* (1623), coincided with rising Protestant antagonism to the proposed Spanish marriage of Charles Stuart, heir to the throne.

Perhaps "tragedy" presents a greater difficulty in matching the two play titles. Again, however, the impediment is hardly disabling. The 1623 First Folio places *The Tempest* with the comedies; today it is typically considered a romance, a genre not found in the folio. As Lucas Erne has recently emphasized, early-modern "generic descriptions are notoriously loose."[16] A rich critical tradition, including such leading Shakespearean scholars as John Dover-Wilson and E. M. W. Tillyard, testifies to the play's ambiguity of form and its close affinity to the conventions of early-modern tragedy. With the exception of Antonio's decision to exile rather than execute Prospero, the plot is "entirely typical of Elizabethan revenge tragedy," and the play consequently "more typically *tragic* in the fashion of its age than *The Winter's Tale*."[17] Signet editor Langbaum agrees: the play "contains the subject matter of tragedy, and it gives us throughout the sense of omniscience, of surveying all life, that we get only at the highest points of illumination in the tragedies."[18] One might add that the play's ambiguous epilogue, which leaves Prospero stranded within the confines of a magic circle of his own creation, contributes significantly to its amorphous form and affinity with tragedy. Will Prospero be released through the "indulgence" of his audience? If not, the play definitely qualifies as a tragedy, at least for its protagonist.

Doubtless the most germane classification of Shakespeare's play would be that of tragicomedy, as defined in the contemporaneous induction to Fletcher's *Faithful Shepherdesse*:

> A tragic-comedy is not so called in respect of mirth and killing, but in respect it wants deaths, which is enough to make it no tragedy, yet brings some near it, which is enough to make it no comedy....[19]

But perhaps the original scribe, a functionary who spelled the great playwright's name as "Shaxberd," may be excused for lacking the critical vocabulary of John Fletcher and consequently mistaking a tragicomedy that "contains the subject of matter of tragedy," and is in many respects "entirely typical of Elizabethan revenge tragedy," for a tragedy pure and simple.[20]

Whether *The Tempest* was originally known by an alternative title is ultimately unprovable, barring further discovery. But if the play originally was known as *The Spanish Maze*, it is easy to see why it would have been revived with a different title, one that reflected the needs and expectations of a mid–Jacobean Whitehall audience. In the words of David Lindley, "It is indisputable that for an audience in 1611 the apparent parallel [to the Bermuda wreck] would have given the play an irresistible topicality."[21] Indeed the months leading up to the third Virginia Supply (June 1609) were a time of heightened ideological conflict between the stage and the Virginia Company. Theatrical parody of the adventurers was big business, but the authorities of the Company were not amused. William Crashaw, in a sermon delivered 21 February 1609 before Lord De La Warr "at the said Lord General his leave-taking of England his Native country, and Departure for Virginia," lashed out at the players for their topical travesties:

> As for players: (pardon me right honorable and beloved, for wronging this place and your patience with so base a subject,) they play with Princes and Potentates, Magistrates and Ministers, nay with God and Religion, and all holy things: nothing that is good, excellent or holy can escape them: how then can this action? But this may suffice, that they are Players: they abuse Virginia, but they are but Players: they disgrace it: true, but they are but Players, and they have played with better things, and such as for which, if they speedily repent not, I dare say, vengeance waits for them.[22]

Crashaw's thundering critique illustrates the sociological divide between the extravagant practices of the stage and the sober norms of the predominantly Puritan colonists. He compares New World parodies to the disruptive antics of players traducing the early-modern social hierarchy by adopting the fancy dress and mannerisms of their social superiors. In Crashaw's world, unrepentant players (and, by implication, the playwrights who supply them with their "disgraceful" scripts), will be dealt divine vengeance. As a leading public advocate for the Company, Crashaw puts paid in this outburst to the popular fantasy in which a secretive (and invisible) Shakespeare, privy to the inside gossip of the Colonists, joins forces with the Virginia Company to promote a New World colonization scheme in his play. To the contrary, all the available evidence suggests that Company authorities would have responded to Shakespeare's *Tempest* with the same hostility Crashaw directs against the "players" in his sermon. The author of the *Tempest* was the last person in the world they would have wanted to enlist in their activity by supplying the latest inside news of the Bermuda wreck in the form of the manuscript of Strachey's *Repertory*.[23]

Not surprisingly, theatrical representation of the New World seems to have reached a crescendo around the time of the third Jamestown supply and Bermuda wreck. The anonymous author of the Virginia pamphlet *True Declaration* (registered November 1610) refers to the Third Supply's tempest-driven diversion to the Bermudas as a "tragical Comedy." Traditional *Tempest* scholars have steadfastly resisted the implications of this striking passage, which gives every sign of the author's knowledge of Shakespeare's play over a year before its first recorded performance:

> Consider all these things together. At the instant of need, they descried land, half an hour more, had buried their memorial in the Sea. If they had fell by night, what expectation of light, from an uninhabited desert? They fell betwixt a labyrinth of rocks, which they conceive are moldered into the Sea, by thunder and lightning. This was not Ariadne's thread, but the direct line of God's providence.... What is there in all this tragical Comedy that should discourage us with impossibility of the enterprise? when of all the Fleet, one only Ship, by a secret leak was endangered, and yet in the gulf of Despair, was so graciously preserved. *Quæ videtur pæna, est medicina*, that which we accompt a punishment of evil, is but a medicine against evil.[24]

This reference to a "tragical Comedy" has sometimes been regarded[25] as one of Shakespeare's inspirations for a tragicomedy about the New World. But the literary references to Ariadne's thread and the labyrinth, while mere surface details in *Declaration,* form the mythopoeic substructure of Shakespeare's play. As Barbara Mowat has noted, the play is rooted in the Ovidian and Virgilian traditions of "that most infamous of mazes, created by Daedalus to enclose the Minotaur."[26] Echoing Crashaw's denunciation of the players in a more temperate mode, the author of *Declaration* contrasts this pagan labyrinth to the "direct line of God's providence" followed by the Virginia colonizers. Like Crashaw, he is evidently participating in an ideological battle between the stage and the colony. He appears to respond directly, almost conversationally, to the symbolism of Shakespeare's play.

If such references to theatrical representations of the Virginia colony as those of Crashaw's sermon and *Declaration* tend rather to support than invalidate an early date for *The Tempest,* they also confirm that plays about New World voyages were in vogue well before the time of the Third Supply. Such plays dated back at least to *Eastward Ho,* the flamboyant collaboration of Marston, Jonson, and Chapman, first produced in 1605. The collaborative satire, which lampoons several Shakespeare plays — including, as we shall see, *The Tempest* itself — appealed to public curiosity about a colonization enterprise that had been unfolding since the 1580s on the quays of London and

Plymouth, and had long since been memorialized in print in the first volumes of Hakluyt's *Principal Navigations*, published 1598–1600. Most importantly, these references also suggest a plausible reason why a late Elizabethan-era play originally titled *The Spanish Maze* might by 1611 be renamed *The Tempest*. A play that in 1603 would have recalled the recent death of Phillip II in parodying the Spanish attempt to master the New World was put to alternative service in 1610–11 in the wake of the Gates disaster. The Spanish threat to English colonization of North America was waning. By the "direct line of God's providence" the colony at Jamestown had survived a horrible winter. But all of London *was* buzzing with news of the Bermuda disaster and the pitiful wreck of the *Sea Venture*.

While these considerations are in themselves intriguing, they also suggest opportunity for further inquiry. If *The Tempest* was once known as *The Spanish Maze*, and the latter play was produced for Shrovetide in 1604/05, does Shakespeare's play preserve any trace of Shrovetide symbolism?

6

Prospero's Labyrinth

If the travel narratives and literary precedents discussed in previous chapters have furnished the imaginative topography of Shakespeare's "New World" island, the genesis of the play's form and symbolism must be sought in the liturgical conventions that shaped Shakespeare's age. The Christian liturgical cycle served as a template for organizing the symbolic and devotional life of early-modern theatrical audiences; many early-modern plays, like their medieval antecedents, owe their form and symbolism to corresponding liturgical associations. Many decades ago Sir E. K. Chambers noted the "persistent correlation between the dates of dramatic performance at Elizabeth's court and certain liturgical festivals in the English church year."[1] Plays were chosen, and sometimes written, for specific liturgical contexts: in England, of 328 Elizabethan recorded court performances from 1558 to 1603, 289 — 88 percent — occurred on one of seven major festival days.[2] Partly with this in mind, R. Chris Hassel urged that close study of the devotional patterns of the English church year would "establish a new and major context for the understanding of Renaissance drama."[3] A flood[4] of subsequent studies attests to the potential of such a perspective for transforming our critical awareness of the design and symbolism of early-modern drama.

Among the most prominent festivals, in England and on the continent, was pagan Carnival, appropriated by the Catholic Church as a period of license immediately preceding Lent and renamed Shrovetide, which fell between 3 February and 9 March, varying with the date of Easter. The name derives from the Middle English verb *schriven,* referring to the penitential practices preceding Lent[5]; however, consistent with its pagan roots, Shrovetide is an "inversion ritual," in which normative social roles and patterns of behavior are temporarily suspended or reversed. A season of indulgence and symbolic rebellion,[6] Shrovetide was an officially sanctioned release from, and compensation for, the approaching deprivations of Lent. As described by Ronald Hutton,

In medieval and early-modern high society, Shrovetide marked the end of the chain of cold season celebrations which had commenced with the Twelve Days of Christmas and continued at Candlemas [Feb. 2]. From the time at which royal, aristocratic, and episcopal household accounts become abundant, in the 14th century, payments for food, drink, and entertainment at this time rank only behind those at Christmas. 16th century accounts for the English and Scottish royal revels show regular and heavy expenditure upon plays, music, and masquerades for Shrove Tuesday.[7]

In both the literary and the pictorial arts the paradox of Shrovetide, with its unique fusion of libidinal excess and pious deprivation is emblematized as the "Battle of Carnival and Lent,"[8] exemplified in Brueghel's painting by that name. The theme was a popular one in the pictorial arts, repeated by Jan Miense Molenaer around 1633 (Figure 6.1). And, less famously, in Thomas Neogeorgus' anti-papist lampoon, translated and published in English in 1570:

> Now when at length the pleasant time of Shrovetide comes in place,
> And cruel fasting days at hand approach with solemn grace:
> Then old and young are both as mad, as guests of *Bacchus* feast,
> And four days long they tipple square, and feed and never rest.[9]

> [They] seek their Shrovetide Bachanal, still crying everywhere,
> Where are our feasts become? alas the cruel fasts appear.
> Some bear about a herring on a staff, and loud do roar
> Herrings, herrings, stinking herrings, puddings now no more.
> And hereto join they foolish plays, and doltish doggerel rhymes.
> And what beside they can invent, belonging to the times.[10]

By the Middle Ages Shrovetide had attained a prominence matched only by Christmas as an occasion for merry-making and theatrical indulgence. During the 15th century the secular drama of Continental Europe was "chiefly represented by the Shrovetide play [Germ. *Fastnachtspiel*]," named from its origin in the "mummeries and the coarse fun-making indulged in on special occasions, notably on Shrove-Tuesday."[11] Paradoxically, brothels and theatres were popular targets of Shrovetide iconoclasm and were often "at the mercy of the traditional rowdiness of the prentices on Shrove Tuesday."[12] In London crowds of apprentices and other young men — drinking, masked, costumed and led by the Shrovetide equivalent of the "master of 'merry disports' with his retinue of ragged revelers"[13] — raised havoc in the streets and sometimes rioted. In *Time Vindicated* (1623) Ben Jonson has Fame denounce "lawless Prentices, on Shrove Tuesday" who "compel the Time to serve their riot: for drunken Wakes, and strutting Bear-baitings, that savor only of their own abuses."[14] Here art was imitating nature. On Shrove Tuesday, 1617, a crowd of apprentices sacked Christopher Beeston's Cockpit theatre on Drury Lane.[15]

Figure 6.1. The battle of Carnival and Lent by Jan Miense Molenaer, c. 1633 (Indianapolis Museum of Art, purchased in honor of A. Ian Fraser, with additional funding provided by the David L. Chambers, Jr. Fund for Dutch and Flemish Art, the Dr. V. K. Stoelting Art Fund, and Mrs. Jane. W. Myers).

In another 1618 account "bands of prentices, 3,000 or 4,000 strong ... on Shrove Tuesday and 1 May [perform] outrages in all directions,"[16] and in 1630 "youths armed with cudgels, stones, hammers, tools, trowels, and handsaws, put the Playhouses to the sack and Bawdyhouses to the spoil."[17]

The tradition of Shrovetide dramatic performance was particularly strong in Germany. Most extant *Fastnachtspiel* manuscripts are anonymous productions of the 15th century, but the genre achieved its greatest success at the hands of Hans Sachs (1494–1576), Macropedius (1487–1558), and Jakob Ayrer (1543–1605). Ayrer became famous as one who "blended the tradition of the Shrovetide play with the innovations of the English comedians in his dramatic works."[18] In England the list of early-modern plays known or suspected to have definite Shrovetide associations[19] includes many prominent titles, among them *Hamlet*,[20] *Staple of News*,[21] *Merchant of Venice*,[22] *As You Like It*,[23] *Sapho and Phao*,[24] and *Love's Labour's Lost*.[25]

In England and on the Continent, Shrovetide performance both expressed and imitated the passions of the season. In his study of the eight masques known to have been produced at Shrovetide, Hassel finds an unusual "intensity and frequency of correlation" between theatrical forms and the "liturgical and sociological motifs" of the festival.[26] More specifically, "the tension between [the] interwoven if contradictory festival strands" of license and penitence was found prominently expressed in the Shrovetide productions; this tension would exert "a significant influence upon the Shrovetide entertainments at court."[27]

By the age of Shakespeare, from a theatrical as well as a sacramental or popular perspective, Shrovetide had come to mark a critical transition in the English calendar. During Lent secular plays, like marriages,[28] were traditionally proscribed. On Ash Wednesday, the annual cycle of court revels ended and the public theatres fell silent and remained closed until after Easter. According to Glynne Wickham, "the idea of Lent, as a period of obligatory abstinence and penitential reflection in preparation for the rejoicing of Easter, militated positively against any form of display or festive celebration."[29] By the Elizabethan period, however, the traditional prohibition was weakening, and Lenten plays had to be formally prohibited by Act of the Privy Council on 13 March, 1578/79. Gerald Eades Bentley notes that the proscription was reinforced inconsistently, and by 1615 had noticeably weakened through the use of dispensations, paid to the Master of the Revels, allowing performance during Lent except for Wednesday and Friday, Sermon-Days.[30] But even through the reigns of James and Charles I, Lent remained a low water mark in the annual cycle of dramatic production, and "the London theatres were not open for business as usual during the weeks before Easter."[31]

The Tempest is of course not liturgical in the medieval sense of a play designed to dispense official Church doctrine through seasonal symbolism. As Grace Hall emphasizes, it instead enacts a burlesque parody of traditional religion:

> Drunk Caliban's High-day mocks a Christian ritual. All of the occupants of the "ship of souls" are immersed (baptized). A banquet, symbolizing communion, appears, but is not available to the "three men of sin." A wedding [masque] is performed. Caliban is taught a supreme lesson in mastership and becomes a candidate for "grace"—confirmation. A "holy" man and the king enter the magic circle to receive orders of a kind.... Alonso undergoes a sea-change, a spiritual form of extreme unction. As penance, Caliban, Trinculo, and Stephano trim Prospero's cell "handsomely."[32]

Hassel also endorses the idea that *The Tempest* might exemplify a liturgical design reflecting a fall Hallowmas production rather than a spring Shrovetide connection. He speculates that the Hallowmas audience could have perceived that Prospero ideally exemplifies both the private and the public dimensions of [Hallowmas] commandments of the blessed as he deals with Caliban's depraved troop and Alonso's with justice and mercy.

Hassel goes on to claim that "in [its] elaborate context of liturgical and sociological associations, *The Tempest* evidences a complex relationship to the festival."[33] Hall, likewise, tries valiantly to connect the play to the Hallowmas installation of the Lord of Misrule in the great houses of England, suggesting that "the custom can be applied to the play on several levels."[34] Unfortunately such theories have tended more to discredit the entire idea of the relevance of liturgical context to interpretation — a topic on which Hassel elsewhere writes with great conviction and insight — than to substantiate their own premises. But, in an entire book focused on detailed study of the theological dimensions of *The Tempest* Hall devotes only two unconvincing pages to the play's liturgical context.[35] In a book that brilliantly reveals the symbolic implications of the liturgical and sociological context of early English drama in general, Hassel's analysis of *The Tempest* is remarkably abbreviated and ultimately, unlike his general argument, unconvincing. No careful reader can agree that Hassel makes the case for an "elaborate context of liturgical and sociological associations" between *The Tempest* and a hypothetical Hallowmas context.

The reason for these failures is apparent. Misplaced confidence in the completeness of the documentary record has led scholars to assume that *The Tempest*'s first *recorded* performance, 1 November 1611, was its first *actual* performance. Anyone who has studied early-modern theatrical records knows how precarious such an assumption is. Literary historians are aware that these records are notoriously incomplete.[36] Even if we assume that complete records ever existed, what has come down to us is only fragmentary.

As we shall see, however, the Shrovetide dimensions of *The Tempest*, properly contextualized, are as obvious and profound as those of such acknowledged Shrovetide plays as *The Merchant of Venice* or *As You Like It*. Recognizing the true liturgical context of the play will provide a ready explanatory construct for many otherwise puzzling passages and open fresh vistas on the play's structure, genesis, themes, and symbolism. A shipwreck precipitated by a tempest is an apt prelude to a play written for special performance during an inversion festival. In medieval iconography, the ship was a customary image of both church and state, and it was the authority of these two institutions that was most jeopardized by the libidinous populism of the inversion festivals. Just as Shrovetide precipitates a symbolic conflict of authority on land, the storm provokes a conflict of authority on the ship: the king is over-ruled by the boatswain, but both king and boatswain are deposed when the ship goes down. This "who's in charge" theme permeates the play but is never resolved, as the magus Prospero, in his final words, transfers power to the audience when he begs them to decide his fate.

The idea of the tempest as a naturalized emblem of Shrovetide license appears in contemporaneous sources such as Neogeorgus' vivid account of German Shrovetide festivities: "with all their force throughout the streets and marketplace they run,/as if *some whirlwind mad, or tempest great* from skies should come."[37] This carnival of the elements, orchestrated by Prospero just as real storms were believed to be inflicted by God, precipitates Lenten penitence in the passengers: "the king and prince [are] at prayers. Let's assist them, for our case is as theirs" (1.1.46–47). Penitence, and with it forgiveness, becomes a leitmotif of the play, culminating in Prospero's final appeal to the audience: "As you from crimes would pardon'd be,/ Let your indulgence set me free" (epi. 19–20).

The Janus-faced word *indulgence* is freighted with relevant liturgical ambiguity. In the sense of license, indulgence was a leading motif of Shrovetide festivities; Caliban's "work to rule" resistance to Prospero's labor regimen and enthusiasm for drunken merriment express the popular view of Shrovetide as a time for escaping work and indulging the appetites. But *indulgence* also recalls the selling of religious pardons, a controversial practice that by the time of Martin Luther had become one of the most inflammatory theological disputes of the age. For Catholics, Lent, when the mind of the parishioner was focused on penitence and salvation, was the primary season for the buying of indulgences.[38]

The conflict between Carnival and Lent is a frequent theme in early-modern theatre. François Laroque, for example, identifies the central tension of *Love's Labour's Lost* as "the long struggle between Carnival and the love-making that goes with it on the one hand, and on the other Lenten meditation and study." He finds that "oppositions of this kind ... are the very substance of festive comedies such as Nashe's *Last Will and Testament*, [and] are certainly particularly used by Shakespeare in his earliest comedies."[39] This pattern is also used by Shakespeare in *The Tempest*, and is more specifically related in that play to a Shrovetide festival context. Stephano, Trinculo and Caliban, celebrating Caliban's "high-day" (2.2.181) with drinking, sacrilegious jesting, and a procession through the mire, exemplify the riotous indulgence of Carnival. Carnival love finds expression in the courtship of Miranda by Alonso's son Ferdinand. Most significantly, the play's plot even originates in Antonio's exploitation of Prospero's Lenten retreat into meditation and "secret studies" (1.2.77). Throughout, the balanced juxtaposition of license and penitence constitutes a powerful integrating principle that accounts for much of the play's dramatic unity and force.

Because of its particularity, another powerful thematic connection between *The Tempest* and the practices of the Shrovetide season — the period from Shrovetide through Lent and Easter — is the play's iconography of the labyrinth. Treading the labyrinth was traditional at Lent, when the Christian penitent followed "the way,"[40] and this practice of using the labyrinth as a contemplative device, originating in very ancient times, still occurs in both pagan and Christian contexts throughout Europe and the near east, often at Lent.

Colin Still, analyzing the mystery-play elements of *The Tempest*, relates the role played by the maze in two ancient initiatory modes:

> While the Lesser Initiation was concerned with life and purgation from sin, the Greater Initiation was concerned with death and rebirth. For, as in the former, the aspirant trod the winding paths of an intricate maze that signified our mortal life, and came at last through repentance to that clarity of intellect which is self-finding and self-mastery, so in the latter he was deemed to go through the grave itself, that thereby he might come face to face with the Gods and learn the ultimate mysteries of existence....[41]

The Christian maze or labyrinth[42] of the Middle Ages appears to have served an analogous ritual function. By the 15th century walking the labyrinth had replaced the Easter pilgrimage to Palestine for Christians unable to undertake the hazards and hardships of the actual journey.[43] The famous labyrinth at Chartres, originally constructed in the 13th century, even became known as the "chemin de Jerusalem,"[44] or "chemin de paradis."[45] Arriving at the cathedral, the pilgrim entered the labyrinth and traced the route to the center rosette, pausing to pray at each one of the fourteen labyrs, or turning points.[46] As well as replicating the pilgrimage to Jerusalem and following the path of life, the Christian treading the labyrinth also recapitulated Christ's journey during the Passion. Reaching the center symbolized remission from sin, release from purgatory and, ultimately, salvation (Figure 6.1).

This pattern of peripatetic salvation, so familiar from the popular iconography of Lent, is duplicated in *The Tempest*. The pilgrimage through Prospero's maze of illusions not only forms a microcosm of the larger "life" journey to Tunis and back to Naples and Milan but also symbolizes redemption through death and rebirth. Indeed, according to several critics, the maze forms one of

Opposite: **Figure 6.2. Labyrinth of Christian Life, Francis Quarles, *Emblems* (1635) (reproduced with the permission of Rare Books and Manuscripts, Special Collections Library, Pennsylvania State University Libraries).**

II.

Oh that my wayes were directed
to keepe thy Statutes. Ps.119.5.

W. Simpson Sculp:

the play's central metaphors. To Barbara Mowat the metaphor is deeply rooted in the play's classical sources as well as pivotal to its action and symbolism: "Prospero is the creator of *the maze in which the other characters find themselves....* Gonzalo's 'Here's a maze trod indeed' ... picks up suggestively Ovid's description of that most infamous of mazes, created by Daedalus to enclose the Minotaur..."[47]

This association between the Shrovetide season and the labyrinth is conventional in early-modern drama and would have been readily recognized by Shakespeare's audience. Daedalus even appears as the narrative voice of Jonson's Shrovetide masque, *Pleasure reconcild with Virtue* (1618) constructing a knot so cunningly interwoven that "ev'n th' observer scarce may know/Which lines are pleasures and which are not,"[48] so that "all actions of mankind/are but a Labyrinth, or maze."[49] Hassel calls Jonson's Daedalus the "most important interpreter of the Shrovetide festivities,"[50] a character who "understands [the paradoxical merging of pleasure and virtue] better than any ... subsequent interpreters of this Shrovetide tradition."[51]

The maze constitutes the primary technology of Prospero's magic, and its figure, as a symbolic structure, informs the entirety of the play, explaining many curious features of plot and language. According to Vaughan and Vaughan, the play's action largely consists of circumscribed

> geographic movement writ small. The first four acts conclude with an invitation to move on: "Come, follow" [1.2.502]; "Lead the way" [2.2.183]; "follow, I pray you" [3.3.110]; "follow me and do me service" [4.1.266]... The characters perambulate in small groups from one part of the island to another; only at Prospero's final invitation, "Please you, draw near" [5.1.319], do they join in one place. Although their physical and psychological journeys through the island's maze have ended, the play concludes with plans for a sea journey back to Milan...[52]

Each of the play's three shipwrecked parties wanders in Prospero's maze until reunited with the other two in the fifth act. In act two Ariel leaves Ferdinand "cooling the air with sighs in *an odd angle* of the isle, sitting/his arms in this sad *knot*"[53] (1.2.22–24: emphasis ours). In the court party, the maze references are less camouflaged. By the third act, the wearied Gonzalo announces,

> By'r lakin, I can go no further, sir;
> My old bones ache: *here's a maze trod, indeed,*
> Through *furth-rights and meanders!*[54] [3.3.1]

Into the medieval fabric of labyrinth initiation symbolism Shakespeare has woven the emergent historical theme of New World exploration, conflating Mediterranean and New World topographies. The play maps the Lenten theme of ritual pilgrimage onto the emergent paradigm of New World exploration and colonization. The confused wandering of *Tempest* characters through the Old-New World maze of Prospero's island explicitly recalls the missionary rhetoric of Peter Martyr, who justifies New World Christian evangelism as an antidote to "the illusions wherewith the people of the Island have been seduced after the errors of the old gentility, and wandered in the ignorance and blindness of human nature corrupted by the disobedience of our first parents, which hath remained in all nations...."[55]

In the fifth act, as the pilgrims approach Prospero's cell, at last nearing the sacred center of the labyrinth, Gonzalo's weariness is transfigured by the promise of new life that is characteristic of the symbolic movement from Shrovetide through Lent to Easter. This inspires a benediction for Miranda and Ferdinand in which the maze symbolism explicitly resurfaces: "Look down, you gods,/And on this couple drop a blessed crown;/For it is you that have *chalked forth* the way" (5.1. 201–03; emphasis added). David Lindley glosses the phrase "chalked forth the way" as marked out "as a course to be followed."[56] More specifically, the image invoked is that of a divinely sanctioned maze, marked out in chalk, as English turf mazes have been since time immemorial. Treading the maze has brought Alonso face to face with his wronged nemesis Prospero, led the revelers through the baptism of a horse-piss swamp, and yoked together Ferdinand and Miranda in a betrothal, prefiguring the sacrament of marriage and the union of two competing dynasties.

Astrologically inclined Elizabethans would have recognized Alonso's descending crown, recalling Prospero's "most auspicious star" (1.2.182), as an apt allusion to the *Corona Borealis*, also known as Ariadne's crown. The constellation, which closely circles the polestar and "zenith" (1.2.181) of the northern hemisphere, was named after the legend of Theseus and Ariadne in the labyrinth, to which *Declaration* alludes in the same passage referring to the "tragi-comedy" of New World colonization (see Chapter 5). No wonder that Alonso moralizes: "This is as *strange* a *maze* as e'er men trod" (5.1.241–44: emphasis supplied). This spiritual journey of the court party is shadowed by the drunken perambulations of the revelers. Caliban, Stephano, and Trinculo wander through fen and bramble, following the same pattern of "geographic movement writ small."[57]

Wonder is an appropriate response to the illusory "subtleties" (5.1.134)[58] of Prospero's labyrinth, as well as the prerequisite to self-revelation: a maze induces a-maze-ment,[59] and as the characters wend their way toward Prospero's cell, the symbolic center of both island and maze, each one circumnavigates a world of illusions that expresses his own subjectivity and nature. As James Walter has eloquently summarized, "The figures that establish the setting, oppositions of characters, and progression of plot in *The Tempest* make visible certain archetypal desires, states, and actions common to the experience of Christian pilgrims."[60] The physical perambulations are thus only the outward manifestation of a psychological journey of "torment, trouble, wonder and amazement" (5.1.104–5). As Gonzalo's synopsis unfolds, the "metaphor of unclarity"[61]— the maze — yields the rich fruit of self-knowledge:

> O, rejoice beyond a common joy, and set it down
> With gold on lasting pillars: in one voyage
> Did Claribel her husband find at Tunis;
> And Ferdinand, her brother, found a wife
> Where he himself was lost; Prospero his dukedom
> In a poor island; and all of us ourselves
> When no man was his own [5.1.206–13].

7

A Movable Feast

The masque is a traditional Shrovetide genre. For this reason it is small surprise that Prospero's masque, the *Tempest*'s "play within a play," reflects the play's original Shrovetide context by staging the war of Carnival and Lent in a mythological register. The masque contrasts the Lenten sobriety of Iris' "cold nymphs chaste crowns ... [the] dismissèd bachelor ... [and] sea-marge, sterile and rocky hard" (4.1.66–69) with the harvest abundance of Ceres' betrothal song, celebrating "honor, riches, marriage blessing ... earth's increase, foison plenty, barns and garners never empty" (106–11).

As Ernest Gilman has noted, moreover, Prospero's masque — framed by the disruptive threat of "Caliban's antimasque conspiracy"[1] — inverts the Jonsonian ideal in which the anarchic impulses of the anti-masque are subordinated to the measured harmonies of the main production. In the *Tempest* "anti-masque" the carefully scripted rhetoric of Prospero's dramatic tableau dissolves into a disorderly improvisation in which the revelers exemplify the antics of Shrovetide rioters, who, during the Shrovetide suspension of sumptuary laws, "run about the streets attired like Monks, and some like kings/ Accompanied with pomp and guard, and other stately things."[2]

Ariel's intervention of baiting the "rabble" (4.1.37) — the word has distinct association with the riots so familiar on Shrovetide and other festivals of inversion[3] — with "glistering apparel" perpetuates the theatrical metaphor by putting the elaborate costumes of the masque to the practical purpose of quelling the upstart revelers. The scene is an extravagant parody of the anti-theatrical iconoclasm of the Shrovetide apprentices; instead of attacking the theatres, the revelers plot to murder the theatrical magus, Prospero.

Prospero strikes back with the art of theatrical costume. The conspirators may "know what belongs to a frippery" (4.1.226), but the temptation of gaudy clothing proves irresistible; through an inversion ritual of theatrical dress-up, their *literal* ambition to kill Prospero and to establish themselves as rulers of the island is subordinated to the immediate gratification of *acting* the parts of kings and viceroys. Only Caliban, the "natural man," remains undistracted by Prospero's theatrical mousetrap, able to recognize "trash" (4.1.225), and to remain focused on the practical goals of the revolution.

A leading characteristic of Shrovetide productions mirrored in *The Tempest* is their tendency to assume the form of what John G. Demaray has termed "spectacles of strangeness."[4] Chapman's *The Memorable Maske of the Two Honorable Houses or Inns of Court*, performed on Shrove Monday, 1613–14, illustrates this trend. Chapman projects the traditional festive dichotomy between license and restraint into a colonial context fraught with geopolitics. In the main masque, a dozen courtly Indians, sumptuously costumed in "bawdricks of gold [and] about their necks Ruffs of feathers spangled with pearl and silver,"[5] and styled as "Princes" and "Knights," celebrate the union of England and Virginia.

The antimasque is populated with grotesque baboons, "attir'd like fantastical travelers, in Neapolitan suits, and great ruffs,"[6] which not only parody Spanish colonialism but enact a New World Shrovetide bacchanal. *Tempe Restord*, a 1632 Shrovetide masque, also replicates this theme of New World strangeness, displaying an antimasque of "Indians, and Barbarians, who naturally are bestial, and other which are voluntaries, and but half transformed into beasts."[7] Like these two later Shrovetide masques, which seem to imitate the Shakespeare play, *The Tempest* stages a "spectacle of strangeness," framing its own classical Apollonian masque within a "brave new world" inhabited by the drunken monster Caliban and conspiratorial Neapolitans — "attired like fantastical travelers." Anyone familiar with *The Tempest* will immediately recognize the relevance of this widely attested and symbolically potent association between New World spectacles of wildness and Shrovetide entertainment.

Not only does *The Tempest* contain a masque, one which illustrates the themes characteristic of extant Shrovetide masques, but the play as a whole exhibits an impressionistic, masque-like design. Shrovetide was one of six festival holidays that "would have been incomplete without masquing and disguising."[8] More than any other dramatic form, the masque mirrored the aesthetic of the holiday by disintegrating the conventional antithesis between audience and performer, enacting a scripted Carnival for a select group of participants. The association between the play and the festival of Shrovetide therefore goes very far to account for the widely acknowledged "direct and large influence" of the masque genre in "shaping *The Tempest*."[9]

It has sometimes been supposed that the masque is an afterthought, added to *The Tempest* to honor an aristocratic marriage.[10] The symmetrical placement of the scene as the play's "crucial emblematic tableau"[11] contradicts this hypothesis: framed on each side by three equivalent and juxtaposed scenes, respectively featuring the lovers and Prospero (1.2; 4.1); the court party (2.1; 3.3); and the revelers (2.2; 3.2); and together constituting "an extraordinary triple frame comprised of distinct character groups"[12] (Figure 7.1), the masque is both a structural and a thematic focal point. The Shrovetide associations of these framing scenes are as rich as those in the play's central masque tableau. In preparation for the play's Eastertide climax each of the three main groups of characters undergoes a ritual experience analogous to the socially disruptive practices of Shrovetide and the penitential mortifications of Lent. Ferdinand's rash love for Miranda is tested by the Lenten impositions of his prospective father-in-law; the court party descends into a state of political anarchy and potential regicide before Ariel, in the form of an avenging harpy, confronts Alonso, Sebastian, and Antonio with their vices; the revelers Trinculo, Stephano, and Caliban, in drunken quest of "the tune of our catch played by the picture of Nobody" (3.2.126–27), are baptized in a pool of horse-piss.

The closer we look, the more apparent it becomes that the opposition between Shrovetide and Lent that Laroque has identified as the festival pattern of many plays runs throughout *The Tempest*. It has been ignored largely because the theme is incompatible with a Hallowmas performance context. Even the conflict between the play's two leading emblematic characters, Caliban and Prospero, embodies the Shrovetide paradox. Whether Caliban is seen as the embodiment of the New World "savage" as found in early 16th century Spanish travel narratives, or as an ancestral memory of Europe's own green man,[13] he expresses the cacophonous music of Shrovetide rebellion, staging and satirizing the revolt of the apprentice mobs that so often disrupted

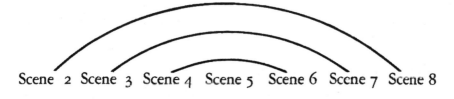

Scene 2   Scene 3   Scene 4   Scene 5   Scene 6   Scene 7   Scene 8

Prosp.,	Alonso,	Caliban,	Ferd.	Caliban,	Alonso,	Prosp.,
Ferd.,	Sebas.,	Steph.,	and	Steph.,	Sebas.,	Ferd.,
Miranda	Anton.	Trinc.	Miranda	Trinc.	Anton.	Miranda

Figure 7.1. The Symmetrical Design of *The Tempest* (after Mark Rose) (reprinted by permission of the publisher from *Shakespearean Design* by Mark Rose, p. 173, Cambridge, MA: Belknap Press of Harvard University Press, copyright by the President and Fellows of Harvard College, 1973).

public order during the season: "Ban, Ban, Ca-caliban, has a New Master—Get a New Man!" (2.2.160–61). In his relations with Caliban (as well as Ferdinand) Prospero personifies Lenten restraint and sometimes repression.

When Sebastian and Antonio exchange barbs with the loquacious Gonzalo in the curious scene (1.2) of the court party's landfall, Shrovetide supplies both form and content for the exchange. Commentators since Pope—who regarded it as composed of "impertinent matter"—have often puzzled over the scene's linguistic labyrinth. Gonzalo strikes the first festive note when he exhorts Alonso to "be merry" (2.1.1) despite the loss of Alonso's son,[14] and later echoes the phrase in his irritable allusion to the "merry fooling" (2.1.174) of his interlocutors. Such language was characteristically associated with Shrovetide: "'Tis merry in hall, when beards wag all/And welcome merry Shrovetide."[15] After Alonso declines Gonzalo's advice to adopt a cheerful disposition, Sebastian envisions his monarch as a Lenten faster, forced to eat "comfort like cold porridge" (2.1.10).

The scene is Shakespeare's comically erudite version of the popular medieval form of the seasonal *certamen* (debate).[16] The high literary genealogy of the form, going back to the eclogues of Theocritus and Virgil, reflects a parallel folk practice, indigenous to early-modern Shrovetide. *Flyting*, similar to the modern African-American tradition of "playing the dozens," was a sport of the season, if we may trust the evidence of manuscripts surviving from both Sweden[17] and Mediterranean Europe,[18] which connect the practice to Shrovetide.

The *flyting* continues when Sebastian and Antonio mock Gonzalo and Adrian as the "cock" and "cockerel," and take wagers for the ensuing "cock fight." Cock fighting with its associated gambling was the traditional sport of Shrove Tuesday, when the custom was augmented by the brutal additions of cock thrashing—a sport in which a cock was tied to a stake, while young men threw rocks or sticks at it—and cock throwing.[19] "Bat-fowling" (2.1.191), a mode of catching birds at night by holding a torch and beating the bush until the birds flew into the light and were caught with nets, is a kind of primal cock-thrashing and therefore also corresponds to the pattern of the play's Shrovetide symbolism. These rituals were justified by the belief that the cock was an emblem of parricide.[20]

From the start the exchange among the four courtiers continues the predominant theme of festival contraries:

> **Seb.** Look, he's winding up the watch of his wit,
> By and by it will strike.
> **Gonz.** [to Alonso] Sir—
> **Seb.** One: tell.

Gonz. When every grief is entertained
That's offered, comes to the entertainer —
Seb. A dollar.
Gonz. Dolour comes to him indeed. You have spoken truer than you pur-
posed [2.1.12–20].

The debated themes — entertainment/grief and dollar/dolour — again reflect
the antithesis between Shrovetide abundance and Lenten regret. *Dolour* recalls
the *via dolorosa,* the path of Christ's passion recapitulated in the Stations of
the Cross, another Lenten pilgrimage closely associated with the idea of the
Christian labyrinth. It also puns on the word "dole" — as in the dole or charity
given to the poor — a word with distinctive Shrovetide associations, as Ronald
Hutton has shown in his authoritative study, *The Stations of the Year: A History
of the Ritual Year in England* (Oxford, 1996).[21] The conclusion of the wager
is a *tour de force* of *flyting* wit; instead of betting either dollars or dolours, the
two cynics wager *a laughter* (2.1.27–36). The unexpected word, punning on
a clutch of eggs,[22] trumps the Shrovetide symbolism. It not only extends the
cock/cockerel imagery, as critics have recognized, but also reconciles the contraries of Shrovetide and Lent in a Janus-faced metaphor that looks *back* to
Egg Saturday[23] as well as *foreshadowing* the Christian epiphany at Easter. But
laughter in the mouth of a cynic soon turns to tragedy. Sebastian and Antonio's
jocular "cock-throwing" of Gonzalo reverts to regicide as soon as the other
courtiers fall into a dead sleep.

Sex and digestion were two dominant themes of the continental *fastnachtspiel,* both "bandied about all over Europe to the last shred of vulgarity,"[24]
and predictably both festival themes are prominent not only in Prospero's
masque but in *The Tempest* as a whole. Because Shrovetide festival excess originated in rites of fertility,[25] and marriages were traditionally proscribed during
Lent, Shrovetide was a popular time for marriages and marriage masques[26] as
well as excessive feasting. Performed during Shrovetide, Jonson's Haddington
wedding masque of 1608 (Figure 7.2), like the *Tempest* masque, anticipates a
harvest: "in nine moons, there may be born/A babe, to uphold the fame/Of
Radcliffe's blood and Ramsey's name." Unsurprisingly, a thread of bawdry
runs through *The Tempest*: Caliban's predatory but procreative lust for
Miranda — "would't had been done" (1.2.349) — or his promises to award her
to Stephano — "she will become thy bed ... /and bring thee forth brave brood"
(3.2.96–97) — contrast with the masque's masturbatory imagery of

> ... broom groves,
> Whose shadow the dismissèd bachelor loves [4.1.67].

The implied homoeroticism of Caliban, Trinculo, and Stephano under the
gabardine receives repeated comic emphasis that recalls the libidinous excesses

THE
DESCRIPTION OF
THE MASQVE.

With the Nuptiall songs.

At the Lord Vicount HADINGTONS
marriage àt Court.

On the Shroue-tuesday at night. 1608.

He worthy cuſtome of honouring worthy *marriages*, with theſe noble *ſolemnities*, hath, of late yeeres, aduanc'd it ſelfe frequently with vs; to the reputation no leſſe of our *court*, then *nobles*: expreſſing beſides (through the difficulties of expence, and trauell, with the cheerefulneſſe of vnder-taking) a moſt reall affection in the *perſonaters*, to thoſe, for whoſe ſake they would ſuſtayne theſe *perſons*. It behoues then vs, that are truſted with a part of their honor, in theſe *celebrations*, to doe nothing in them, beneath the dignitie of either. With this prepoſed part of iudgement, I aduenture to giue that abroad, which in my firſt conception I intended honorably fit: and (though it hath labour'd ſince, vnder cenſure) I, that know *Truth* to be alwayes of one ſtature, and ſo like a rule, as who bends it the leaſt way, muſt needes doe an iniurie to the right, cannot but ſmile at their tyrannous ignorance, that will offer to ſlight me (in theſe things being an *artificer)* and giue themſelues a peremptorie licence to iudge, who haue neuer touch'd ſo much as to the barke, or vtter ſhell of any *knowledge*. But, their daring dwell, with them. They haue found a place, to powre out their follies, and I a ſeate, to ſleepe out the paſſage.

Figure 7.2. Jonson's Shrovetide Haddington Masque (courtesy Wikimedia Commons).

of Carnival. Caliban is conceived as an erect "poor john" (2.2.27)[27]; Stephano asks Caliban to "bear [his] bottle" (2.2.152); responding to the image of Stephano as the man in the moon, Caliban declares "I have seen thee *in her.* I do adore thee. My mistress showed me thee, and thy dog, and *thy bush*" (2.2.118–19, emphasis supplied).

In the corresponding scene with Ferdinand and Miranda this Shrovetide ribaldry is concealed behind the veil of romantic decorum and Lenten abstinence. But Ferdinand's log carrying, a Lenten penitence imposed for his alleged rebellion, is also a Shrovetide joke on the male erection, as Miranda unconsciously acknowledges in her comical innocence: "If you'll sit down, I'll bear your logs the while" (3.1.24–25).

While sexual imagery connects *The Tempest* to the *fastnachtspiel*, the themes of eating and digestion,[28] by their arbitrary repetition, confirm the link. In one of his first lines, Caliban, the play's emblem of the appetitive impulse, announces the theme: "I must eat my dinner" (1.2.332). Several of his subsequent speeches concern the obtaining of food on the island, but, like the question of authority, the issue of whether the island provides Shrovetide abundance or Lenten dearth is never resolved. Alonso, likewise, objects to Gonzalo's exhortations to Shrovetide cheerfulness, with a striking gustatory metaphor: "you *cram* these words into my ears against *the stomach* of my sense" (2.1.101–02: emphasis supplied). For his part, Prospero condemns Ferdinand to fast on the island's Lenten fare: "Sea water shalt thou drink. Thy food shall be/The fresh brook mussels, withered roots, and husks wherein the acorn cradled" (1.2.461–63); as previously mentioned, Trinculo, anatomizing his sensory responses to Caliban's "fish-like" smell, calls him a "poor-john" (2.2.26) — a salted fish emblematic of Lenten dietary prescriptions.

Within the court party, food becomes a subject for *flyting.* Gonzalo, echoing the optimistic vision of New World abundance expressed by his idealistic namesake Gonzalo Oviedo in Eden's book, invokes the Shrovetide theme of nature's plenitude. He expects that "nature should bring forth/Of its own kind all foison, all abundance/To feed my innocent people" (2.1.159–61). His antagonist Antonio, plotting the assassination of Alonso, ironically inverts Gonzalo's gustatory idealism in a series of food metaphors revealing the iniquity of his own nature: conscience shall be "candied" (2.1.276), Gonzalo is an "ancient morsel" (2.1.283) fit to be devoured, and the rest of the court party will "take suggestion as a cat laps milk" (2.1.285).

Not to be outdone, and recalling Gonzalo's utopian vision of the New World as cornucopia, Caliban regales the revelers with the culinary wonders of the island:

I'll show thee every fertile inch o'the isle ... I'll show thee the best springs; I'll pluck thee berries; I'll fish for thee ... bring thee where crabs grow ... dig thee pig-nuts,/Show thee a jay's nest, and instruct thee how/to snare the nimble marmoset. I'll bring thee to clust'ring filberts... [2.2.125–48].

But after falling out with Trinculo, Caliban imitates Prospero's Lenten discipline of deprivation: "He shall drink nought but brine, for I'll not show him/Where the quick freshes are" (3.2.60–61).

While Caliban punishes his enemies by depriving them of fresh water, the better part of his time with Stephano and Trinculo is devoted to drinking, jesting, and singing. Bacchanalian excess is another "indulgence" of Shrovetide burlesqued in *The Tempest*, and one that completes the parody of the Christian liturgy. Stephano's wine bottle is both an ironic substitute for the Bible (he commands Caliban to "swear by" it [2.2.121]) and a parody of the offering of the wine (he asks Caliban to "bear my bottle" (2.2.152)) in the Eucharist. Again the symbolism fits a Shrovetide play, since the Eucharist commemorates both the last supper, an event falling on the cusp between Lent and Easter, and the resurrection of Christ.

Perhaps the most compelling instance of liturgical symbolism reflecting the semiotic conventions of the pre–Easter season, however, is Ariel's appearing and disappearing banquet (3.3), which enacts a literal "movable feast" (Shrovetide) followed by a period of abstinence (Lent). After the dancers bring on the banquet, the exchange between Francisco, Sebastian, and Alonso underscores the scene's liturgical symbolism:

> **Fran.** They vanished strangely.
> **Seb.** No matter, since
> They have left their viands behind, for we have stomachs!
> Will't please you taste of what is here?
> **Alonso.** Not I [3.3.39–42].

Sebastian's gratuitous emphasis on anatomy — for "we have stomachs" — recalls the sensuous indulgences of the *fastnachtspiel*. Generically, *Viands,* from the French *la viande*, means food, including bread (in which case it might support a reading of the scene as a dark parody of the Christian Eucharist, as Grace Hall has suggested), but more narrowly it denotes "meat." The table is left onstage throughout Ariel's speech and is only removed by the spirit dancers after he vanishes in a clap of thunder, a feature that underlines the liturgical character of the entire episode by recalling doctrinal debates over the communion table, which after the 1552 Prayer book was substituted for the altar. In this reading Alonso's refusal acquires a religious meaning specifically suited to a play staged on the eve of Lent: he will not break his Lenten fast for Ferdinand's death to consume forbidden food.

Like the festival of Shrovetide itself, Ariel's feast is even — literally — "movable." When the banquet suddenly "vanishes" (3.3.s.d.@52), signifying the onset of Lent, Ariel appears dressed as the avenging harpy. He launches into a fiery denunciation of the courtiers that imitates the brimstone sermons characteristic of the Lenten season.[29] Standing on the table that once contained the vanished feast, he pursues the emphasis on food and its digestion, condemning Alonso, Sebastian and Antonio as "three men of sin, whom ... the *never surfeited* sea/Hath caused to *belch* up you" (3.3.53–56: emphasis supplied). Eventually Prospero even commends Ariel for his "devouring" (3.3.84) performance.

At Shrovetide the beast became the symbol of man's own sinful nature, and like all Christian holy days the season possessed a characteristic bestiary, as described by Neogeorgus:

> Some like wild beasts do run abroad in skins that diverse be
> Arrayed, and eke with loathsome shapes, that dreadful are to see:
> They counterfeit both Bears and Wolves, and Lions, fierce in sight,
> And raging Bulls. Some play the Cranes with wings & stilts upright.[30]
> Some like the filthy form of Apes, and some like fools are dressed,
> Which best beseem these Papists all, that thus keep Bacchus feast.[31]

This pattern, like so many other Shrovetide motifs, is evident in extant dramas written for special performance during the festival. *Tempe Restord* includes an episode of Circe transforming a young man into a lion, followed by an anti-masque of Circe's other beasts.[32] The theme is also evident in Thomas Carew's *Coelum Britannicum* (1634), another Shrovetide masque, which includes an antimasque of "monstrous shapes ... of Natural deformity."[33] Hassel remarks that "the familiar emblems of bestiality that have so often been paraded and shriven in the other Shrovetide masques"[34] play a significant role in Carew's production.

The Tempest follows this festival bestiary pattern. We have already mentioned the significance of the cock as a scapegoat in 2.1; the *crowing* cock, which occurs in satiric form in Sebastian and Antonio's wager (2.1.27), and in lyric form in Ariel's song (1.2.385–86), would no doubt have been recognized by Shakespeare's contemporaries as a reference to Peter's threefold denial of Jesus before the passion.[35]

Ariel's disappearing banquet induces in Sebastian the invocation of two further emblems in the bestiary that share a special connection to the Lenten/Easter liturgy: "Now I will believe that there are unicorns; that in Arabia/There is one tree, the Phoenix throne; one Phoenix at this hour reigning there" (3.3.21–24).[36] The mythology, ostensibly fitted to the play's pagan otherworldliness and appeal to the exotic, masks an esoteric Christian implication: the unicorn is a symbol of Christ, and the story of the unicorn, and the hunt for it, was conventionally "read as an allegory of the Passion of Christ."[37]

The Phoenix, a prominent symbol of the Christian Passion, also corresponds to a liturgical festival that anticipates Easter, as the Aberdeen Bestiary relates:

> On the ninth day after [constructing its own funeral pyre], the bird rises from its own ashes. Our Lord Jesus Christ displays the features of this bird, saying: "I have the power to lay down my life and to take it again" (see John, 10:18). If, therefore, the phoenix has the power to destroy and revive itself, why do fools grow angry at the word of God, who is the true son of God, who says: "I have the power to lay down my life and to take it again?" For it is a fact that our Saviour descended from heaven; he filled his wings with the fragrance of the Old and New Testaments; he offered himself to God his father for our sake on the altar of the cross; and on the third he day he rose again.[38]

Caliban, the "half fish, half man," "mooncalf," and "monster of the isle with four legs" (2.2.59), completes the Shrovetide tableau by serving as a symbolic mediation between man and beast, between Christ and the devil.[39] Among the most popular emblems of the season was Jack-a-Lent, a puppet made from a Leek and a Herring and set up on Ash Wednesday as a scapegoat for the deprivations of Lent. Decorated with herrings and pelted with missiles, he became "both a manifest and a ubiquitous symbol of the long period of austerity and at the same time operated as a kind of safety valve."[40] Caliban's likeness to this "ubiquitous" Lenten scapegoat, half man and half fish, hardly requires emphasis.[41] On the other hand, Stephano and Trinculo's insistent labeling of Caliban as a "fish"—"legged like a man and his fins like arms" (2.2.30–31) also identifies him, paradoxically, with the figure of Christ in his most traditional animal aspect.[42] In this reading, Caliban becomes a dangerous jest on Christian religious practice as well as furnishing, in Christ's body, a symbolic complement to the bread and wine of the Eucharist.[43]

Trinculo, the play's English realist, has profit on this mind: he thinks of Caliban as a circus animal, exploitable for financial gain, and even considers importing him to England as a tobacco-store Indian,[44] like one of the noble savages of Chapman's 1613 Shrovetide "spectacle of strangeness." Antonio agrees: "A plain fish and, no doubt, marketable" (5.1.265).[45] But Caliban is not just a commodity, and in the end it is he, more than any other reveler, who articulates the play's moral vision when he repudiates his idolatry of Stephano and promises to "seek for grace" (5.1.296).

Stephen Sohmer has noted Shakespeare's propensity for "calendrical design"; in The Tempest this focus on the ritual divisions of time as a method of dramatic exposition is not only structurally conspicuous but is inscribed in the etymology of "tempest." The word is closely cognate with words for time in several indo–European languages. *Etymology Online* derives it from

> O.Fr. *tempeste* (11c.), from V.L. **tempesta* from L. *tempestas* (gen. *tempestatis*) "storm, weather, season," also "commotion, disturbance," related to *tempus* "time, season," stating that the evolution is from "period of time" to "period of weather," to "bad weather" to "storm." Words for "weather" were originally words for "time" in languages from Russia to Brittany.[46]

The ominous temporal emphasis in Prospero's speech to Miranda, "The hour's now come;/the very minute bids thee ope thine ear;/Obey, and be attentive" (1.2.36–38), echoes Christ's phrase on the cross — "the hour is come" (John 17.1 et seq.)[47] — and reminds the listener of the play's religious and allegorical dimensions. As Grace Hall has observed,[48] the emphatic focus on *now* anticipates a hierophantic climax: sailors are restored to life, Miranda and Ferdinand are united in holy matrimony, the revelers undergo spiritual rebirth, and Prospero is restored to his Dukedom. The symbolic act of the release from bodily bondage of Ariel, which recapitulates Jesus' release of his spirit to God in the crucifixion, completes the play's liturgical symbolism.

While it is customarily believed that *The Tempest* adheres to the unities of time and place, Prospero *twice* declares that the elapsed time between the play's second scene and Ariel's release is actually "two days" (1.2.299; 1.2.419–20).[49] We have no definitive answer to the significance of this temporal marker; that it is significant seems impossible to deny, and there are several interesting possibilities. Perhaps the play was written to be enacted two days before the onset of Lent. Another possibility is that Prospero's words — again — recall the gospel story of the passion, which would have been on the minds of all Christian parishioners at this time, when Jesus declares that his own crucifixion is imminent: "Ye know that *after two days* is the Passover, and the son of man is betrayed to be crucified" (Matt. 26:2).[50] Perhaps most significantly, two days is also the elapsed time between the crucifixion and resurrection, as on "the third day" it is said Jesus rose from the dead (I Cor. 15.4).

A third temporal marker related to the play's liturgical symbolism is activated when Prospero announces that the time of Ariel's release will be at "six" (1.2.240); the marker is later repeated for emphasis by Ariel as "the sixth hour, at which time my Lord, you said our work should cease" (5.1.4–5). In ancient and medieval traditions of liturgical time, the *hora sexta*, "sixth hour" or *sext,* corresponded to the modern twelve o'clock, usually mid-day. In pre–Christian times, the hour was already considered the most propitious time for prayer. In the Christian calendar, however, it came to have a particular significance during Lent. Originally, the Lenten fast was broken after vespers in the evening, but the strictness of the practice was relaxed until, by the time of Charlemagne in the 8th century,[51] the fast was often broken at *nones* in the mid-afternoon. At an even later period, *nones*— the root of our modern English word, *noon*— itself slipped back to the position of the *hora sexta*, and both the breaking of the Lenten fast and vespers became offices of mid-day. Most significantly, as Grace Hall has observed,[52] the Christian sixth hour was also the traditional moment of the crucifixion.[53] Thus, three major temporal markers of *The Tempest* manifestly connect the play to its original liturgical context.

Perhaps for the reasons examined by Anthony Gash, critics have been slow to comprehend *The Tempest*'s richly constructed syncretism. Gash argues that contemporary criticism has suppressed "the convergence of Christian theology with the terms in which Bakhtin describes the logic of carnival."[54] But if we return to the early-modern frame of reference we can easily see that the interpenetration of Christian and pagan symbolism must have been habitual. As we have noted, for example, the phoenix forms a significant element in the play's pagan bestiary. It is also an emblem for the play's larger theme of death and resurrection. As such it illustrates a fundamental metaphysical principle of *The Tempest*'s symbolic design: the elaborate interweaving of Christian and pagan symbolism, through which many ostensibly Pagan motifs and metaphors contain concealed Christian counterparts and vice-versa.

Long before the advent of Christianity, the motif of resurrection had been a characteristic theme of the Carnival season, celebrated in the figure of the fool, who was traditionally subjected to a mock execution and resurrection/rebirth. With the advent of Christianity, the fool had also come to prefigure the cycle of death and resurrection as enacted at Easter. This theme, manifest in many curious and particular ways, is central to *The Tempest*.[55] The most obvious resurrection is Prospero's; having been usurped as Duke of Milan, exiled and thought dead, he reveals himself and is ultimately promised restoration of his dukedom by a repentant Alonso. Characters on the ship are drowned in the "dire spectacle of the wrack" (1.2) but are reborn after a baptism "full fathom five." The master, boatswain and crew sleep through the action but are awakened at the end; Ferdinand and Alonso each suppose the other dead, but are reciprocally "resurrected" when they at last behold each other alive; the three revelers descend into the "filthy mantled pool" and are reborn in a parody of baptism.[56] Even the failed murders of Alonso and Gonzalo by Sebastian and Antonio, and Prospero by the revelers, are mocking variants of the execution and resurrection theme.

For more than two centuries, the retrospective tone of the concluding two scenes of *The Tempest* has been interpreted in a biographical context.

Even scholars reluctant to engage in "biographical heresy" have often been unable to resist the temptation to conceive Prospero as a projection of the author's own persona, and the play as his "farewell" to the stage. That tradition goes back at least to the 18th century,[57] and since the 19th has seemed to verify the commonly accepted 1611 date for the play's composition.

Although we too appreciate the significant biographical implications of an authorial Prospero, focus on the *Tempest*'s original Shrovetide context reveals a more objective register of meaning accessible to an early-modern audience adapted to the seasonal nature of theatrical performance. Each year at Shrovetide the winter cycle came to a sudden halt; Shrove Tuesday represented "the last taste of Christmastide"[58] and "a final explosion of riotous misrule just before the somber restraints of Lent."[59]

In such a context, *The Tempest*'s original Shrovetide audience would surely have recognized Prospero's announcement, "our revels now are ended" (4.1.148), as proclaiming a conclusion to the Christmastide revels' season. Just before Ash Wednesday, Prospero's actors are reduced to "spirits ... melted into ... thin air" (4.1.150) as the "pageant" ends, leaving "not a rack behind" (4.1.171).[60] It is difficult to imagine a more apt illustration of Shakespeare's uncanny genius for dramatic timing.

If the chaos of carnival imbues *The Tempest* with its characteristic formlessness, so that its representations of Shrovetide, Lent and Easter vie with one another through successive scenes, the play also maps the stations of Christian devotion in a linear fashion. It moves from the Shrovetide revelry of Stephano, Trinculo, and Caliban — mirrored in the murderous rebellion of Sebastian and Antonio — through the Lenten imposition of the disappearing banquet, the repentance of Alonso and Caliban, and the "recalled to life" reunion of Alonso and Ferdinand. Prospero has plunged the shipwrecked parties into a maze, inducing in them the state of penitent wonder that is the purpose of Lenten discipline: "They being penitent,/The sole drift of my purpose doth extend/ Not a frown further. Go, release them, Ariel" (5.1.28–30).

Given the liturgical context, it seems only logical that *The Tempest*'s sixth hour climax, when Prospero separates from Ariel, replicates the crucifixion; in the epilogue Prospero appears as the high priest of Lent[61] who has forgiven others their sins but requires reciprocal forgiveness from his congregation. When he begs the audience for redemption, his words — "release me from my bands/with the help of your good hands" (ep. 9–10) — recall the gospel of Luke: "Father, into thine hands I commend my spirit" (23.46). Only in this case, in a Brechtian turn breaking the fourth wall, it is into the hands and the hearts of *the audience* that Prospero commends his spirit.

Some might argue that the correspondences between the festival patterns documented in this chapter and *The Tempest* would be suited to any number of liturgical occasions, not specifically to Shrovetide. According to François Laroque the theme of the clash of contraries is found in many Elizabethan dramas and even constitutes "the very substance of festive comedies."[62] But many aspects of the symbolic design identified in this and the previous chapter — the oscillating pattern of Lenten penitence and Shrovetide excess, the metaphor of the labyrinth, the recurrent imagery of food and digestion, and the scenes of Shrovetide anti-theatricality — match no festival occasion *except* Shrovetide. Efforts to associate the play with other festival occasions such as Hallowmas, by contrast, have yielded a very "bad harvest."

In sharp contrast to this tradition of failed attempts to fit *The Tempest* into a liturgical category to which it does not belong, our study reveals an abundance of symbolic associations between Shrovetide and Lenten practices on the one hand, and the design of Shakespeare's play on the other. These are so rich and detailed that it may safely be concluded that it was in fact written, as R. Christopher Hassel has said of Jonson's epiphany masques and *Twelfth Night,* "with the major outlines of the festival season firmly in mind."[63]

8

Where in the *World*?

Of the 36 plays collected in the 1623 Shakespeare First Folio, *The Tempest* is, geographically speaking, unique: while it in a sense takes the entire world for its stage,[1] the main action occurs in a single circumscribed location that remains stubbornly indefinite. Among the most obvious geographical markers, Prospero sends his messenger-sprite Ariel to "fetch dew" from the "still-vexed bermoothes" (1.2.267).[2] The Bermuda islands, discovered by Juan Bermudez only in 1503, were at that time widely considered "the furthest of all the Islands ... found at this day in the world" (Eden 203v).[3] All the other characters in the play, however, seem to be wandering within the confines of an island maze.

Notes to the First Folio — the only received original text — do little to clarify the geographical ambiguity, identifying the locale of these peregrinations only as a generic "un-inhabited island," an unlocalized space, occupying an imaginary "nowhere." Paradoxically, however, this ambiguous domain is surrounded on every side by markers of human geography. For example, when Trinculo and Stephano discuss transporting Caliban back to England, it seems that this is their native land. In England, announces Trinculo, every "holiday fool" will "give a piece of silver" to see Caliban:

> ... there would this monster make a man; any strange beast there makes a man: when they will not give a doit to relieve a lame beggar, they will lay out ten to see a dead Indian [2.2.32–37].

Stephano's get rich quick plan to market in Old World England such New World exotica as a "dead Indian" is only one sign of the play's well known "American" atmosphere. The ambience is further attested in numerous textual particularities, among them Caliban's reference to his mother's god, "Setebos," a word drawn — as we have seen — from contemporary accounts of American exploration and colonization, and Miranda's encomium to a "brave new world" that "hath such creatures in it." Yet the play's frequent and obvious Mediterranean markers dwarf its generally vaguer Atlantic associations. Wherever Ariel may be sent in search of "dew," it is obvious that all the other characters are confined within a stone's throw of such familiar Mediterranean landmarks as Argier (2x),[4] Tunis (9x),[5] Carthage (4x),[6] Milan (17x),[7] and Naples (20x).[8]

As recent *Tempest* studies acknowledge, such references contradict a long-standing tradition of scholarship that has focused on the play's New World ethos. William Sherman and Peter Hulme's collection of critical essays, *The Tempest and Its Travels* (2000), for example, expresses a renewed appreciation for the topographical complexity of Shakespeare's imaginative landscape and invites a return to critical exploration of the play's Mediterranean context. The articles anthologized in their volume, along with other recent scholarship, stress sources and symbolism that connect *The Tempest* as much to the Old World of Virgil's Aeneas as to the New World of Christopher Columbus. In the words of David Lindley, "the [Americanist] colonial reading of the play masks the Mediterranean contexts which are much more obvious on the play's surface."[9] To Meredith Anne Skura, Americanist criticism has "flatten[ed] the text into the mould of colonialist discourse and eliminate[d] what is characteristically 'Shakespearean' in order to foreground what is 'colonialist.'"[10] Writing more recently, Leo Salingar agrees that new historicist readings of the play which emphasize its connection to the literature of British colonization "distort Prospero's project of returning to Milan ... and mask the play's affinity with other contemporary romances, whether Shakespeare's own preceding work or the scattered international romances featuring Island magicians."[11] And Barbara Fuchs argues that the critical privileging of the Americanist reading, while it has made the play more relevant to a twentieth century audience, has done so at the cost of obscuring relevant early-modern context, including "the very real presence of the Ottoman threat in the Mediterranean in the early 17th century."[12] It seems that David Scott Wilson-Okumura expresses a contemporary consensus when he calls for a "literary criticism that does justice to the play's Mediterranean setting without neglecting the obvious references to Atlantic exploration and colonization."[13]

These critics recognize that Shakespeare not only superimposes his study of the ideological drama of New World voyage and conquest onto an Old World Mediterranean topography, but also includes frequent and clearly deliberate allusions — integral elements of the play's symbolic design — to such pertinent old world texts as Ovid's *Metamorphoses* and Virgil's *Aeneid*.[14] That this Mediterranean landscape would have meant something very different to Shakespeare's audience than it does to his modern readers is obvious. John Gillies argues that a prevailing practice of the plays is Shakespearean "typo-geography," a "form of geographic moralization" in which places are designated in terms of their "moral (or historical, or epic, or mythological) significance."[15] An example of this process is the curious exchange about the collocation of Tunis and Carthage: "Because modern Tunis recaps ancient Carthage, the marriage of Claribel to the African recaps the ill-starred relationship of Dido to Aeneas."[16] To Gillies such typo-geography shows that Shakespeare is "demonstrably conversant with a variety of geopolitical discourses and a variety of cartographic genres."[17]

Tempest typo-geography is complicated by Shakespeare's agile imagination, which superimposes a Renaissance frame over a landscape saturated with ancient history. During the Renaissance the concept of a pan–European identity was being forged in the cauldron of Mediterranean geopolitical conflict, in dialectical relationship to an "other" largely consisting of the peoples of North Africa and the Levant. This process was the most current phase of a larger dynamic that could be traced back to the days of Virgil. For Shakespeare "this Tunis" not only *"had been"* — but in a sense still *was* — "Carthage," the site of an ancient but still very lively contest between the aspirations, desires, myths, and symbols of "east" and "west." Here wily Aeneas got the better of tragic Dido; but Hannibal, returning to haunt Roman hubris, would remind "the west" that it was not omnipotent.

Like a palimpsest, *The Tempest* writes its more immediate 16th century "typo-geography" of contemporary politics over such classical precedents. For Shakespeare's 16th century audience, the displacement of cultural frames of reference invoked in the contrast between Carthage and Tunis would have called to mind the contemporary cause of Constantinople. In 1453, after serving for more than a millennium as the center of the Eastern Orthodox Church, the city had fallen to the Ottomans. Throughout the 16th century, conflict between Christianity and Islam intensified as the Ottomans extended their power westward, eventually besieging Vienna and formally gaining control over Hungary. In 1492, Christians had retaliated for the loss of Constantinople by expelling all "Moors" from Spain. The Ottomans took their revenge seven years later when they smashed the Christian fleet at Lepanto; the tide of naval supremacy did not begin to turn until Don John of Austria's 1571 victory, also at Lepanto, began to restore Christian influence in the region's shipping lanes.[18]

The action of *The Tempest* unfolds on a Mediterranean island in this mythologized and historically contested region, somewhere between Tunis and Naples. Given such a location, unless Shakespeare created a wholly imaginary island, Caliban's kingdom has to be identified with one of the three Pelagie islands (Lampedusa, Linosa, and Lampione), located 113 km northeast of modern day Tunisia.[19] For a Jacobean audience, Lampedusa was, significantly, located in the heart of the most frightening region of the known world, an area if not "beyond man's life," at least beyond the zone of imaginable safety: the Barbary territory of the North African coast. During the early 16th century, English mariners aggressively exploring Mediterranean trade routes first ran afoul of North African pirates, and by the time of Shakespeare's play the threat to English shipping interests had become a significant deterrent. Richard Wilson argues that "to sail in the Ottoman Regencies of Algiers, Tripoli and Tunis, was to traffic in an entire economy driven by the corso (or lottery) of the slave market ... run ... for the lucrative turnover of capture and ransom."[20] Emboldened by the conquest of Constantinople in 1453, by the 1590s the Barbary pirates had become a serious diplomatic and commercial problem for the northern European maritime powers. One source estimates that between 1609 and 1616 England lost as many as 466 ships to Barbary piracy.[21] According to the redemptionist priest Pierre Dan, as cited in Wilson's account, by 1611 over a million Europeans had experienced some form of North African bondage; a white slave population of 25,000 existed in Algiers and 7,000 in Tunis.

Although Lampedusa had been nominated for the locale of *The Tempest* as early as 1839 by Joseph Hunter, neither the island nor Hunter's pioneering research have, to our knowledge, been mentioned in *any* of the literature of the Mediterranean *Tempest* revival of the last fifteen years.[22] And yet, according to Hunter, Lampedusa

> is precisely in the situation where the circumstances of every part of the story require. Sailors from Algiers land Sycorax on its shores; Prospero, sailing from an Italian port, and beating off the mercy of the waves, is found at last with his lovely charge at Lampedusa; Alonso, sailing from Tunis, and steering his course for Naples, is driven by a storm a little out of his track and lights on Lampedusa.[23]

Such a setting strikingly demonstrates Shakespeare's ability to shape dramatic action through geographical context, for Lampedusa was a privileged *topos* in the early-modern European geographical imagination long before Shakespeare's muse arrived there. By the Elizabethan age, the island had acquired a range of historical and literary associations that made it the ideal staging ground for *Tempest*'s "typo-geographical" rhetorical strategies. The location was infamous for its stormy weather, frequent visitations of St. Elmo's fire, and historical shipwrecks: several ships from the Fleet of Charles V, commanded by Admiral Andria Doria, wrecked on the island in 1551 while pursuing the notorious pirate Barbarossa. Most significant, because of its strategic location off the coast of Tunisia in seas belonging neither to Africa nor Europe, the island was the staging ground for a number of historic confrontations, both real and imaginary, between Christian crusaders and Muslim warriors during centuries of conflict for control of the Mediterranean basin.

Hunter's theory identifying Caliban's island with Lampedusa was inspired at least in part by William Henry Smyth's *Memoir Descriptive of the Resources, Hydrogaphy, and Inhabitants of Sicily and Its Islands* (1824), which recorded a number of Lampedusan traditions that must have struck Hunter as extraordinary coincidences linking the island to the imaginative geography of Shakespeare's play. In Smyth's representation, the island was once inhabited by a Prospero-like recluse, known as the "hermit of Lampedusa," who lived in a grotto and served as a caretaker for the island's Christian chapel.

To this day, Lampedusa is filled with "grottos" and "troglodytic caves"[24]; any early-modern Christian unlucky enough to be stranded there would face a double jeopardy, of being sold into Ottoman slavery and of being haunted by "horrible specters,"[25] "formidable apparitions," and "frightful dreams that fatally afflict with death-like terrors."[26] Although the island today is almost barren of vegetation (in part because of the extensive deforestation that has destroyed native groves of olive and juniper that existed up until the 19th century), Hunter was further intrigued by Smyth's account that "a good deal of firewood is cut and sent to Tripoli and Malta."[27]

Such early traditions of Lampedusa contain much that is evocative of Shakespeare's "un-inhabited island." To English readers the most important 16th century source on the Eastern Mediterranean region available, including the history and traditions of Lampedusa, is Martin Crusius' *Turco Graecia* (1584),[28] which contains the earliest extant account of the island after Pliny's mention of it in the 1st century. The tradition recorded by Smyth that "no one can reside in this island on account of the phantasms, specters, and horrible visions that appear in the night, repose and quiet being banished by formidable apparitions and frightful dreams" dates back at least to Crusius, who in 1584 had already remarked that "the nights here are [filled with] wild and disturbing specters."[29] The tradition of haunting may be related to unusual weather patterns around the island. According to the 16th century commentator Fazellus, St. Elmo's fire was so frequent a local occurrence that it accounts for the names of Lampedusa and Lampione, both derived from the Latin (originally Greek) word *lampa* (lamp), because of the frequent shinings and lights ("spessi baleni e lampi") which sailors reported there.[30]

The natural history and the cultural traditions of the island have both left a distinctive mark on *Tempest* symbolism. Extant in a 1679 anonymous French account is the fact that sailors kept the island stocked with food and provisions that

> could be used by those who landed there, and which they could partake of freely
> if they needed it to complete their voyage, but could not take if they had no
> need of it, because punishment would swiftly follow their crime, and they would

not be able to leave the island until after making restitution for what they had taken.[31]

This practice dates back to Shakespeare's time, as shown by a version included in Crusius. After describing the Christian and Turkish practice of leaving oblations at their respective shrines on the island, he remarks that "they say that those who fail to make an offering, or who take something away without restoring it, are not able to leave the island."[32] The custom of leaving provisions for shipwrecked sailors seems uncannily relevant to a play that takes place on an "un-inhabited island" that is mysteriously stocked with food and clothing capable of supplying the needs of a shipwrecked party.[33] In Act 3, scene 3, Alonso and his shipwrecked court discover a "disappearing banquet," catered by "strange shapes" and "monsters of the isle." Should they eat? Like the sailors in the accounts of Anon and Crusius, they are not truly in need and therefore are violating the custom of the island when they do, which provokes Ariel's fire and brimstone denunciation of them as "three men of sin" (3.3.53). A clue to the exotic Ottoman ambience of the island and its inhabitants — the beneficent dancers — who assist in Ariel's display may be discerned in Sebastian's associations: "Now I will believe there are Unicorns; that *in Arabia* there is one tree, *the Phoenix* throne..." (3.3.26–29).

Another item traditionally left on Lampedusa for the use of needy sailors was clothing[34] — which, like food and eating, becomes a major *Tempest* motif.[35] In Act 4, scene 1, the revelers discover a "wardrobe" suspended from a clothesline (or, alternatively, a "Lime" or "Line" tree). This "frippery" not only burlesques the anti-establishment merriment of Shrovetide and the theatrical violation of sumptuary laws, but might also have partly been inspired by the Lampedusan tradition of leaving clothing for shipwrecked sailors. The islander Caliban exemplifies this tradition in his own perverse way, warning of the dangers associated with frivolous appropriation of gaudy apparel: "Let it alone, thou fool; it is but trash" (4.1.224).

Perhaps most important, Lampedusa lays claim to a history rich in 16th century literary associations to Ariosto's *Orlando Furioso* (1516). Largely unknown to modern readers, Ariosto's comic epic was in its time among the most influential works in all of European literature. Telling the story of the defense of the values of Christendom from Islam by the paladins of Charlemagne, the sprawling narrative achieves coherence through Ariosto's moral vision of a Europe united against the threat of Ottoman invasion. Significantly, it is also a prominent 16th century rewriting (in an ironic key) of Virgil's *Aeneid*, a work known to have furnished a template and precedent for *The Tempest*.

Lampedusa features as the site of Ariosto's narrative climax in cantos 41–

43, the confrontation of the six knights, three Christian and three Muslim, in single combat. In a striking instance of what Barbara Reynolds has termed "the precision with which [Ariosto] represents the real world in which he sets his other world of legend and fantasy" (II: 20), the "little island" is named "Lipadusa" (40.54.2; sic), and later identified as "the island where a test of prowess will conclude the war at last" (41.35.7–8). By the mid–16th century, this association between Ariosto's epic and the island had diffused into the popular lore of the Eastern Mediterranean. Already in Crusius' account the island contained the ruins of an ancient and decrepit tower, known as Orlando's castle.[36]

That Shakespeare was familiar with Orlando's epic, a narrative well known in England and throughout Europe, has never been disputed. By 1591, when Sir John Harrington's fanciful English translation appeared, the book was already available in England in its original Italian. Harrington's expurgated translation popularized the work, and it was shortly followed by Robert Greene's stage version, *The History of Orlando Furioso* (1594). Ariosto's epic would have exercised a strong fascination for an English writer such as Shakespeare, with a sustained interest in both history and romantic epic. While it is primarily a Mediterranean narrative, it contains a major English element through the important character of Astolfo, introduced as the "son of the King of England," as well as over thirty English and Scottish noblemen.

Substantial scholarship confirms Shakespeare's familiarity with *Orlando Furioso*. In his discussion of the sources of *Much Ado About Nothing*, Kenneth Muir suggests that Shakespeare "probably knew [the book] in the original as well as in Harrington's translation."[37] Andrew Cairncross finds unmistakable traces of *Orlando*'s influence not only in *Much Ado* but in *Lear* and *Othello*, and concludes that "it seems reasonable to infer that Shakespeare had at least a reading knowledge of Italian and had read and been fascinated by certain passages of *Orlando* ... which he used ... independently of translations."[38] In a significant concession to Shakespeare's knowledge of European vernaculars, Stuart Gillespie agrees, noting that "the assumption that [Shakespeare] could not read Italian has been weakening in recent years."[39] In view of the general agreement that Shakespeare knew *Orlando Furioso*, and its documented influence in other plays of the canon, it is striking how thoroughly its impact on *Tempest*, the Shakespearean play with which it shares far more obvious features than any other, has been overlooked.

Among the most intriguing connections between *The Tempest* and *Orlando Furioso* is the latter's cast of real world characters drawn from the Milanese and Aragonese elites. Like Peter Martyr, Ariosto had a first-hand connection to the internecine quarrels of the Milanese dynasties that furnish

Shakespeare's back-story and exposition. As with Martyr's *Decades,* Ariosto's narrative refers to these historical protagonists by name. Beatrice d'Este, the sister of Ariosto's two patrons, Alfonso and Ippolito, married Ludovico Sforza. Ludovico, previously noted in our discussion of Martyr's text as a likely inspiration for Shakespeare's own Prospero, reappears in Ariosto as the naively trusting figure "unhappy Sforza of Milan" (46.49) only to be "to the Gaul ... by allies sold" (40.41).[40] Ariosto's Latin tutor, Gregorio of Spoleto, terminated his instruction of Ariosto to obtain employment as the tutor to Francesco Sforza (33.45), the son of Gian Galeazo Sforza and Isabella of Aragon.

Beyond the shared elements of historical contextualization, the two literary texts share many common features that not only suggest Shakespeare's awareness of Ariosto's epic, but also reveal his replication of its themes and symbolism to suit his own purpose. It is impossible within the compass of this short chapter to do full justice to the many specific points connecting *Tempest* to *Orlando Furioso,* but here are a few of them. In both texts

1. An eastern Mediterranean geopolitical landscape shaped by religiously inspired conflict between Muslim and Christian forms the "typo-geographical" context;

2. The Aragons of Naples and the Sforzas of Milan are central players;

3. A shipwreck survivor swims ashore on a deserted Mediterranean island while his ship is miraculously saved from destruction;

4. Critical action occurs on an island (Lampedusa) located off the coast of North Africa;

5. The "amazing" events and ambience of romance are juxtaposed to the psychological realism of fully drawn and believable individual characters;

6. A magician conjures up a "sprite" to perform magic for him;

7. A wicked witch (Alcina; Sycorax) imprisons her enemies or former lovers in a tree; Astolfo is imprisoned in a myrtle by Alcina and becomes "a living spirit, hidden in its bark"[41] and Ariel is imprisoned by Sycorax in a "cloven pine."

8. A vivid account of St. Elmo's fire is included in a Renaissance "storm template," which incorporates such elements as the motif of the pale pilot/helmsman, the loss of ship's rigging and superstructure, high winds, turgid sea, and the tossing of cargo overboard to lighten the load (19.50–51);

9. A ship, apparently lost, is by magic found to be whole and seaworthy (40.60–61);

10. An island hermit who eats only fruits and berries and drinks only water (similar to what Prospero feeds Caliban) threatens wreck survivors, consoles them with Christian piety, and then leads them to higher wisdom (41.52–60).

Perhaps the most obvious and illuminating parallels between *Tempest* and *Orlando Furioso* come into focus when we examine the episodes of *Orlando*'s climactic action, which occur on Lampedusa (or Lipadusa) in cantos 41–43. *The Tempest*, we suggest, stages a rewriting of these critical cantos in an ironic key. In Ariosto's narrative Ruggiero, Orlando, Oliver, and Brandimart all end up, by indirect routes, on Lampedusa. In a passage distinctly recalling Francisco's 2.1.118–25 hypotyposis of Ferdinand escaping the wreck, Ruggiero, sailing "for Africa" (7) to restore freedom to several Ottoman nobles captured in battle, is wrecked in a violent tempest (8–21) and must swim ashore. Compare the passages (Table 8.1 on next page).

With the possible exception of Virgil,[42] nothing remotely comparable to this vivid description of a shipwreck survivor contending with the waves occurs in any other known *Tempest* source. Both Ruggiero and Ferdinand make it safely to shore only to fall under the authoritarian rule of aged island patriarchs. Prospero's harsh schooling of Ferdinand recalls the relationship between the "holy hermit" (41.54.1) and Ruggiero, as Ariosto develops it through subsequent cantos. The hermit rebukes Ruggiero and threatens him with the lash (41.55), but ultimately consoles him with Christian piety: "He schools the knight as to his cell they go" (55–57), leading him "higher and yet higher/in knowledge of our faith and in pursuit of truth" (59). Prospero, likewise, threatens to manacle Ferdinand (1.2.540), and then imposes on him a series of Herculean rites of passage which Ferdinand must complete to win Prospero's approval for his marriage to Miranda (4.1).[43] After christening his young charge, Ariosto's hermit engages Ruggiero in a dialogue concerning his "own affairs/of his posterity and of his heirs" (41.60.7–8); the same themes of dynastic posterity figure prominently in *The Tempest*'s hymeneal masque and other episodes of the concluding scenes.

Just as Ariosto's Lampedusa/Lipadusa is the site of an encounter between the fictionalized ancestor of Ariosto's Este patrons (Ruggiero) and the island hermit, it is also a theatre of chivalry, a stage for the climactic showdown between honorable protagonists of Christendom and Islam. But neither Ariosto nor Shakespeare is a passive copyist of his antecedents. Shakespeare's "typo-geographical" rewriting comically inverts the normative 16th century values of Ariosto's epic, reproducing both strands of the Lampedusan narrative in a satiric register. Having arrived on Lampedusa, the Christian knights of Ariosto's epic proceed to do manly battle with their honorable Ottoman counterparts, but the shipwrecked party of Alonso *et alia*, heedless of their mortal danger on the frontlines of a historic cultural showdown between Christianity and Islam, enact a parody of the Christian fall. Typo-geography, in other words, casts a shadow of tragi-comic irony over the entire misadventure of

Table 8.1. Comparison of the *descriptio* of Ruggiero (*OF*) and Ferdinand (*Temp.*) Swimming Ashore — Both on "Lampedusa"

Orlando Furioso, *41*

Ruggiero will not yield to fear,
His body from the seas embrace he heaves.
He sees the naked rock not far away,
Where all assumed the ship must crash that day. (21–22)

Ruggiero strikes out boldly with each limb
And battles with the overwhelming waves.
The wind and tempest, menacing and grim
(but not his troubled conscience), the youth braves. (47)

His strength redoubled, and with heart undaunted,
Ruggiero struck the waves and pulled them past,
As hard upon each other's trail they flaunted.
One flung him up, another downward cast.
Now he descended, now again he mounted,
With great distress and labor, till at last
He landed; where the hill most gently verged
Towards the water dripping he emerged. (50)

Tempest

Fran. Sir, he may live:
I saw him beat the surges under him,
And ride upon their backs; he trod the water,
Whose enmity he flung aside, and breasted
The surge most swoln that met him; his bold head
'Bove the contentious waves he kept, and oar'd
Himself with his good arms in lusty stroke
To the shore, that o'er his wave-worn basis bow'd,
As stooping to relieve him: I not doubt
He came alive to land. (2.1.118–25)

The Tempest shipwreck. Not just *how,* but also *where* these characters are misbehaving, is part of Shakespeare's design. Instead of the site of heroic knights clashing in formal battle, Shakespeare's island becomes a stage for drunken disorder and attempted regicide. It is no accident that this disreputable behavior takes place in the shadow of Eastern Mediterranean piracy on the site of Ariosto's clash of civilizations. Indeed, as Wilson and several others have recently argued, Shakespeare's early-modern audience would have been painfully aware that the inhabitants of Caliban's island stood in mortal danger of being captured and cast into lifelong slavery. Both the court party and the revelers, however, endure North African shipwreck without a thought of the dangers with which any of their English audience would have associated the locale.

Hotly debated during the 19th century, Joseph Hunter's book has since been ignored, despite its obvious relevance to the new Mediterranean perspective of 21st century *Tempest* criticism. Contemporary *Tempest* scholarship has fruitfully recontextualized the play in a Mediterranean framework, while declining to notice Hunter's pioneering work, or to consider the seemingly obvious possibility that Ariosto's grand epic might have influenced the construction of *The Tempest*.

This is a pity. The Ariosto-Lampedusa axis discovered by Hunter reunites literature with geography. Hunter not only anticipated the revival of scholarship on a "Mediterranean *Tempest*" by over a hundred and seventy years, he identified the play with a specific and revealing Mediterranean location both rich in literary associations and fraught with 16th century geo-political implications.

Such absence of curiosity among literary scholars begs explanation. After the rise of postmodernism in the 1970s, any attempt to identify Caliban's island with a particular locale, no matter how credible, conflicted with prevailing academic habits of thought. To modern scholars, especially those committed to the rise of theory, Hunter was an antiquarian. Moreover, Hunter's literalism blinded even his potential supporters to the deeper implications of his thesis. The connection between the Lampedusan tradition of leaving clothing and provisions for shipwreck survivors and a *Tempest* island supplied with a frippery and a banquet table went unrecognized. Nor did Hunter himself fully appreciate the role that fear of Barbary Coast piracy would have played in shaping the expectations of Shakespeare's contemporary audiences.

Hunter's neglect is relevant to the larger thesis of this book. His great 19th century antagonist was none other than Edmond Malone, credited by Alden Vaughan with being the originator of the "standard thesis" of Strachey's inspiration of *The Tempest*. In pursuit of this thesis, Malone ignored the obvious indices of Mediterranean topography in Shakespeare's play, advanced the idea that the 1611 Bermuda documents constituted a *Tempest* source *sine qua non*, and insisted that the play was not written until circa 1611–12.[44] Perhaps Malone was wrong, not only about geography, but also about chronology.

9

An Elizabethan *Tempest*

One test of a new theory is its power to elucidate answers to emergent questions. With this in mind, the preceding chapters have explored Richard Malim's theory that the play later known as *The Tempest* already existed in 1605 under a different title, *The Tragedy of the Spanish Maze*. As we have seen, a play by this title was performed on Shrovetide 1605, and we confirmed that *The Tempest* was created with a Shrovetide performance date in mind. This conclusion, however, raises yet another question. *The Spanish Maze* production took place more than six years before traditional *Tempest* scholarship insists the play was written. Is there more evidence for a *Tempest* that existed that early? The answer is a resounding "yes."

Following a scenario — that the 1609–10 Bermuda narratives were a primary *Tempest* source — first established by Edmond Malone in the early 19th century, and modified through the successive intervention of Henry Howard Furness, Luce, Gayley, and others, Hallett Smith (1969) summarizes the dominant view, in words that almost all Shakespeareans today still accept as beyond serious dispute:

> *The Tempest* can be dated with some precision, since there is a record of a performance of it at court on November 1, 1611, and since it borrows some details from accounts of the travels and adventures of Sir George Summers in Bermuda which were not available in England before the fall of 1611.[1]

But *if,* as we have seen, the evidence for Shakespeare's reliance on Strachey is now called into serious doubt; *if* much better sources of Shakespeare's New World imagery can be found in Richard Eden's 1555 translations; *if* the play was originally written for a Shrovetide performance; and *if* a play fitting the description of *The Tempest* but known by another title was performed as early as 1605, then this traditional scenario can no longer be accepted uncritically. Let us return to the literary record to see if the hypothesis of an earlier *Tempest* can be substantiated from external evidence of a more direct nature.

Because the chronological coincidence of the earliest recorded performance date and the supposedly influential contemporaneous reports of the Bermuda wreck are often invoked as conclusive evidence, it must again be noted that records of performance or publication, unlike sources, establish only a *terminus ad quem*, a date *before which* the play must have been written. For this reason the case for a 1610 *terminus a quo*—a date *after which* it must have been written—*logically*, rests *solely* on the alleged influence of the Bermuda shipwreck literature, in particular Strachey's *Reportory* (f.p. 1625). Recognizing the incomplete nature of early-modern theatrical records,[2] scholars know that many plays were written long before their first date of publication or first known record of performance.[3] That this might also be true of *The Tempest* is an alternative few have considered; even fewer have paid any attention to the factual and logical problems raised by the traditional view.

A survey of past attempts to establish a definitive *Tempest* composition date fails to inspire confidence in the logic of the traditional view. Throughout most of the 20th century, the need to preserve a chronology which "fit[s] [the works] into the facts of Shakespeare's dramatic career" so as to "provide a fairly even flow of production"[4] circumscribed critical inquiry, emboldened speculation, and suppressed consideration of plausible alternative scenarios. Until very recently, this trend has accelerated. With few exceptions, impressive evidence supporting a much earlier composition date for *The Tempest,* which has steadily accumulated over almost two centuries of scholarship, has been excised from critical consciousness. E.K. Chambers, predictably, was one of the few who preserved some note of skepticism; endorsing the late date only with explicit reservations, he noted that "Malone's date of 1611 ... *remains reasonable,*"[5] and went on to acknowledge that "the notion of an early date for *Tempest* in some form has been encouraged by its analogies to the play *Die Schöne Sidea,*"[6] a work written before 1605. As Chambers admonished, moreover, citing a familiar principle: "As a rule, the initial dates are much less certain than the terminal ones."[7]

Skepticism of the validity of the Bermuda pamphlets as a chronological marker never disappeared entirely. Writing in 1977, Kenneth Muir kept the door open to an earlier date, voicing the conviction that "the extent of the verbal echoes of [the Bermuda] pamphlets has been exaggerated."[8] More recently, Andrew Gurr,[9] Penny McCarthy[10] and others have questioned elements of the Malone-Furness dating, McCarthy even arguing that the play might have been written as early as 1599. Picking up where Chambers left off, she identifies the Achilles heel of the orthodox view, noting that

> the whole edifice of what is here for short-hand called "the consensus" [of
> the chronology of the plays] rests dangerously on the assumption that date

of composition must be close to date of first performance/publication/ mention.[11]

She goes on to insist that "there is no reason why Shakespeare's plays should have been originally written close to the first record of their existence."[12]

In addition to the Bermuda pamphlets, it has sometimes been argued that *The Tempest* must be dated circa 1611 because, in the words of David Kathman, "the debate among Gonzalo, Antonio and Sebastian in Act 2, scene 1 about the nature of paradise parallels the public debate in England in the wake of the attempted colonization of Virginia beginning in 1607."[13] This line of argument is dubious, for several reasons. It is well known that English pamphleteers were already exploiting the "paradise" *topos* by the 1580s, in the wake of the disastrous Roanoke colonization (1585–88). By 1588 "[Thomas] Harriot is especially concerned to counter the 'many envious, malicious, and slanderous reports' brought back by ... dissatisfied ex-colonists [who] were spreading damaging stories about their hardships in Virginia and the unlikelihood that the land would support civilized life, much less produce profits."[14] The dispute over whether the new world was a paradise or an inhospitable desert, contrary to Kathman's implication, goes back even further in Iberian travel narratives to the earliest decades of the 16th century. It even forms a motif in the narratives collected, translated, and published in English by Richard Eden in 1555, previously identified in chapters 2 through 4 as Shakespeare's primary source of information about the New World.

In short, *assumptions* about a source — not evidence — have inhibited scholarly inquiry and encouraged a false confidence in a particular theory of *Tempest*'s composition date. Fortunately, there are signs that this is beginning to change. As we demonstrate (see chapters 16 through 18), Strachey's narrative in its extant form was almost certainly not completed until after the November 1611 *Tempest* performance and for that reason alone should no longer be construed as Shakespeare's source. Thus it is not surprising that, as we have seen, every claimed instance of Strachey's alleged influence on Shakespeare can more credibly be explained by the playwright's reliance on early Iberian and English travel narratives, and other literary sources such as Ariosto and Erasmus, all available by the mid–16th century.

These findings have further implications for the actual composition date of *The Tempest*. By 1892, when Furness published his Variorum text, evidence for an earlier date — distinct traces of *Tempest* influence in several pre–1611 plays — was already accumulating and was cited by Furness.

Furness was by no means a chronological revisionist. Although he presents abundant evidence for an earlier *Tempest* date, he manages to deflect its powerful cumulative effect. He lists each clue to an earlier date in an *ad hoc* fashion, classifying some items under "chronology" and others under "sources." In retrospect it is apparent that Furness' conservative conclusion, cited earlier, was not the result of a critical method, but a summation and consolidation of previous opinion: "The voice of the majority pronounces in favor of 1610–11. Let us all, therefore, acquiesce, and henceforth be, in this regard, shut up in measureless content."[15]

We prefer Penny McCarthy's contrasting view that "contemporary literary evidence in the form of parody and oblique allusion to Shakespeare has been under-utilized in the search for correct 'dates before which' his plays must have been in existence."[16] We thus decline Furness' invitation to be "shut up in measureless content." Let us take a close look at four works, dated c. 1603–1610, to answer the obvious question: if the traditional basis for a 1611 *Tempest* is no longer set in stone, can we determine with greater accuracy when it *was* written? Each of these texts exhibits distinctive evidence of *Tempest* influence, cumulatively leaving little doubt that Shakespeare's play was known to the London theatre public no later than 1603. How much earlier it may have been written, we do not know. That it existed by 1603 seems, however, certain.

The first hint of a pre–1611 date is the Satyr's speech in John Fletcher's *Faithful Shepherdess*, which closely parallels a passage from *The Tempest* (Table 9.1). The implication of the comparison is supported by Herford and Simpson's percipient description of the Satyr as a character not only influenced by Spenser, but also exhibiting "added touches of Ariel."[18] The parallel threatened to upset Malone's chronology. Published in 1610, Fletcher's play has a *terminus ad quem* of May 1610, but is normally dated to 1608–09.[19] Even Furness acknowledges that "[if] the imitation [had] been unquestionable, it would have played sad havoc with Malone's date of 1611."[20] To preserve the chronology, Furness dismisses the parallel with a sweeping appeal to an undocumented "consensus" about the meaning of the evidence that efficiently abrogates any hint of principle: "Belief in the alleged imitation has never been seriously entertained."[21]

Even if true, this is not a valid argument. Beyond the common pastoral ambiance that already suggests a genetic relationship of some kind, the two plays share several linguistic and symbolic parallels that Furness does not mention but which, collectively, substantiate a definite impression of intertextuality. Fletcher's Satyr, for example, bears the imprint not only of Ariel but also of Caliban. In a passage distinctly recalling Miranda's dismay at the sexual overtures of Caliban, whom Prospero later describes as being "as disproportioned in his manners as in his shape" (5.1.292), Clorin describes the satyr as one who "never knew manners" and whose "heats are rougher than himself, and more misshapen" (1.1.21–24). It is difficult to suppress the impression of

Table 9.1. *Tempest* (1.2.189–193) Compared to
The Faithful Shepherdess, Written Circa 1608–9[17]

Tempest	Faithful Shepherdesse
Ariel. I come to answer thy best pleasure;	**Satyr.** Tell me sweetest,
Be't to fly,	What new service now is meetest
To swim, to dive into the fire; to ride	For the Satyr? Shall I stray
On the curl'd clouds; to do they strong bidding, task	In the middle air, or nimbly take
Ariel, and all his quality. (1.2.189–93)	Hold by the moon, and gently make
	Suit to the pale queen of night
	For a beam to give thee light?
	Shall I dive into the sea,
	And bring thee coral, making way
	Through the rising waves that fall
	In snowy fleeces?
	Dearest, shall I catch thee wanton fawns, or flies
	Whose woven wings the summer dyes
	Of many colors? Get thee fruit,
	Or steal from heaven old Orpheus' lute?
	All these *I'll* venture for, and more
	To do her service all these woods adore. (5.5.240–57)

Fletcher's dependence on Shakespeare when, in the same speech, Clorin echoes Ariel's pied-piper trick of leading the revelers by voice and music through "toothed briars, sharp furzes, pricking gorse and thorns," ending with them "I'th' filthy mantled pool" (4.1.203). Fletcher's Clorin, likewise, complains that she has been led on by "voices calling me in dead of night ... through mire and standing pools" (1.1.118–20).

Finally, as tempting as it may be to dismiss the parallelism between the speech of the Priest of Pan and Prospero's famous "ye elves of hills" imprecation (Table 9.2, below) as an effect of the hypothetical common source in Ovid's *Metamorphoses*,[22] the accumulation of other parallels diminishes the plausibility of such an *ad hoc* recourse. As Shakespeare's passage is distinctly closer to Golding's translation than to Fletcher's, it is unlikely he derived it from Fletcher.

These analogies, collectively considered, establish a firm connection between the two works. In theory either dramatist could be the borrower. But the norm is unmistakable: Fletcher takes from Shakespeare, not the other way around. *The Woman's Prize or The Tamer Tamed* (c. 1611) is an acknowledged sequel to *Taming of the Shrew*; *Philaster* (c. 1610), co-written with Francis

**Table 9.2. Prospero's *Tempest* Imprecation
Compared to the Song of the Priest of Pan
in *Faithful Shepherdess* and Golding's Ovid**

Golding's Metamorphoses	Tempest	Faithfull Shepherdesse
Ye airs and winds: Ye elves of Hills, of Brooks, of Woods alone, Of standing Lakes, and of the night approach ye everyone. Through help of whom (the crooked banks much wondering at the thing). (7.263–89)	Ye elves of hills, brooks, standing lakes, and groves, And yet that on the sands with printless foot Do chase the ebbing Neptune.... (5.1.33–35) Ye nymphs called Naiads of the windring brooks, With your sedged crowns and ever-harmless looks, Leave your crisp channels, and on this green land Answer your summons, Juno does command. (4.1.128–131)	All ye woods, and trees, and bowers, All ye virtues and ye powers That inhabit in the lakes, In the pleasant springs or brakes. (5.5.216–20)

Beaumont, shows the distinctive influence of *Hamlet,* and probably *Cymbeline.*[23] *The Tempest,* in particular, left so durable an imprint on Fletcher's imagination that Dryden disparaged Fletcher's *Sea Voyage* (1622)[24] as a mere copy[25] of Shakespeare's play. Again, both internal and external evidence — objectively evaluated without the *a priori* prejudice of chronological impossibility — support the inference that Fletcher was influenced by a *Tempest* already in existence by 1608.

The evident intertextuality of *The Tempest* and Jakob Ayrer's *Die Schöne Sidea* — a play which Campbell and Quinn acknowledge "reveals many similarities to *The Tempest,* for which no source has been found"[26] — is a second obstacle to the 1611 date. Admission of a close relationship between the two plays is typically accompanied by a claim that the apparent influence is impossible for chronological reasons. Brennecke, following a tradition established by Tieck in 1817, holds that "it has often been pointed out that [Ayrer's] *Die Schöne Sidea* shows certain resemblances in its plot to Shakespeare's *Tempest,* but there is no evidence that the two plays could have influenced each other."[27] Notwithstanding such denials, the parallels in plot and characterization are so evident that the only way to argue against one play influencing the other is to presume a common antecedent in literature or folklore. This, however, is purely a hypothesis. Except for the fact that it conveniently solves the problem of how the two texts came to share so much thematically and structurally, there is no basis for the conjecture; while it is beyond serious doubt that the two plays are drawn on a common pattern, no common antecedent has ever been successfully identified.[28] Following a Shakespearean design established with variation, as Harold Goddard has noticed,[29] in *As You Like It* and *Lear* as well as *The Tempest* and *Die Schöne Sidea,* protagonists in both plays are exiled to a wilderness after having had their thrones usurped by a competing power. To this must be added numerous points of plot detail (see Appendix B for our tabulation, which enumerates seven major parallels between the two plays). Albert Cohn summarizes the pattern:

> The ideal arrangement as well as the single scenes and passages in both pieces display a most unmistakable resemblance. Ayrer's removal of the action into the region of fable is a feature to which we have already alluded. In both pieces then we have two hostile princes, of whom the one ... practices the arts of magic to get the son of the other into his power, in both pieces this prince has a spirit in his service, through whose power the enemy's arms are rendered innocuous, and lastly, in both pieces an attachment is formed between the only daughter of the one prince, and the captive son of the other, which is eventually the means of bringing about reconciliation between the two hostile families. Both pieces are based on the idea of a retributory justice. If these points of resemblance in the fundamental structure are in themselves sufficient to exclude all possibility of an accidental coincidence, the numerous external points of agreement in the course of the two pieces must remove the last shadow of a doubt. In one piece as in the other, the captive son of the prince is obliged to pile up logs of wood, and in both pieces this scene leads to the attachment of the lovers.[30]

The traditional assumption is that if there is no common source, Shakespeare must have borrowed from Ayrer. Even Cohn remarks that "if we agree with most of the commentators that *The Tempest* is one of Shakespeare's later works, there cannot be the slightest doubt that Ayrer's piece was written long before [it]."[31] But if we consider the alternative, all the evidence of context supports the idea that the similarities are due to Shakespeare's influence on Ayrer, whose other works are largely derivative of English dramas, and not the other way around.

Ayrer's *Opus Theatricum* containing *Die Schöne Sidea* was published in 1618, but his death in 1605 demonstrates the contradiction that results from the traditional assumption of the date of Shakespeare's play. If Ayrer borrowed from *Tempest*, then it already existed sometime before 1605.

The probability of Shakespeare's influence can be further inferred from a larger cultural trend, the existence of which is beyond dispute. As is well known, starting in the 1580s companies of English actors touring the Continent were greeted with special enthusiasm in Germany, and by 1590 their influence was so great that Brennecke refers to them as an "invasion in real force."[32]

The invasion continued well into the 17th century. Extant records, undoubtedly fragmentary and incomplete, record early German performances of *Julius Caesar, The Spanish Tragedy, Doctor Faustus, The Jew of Malta, Orlando Furioso, Edward IV, The Maid's Tragedy, The Virgin Martyr, King Lear, The Comedy of Errors,* and *Othello.*[33] Even by the turn of the century, Shakespeare was a special favorite with German audiences, and Cohn documents the "astonishing fact that the Germans became acquainted with the greatest masterpieces of Shakespeare through the medium of the stage, nearly a century and a half before any other nation except of course the English."[34] Brennecke reprints no fewer than five 17th century German productions written in imitation of Shakespearean plays: *Titus Andronicus, Midsummer Night's Dream, Merchant of Venice, Twelfth Night,* and *Hamlet.* To these Cohn adds early German imitations of *Romeo and Juliet, Much Ado About Nothing, Taming of the Shrew,* and *Merry Wives of Windsor.*

Ayrer's own dramatic career typifies this dependence of the German theatre on English exemplars; according to Cohn,[35] Ayrer was acquainted with English actors at least as early as 1595, and by Ayrer's own admission, his plays are conceived "gleichsam auf die neue Englische manier und art"/"just according to the new English manner and style."[36] Cohn goes on to argue that "many of his dramas bear external and internal traces of English models, *and it does not admit of a doubt, that all of Ayrer's literary activity received its direction from his acquaintance with the English Comedians.*"[37] Even Furness, apparently unconscious of the implications, agrees that Ayrer's plays "appear to be merely imitations or reproductions of English dramas ... [and] ... it was from them that Jacob Ayrer drew the materials for many of his plays."[38]

With such robust testimony to the overwhelming influence of the English drama on German playwriting in general, and on Jacob Ayrer in particular, it is strange that scholars have for so long either denied a direct connection between *The Tempest* and *Die Schöne Sidea,* or insisted that if there is one, Shakespeare *must* be the borrower rather than the lender. The reasons for this failure to consider the implications of Ayrer as the borrower are evident. As E.K. Chambers noted, the possibility of Shakespeare's influence on Ayrer has for decades encouraged advocates of an early *Tempest* date, one which seemed to contradict Shakespeare's accepted reliance on Strachey as an inspiration and source. It is clear that these advocates were correct, and that Chambers' reticence about the Malone-Furness chronology was well justified.

An even earlier play exhibiting a definite correspondence to *The Tempest* is William Alexander's *Darius*, a historical tragedy published in Edinburgh in 1603. A topical allegory, *Darius* celebrates the occasion of King James' ascension to the English throne and flatters the new king as a conquering Alexander the Great. The playwright (c. 1570–1640) was one of the Scots who followed James to London for his July 25, 1603, coronation. His command of theatrical rhetoric proved an invaluable asset; he rose steadily in the service of James and was knighted in 1614, receiving a royal charter for the territories that later became Nova Scotia, and in 1633 he was made Earl of Stirling.

One obvious link between Alexander's play and *The Tempest*—Darius' stoic reflection on the transience of earthly power (Table 9.3)—has long been acknowledged.

Table 9.3. Prospero's Speech Compared to *Darius* (1603)

The Tempest	Darius *(1603)*
Pros. These our actors, (As I foretold you) were all spirits, and Are melted into Air, into thin Air, And like the baselesse fabric of this vision, The cloud-cappped towers, the gorgeous palaces, The solemn temples, the great globe itself, Yea, all which it inherit, shall dissolve, And like this insubstantial pageant faded, Leave not a rack behind: we are such stuff As dreams are made on... (4.1.148–157)	**Dar.** Let greatness of her glassy scepters vaunt; Not scepters, no, but reeds, soon bruis'd, some broken: And let this worldly pomp our wits enchant. All fades, and scarcely leaves behind a token. Those golden Palaces, those gorgeous halls, With furniture superfluously fair: Those stately Courts, those sky-encountering walls, Evanish all like vapors in the air. (G4v)

Even Furness admits that "a parallelism" between the passages is "evident" and concludes that "if we believe that Shakespeare 'conveyed' from *Darius*, we obtain a definite early limit, viz.: 1603, after which *The Tempest* must have been written."[39] W. Aldis Wright concurs that the two passages are cognate, but cautiously concludes that there is "hardly enough to justify any inference with regard to the priority of the dates."[40]

As in the previous examples, the similarities between the two plays are not limited to the obvious linguistic parallelism of a single passage. The fact that both plays treat common themes of governance, retribution, and forgiveness, as well as the operations of fortune that direct the rise and fall of kingdoms, can only enhance suspicion of a common genesis. Like Prospero, Alexander's title character has had his kingdom usurped by a conquering rival and becomes a "patron now/Of the unstableness of states and crowns" (c3r). Conspiracy is another conspicuous theme of both plays, and the plot of Nessus and Narbazanes to overthrow Darius (3.3) parallels the plot of Sebastian and Antonio to kill Alonso (as well as the parallel plot of the revelers to kill Prospero), not only dramatically but figuratively: in both passages the senior rebel incites his comrade with the metaphor of "sleepy" conspirators who fail to seize the "occasion" of their own advancement. In retrospect one may reasonably wonder why Furness was so certain that the direction of influence *must*

Table 9.4. The Conspiracy of Nessus and Narbazanes to Overthrow Darius (3.3) Includes the Same Curious Idea of Sleepy Conspirators Awakened by Ambition

Tempest	Darius
Seb. I find not Myself disposed to *sleep...*	**Bes.** *You see occasion call us, whilst we sleep,* And points us out the way to be advanc'd;
Ant. me thinks I see it in thy face, What thou shouldst be: *the occasion speaks to thee,* and My strong imagination sees a crown Dropping upon thy head. **Seb.** What, art thou waking? **Ant.** Do you not hear me speak? **Seb.** I do; and surely It is a sleepy language and thou speak'st *Out of thy sleep.* What is it thou didst say? This is a strange repose, to be asleep With eyes wide open; standing, speaking, moving, And *yet so fast asleep.* **Ant.** Noble Sebastian, Thou let'st thy fortune sleep — die, rather; wink'st *Whiles thou art waking.* (2.1.201–216)	Yea blames *our sluggishness* that we cannot keep The course of things which for our weal have chanced. (e3v)

have been *from* Alexander *to* Shakespeare. There is no intrinsic rationale; on the contrary his "confidence" seems to originate in the unspoken but evidently erroneous *assumption* that *The Tempest* could not possibly have been extant by 1603.

Can the case be made for Shakespeare's priority? One axiom for determining the direction of influence between two related texts is the appropriateness of a sign for a particular thematic, symbolic, or linguistic context: Both vocabulary and metaphor should more naturally fit the source text than the imitation.[41] This condition is abundantly fulfilled in the present example. While *Darius* concerns a historic land war between the Persians and the Greeks under Alexander, it reiterates the nautical analogy between state and ship on which *The Tempest*— naturally and appropriately for an island romance — depends[42]: "The state-disturbing blasts of Fortune fall:/Yet each of them some several sorrows move/But *wretch I suffer ship-wreck* in them all" (d2r). Even though they seem arbitrary, as if appropriated from a source for which the nautical imagery would be more natural, images of ships and seas reappear many times in Alexander's play. At least one of these poignantly evokes the *Tempest* theme of Prospero's lost but regained kingdom[43]: "When he hath calm'd *this tempest* now so hot,/And settled Asia with a good success;/He will your kingdoms lost with what he got/Restore: appearance promises no less" (g2r).

Alexander's play explicitly echoes other Shakespearean works, including *Hamlet*. Table 9.5 illustrates Alexander's imitation of Hamlet's metaphor of ambition as the futile "shadow of a dream."

Table 9.5. "Shadow of a Dream" Motif in *Hamlet* and *Darius*

Hamlet	Darius
Ros. Which *dreams* indeed are *ambition,* for the very substance of the ambitious is merely the *shadow of a dream.*	**Dar.** And when th' eclipse comes of our glories light
Ham. *A dream* itself is but *a shadow.*	Then what avails this glory of our name:
Ros. Truly, and I hold ambition of so airy and light a quality that it is but *a shadow's shadow...* (2.2.257–62)	A mere illusion made to mock the sight, Whose best was but *the shadow of a dream* (g4v)

Given the cumulative force of this evidence, we believe a case for Shakespeare's priority is strong. There is certainly no basis for the assumption that Shakespeare "conveyed" from Alexander, and circumstance — Aristotle's argument from antecedent probability — substantiates the impression of Alexander's reliance on Shakespeare. Indeed, the cited parallels in *Darius* collectively project what McCarthy terms the "scatter effect,"[44] in which a single seminal work "impresses itself so forcibly" on the imagination of the imitator that he repeats its words and ideas again and again. This is just what Alexander does with the metaphor of the tempest as an emblem of the instability of human monarchies — an idea we earlier saw Shakespeare may have drawn from Eden, where again it possesses an intrinsic connection to the semantic context, a connection that is missing in *Darius*.

If *The Tempest* were acted as early as 1603, Alexander would have had ample opportunity for imitation. As a cosmopolitan "new man" of the court, who toured Spain, Italy, and France with the 7th Earl of Argyle and studied at the University of Leiden in the Low Countries, he would likely have seen English players performing Shakespeare abroad, in Edinburgh, or even in London. Such a young but ambitious playwright would surely have availed himself of any opportunity for theatrical exposure. He also had an obvious motive to copy Shakespeare; in 1603, while Alexander was still an apprentice playwright, Shakespeare was already the most prominent literary figure of his generation, a dramatist whose works had been performed to public acclaim at least since 1592 and had appeared in print in more play quartos than those of any other writer. Which is more plausible — that a famous dramatist at the height of his literary powers would imitate the first work of an apprentice, or that the apprentice would turn to one of the master's greatest dramas for inspiration?

The early Jacobean satire *Eastward Ho,* a collaborative project of John Marston, Ben Jonson and George Chapman, furnishes another impressive confirmation of the case for an early *Tempest.* Registered on September 4, 1605, it is perhaps best known for its controversial lampoons of the eccentricities of early Virginia investors and explorers, as well as the social climbing of a new generation of Scots' immigrants who followed James I to London. The exceptional appearance of three printings within a year suggests that *Eastward Ho,* although controversial, was extremely popular, in significant measure because of its "ludicrous parodies of other contemporary plays,"[45] including several Shakespearean works, among them *Richard III, As You Like It, Hamlet,*[46] and, it seems likely, *II Henry IV,*[47] *Henry V,*[48] and *Lear.*[49]

To this list must be added *The Tempest,* although the connections have been overlooked because of the controlling assumption that they *cannot* exist. To begin from the obvious, in both plays journey to an exotic destination is interrupted by a nautical disaster. More generally, the ethos of New World exploration, and contemporary debates over the *bona fides* of the colonial enterprise, are as central to *Eastward Ho* as they are to *The Tempest*; Shakespeare's Gonzalo, for example, apparently taking his cue from Gonzalo Ferdinando Oviedo or Montaigne,[50] expects that Prospero's isle will "excel the Golden age" (2.1.165). One suspects a witty parody of this line in Captain Seagull's inversion of Gonzalo's utopianism when he appeals to fantasies of new world treasure in a place where "Gold is more plentiful ... than copper" and even chamber pots are "pure gold" (3.3.25–28).[51]

Lest the reader be tempted to suppose that Seagull is merely parodying the extravagant but generic illusions of English explorers, the same passage furnishes more specific signs of *Tempest* influence. On Prospero's island Gonzalo celebrates the primeval ideal of a world with "no kind of traffic ... no name of magistrate ... riches, poverty ... contract, succession,/Bourn, bound of land, tilth, vineyard, none, nor any use of metal, corn, or wine, or oil" but also believes he himself "would be king on't" (2.1.145–53). Seagull's Virginia is compromised by the same social contradiction. There, likewise, the settler "shall live freely ... without sergeants, or courtiers, or lawyers, or intelligencers" (3.3.40–41), but may also, just as in Gonzalo's fantasy of kingship, "be a nobleman, and never be a slave" (3.3.50–54). Gonzalo's new world, a commonwealth of indolence with "no occupation; all men idle, all" (2.1.151), also becomes a target for *Eastward Ho*'s jesting. Surely it impairs Chapman's reputation for satire[52] and ignores the subtle music of his parody when, in the very next line, he has Seagull describe a Virginia occupied by "a few *industrious Scots*, perhaps, who indeed are dispers'd over the face of the whole earth" (3.3.41–42: emphasis ours).[53] *Eastward Ho*'s well-established reputation as a work that parodies a number of Elizabethan plays, the vast majority of them by Shakespeare, must be considered when evaluating the most plausible direction of influence. Any notion that the correspondences result from both plays coincidentally borrowing from Montaigne or other common sources also is most unlikely in view of this pattern.

The climax of the lampoon occurs in the extended description of the storm scene — written by John Marston[54] — when the butcher's apprentice Slitgut, sitting on top of the infamous Cuckold's Haven tree ("the farthest seeing sea mark in the world" [4.1.285]) witnesses a "furious tempest" that sinks the drunken sailors[55] and voyagers. Comically, they are still in a rowboat on the Thames *en route* to their ship. This vivid scene parodies Miranda's elaborate description of the wreck, and the reference to the "farthest seeing sea mark" may allude to Ariel's excursion to the "still vexed Bermoothes" — since, as we have seen, in a passage that apparently inspired Shakespeare's reference to the islands,[56] Oviedo had famously described them as "the furthest of all the Islands that are found at this day in the world."[57]

Wandering in a daze about this "New World," Petronel and Seagull — the "remnants" of the "unfortunate shipwreck"—convince themselves that they have washed up on the shores of France, Petronel swearing that he recognizes their location "by th' elevation of the Pole; and by the altitude and latitude of the Climate" (152). In a comic dialogue reminiscent of the "broken French" used in the wooing scene between Katherine and Henry V (*Henry V*, 4.2.160–167), Petronel and Seagull encounter two gentlemen walking along the shore:

> **Sea.** Pray you, do you beg on 'em then; you can speak French.
> **Pet.** *Monsieur, plaist il d'avoir pitie de nostre grande infortunes? Je suis un povre chevalier d'Angleterre qui a souffri l'infortune de naufrage.*
> **1 Gent.** *Un povre chevalier d'Angleterre?*
> **Pet.** *Oui, monsieur, il est trop vraye; mais vous scaves bien nous sommes toutes subject a fortune.*
> **2 Gent.** A poor knight of England?—A poor knight of Windsor, are you not? Why speak you this broken French, when y' are a whole Englishman? On what coast are you, think you?
> **Pet.** On the coast of France, sir.
> **1 Gent.** On the coast of Dogs, sir; y' are i' th' Isle a' Dogs, I tell you. I see y' ave been wash'd in the Thames here, and I believe ye were drown'd in a tavern before, or else you would never have took boat in such a dawning as this was... (4.1.160–76).

Much like Ferdinand in *The Tempest*, Quicksilver proceeds to wander about the Isle in search of his comrades:

> I will walk this Bank,
> And see if I can meet the other relics
> Of our poor ship-wrack'd Crew, or hear of them [4.1.131–33].

The fresh and unblemished clothing of the sea-drenched survivors in *Tempest* is among the most telling motifs parodied in *Eastward Ho*. It receives repeated emphasis in *The Tempest*. When Ariel tells Prospero of the precautions he took to ensure the survivors' safety, he warrants that "on their sustaining garments [is] not a blemish, but fresher than before" (1.2.218–19), and Gonzalo later expresses his wonder that "our garments being, as they were, drenched in the sea, hold notwithstanding their freshness and glosses, being rather new-dyed than stained with salt water" (2.1.59–61). This imagery of clean clothing on characters fresh from the Tunisian marriage of Claribel is drawn from the admonition of the 1559 Book of Common Prayer, urging the communicant to come "holy and clean to a most godly and heavenly feast ... in no wise ... but *in the marriage garment,* required of God in Holy Scripture."[58] Marston transforms this *Tempest* motif into a hilarious lampoon when he has Petronel, urged by Seagull to change out of his drenched clothing, announce: "Nay, by my troth, let our clothes rot upon us, and let us rot in them" (4.1.192–93).

Like the *Tempest*, *Eastward Ho* ends with penitence and pleas for forgiveness from the wicked characters and magnanimous displays of charity from the good ones. The prodigal apprentice Quicksilver, whose name and actions seem to parody the rebellious Ariel[59] in the form of a London apprentice, admits that he "thought by sea to run away,/But Thames, and tempest did me stay" (5.5.70–71). Playing the part of Prospero to Quicksilver's Ariel, Touchstone is struck to the quick by this confession, announcing, "Heaven pardon my severity!" Later he declares to the penitents Quicksilver and Petronel, "Speak no more; all former passages are forgiven; and here my word *shall release you*" (5.4.136: emphasis supplied). These lines imitate the ethical turning point of the *Tempest*, including Prospero's transformation from curmudgeonly tyrant to forgiving father, and his announcement that his enemies "being penitent/The sole drift of my purpose doth extend/Not a frown further. Go *release them*, Ariel" (5.1.28–30).[60]

In what must have been an inviting target for satire, Gonzalo in Act 5 offers a synopsis of *The Tempest*'s tidy ethical consummation:

> In one voyage
> Did Claribel her husband find at Tunis,
> And Ferdinand, her brother, found a wife
> Where he himself was lost, Prospero his dukedom
> In a poor isle and all of us ourselves
> When no man was his own [5.1.206–13].

Touchstone's travesty of Gonzalo apparently adopts from *The Tempest* the nautical image of the hourglass,[61] appropriating the prominent *Tempest* theme of *time*—as he carefully delineates for his London audience the moral of his own play:

> *Touch.*… Now, London, look about,
> And in this moral see thy glass run out:
> Behold the careful father, thrifty son,
> The solemn deeds, which each of us have done;
> The usurer punish'd, and from fall so steep
> The prodigal child reclaim'd, and the lost sheep [5.5.205–10].

Eastward Ho's parody of *The Tempest* carries through to Quicksilver's farewell and epilogue, which travesties the self-reflexive allusions to theatrical artifice and the London environs in Prospero's Act 4, scene 1, "cloud capped towers" speech. *Eastward Ho* inverts the otherworldly romanticism of Prospero's speech, which alludes to London in its nostalgic language of an enchanted world of "gorgeous palaces" (Whitehall) and "solemn temples" (St.

Paul's ,Westminster, or Inns of Court "temples"), and the "great Globe itself" (theatres). In place of this *Eastward Ho* recreates the gritty comic realism of a London city play, correspondingly reducing the diction to a comic register, bidding "Farewell, Cheapside; farewell sweet trade/of *Goldsmiths* all, that *never shall fade.*" Quicksilver's double reference to the "pageant" of the release of the prisoners reveals *Eastward Ho*'s evident dependence on Shakespeare's drama, in which Prospero has lamented "this insubstantial *pageant faded/* leav[ing] not a rack behind" (4.1.155–56). Compare the passages as given side-by-side in Table 9.6.

Table 9.6. The *Eastward Ho* Epilogue Travesties Prospero's Theatrical Rhetoric

Tempest	Eastward Ho
The cloud-capp'd towers, the gorgeous palaces, The *solemn* temples, the great globe itself, Ye all which it inherit, *shall dissolve* And, like this insubstantial *pageant faded,* Leave not a rack behind (4.1.148–56)	Farewell, Cheapside; farewell sweet trade of Goldsmiths all, that *never shall fade...*[62] See, if the streets and the fronts of the houses be not stuck with people, and the windows fill'd with ladies, as on the *solemn day of the pageant!* Oh, may you find in this our *pageant* here, The same contentment which you came to seek; And, as that show but draws you once a year, May this attract you hither once a week. (epilogue)

Penny McCarthy's axiom of *lectio facetior* ("the wittier reading") applies to *Eastward Ho*'s parodic inversions of Shakespeare's play. Parody thrives by transmuting romance (or tragedy) into farce; the "wittier reading" depends on the reader's apprehension of an intentional relationship between parody and object. Translating the mysterious locale of Prospero's island into the familiar *topos* of the Thames River and depositing the shipwrecked survivors on the Isle of Dogs, *Eastward Ho* achieves a full measure of comic effect, reducing Shakespeare's exotic locale to the homely realism of the controversial Thames river site.[63] Only chronological presumption — the unquestioned belief that Shakespeare's play "can be dated with virtual certainty [to] between late 1610 and mid-to-late 1611"[64] — can account for the failure to recognize that these passages lampoon *The Tempest,* just as other passages in the same play are known to parody *Hamlet* and *Richard III.*[65]

Close comparison reveals that the populist rhetoric of *Eastward Ho*'s dedication to the city, lampooning of the nobility, and relentless parodies of Shakespearean texts, are as much marketing strategy as ideology or aesthetics. As we have seen, *The Tempest* was written for Shrovetide performance; the holiday themes, from licentious revelry to penitential shriving, from "spectacles of barbarian strangeness" to the contemplative practices of the labyrinth, feature conspicuously in Shakespeare's play. In language that explicitly refers to the annual character of a Shrovetide performance Prospero concludes his marriage masque with the climactic pronouncement that "our revels now are ended," concluding the "spectacle" of a play that "leaves not a rack behind" (4.1.148–156).

Inverting the logic of *The Tempest* denouement, the *Eastward Ho* epilogue assures the audience that while an unnamed rival play only "draws you once a year," this one may "attract you hither once a week." *Eastward Ho* trumps Prospero's allusion to the theatre and the actors going home for the solitary rites of Lent, by invoking a swelling "multitude" — an audience overflowing the galleries — that has gathered to witness the liberation of Quicksilver, Flash, and Security from their imprisonment in jail. This scene is replete with ladies in the "windows" (gallery), groundlings in the "streets" (pit), and reference to the "fronts of houses" (the area for the audience in front of the stage).[66]

While at the conclusion of Act 5, Prospero's actors melt away (only to return again at another Shrovetide season a year later), on London's Bankside the homely diction of this materialist satire is just getting started. A throng of customers, anxious to witness the homecoming of the impecunious knight with an encumbered East Anglia castle and a mercurial apprentice, are only now gathering to purchase tickets for the next performance.

Doubtless, each of these instances of apparent *Tempest* influence on the discourse of colonization and the Jacobean drama, considered in isolation, is susceptible to *ad hoc* skepticism. But to us, the accumulation of evidence damages the precarious edifice of the orthodox "consensus" chronology beyond repair. Indeed, judging by the evidence cited, *The Tempest* was among the most influential of Shakespeare's late plays. To recognize that it must have been performed at least by 1603, when *Darius* imitates both its ethos and distinctive language, and possibly even as early as 1598–99 when Tom Nashe's *Lenten Stuffe* seems to already parody the image of Miranda and Ferdinand at chess,[67] is to invite rereading *The Tempest* with fresh eyes. It implies that *The Faithful Shepherdesse, Die Schöne Sidea, Eastward Ho,* and much of the New World and nautical symbolism of the Jacobean masque[68] are in significant respects derivative of Shakespeare's seminal work. It also restores the play to an original theatrical context that gives meaning to otherwise irrelevant imagery. Sebastian's pointed allusion to "one tree [in Arabia], the Phoenix throne: one Phoenix at this hour reigning there" (3.3.21–24) can now be appreciated — as it would be in any play dated before 1604 — as a topical compliment to an elderly Queen known as the Phoenix, Elizabeth I (1533–1603).[69]

10

A "Standard Thesis"

Our argument that Strachey's manuscript could not have been a significant source for a play written no later than 1611 first appeared in the fall 2007
issue of *Review of English Studies (RES)*.[1] Within a year Alden Vaughan challenged it in a *Shakespeare Quarterly* article,[2] "William Strachey's 'True Reportory' and Shakespeare: A Closer Look at the Evidence." Soon afterwards Tom
Reedy, also writing in *RES*,[3] further critiqued our argument. Both *Shakespeare
Quarterly* and *RES* refused our subsequent requests to rebut their arguments
(some of them highly technical in nature), which uncompromisingly defended
the traditional view of Strachey's temporal priority and importance as Shakespeare's *Tempest* source.

As a senior Shakespearean scholar, and co-editor of the 1999 Arden edition of *The Tempest*, Vaughan's entry into the discussion signaled that our
article had struck a nerve. Advertised as a "closer look at the evidence,"
Vaughan's essay fell far short of such an accomplishment. Over the next several
chapters, we detail the many errors made by Vaughan and Reedy in defense
of what Vaughan terms the "standard thesis" of Strachey's influence.

Vaughan's view of the history of the case for Strachey's influence[4] on *The
Tempest* is Manichean: there are heroes such as Edmond Malone[5] and Morton
Luce, who advocate the "standard theory," and there are "people determined
to find a date earlier than 1604 for the *Tempest*'s composition,"[6] who are "in
denial of the obvious."[7] Unfortunately, this focus on chronology misinterprets
the basis for doubting the "standard thesis" and oversimplifies the history of
the debate. It substitutes an *ad hominem* approach, challenging motives rather
than responding to arguments, for a reasoned defense of the traditional view.
Before further examining Vaughan's critique, it is useful to review the logical
relationship between theories of influence and those of chronology, which is
by no means as simple as Vaughan implies. Of course, if advocates of the
"standard thesis" could conclusively prove Shakespeare's dependence on Strachey's

text, it would require the play to have been written during or after the fall of 1610, but *the reverse does not hold*.

In other words, while the argument that Shakespeare did not depend on Strachey *opens the door to* theories of earlier composition, too closely connecting the Strachey question with chronology leads to confusion and misunderstanding. Proof that an author used a particular source can only establish a terminus *a quo* (often much earlier than the actual composition date), never a terminus *ad quem*. It would thus not be illogical for one to believe that, even if Shakespeare did not make use of Strachey, he still could have written *The Tempest* in 1609, 1610, or even 1611. Advocates of an earlier *Tempest* date will need stronger evidence than merely demonstrating that Shakespeare did not need, or did not use, the 1609 Bermuda shipwreck literature. (We believe, of course, that we have presented such "stronger evidence" in Part One of this book to show that *The Tempest* was indeed written well before 1609.)

Vaughan's emphasis on chronology as the sole source of doubts about Strachey's influence also oversimplifies the history of skepticism. While Karl Elze[8] advocated a *Tempest* date as early as 1604, other critics of the Bermuda theory have been neutral about the possible chronological implications. Kenneth Muir (1977) was hardly engaging in chronological revisionism when he expressed the conviction — without ever wholly repudiating a link between *The Tempest* and the Gates shipwreck — that "the extent of the verbal echoes of [the Bermuda] pamphlets has been exaggerated."[9]

More recent skeptics of the Strachey theory include David Lindley and Andrew Gurr.[10] Neither, to our knowledge, has advocated a *Tempest* composition date earlier than 1608–09. In Lindley's view, though "the Strachey letter is a *possible* source for *The Tempest*, it is not a *necessary* source, in the way that Ovid or Montaigne both are, nor does it provide a particular point of reference in the way that *The Aeneid* does."[11] In his Cambridge edition of the play, Lindley confirms that "in fact, there is virtually nothing in these texts [Jourdain, *Declaration*, and *Reportory*] which manifests the kind of unambiguous close verbal affinity that we have seen in [Virgil, Ovid, or Montaigne]."[12] Lindley is discussing only the direct evidence "from sign" for Strachey's influence on *Tempest*, not the entirely separate question of whether Strachey's text could have been completed in time for it to have even been a "possible" source.

Other contemporary scholars such as Penny McCarthy have gone far beyond this skepticism to propose earlier dates for *The Tempest* without even considering the Strachey question. McCarthy, as we have noted previously, is sharply critical of the "consensus" idea that "date[s] of composition must be close to date[s] of performance/publication/mention."[13] McCarthy's argument exemplifies the well-understood principle, applicable to all historical sciences, that surviving evidence for innovation (including the composition dates of plays) always constitutes a date *before* which, not a date *after* which. Evidence degrades over time[14]; where it is scarce or fragile (as are early-modern theatrical records, for example), the earliest exemplars in a series are more likely to degrade or to be lost than later ones.[15]

To this general consideration it must be added that, during the period in question, the English commercial theatre was in its infancy, and early-modern record keeping was rapidly changing. Early-modern theatrical records are notoriously incomplete. From the entire period 1580–1612 official records of performances at court, although strictly kept, survive for only two short periods —1604–05 and 1612–13. Even more surprising, almost all of the revels documents from the later tenure of Sir Henry Herbert (MR 1623–1673) are still missing, despite the fact that they came to light in 1789 (long after the Great Fire) only to "for the most part disappear" only thirty years later, without ever having been transcribed.[16]

Vaughan's confusion, even over the definition of such key terms as the "standard thesis" he is defending, bodes ill for the cogency and consistency of his analysis. He explicitly defines this as "the assumption" that has "long persisted" that "somehow Shakespeare read Strachey's manuscript (or a copy) and that the [*Tempest*] reveals its influence."[17] Surprisingly, given this definition, Vaughan goes on to assert that the two "principal authors"[18] of the thesis are Edmond Malone (1808) and Arden editor Morton Luce (1901). This is incorrect. Malone did (as Vaughan subsequently qualifies) posit the 1609 Bermuda wreck, *generally construed*, as "the determining evidence for the *Tempest*'s date of origin,"[19] but he was *not* an advocate of the standard thesis as defined by Vaughan. On the contrary, Malone argued primarily for the influence of a different Bermuda text, Sylvester Jourdain's *Discovery of the Bermudas* (1610). Indeed, the reader of Vaughan's article will be surprised to learn that, although Malone lists fourteen texts related to the Virginia exploration and Bermuda wreck as possible *Tempest* sources, Strachey's *Reportory* is not one of them; indeed, it appears that Malone may not have known of its existence.[20]

Such debates over terminology may seem inconsequential, but for those who believe that rigorous scholarship depends on clear and consistent definitions of key terms, this is not an auspicious beginning. Vaughan not only conflates the distinctive positions of Malone (1801) and Luce (1901), but effectively writes off the complex exchanges of the intervening years, sidelining such major figures as Furness, Elze, and Hunter as irrelevant to *Tempest* critical history, thereby concealing their critical role in shaping what was to become the "standard thesis." Instead, he constructs a monolithic orthodoxy that never existed, overlooking the process by which the orthodox tradition was transformed over decades of revisionism, during which one implausible theory, originally Malone's, was brought into doubt, rejected, and then replaced with an alternative, all with very little explicit acknowledgment of how the theory had evolved.

Vaughan begins his case by identifying Malone as an advocate of the "standard thesis" and concludes by stating that "Malone and Luce were right."[21] The claim is as inaccurate as it is unqualified. Malone and Luce shared the belief that the Gates/Summers wreck influenced Shakespeare, but they held contrasting views of how the incident exercised this alleged influence. Indeed, Luce is highly critical of Malone's errors and omissions, and would no doubt be surprised to find himself lumped in with Malone as one of the two founders of the modern "standard thesis."

The development of the theory of Strachey's influence, up to and including Vaughan's own article, constitutes a tangled web of assumption and error, involving the critical intervention of at least half a dozen scholars, among whom Luce is only one critical link in the chain (see Chapter 15). *Reportory* was not even named as a possible *Tempest* source and hypothetical alternative to Malone's fourteen unfruitful speculations until the Furness 1892 Variorum edition. It was not until Luce's 1901 Arden that Furness' own speculations — for that is clearly what they were — were transformed into what would eventually become the "standard thesis" as defined by Vaughan. With this in mind, let us review the actual merits and weaknesses of the case Luce made for Strachey's influence on *Tempest,* rather than accepting it unquestioningly.

Unlike Malone, Luce was an advocate of the Strachey theory. But although he was the first of several to attempt a detailed exposition of the alleged echoes of Strachey's document in *The Tempest,* he appears to have obtained the idea of *Reportory*'s significance from Furness.[22] An accurate critical history should therefore consider the implications of Furness' role in the development of the "standard thesis," rather than concealing Furness' relevance behind nebulous phrases implying that he was "ambivalent"[23] about the alleged influence of *Reportory.* Furness could hardly have been "ambivalent" about a source he had never seen and for which he did not even know the correct date. As we detail in Chapter 15 Furness apparently turned to Strachey as a possible source only because Elze and Hunter had already undermined Malone's chief nominee, Jourdain, as a plausible candidate for *Tempest* influence.[24] Furness not only summarizes but also seems to agree with the view of Elze and Hunter — among others — that "the parallelisms which were to Malone so remarkable and so convincing in the Jourdain pamphlet were either commonplace or non-existent."[25] Charles Mills Gayley, agreeing two decades later, concedes that "from none of [alleged parallels in the first pages] should we conclude that [Shakespeare] was dependent on Jourdain," and in the remainder of the book "there is nothing uniquely suggestive of any feature of Shakespeare's *Tempest.*"[26]

Critical scrutiny of Luce's methods confirms the frailty of the traditional view of the influence of the Bermuda documents as transmitted (with modification) from Furness. In his introduction, Luce says that the Bermuda adventure "must have left a deep impression throughout England," and that "news of the storm" had already "reached England before the end of 1609."[27] Luce identifies "three pamphlets" of the wreck: Jourdain's *Discovery*, which he dates 13 October 1610; *Declaration,* dated "autumn of 1610"; and a third, untitled, "of earlier date," but by William Strachey, who had not only "lived in the 'Blackfriars,'" but wrote poetry, "and very possibly had talk with Shakespeare."[28]

Luce inaccurately terms Strachey's text a "pamphlet" — and opines that it is "of earlier date" than *Discovery* and *Declaration.* This is based on a misconception. Unlike the two other dates given by Luce, the 15 July 1610 date for *Reportory* is not a date of registration or publication,[29] but a date *internal to the document*, subsequently copied, presumably in 1625 by editor Purchas,[30] and perpetuated over many decades of academic error as a definitive composition date. The relevance of this distinction becomes apparent when we notice that Luce fails to mention the availability of a comparable internal date for Jourdain's *Discovery,* which breaks off its narrative on or about 19 June 1610, when Sir George Summers departed from Jamestown to fetch supplies from Bermuda. This is *three and a half weeks before Reportory's* July 15 date. In other words, the facts contradict Luce's argument that *Reportory* antedates *Discovery.*

In *Tempest* criticism, such errors have long half-lives. Luce's faulty reasoning is still evident in Tom Reedy's 2010 attempt to rebut our 2007 *RES* article. Indeed, both Reedy and Vaughan follow the pattern established by Luce of mixing dates of publication or registration with dates internal to the documents themselves, without acknowledging this confused methodology. This has the effect of promoting an unjustified confidence in the composition order of the documents, which is used to paper over otherwise doubtful interpretations. Both Vaughan and Reedy would have us believe that the order is indisputable. Consequently, their argument for the "standard thesis" largely owes its plausibility to free use of the fallacy of circular proof. Only through careful selection of incommensurable dates can Reedy maintain that Jourdain's *Discovery* definitively postdates *Reportory* and establish an *a priori* assumption of Strachey's temporal priority. The mistake, which Reedy repeats in almost all of his tables, is illustrated in his table, "Description of the Leak" (536), which reconstructs the following sequence:

- Strachey B, 7 June 1610
- Summers' Letter, 15 June 1610
- *Reportory*, 15 July 1610 [internal date]
- Jourdain's *Discovery*, 13 October 1610 [date of dedication]
- *True Declaration*, 8 November 1610 [S.R. external date]

As we have seen, using comparable internal dates would require that Jourdain be placed at 19 June (when his narrative ends), almost four weeks before the 15 July *Reportory* date. This alone refutes the argument that any actual or alleged parallels must be attributed to Jourdain's copying from Strachey. Reedy's chronology combines the internal date from *Reportory* with the publication date of Jourdain, which not only reverses the correct order of the two documents, but introduces an error of at least a month into the calculations. In fact, if the 15 July internal date of *Reportory* is not really its compositional terminus — as we *know* the 13 October and 8 November dates are for *Discovery* and *Declaration*— then Reedy's relative dates for *Reportory* and *Declaration* are even farther off. Like Luce before him, Reedy creates an illusion of chronological comparability where none in fact exists. Using comparable internal dates produces a very different arrangement of the documents:

- B (earliest possible date of completion), 10 June 1610
- *Discovery*, 19 June 1610
- *Reportory*, 15 July 1610

If, on the other hand, we employ the method of using "hard" external dates of publication or registration, the list looks like this:

- *Discovery*, 13 October 1610
- *Declaration*, 8 November 1610
- *Reportory*, 1625

Reedy's confusion about chronology is apparently traceable to Luce's interpretative errors. Like so many mistakes in the history of *Tempest* studies, they have been uncritically copied over several generations of scholarship.

Neither the confusion over terminology nor these mistakes of chronology are by themselves decisive in establishing the failure of the traditional paradigm; however, by now it should be evident that Luce, like Malone before him, supplied an inauspicious predicate for an analysis credited with establishing the "standard thesis" of Strachey's influence. Luce's bibliographical standard for the three documents is inconsistent and misleading. The first two —*Discovery* and *Declaration*— are named and dated; the third, only later identified as "Strachey's Letter or Reportory,"[31] is nameless but is said — incorrectly, as we have seen — to be earlier than the other two, and to be a "pamphlet." In fact, Strachey's narrative was not published until 1625, and then as a 24,000-word chapter in Samuel Purchas' sprawling *Purchas His Pilgrimes*. Compounding these bibliographical errors, Luce assures us, of Strachey's literary associations and — entirely without evidence — his intimacy with Shakespeare.

Close reading of Luce's Appendix 1, which provides further particulars of the alleged Strachey link, confirms that something is deeply amiss. Here Luce reprints bibliographical particulars about eighteen possibly relevant Virginia or Bermuda publications, dated 1608–13.[32] All but one — the manuscript of Lord De La Warr's dispatch of 7 July 1610[33] — are published documents, including, of course, Strachey's *Reportory*. All of them, *except for Strachey's document*, are accurately listed under their dates of registration or publication. Only Strachey is cited with the *internal* date of 15 July 1610 that appears towards the end of the manuscript (reproduced in the 1625 editorial apparatus, and repeated by modern scholars at least since Luce as the composition date: *see Figure 10.1*). No other item in the list — excepting the De La Warr letter, dated 7 July and evidenced to have gone back to England by September 1610[34] — is designated by a date other than that of its actual publication or registration.[35]

Surely Luce, somewhere in his Arden edition, makes clear that Strachey's document was not published until 1625? We were surprised — and disappointed — to discover that the answer is "no." A reader will search Luce's book in vain — through a dozen mentions of the name Purchas — for any reference to the pertinent but troubling fact that the text which Luce would make the foundation of his case for *Tempest* influence is not merely "too late." It was not published until *fourteen years after* the 1611 production of Shakespeare's play. Luce does acknowledge that, "apart from Purchas, which of course is too late for *The Tempest*, I cannot trace any printing or publication of this *letter*."[36] The admission reveals the extent to which Luce struggled to resolve the apparent contradiction between the 1625 publication date of Strachey's manuscript and his desire to read it as Shakespeare's source. That Luce resolved the struggle by excluding from his Arden edition the most critical fact of all about *Reportory*, which he could not reconcile with his theory, constitutes a sobering reminder of dangers of the scholarly temptation to gloss over or omit inconvenient facts. Luce never admits the problem. But the absence of a published version in 1611 does force him to conclude that Shakespeare must have read the document in manuscript.[37] Without embarking on the kind of elaborate and imaginative narrative later devised by Vaughan among others to explain Shakespeare's access to this document, Luce lays the foundation for further "inquiry." He notes not only that "the original document is said to have been one of the manuscripts preserved by Hakluyt,"[38] but — most significantly — introduces Strachey as an associate of the Blackfriars theatre and undoubted confidante of the bard.

11

B to the Rescue

The orthodox tendency to construct elaborate circular arguments becomes apparent when we consider the uses to which the "B" manuscript draft of Strachey's text has been put since its discovery in 1983. Surely Alden Vaughan is correct that the manuscript "raises intriguing possibilities."[1] That it represents an anterior state of *Reportory,* containing "clear internal evidence that it is not simply a poor transcript of the Hakluyt-Purchas version"[2] also seems highly probable. Vaughan's assumption that the B manuscript can rationally support the "standard thesis" is, however, another matter.

Vaughan claims that "overwhelming ... internal evidence"[3] substantiates Strachey's authorship of both documents. This is at best doubtful. Certainly Hume offers none.[4] Indeed, his eleven-page introduction to B *assumes*, from start to finish, that Strachey is the author of both texts. He makes almost no effort to support this assumption, instead merely asserting that "there is ... ample evidence, both semantically and historically, that Strachey wrote both accounts."[5] However, the "evidence" to which both Hume and Vaughan allude is in reality the mere *assumption* that because *Reportory* is manifestly *based on* B, and because *Reportory* is attributed to Strachey, one must therefore conclude that Strachey is also the author of B.

Consistent application of Vaughan's reasoning would oblige us to also conclude that Strachey wrote Smith's *Map of Virginia* as well as James Davies' "The Relation of a Voyage into New England," both of which accounts Strachey reproduced verbatim, or nearly so, in *History of Travel*. Mainstream scholars of the age of exploration have long known of Strachey's plagiaristic habits. Moreover, the discovery of the extent of Strachey's plagiarism has been a historical process, suggesting that further revelations may come: like the B manuscript, not discovered until 1983, Davies' account lay undiscovered until 1880.[6] Until then, it was assumed that Strachey himself was the author of passages now known to be originally by another hand, probably Davies'.[7]

Vaughan's narrative is exempt from such well-documented complications. He is confident that Strachey not only "saw an opportunity for further advancement" through his pen, but understood that the Bermuda shipwreck narrative "was bound to be popular back home," and set out while still in Jamestown to expand the document, "borrowing more freely from other writers (by memory or, more probably, from books available in Jamestown)." As appealing as this scenario may sound, however, it is fancifully improbable for several reasons. For one thing, the available evidence contradicts Vaughan's assumption that the books Strachey needed would have been available in Jamestown.[8] Moreover, as Vaughan acknowledges, the scenario it depends on raises a glaring contradiction: "Why Strachey did not foresee the Company's displeasure at his account of those weeks is hard to fathom."[9] Most important, as we have seen, the B manuscript tends to confirm that *Reportory* in its published form did not go back to England on the July 1610 Gates voyage, contradicting a scenario Vaughan identifies as not only "obvious," but "virtually certain."[10]

On the contrary, the B manuscript represents impressive evidence supporting our alternative scenario. Many evident characteristics of B are more consistent with the interpretation that it (or, rather, a lost manuscript on which it is based or from which it is copied), not *Reportory*, was the text that returned on the Gates voyage. Comparison of the two texts reveals that *Reportory* was completed with the assistance of reference materials that were apparently unavailable to the B writer. Table 11.1, for example, shows that the author of *Reportory* must have had direct access to a copy of Eden. He cites the passage almost verbatim, while the briefer version in B omits a number of details, suggesting that the author may have relied on memory.

The B version, as we know, is not addressed to a "noble lady" or anyone else.[11] In short, no one would ever think of saying, as Watson says of *Reportory*, that the author "sat him down" to compose it, "writing at ease with attention to literary effect."[12] On the contrary, it reads like an experiential account of a real event, only later revised by Strachey with an eye toward a particular audience who would be entertained and enlightened by a "philosophical commentary" on the episode, embroidered with an elaborate historical contextualization drawn from other printed and manuscript sources. If *some version* of the Strachey document returned on the 1610 Gates voyage, it was more likely a highly abbreviated text, far closer to B than the *Reportory* published fifteen years later by Purchas.

When one adds to all these considerations Strachey's own 1612 dedication of *Lawes*, testifying to the existence of an unperfected narrative of his experience as "a sufferer and an eyewitness," in the "Bermudas ... and ... Virginia,"

Table 11.1. B's Impressionistic Use of Eden Compared to the More Accurate Version in *Reportory* Suggests a Shift from Oral Recall to Consultation of the Printed Text

Eden	*B*	Reportory
[Oviedo in Eden, *The History of the West Indies*, dedicated to Emperor Charles V]	Oviedo, in his history of the West Indies addressed to the Emperor Charles 5th, thus expresses himself:	It should seem by the testimony of Gonzalus Ferdinandus Oviedus in his book entitled, The Summary or Abridgement of His General History of the West Indies, written to the Emperor Charles the Fifth, that they have been indeed of greater compass (and I easily believe it) than they are now; who thus sayeth:
In the year a thousand and five hundred fifteen when I came first to inform Your Majesty of the state of the things in India, and was the year following in Flanders in the time of your most fortunate success in these your kingdoms of Aragon and Castile, whereas at the voyage I sailed above the island Bermuda, otherwise called Garza, being the furthest of all the island that are found at this day in the world, and arriving there at the depth of eight yards of water, and distant from the land as far as the shot of a piece of ord-nance, I determined to send some of the ship to land, as well to make search of such things as	In the year 1515, when I first came to inform your majesty of the state of things in India, I observed that in my voyage when to wind-ward of the Island of Bermudas, otherwise called Garza, being the most remote of all the Islands yet found in the world; I determined to send some of the people ashore, both to search for what might be there, and to leave certain hogs upon it to propa-gate. But on account of a contrary wind I could not bring the ship nearer than cannon shot. The island was 12 leagues in length, 16 in breadth and about 30 in circuit. (74)	In the year 1515, when I came first to inform Your Majesty of the state of the things in India, and was the year following in Flanders in the time of your most fortunate success in these your kingdoms of Aragon and Castile, whereas at that voyage I sailed above the island Bermudas, otherwise called Garza, being the farthest of all the islands that are yet found at this day in the world, and arriving there at the depth of eight yards of water, and distant from the land as far as the shot of a piece of ord-nance, I determined to send some of the ship to land, as well to make search of such things as were there, as also to

---

Table 11.1. (cont.)

were there, as also to leave in the island certain hogs for increase. But the time not serving my purpose, by reason of contrary wind, I could bring my ships no nearer the island, being twelve leagues in length and six in breadth and about thirty in circuit, lying in the 33 [unreadable symbol] degree of the north side. (203v)	leave in the island certain hogs for increase but time not serving my purpose, by reason of contrary wind, I could bring my ships no nearer. The island, being twelve leagues in length and sixteen in breadth and about thirty in circuit, lying in the 33 degrees of the north side. (18–19)

---

and promising that "*the full story of both in due time* [I] shall consecrate unto your views ... [and] deliver ... perfect unto your judgements,"[13] it is difficult to avoid a troubling conclusion: Strachey did not complete his revisions of what would later be included in the Purchas publication until 1612 or later.

Vaughan struggles to avoid reaching this commonsense conclusion, instead inventing a scenario in which "the shorter letter ... was intended ... for a relative or a friend when Strachey's fate — and everyone else's on Bermuda — was still uncertain."[14] It appears that Vaughan may not have read the B text with any care, as he gives a mistaken account of its contents and genesis. He implies, impossibly, that its original was actually written in Bermuda. It was not, nor was it written when the fate of the Bermuda survivors was "still uncertain." In fact, the B manuscript makes reference to events that occurred in Virginia long after the survival of the marooned Bermuda crew and passengers was assured. The B author recounts that on 21 May, when the survivors arrived at Fort Algernon in the Virginia colony, there was a thunderstorm, adding that the Bermuda survivors also "learned that most of the fleet bound from England for Virginia [had] arrived in safety."[15] Like the author of *Reportory*, he also describes the devastation that greeted the survivors when they finally reached Jamestown on 23/24 May[16]:

> The Colony was in a distressed condition, the buildings going to waste, & the scarcity of provisions daily increasing...[17] Indiscretion in the management, added to the conduct of the colonists, produced those evils to which may be added the jealousy of the natives & the unexpected failure that was expected to be easily obtained.[18]

As Vaughan subsequently admits, the B manuscript continues its narrative up until at least the 10 June arrival of Lord De La Warr from England:

> All the arms, stores, and people were therefore embarked in vessels which set sail on the 7th, but next afternoon very unexpectedly falling in with Lord Delaware, who had been sent from England to take the Government, the intentions of the colonists were altered and the settlement established anew.[19]

Taking all of this into consideration, we believe that the most intriguing aspect of the B manuscript is that it provides a window on the compositional process which resulted in the published *Reportory*— one that strongly supports the view that a variant of B, not *Reportory*, may have gone back to England in 1610 with Gates. While many details are murky, others have been clarified by the emergence of the new document, and none of them to the advantage of the unexamined "just so" story of how Strachey's narrative influenced *The Tempest*. It is now evident that the finished *Reportory* was based on a pre-existing draft which contained a straightforward account of the shipwreck, survival, and return to Jamestown of the *Sea Venture* passengers and crew. The original version contained little religious moralizing, literary flourish, or study of the history and natural resources of the islands. It was a raw, firsthand account of an actual event. In revising the original document Strachey enlarged a text of less than 6,000 words to one four times that length, in the process supplying a more detailed account to flesh out the bare bones of the original narrative. This includes an abundance of entirely new material, some of it shared with De La Warr's 7 July dispatch. Some of it, with overlap from De La Warr, appears specifically to respond to several questions contained in Richard Martin's December 1610 letter to Strachey, who was still in Jamestown (see Chapter 16).

Far from being an asset to the traditional view of Strachey's influence, as Vaughan would have it, the B manuscript has only driven advocates of the "standard thesis" to undertake increasingly implausible flights of fancy — all of them aimed at circumventing the much more plausible inference that some version of the B manuscript, not *Reportory*, was sent to England on 15 July. This substantiates our original argument in the 2007 *RES* article, that Strachey's manuscript was revised to include answers to questions that he received in Jamestown in spring 1611, months after advocates of the "standard thesis" claim the "letter" was sent to England.

12

Who Made the Addendum?

In the 1625 edition of *Purchas His Pilgrimes*, at the end of Strachey's "letter" is appended a 1700 word excerpt from *Declaration* (first published in 1610). Our *RES* article challenged the longstanding theory of Louis B. Wright, which had more or less summarily identified the responsible party as Purchas. For several reasons, we suggested that the addition was probably added by Strachey; if true, this would *ipso facto* confirm that Strachey was still fiddling with his text in 1611 or later. For that reason Vaughan is anxious to dissociate the passage from Strachey. One reason we felt the theory of Strachey as the appender was at least plausible is that close examination of the actual design of Purchas' page visually connects the transitional "I have here inserted" passage to the main body of Strachey's text.

The italics begin following a break only at the point of the excerpt, suggesting — without proving — that the author of the preceding portions of *Reportory* is also the "I" of the inserted material from *Declaration*. We have seen that if the *Declaration* passage was added by Strachey, that would prove that the published version was not completed until after 1610; on the other hand, if added by Purchas, as Wright insists it was, it raises questions about what else Purchas might have added or deleted in his role as editor, thus calling into question the text's status as a pristine source available to Shakespeare in 1611. To these two theories, Vaughan adds a third, asserting that Hakluyt is the responsible party and that the addition was made in or around 1610. Reedy, disagreeing with Vaughan, follows the original view of Wright that Purchas is responsible for the addition. Both, however, agree that whoever added the material, it could not have been Strachey. Denying Strachey's responsibility for the addition is essential to Vaughan and Reedy's joint defense of the "standard thesis," for if Strachey made the appendix, he was still working on the manuscript in 1611, and the theory of its influence on Shakespeare evaporates into thin air.

To support his hypothesis, Vaughan relies on two formal characteristics of Purchas' published text, in the process revealing his faulty understanding of Purchas' editorial practices. In his table of contents Purchas explains that narratives modified by Hakluyt are identified by an appended "H"; those modified by himself are identified with a "P"; those to which both men made significant contributions are labeled with both initials. To Vaughan, the fact that Strachey's narrative lacks the editorial "P" proves that Purchas cannot be the emendor. For Purchas "to substantially alter a text he received from Hakluyt without adding a 'P' in the table of contents would have compromised his stated rules and denied a collaboration of which he would have been proud."[1]

While this may sound plausible, analysis of Purchas' actual practices reveals that Vaughan's *assumption* of Purchas' editorial consistency is contradicted by the demonstrable *facts* of Purchas' editorial habits. In other words, Vaughan not only fails to clarify what Purchas' nomenclature was even *supposed* to denote, but neglects the fundamental problem of whether Purchas applied his own system consistently. On this score the facts are clear: He did not.

In fact, *Purchas His Pilgrimes* contains several clear examples of Purchas doing exactly what Vaughan insists he would never do. The table of contents entry for Sir Arthur Gorges' "Large Relation of the Said Island Voyage,"[2] provides a case in point. Neither "H" nor "P" is prefixed to the entry, and in a side note to the text Purchas declares, "I have not added a word of mine but the title and marginal notes."[3] Nevertheless, in his introduction Purchas also states, "for the more plain manifesting of the message, I have thought it not amiss, here *to insert the true copy of the instructions verbatim* that our general sent by Master Robert Knolles into England...."[4]

Likewise, in his "Historie of Lopez Vaza Portugall,"[5] Purchas states in a side note "Part of this discourse was published by M. Hak, out of a written copy containing the whole. *I have added and inserted those things which I thought fit*, leaving out such as before have been by others delivered."[6] Again, neither H nor P is appended to this section. Such contradictions make it obvious that Vaughan's assumption of Purchas' editorial consistency is misplaced.

On the contrary, such examples prove that the absence of a "P" does not always mean, as Vaughan assumes, that Purchas merely reprinted a received Hakluyt text unmodified. Indeed, the extent of the modification required to justify, in Purchas' own mind, the addition of the "P" is unclear. There is no real evidence for Vaughan's assumption, for example, that Purchas would not append the *Declaration* conclusion to the Strachey document as descended through Hakluyt without adding a "P" to the chapter's Table of Contents entry, or that even if he intended to do so, he would remember his plan in every case. Vaughan's justification that Purchas would not have failed to annotate his own modifications because he would have been "proud" of his "collaboration" with Hakluyt is to confuse a possibly credible theory of Purchas' motivation with Vaughan's own need to assure the reader that his scenario is the only plausible one. It is not.

Vaughan also argues that Hakluyt is the responsible editor because the concluding *Declaration* extract is "printed in italics, so readers cannot miss [its] separate identity"[7]; by "separate identity," he means that Strachey cannot be responsible for the quote. He will later go on to chastise scholars who, because they depend on modern editions, fail to "understand the signals included in early-modern printing."[8] Tom Reedy, likewise, argues that the italics are a categorical impediment to the theory of Strachey as the amender:

> The material reprinted from the Company pamphlet is set entirely in italic type, as distinct from the Strachey text, which uses italic only for proper names, chapter titles, Latin phrases, and short quotations, standard early-modern printing practice. When considered altogether, these textual characteristics authoritatively establish that Strachey's original letter ends with its formal closing address to the Lady.[9]

Both Reedy and Vaughan have failed to understand the implications of the volume's actual typographical conventions. Italics in fact occur *throughout Reportory*— and in many other narratives in Purchas — to denote material that is being quoted, apparently by the author himself, from external sources (see Figure 12.1).

For this reason, the italics of the concluding excerpt from *Declaration* fail to prove Vaughan and Reedy's point that the emendation is not by Strachey. They suggest a highly selective method of presenting evidence. Examination of Hakluyt's and Purchas' published works, on the contrary, reveals that the language of the transitional phrase — "I have here inserted" — directly controverts Vaughan's theory of Hakluyt as the responsible party. Using word search functions, Lynne Kositsky and Tom Reedy[10] determined that Hakluyt very rarely uses the word "inserted" in his transitional introductions[11]; he strongly prefers the word "annexed." Purchas, on the other hand, frequently uses "inserted."[12]

Tom Reedy, in an unpublished manuscript, observes that there are several excerpts and letters in Purchas that appear to be added by the author, using the word "inserted," and that in other cases of such insertions the genesis is indeterminate. Authors inserting material themselves, according to Reedy, include Captain John Saris (1.4.337.3) George Sandys (2.8.1287.56–57), Marc Lescarbot or his translator (4.8.1621.21), and Edward Monoxe (2.10.1797.44),

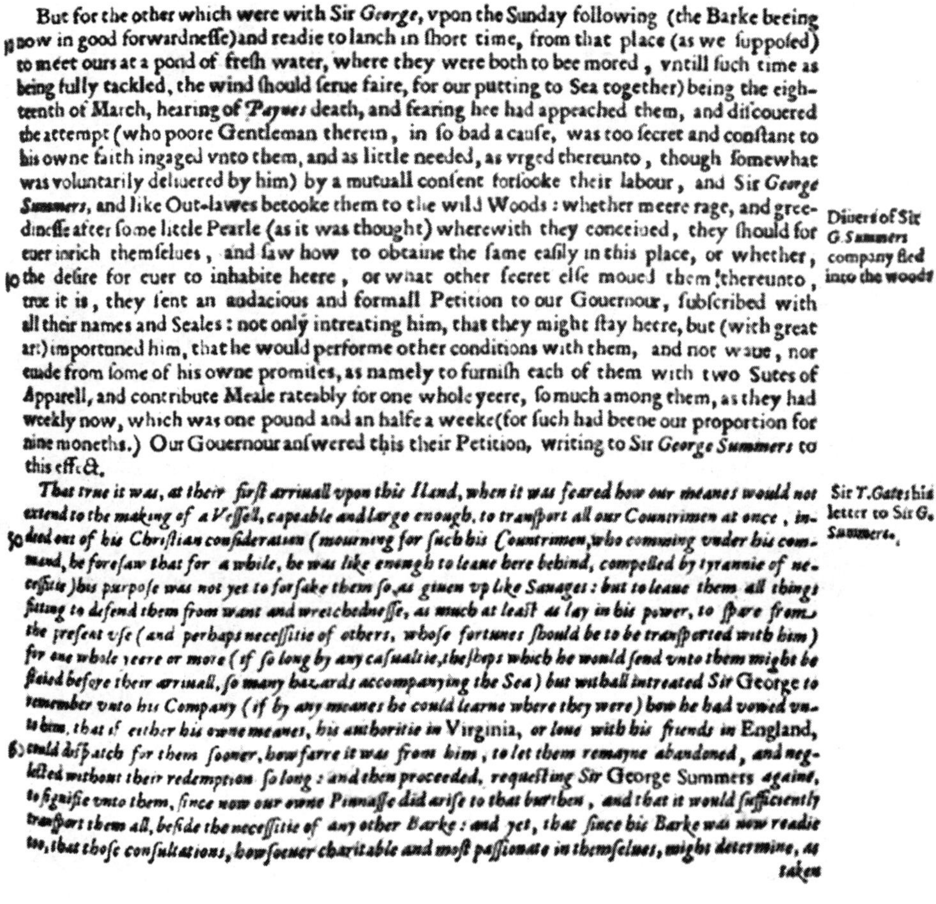

But for the other which were with Sir *George*, vpon the Sunday following (the Barke beeing now in good forwardnesse)and readie to lanch in short time, from that place (as we supposed) to meet ours at a pond of fresh water, where they were both to bee mored, vntill such time as being fully tackled, the wind should serue faire, for our putting to Sea together)being the eighteenth of March, hearing of *Paynes* death, and fearing hee had appeached them, and discouered the attempt (who poore Gentleman therein, in so bad a cause, was too secret and constant to his owne faith ingaged vnto them, and as little needed, as vrged thereunto, though somewhat was voluntarily deliuered by him) by a mutuall consent forsooke their labour, and Sir *George Summers*, and like Out-lawes betooke them to the wild Woods: whether meere rage, and greedinesse after some little Pearle (as it was thought) wherewith they conceiued, they should for euer inrich themselues, and saw how to obtaine the same easily in this place, or whether the desire for euer to inhabite heere, or what other secret else moued them thereunto, true it is, they sent an audacious and formall Petition to our Gouernour, subscribed with all their names and Seales: not only intreating him, that they might stay heere, but (with great art)importuned him, that he would performe other conditions with them, and not waue, nor made from some of his owne promises, as namely to furnish each of them with two Sutes of Apparell, and contribute Meale rateably for one whole yeere, so much among them, as they had weekly now, which was one pound and an halfe a weeke(for such had beene our proportion for nine moneths.) Our Gouernour answered this their Petition, writing to Sir *George Summers* to this effect.

Diuers of Sir G.Summers company fled into the woods

That true it was, at their first arriuall vpon this Iland, when it was feared how our meanes would not extend to the making of a Vessell, capeable and large enough, to transport all our Countrimen at once, indeed out of his Christian consideration (mourning for such his Countrimen, who comming vnder his command, be foresaw that for a while, be was like enough to leaue here behind, compelled by tyrannie of necessitie)his purpose was not yet to forsake them so, as giuen vp like Sauages: but to leaue them all things fitting to defend them from want and wretchednesse, as much at least as lay in his power, to spare from the present vse (and perhaps necessitie of others, whose fortunes should be to be transported with him) for one whole yeere or more (if so long by any casualtie, the ships which he would send vnto them might be staied before their arriuall, so many hazards accompanying the Sea) but withall intreated Sir George to remember vnto his Company (if by any meanes he could learne where they were) how he had vowed vnto them, that if either his owne meanes, his authoritie in Virginia, *or loue with his friends in* England, *could dispatch for them sooner, how farre it was from him, to let them remayne abandoned, and neglected without their redemption so long: and then proceeded, requesting Sir* George Summers *againe, to signifie vnto them, since now our owne Pinnasse did arise to that burthen, and that it would sufficiently transport them all, beside the necessitie of any other Barke: and yet, that since his Barke was now readie too, that those consultations, howsoeuer charitable and most passionate in themselues, might determine, as taken*

Sir T.Gates his letter to Sir G. Summers.

Figure 12.1. Use of italics within the main body of *Reportory* (4:1745–46) (courtesy Library of Congress Kraus Collection).

who writes: "The certainty of the treaty I had no means to know, yet what I heard reported shall be here inserted."

Vaughan does not acknowledge these instances of particular Purchas authors appending materials to their individual contributions, or, as we have seen, that the portions of *Reportory* he and Reedy attribute to Strachey frequently use italics to mark Strachey's own interjections from third party sources.

Finally, Vaughan's confidence that Hakluyt is responsible for the emendations to Strachey's text, including the final *Declaration* excerpt, is called into question by existing Hakluyt scholarship which unambiguously supports a contrary view. Hakluyt scholar George Bruner Parks, for example, comments extensively on the differences in style and temperament between the two editors:

What Hakluyt *did not* [characteristically] do was to cut down the narrative itself. Purchas, his successor, did and was praised for it by our eighteenth century critic. The difference between the two men and their methods is radical. Purchas, using in large part Hakluyt's own collections, was to write a history of travel and so to satisfy the amateur reader... *Wherever possible he used the work of others, weaving it into his own frame.* But Hakluyt was not writing a history. He was compiling archives of history and was obliged to print his documents complete.[13]

Adds Parks: "'Tedious' was a favorite editorial word of Purchas; and, when a manuscript was 'tedious' he abridged it or even omitted it entirely."[14]

Notwithstanding such testimony, Vaughan confidently assures us that Hakluyt is not only responsible for the appended extract from *Declaration*, but also "probably ... for *the one deletion* in Strachey's text."[15] For several reasons this seems, at best, problematic. C.R. Steele's analysis of the conveyance of material from Hakluyt to Purchas[16] shows that of 73 entries marked "H" by Purchas, 39, or 53 percent, were significantly abbreviated by him.[17] For example, *A large relation of the Port Ricco Voiage*[18] is marked only with an "H" in Purchas' Table of Contents, even though Purchas has clearly intervened with major deletions, and even the title concludes with the phrase "very much abbreviated." Purchas' long introduction also acknowledges his extensive abridgement:

[This] is a copious discourse, which we have somewhat abridged; both in the former part of the History, which you already have from Him which best knew it; and in the rest, in some superfluities or digressions (seeming such at least to me, who having so much work, make myself more to make my reader less) providing nevertheless that not a drop of necessary blood be lost....[19]

Steele's statistics reinforce the portrait of Hakluyt's conservatism as given by Parks and contradict the unacknowledged assumptions which lie behind Vaughan's argument; Hakluyt rarely engaged in significant deletions, but Purchas often did. One might wonder, finally, how Vaughan can be so confident that this is *the only* deletion to Strachey's text. To transform the only *acknowledged* deletion into the *only* deletion, ignoring the possibility that others may have occurred without editorial notification, is to engage in a style of discourse antithetical to the spirit of genuine historical inquiry.

In the effort to establish the unlikely scenario of Hakluyt as the amender, so thoroughly contraindicated by Steele and Parks as well as contradicted by most of the available evidence, Vaughan introduces a number of straw man arguments, attributing to us (overtly or implicitly) positions that we never held. For example, "in 1625, there was no earthly reason to append anything to *Reportory* that was not already there, and certainly no purpose in changing the document's date."[20]

The implication — that we said that Purchas changed the document's date from some ulterior motive — is false. On the contrary, we explicitly stated that there is no reason to think that Purchas knew the manuscript's detailed history, and that in lieu of more specific information, Purchas (or, possibly, Hakluyt) did the best he could as editor: He appended, as the document's date, a date internal to his manuscript source. This editorial date is no more than a long-after-the-fact approximation, inserted to support the chronological coherence of Purchas' larger narrative, of which Strachey's document as published constitutes merely a chapter. For his purposes, the date was *close enough*, and he cannot be faulted for using it; by the same token, it is *not* close enough for modern scholars seeking to prove by it that *Reportory* was really completed in 1610. By no means can it be used to disprove the alternative theory, based on a significant preponderance of evidence, that the Strachey manuscript was not actually finished until circa 1612.[21]

In view of these manifold problems, it is safe to conclude that Vaughan's theory that Hakluyt appended the concluding *Declaration* excerpt is *the least likely* of the three possible explanations. We feel confident in concluding that it is wrong, but less confident in assigning the *Declaration* appendix to either Strachey or Purchas. Wright's original theory of Purchas as the amender is supported by Purchas' habit of meddling with his received texts and by the frequency with which he uses the locution "inserted" when doing so. On the other hand, the fact that significant portions of the *Declaration* appendix, including those reproduced in the body of *Reportory*, have been deleted, suggests that the amender was paying very close attention to the continuity of the entire text in order to avoid repetition. This seems to us more likely to have been something done by Strachey, but we must acknowledge that Purchas himself in the quote already given above admits not only to having "*added and inserted* those things which I thought fit," but simultaneously "*leaving out* such as before have been by others delivered."[22]

If Strachey was responsible for appending the *Declaration* text to *Reportory*, he would only have been following a practice for which he is already well known. Culliford notes Strachey's habit of taking extensive excerpts from a source acknowledged only in one local context, a practice that has the effect of camouflaging his earlier (or subsequent) excerpting behind a veneer of appropriate citation while concealing the full extent of his indebtedness. In the case of his numerous excerpts in *Travel* from Smith's *Map*, two overt citations of Smith "would lead a reader to believe that Strachey was indebted to Smith only for the map and the two passages above,"[23] whereas in fact "one third of his first book consists of extracts [from Smith], rearranged, in a few places condensed, and in a few expanded, but in no way rewritten."[24]

13

Shortcuts Make Long Delays

During the early-modern period, delays between composition of works and their publication were common,[1] but in the case of a highly topical and dramatic subject like the Bermuda wreck, an apparent hiatus of fifteen years deserves explanation. Why would Strachey's *Reportory*, a document allegedly completed in 1610, containing a detailed description of a highly dramatic event — the "most newsworthy event of the day,"[2] according to Vaughan — remain unpublished for so long after being put in its final literary form? If Vaughan, Reedy, and others insist that Strachey's manuscript was completed in 1610, such a delay must be explained. Characterizing it as a controversial or "subversive" account of the colonization effort would be a convenient explanation. And that is just what Vaughan asserts: "Strachey's letter would not have pleased the Virginia Company in 1610 or for many years thereafter."[3] Reedy supplies further detail, noting that

> Virginia historians have long thought that Strachey's letter was kept out of print by the Virginia Company because it wished to suppress news of unfavorable incidents, such as the rebellion on Bermuda, the apparent rift between Summers and Gates, the grisly accounts of starvation caused by bad colonial management, and the full extent of the hostility of the Indians.[4]

While these claims may seem reasonable at first, a closer examination of the circumstances of the narrative's delay provides reason for doubt. First, publishers and Virginia promoters seemed to have encouraged shipwreck survivors to publish their accounts. When William Welby, publisher for the Virginia Company, reprinted Jourdain's *Discovery* in 1613, he advertised a forthcoming Virginia/Bermuda pamphlet containing a "more full and exact description of the Country, and Narration of the nature, site, and commodities, together with a true History of the great deliverance of Sir Thomas Gates and his Company upon them."[5] Reedy points out that both Gary Schmigdall and Hobson Woodward link Welby's promise of a narrative of the wreck to

Strachey's then unpublished *Reportory*. Welby in the same year also published *Good News from Virginia*, in which the author, sometimes thought to be William Crashaw, requests "a full, complete, and plain narrative of that whole action, both danger and deliverance, be published to the world."[6]

According to Reedy, "Crashaw was *clearly* referring to Strachey's account, since he used similar language and cited incidents mentioned only by Strachey."[7] While this claim also seems plausible at first, and might be used to bolster our conclusion that *Reportory* was not completed until 1612, it also raises the specter of complications Reedy does not acknowledge. Once again the adverb "clearly" becomes a convenient shortcut that ignores other relevant possibilities: As we noted in Chapter 1, in 1614 Raphe Hamor, another Bermuda "sufferer and eyewitness," promised to publish "the full and unstained Reportory of ... the miraculous delivery of the scattered company, cast upon the Bermudas."[8] Neither Vaughan nor Reedy mention this striking allusion, which closely echoes Strachey's own promise of a Bermuda narrative in the introduction to *Lawes*. Is Hamor referring to a manuscript competing with Strachey's own, or to the *Reportory* narrative itself, then possibly in his own possession? It is impossible to know but it does again indicate a strong public demand in 1612 for an account of the Bermuda wreck. Without knowing the contents of Hamor's manuscript, an honest historian cannot conclude that Crashaw's reference was "clearly" to Strachey's *Reportory*.

The suppression hypothesis does, however, have one doubtful merit. It props up Vaughan's theory of Hakluyt as the editor responsible for appending the *Declaration* extract to Strachey's *Reportory* as published in 1625. To make Strachey's tract more acceptable to the Virginia Company, asserts Vaughan, Hakluyt appended the *Declaration* extract, effectively "palliating" Strachey's "grim picture" of the Virginia Colony. Unfortunately for Vaughan, this argument introduces a patent contradiction: If Hakluyt had in 1610 successfully "palliated" Strachey's excesses by appending the *Declaration* material, why was publication delayed another fifteen years? If the manuscript as amended was still objectionable to the Virginia Company, on the other hand, one may wonder if Hakluyt had actually "palliated" anything.

The passage from Strachey's *Reportory* that would likely have been most objectionable to the Company is his vivid description of the desperate condition of Jamestown when the Bermuda survivors arrived there in late May 1610. With slight variations, that description also appears in Governor De La Warr's 7 June dispatch to the Company:

> Viewing the fort, we found the palisades torn down, the ports open, the gates from off the hinges, and empty (which owner's death had taken from them) rent up and burnt, rather than the dwellers would step into the woods a stone's cast

off from them to fetch other firewood. And, it is true, the Indian killed as fast without, if our men stirred but beyond the bounds of their blockhouse, as famine and pestilence did within.[9]

While the Virginia Company authorities may have opposed the publication of such a description — as they might also have opposed the publishing of Strachey's independent and sometimes critical attitude toward the governing Virginia powers — similar vividly negative reports of colonial life were routinely published and are easily found. For example, *The New Life of Virginea*,[10] a work "Published by Authority of his MAJESTY'S COUNCIL of Virginia" in 1612, describes Jamestown as

> a hostile Camp within itself: in which distemper that envious man stepped in, sowing plentiful tares in the hearts of all, which grew to such speedy confusion, that in few months, ambition, sloth and idleness had devoured the fruits of former labors, planting and sowing were clean given over, the houses decayed, the Church fell to ruin, the store was spent, the cattle consumed, our people starved, and the poor Indians by wrongs and injuries were made our enemies, two of the ships returning home perished upon the point of Ushant, the rest of the fleet came ship after ship, laden with nothing but bad reports and letters of discouragement.[11]

It is difficult to see why, if this account was published on the authority of the Company, the *Reportory* manuscript would have been withheld to protect the public image of the colony. Vaughan's theory is further contradicted by the contents of the appended *Declaration* extract. Although somewhat abbreviated, these hardly "palliate" Strachey's negativism and indeed contain the most grisly elements of *Reportory*. The *Declaration* excerpt republished in *Reportory* recounts, among other Jamestown horrors, "miseries ... violent storm ... dissension ... woes ... negligence ... idleness ... improvidence ... mutinous loiterers ... treasons ... conspiracy ... famine ... penury ... piracy ... ambush and murder by the Indians" and "embezzlement of ... provisions."[12] Surely, for Vaughan to suggest that adding such a piece of narrative to Strachey's own account was done to "palliate" the image of the Jamestown colony is to run *ad hoc* from the Scylla of one uncomfortable proposition into the Charybdis of another.[13]

But Vaughan does not linger over such complications. He assures us not only that Strachey's letter would have incurred the official displeasure of the Virginia Company, but that the published Bermuda documents by contrast reflect Company policy: if *Declaration* supplied the antidote to Strachey's excess, Jourdain's *Discovery* was a piece of orthodox "company propaganda."[14] According to Vaughan's logic, in other words, anything published bore the Company's stamp of approval, and anything unpublished was withheld at the Company's insistence.

Even worse, Vaughan's need to use *Discovery* to explain why Strachey's own narrative was not published leads him into demonstrable errors, such as his insistence that Jourdain said "nothing at all about conditions in Virginia, even the abandonment of Jamestown on the eve of De La Warr's arrival."[15] Although abbreviated and sanitized compared to Strachey's, Jourdain's account *certainly does* discuss the decision of the demoralized and hungry colonists to return to England on the eve of De La Warr's arrival:

> When all things were made ready, and commodiously fitted, the wind coming fair, we set sail and put off from the Bermudas, the tenth day of May, in the year 1610, and arrived at Jamestown in Virginia, the four and twentieth day of the same month: where we found some threescore persons living. And being then some three weeks or thereabouts passed, and not hearing of any supply, it was thought fitting by a general consent to use the best means for the preservation of all those people that were living, being all in number two hundred persons [including those arriving from Bermuda]. And so upon the eight of June 1610, we embarked at Jamestown, not having above fourteen days victual, and so were determined to direct our course for New-found-land, there to refresh us, and supply our selves with victual, to bring us home; but it pleased God to dispose otherwise of us, and to give us better means. For being all of us shipped in four pinnaces, and departed from the town, almost down half the River, we met my Lord De La Warre coming by with three ships, well furnished with victual, which revived all the company, and gave them great content.[16]

Vaughan is on even less secure ground when he tells us that Virginia Company authorities also frowned at Strachey's document, paradoxically, because of its extravagantly rosy description of Bermuda,[17] for fear that public praise of the Island would attract the unwanted attention of Spanish rivals for New World colonization. Vaughan goes on to claim that Jourdain's "praise of Bermuda [in *Discovery*] was less fulsome than Strachey's."[18] But Vaughan does not mention that King James in 1612 extended a Summers Island patent to the Virginia Company to colonize Bermuda, and by 1615 these former Virginia Company shareholders were licensed to form their own separate Summers Island Company.[19] It therefore seems more likely that the Company would support, rather than oppose, publication of a document that reported favorably on the potential for Bermuda settlement. Moreover, the actual contents of Jourdain's *Discovery* contradict Vaughan's belief that Strachey's overly optimistic account of Bermuda could have prevented or delayed its publication; Jourdain's treatment of the idylls of the islands, although less detailed than Strachey's, reads like a Jacobean version of a modern travel brochure:

> For the Islands of the Bermudas, as every man knows that has heard or read of them, were never inhabited by any Christian or Heathen people, but ever esteemed, and reputed, a most prodigious and enchanted place ... yet did we find

there the air so temperate, and the Country so abundantly fruitful of all fit nec-
essaries for the sustentation and preservation of mans life ... out of the abundance thereof, provided some reasonable quantity and proportion of provision,
to carry us for Virginia, and to maintain our selves, and that company we found
there, to the great relief of them, as it fell out in their so great extremities, and in
respect of the shortness of time, until it pleased God, that by my Lord de la
Warre coming thither, their store was better supplied. And greater & better provision we might have made, if we had had better means for the storing and
transportation thereof. Wherefore my opinion sincerely of this Island is, that
whereas it has been, and is still accounted, the most dangerous, unfortunate, and
most forlorn place of the world, it is in truth the richest, healthfullest, and pleas-
ing land, (the quantity and bigness thereof considered) and merely natural, as
ever man set foot upon.[20]

Jourdain's narrative goes on to advertise the fecundity of the Bermuda landscape, where colonists may easily enjoy nature's repast of rockfish, mullets,
large birds and eggs, tortoises and their eggs, mulberries, Palmetto tree berries,
whales, "diverse" fruits, hogs, hawks, tobacco, etc.

Vaughan also assumes that because it appeared in print and *Reportory*
did not, Jourdain's *Discovery* had to have been approved by the Virginia Company. Malone, however — who is not trying to construct a wishful tale in
which *Declaration* constitutes an authorized version of Strachey's unacceptable
realism — notes that *Discovery* does not appear in the Stationers Register. He
proposes, credibly enough, that this absence is a sign of "apprehension ... that
[Jourdain's] publication might have been forbidden by authority."[21] We do
not profess to know who is correct. The Company certainly did authorize the
second, 1613 edition of Jourdain's pamphlet, although he is no longer named
as the author. But it is also conceivable that an authority that initially viewed
publication with some reluctance eventually saw its benefit and subsequently
supported publication of the second edition. It is evident that the title page
of the first edition of Jourdain's pamphlet goes out of its way to advertise a
connection to Company authority that may indicate an underlying anxiety
(Figure 13.1), even going so far as to preemptively advertise a document "set
forth for the love of my country" — as if anticipating an objection to the contrary.[22] Malone's analysis casts further doubt on the implausible notion that
opposition of the Virginia Company to Strachey's manuscript, even if it
existed, would be sufficient to explain the long hiatus between *Reportory*'s
composition and its publication.

Such contradictions become most acute when we consider the role
Vaughan assigns to Hakluyt, who, in his imaginative scenario, is responsible
for preparing Strachey's "subversive" account for publication. Vaughan seems
unconscious of the additional contradiction posed by this scenario: Why

XVI.

A

DISCOVERY

OF THE BARMV-

DAS, OTHERWISE

called the Ile of

DIVELS:

By Sir T͟H͟O͟M͟A͟S͟ G͟A͟T͟E͟S, Sir
G͟E͟O͟R͟G͟E͟ S͟O͟M͟M͟E͟R͟S, and Cap-
tayne N͟E͟W͟P͟O͟R͟T, with
diuers others.

Set forth for the loue of my Country, and also for the good of the
Plantation in Virginia.

S͟I͟L. I͟O͟V͟R͟D͟A͟N.

LONDON,

Printed by *Iohn Windet*, and are to be sold by *Roger Barnes*
in S. *Dunstanes* Church-yard in Fleet-streete, vnder the Diall. 1 6 1 0.

Figure 13.1. Title page of Sylvester Jourdain's *Discovery* (courtesy Wikimedia Commons).

would Hakluyt, a loyal and influential Company member, attempt to "pal-liate" Strachey's document[23] by appending a second narrative such as *Declaration*, which not only recites the previously mentioned colonial woes,[24] but even features prominently the "tragical history of the man eating his dead wife," and details that the husband "cut her in pieces and hid her in diverse parts of his house"?

Vaughan's argument ties itself up in knots; according to him, Hakluyt undertook the insertion of the *Declaration* passage with the aim of achieving "the widest possible circulation"[25] for Strachey's controversial manuscript. In the end, however, the loyal and talented Hakluyt only produced a document that, even after his palliations, "would not have pleased the ... Company in 1610 or many years thereafter."[26] It also seems most implausible that, despite the document's "damaging contents" about conspiracies, starvation, and other Virginia woes, the same Company officers who suppressed the publication would have been happy to transmit the same document to Shakespeare for him to depict the very matters they wanted suppressed in a stage play.

14

William Strachey, Plagiarist

Literary historians have questioned the extent to which modern concepts of originality and "plagiarism" are relevant to early-modern literary practices. There is no doubt that the principle of imitation took precedence over the idea of originality in early-modern compositional practice. Tom Reedy summarizes the standard view on this subject in his response to our *RES* article:

> Stritmatter and Kositsky's characterization of Strachey as a "plagiarist" lends no evidentiary weight to their argument. Writers of the time — especially travel writers — routinely appropriated material from other writers without crediting their sources.[1]

The argument has merit. There was no legal remedy for plagiarism, copying (with or without attribution) was indeed commonplace, and modern notions of individualism were greatly inhibited. But Reedy's implication that the concept of plagiarism was unknown is demonstrably wrong; in fact, due at least in part to the unique and highly salable character of the early-modern travel narrative, travel writers seem to have been unusually possessive about their works, and unauthorized copying of such literature produced consternation and protest. "I am extremely astonished," writes Peter Martyr in an early edition of his *De Orbe Novo*, the first book to describe the voyages of Christopher Columbus,

> that a certain Venetian, Aloisio Cadamosto, who has written a history of the Portuguese, should write when mentioning the actions of the Spaniards, "we have done; we have seen; we have been"; when, as a matter of fact, he has neither done nor seen any more than any other Venetian. Cadamosto borrowed and plagiarized whatever he wrote, from the first three books of my first three decades.[2]

As we have noted, Strachey's own habit of plagiarism is well established by modern critical scholarship. Contrary to what Vaughan and Reedy imply, this is not something we invented in our *RES* article. Although Reedy's argument

141

for the ubiquity of early-modern borrowing helps contextualize Strachey's widely acknowledged reputation as a plagiarist, it also misses the point. From a logical perspective, Strachey's plagiarism matters a great deal, especially as several passages in which he is alleged to have furnished ideas or language for Shakespeare are themselves borrowed from other sources. Even Vaughan acknowledges that Strachey "borrowed freely, unashamedly, and often without specific attribution,"[3] and more specifically admits that *History of Travel* "borrowed extensively from Captain John Smith's writings," as "has long been recognized."[4]

An assessment of Strachey's borrowing habits should begin with his *History of Travel*, where his plagiarism is by no means limited to these well-known appropriations of Smith, and goes far beyond the examples Vaughan and Reedy acknowledge.[5] According to B.F. Da Costa,[6] the journal of Mr. James Davies, recounting a voyage to Kennebec in 1607, "was found to be the source whence Strachey drew his account of the [Virginia] colony, large portions of which he copied verbatim, giving no credit."[7] Culliford remarks that Strachey's method in this instance was to reproduce Davies' account "almost in full, merely changing it from the first to the third person."[8] Numerous similar quotations throughout the literature of the voyagers corroborate the finding that Strachey was among the least original of all the early-modern travel writers. His regular habit, illustrated in Table 14.1, where his source-text alternates between Smith and Percy, was to conflate excerpts from various sources, often enlarging on them with his own observations.

Culliford gives perhaps the most comprehensive picture of the habitual nature of Strachey's plagiarism: Strachey's *Travel* "is a compilation rather than an original work,"[9] providing a

> description of [Virginia] and ... account of exploration and settlement from Raleigh's first voyage in 1584 to an abortive attempt to settle New England in 1606, a work in every way typical of these popular collections of voyages.... The work is purely a compilation of material to be found in Willes' *History of Travail in the West and East Indies*, and Hackluyt's voyages, brought more up to date by the addition of condensations of two printed accounts—John Brereton's *Briefe and true relation of the discoverie of the north part of Virginia*, published in 1602, and James Rosier's *true relation of the most prosperous voyage made ... by Captaine George Waymouth, in the discovery of the land of Virginia*, published in 1605—and one manuscript account reproduced in full, James Davies' *Relation of a voyage into New-England*. Even his first book, in which he describes the country, its products, and its inhabitants, is based on John Smith's *Map of Virginia*, of which Strachey incorporates the greater part unchanged.[10]

Culliford goes on to detail specific instances of Strachey's plagiarism in *Travel*: "The 6th chapter of Strachey's 2nd book, describing the voyage of captain

Table 14.1

Percy 1606 Observations	*Smith 1612* Map of Virginia	*Strachey 1612* Travel
	The women and children do the rest of the work. They make mats, baskets, pots, mortars; pound their corn, make their bread, prepare their victuals, plant their corn, gather their corn, bear all kind of burdens, and such like. (162)	The women ... make mats and baskets, pound their wheat, make their bread, prepare their vessels, bear all kinds of burdens, and such like, and to which the children set their hands, helping their mothers.
There is notice to be taken to know married women from Maids, the Maids you shall always see the fore part of their head and sides shaven close, the hinder part very long, which they tie in a plait hanging down to their hips. The married women wear their hair all of a length, and is tied of that fashion that the Maids are. (*Virtual Jamestown*, n.p)		There are notes to be taken by which may be discerned a married woman from a maid: the maids have the forepart of their heads and sides shaven close, the hinder part very long, which they wind very prettily and embroider in plaits, letting it hang so to the full length: The married women wear their hair all of a length, shaven as the Irish by a dish. The women have a great care to maintain and keep fire light still within their houses, and if at any time it go out, they take it for an evil sign.
	Their fire they kindle presently by chafing a dry pointed stick in a hole of a little square piece of wood, that firing it self, will so fire moss, leaves, or any such like dry thing that will quickly burn. (162)	But if [the fire] be out they kindle it again presently, by chaffing a dry pointed stick in a hole of a little square piece of wood; that fire in itself will so fire moss, leaves, or any such like thing that is apt quickly to burn. (112)

Bartholomew Gosnold in 1602 is condensed directly from [John Brereton] and has no other source" (177); "The 2nd chapter describing the voyage of Captains Amadis and Barlowe, is taken entirely from Hakluyt, rearranged and condensed ... the whole chapter can be paralleled ... from Hakluyt" (176); "A condensation of James Rosier['s] work occupies about half of Strachey's 7th chapter in book 2" (177); "Strachey borrowed about four fifths of Smith's *[Map]* and included every passage actually describing the people, the country, or its products" (178); "Smith's *Map of Virginia* provided the basis of the whole of Strachey's 1st book" (179).

Both Vaughan and Reedy insist on erecting a firewall between *Reportory* and Strachey's other works when it comes to plagiarism. According to them, any pattern of plagiarism in Strachey's other works is irrelevant to ascertaining the extent to which *Reportory* copies from other documents. At the same time, however, even Vaughan concedes that this was Strachey's method. Given this contradiction, Vaughan was obliged to stand our *RES* argument on its head by mistaking conclusions for premises: "Stritmatter and Kositsky's parallel column charts that purport to show Strachey purloining words and phrases from other texts are *based on the erroneous belief* that *Reportory* came last in the chronological sequence."[11] He also refers to our "*mistaken belief* that *Reportory* was not completed until 1612."[12] According to Vaughan, this "mistaken belief" led us to "accuse Strachey of plundering most of his narrative and his subsequent *Virginia Britannia* from earlier or contemporaneous writers."[13]

There is no basis for these assertions. Simply put, we did not *assume* a 1612 composition date; we demonstrated it as a logical *conclusion* grounded in abundant relevant evidence. Nor did we "accuse Strachey of plundering *most of his narrative* ... from earlier or contemporaneous writers"; we only made the case that Strachey *was the likely borrower* of some elements of his narrative from texts that could not have been available to him until after his return to England in late 1611, and stressed the relevance of his longstanding pattern of copying from other works. What Vaughan refers to as our "belief," in other words, was a carefully elaborated hypothesis based partly on the acknowledged reality of Strachey's plagiaristic habits. The better part of our essay was devoted to challenging the longstanding *assumption*, never grounded in a legitimate critical method, that *Reportory* was actually completed on 15 July 1610. Instead, we argued, a preponderance of the evidence suggests a completion date of sometime in 1612.[14] Rather than demonstrating that our argument is mistaken, Vaughan advances an entertaining but implausible narrative that steadfastly ignores our real argument in favor of one of his own invention (see Chapter 18). To Vaughan the fact that Strachey is long known to have appropriated large portions of Smith's *Map* among numerous other works in constructing *Travel* "has nothing to do with 'True Reportory.'"[15] Such statements involve changing the rules to accommodate inconvenient evidence. Because Strachey's account is that of an "eyewitness," it must remain untainted by the library, especially by books that might not have been available until 1612. This avoidance pattern suggests that, contrary to Reedy and Vaughan's assertions, Strachey's habit of plagiarism does matter.

Most importantly, Strachey's plagiarism in his other book establishes a pattern. There is every reason to hypothesize, and sufficient evidence to substantiate, that he employed the same practice in constructing *Reportory*. In the chapters which follow we will show that Strachey borrowed from Smith's 1612 *Map of Virginia* in composing *Reportory*, as well as from *Declaration* (published November 1610), and, probably, Jourdain's *Discovery*. This is not only what we should expect from Strachey, but what the empirical evidence confirms.

Thus, although Vaughan and Reedy deny its significance, Strachey's plagiarism is certainly relevant to Shakespeare's alleged reliance on *Reportory* as a source. In composing his work, Strachey drew extensively from Richard Eden's 1555[16] compilation and translation of several classic works of the Iberian voyagers of the late 15th and early 16th centuries. Paramount among those works were the voyages of Christopher Columbus as set down by Peter Martyr in his *Decades of the New World*, Gonzalo Ferdinand Oviedo's *History of the West Indies*, and Antony Pygafetta's *Voyage Round About the World*, recording Magellan's circumnavigation of the globe. Eden, as we have seen, was the source from which Shakespeare drew much of the inspiration and New World ethos which shaped *The Tempest*. In several cases — St. Elmo's fire, to name just one — in which Shakespeare is alleged to have relied on Strachey, the evidence demonstrates that the playwright drew directly from Eden, Erasmus, or Ariosto, not from Strachey.

Apparently, the stakes are high; Vaughan labels us as being "in denial" of an "obvious" scenario. At the same time, he avoids such telling elements of circumstantial evidence as Strachey's own published dedication to *Lawes*. The dedication — which Vaughan fails to mention in his article — strongly implies that Strachey was still completing *Reportory* in 1612, when he had access to Smith's *Map* and other later sources apparently incorporated into his narrative.

One advantage of such an inference is that it may help to explain Strachey's poor track record in publishing his works. Indeed, Strachey's plagiaristic habits may explain why he could not find a publisher for *History of Travel*; though it circulated in at least three Jacobean manuscripts, it was not actually printed until the 19th century.[17] His contemporaries, including the elite of the Virginia Company (who apparently no longer wished to employ him after his brief service as the Colony's secretary 1610–11),[18] may well have looked askance at his copying habits, particularly as he often copied from already published narratives, including narratives that had previously passed through the hands of those whose patronage he solicited. If so, this model might also help to explain *Reportory*'s delayed publication.

15

A History of Error

The contemporary errors of *Tempest* critics such as Alden Vaughan and Tom Reedy are grounded in a misreading of the play's critical history that constructs a monolithic "standard thesis" which never existed, mystifying the convoluted history by which William Strachey came to be accepted as the ultimate *Tempest* source. The story of how this happened in itself constitutes an intriguing chapter in the history of ideas and provides an understanding of the present moment in *Tempest* scholarship. From the origins of the Bermuda pamphlet hypothesis in Edmond Malone's 1808 tract[1] through Vaughan and Reedy's 21st century efforts to prop it up, the "standard thesis" has been flawed in ways its advocates have never been pleased to acknowledge. Starting with Malone, basic historical context that should have been impossible to confuse has been continuously misrepresented:

> Though some account of the Bermuda Islands, which are mentioned in this play had been published (as Dr. Farmer has observed), yet they were not generally known till Sir George Summers arrived there in 1609. *The Tempest* may [therefore] fairly be attributed to a period subsequent to that year.[2]

Both Malone's claims of fact and his logic were wrong. But rather than correct his errors, decades of scholarship have instead compounded them, piling surmise on error to produce a critical scholarship on *The Tempest* that often bears only slight resemblance to historical reality. As is now widely known, the Bermudas had been described and mapped for nearly a century by the time Sir George Summers and Sir Thomas Gates and their party of 150 colonists were shipwrecked there in July, 1609. Within just a few years after Juan Bermudez discovered them in 1503, the first Latin edition of Martyr's *De Orbe Novo* (1511) had mapped the islands (Figure 15.1), and already they were gaining a reputation as an exotic and dangerous locale.

Although the map itself was not reprinted in the 1555 or 1577 English editions of Martyr's work, the islands remained a topos of ambivalence, even

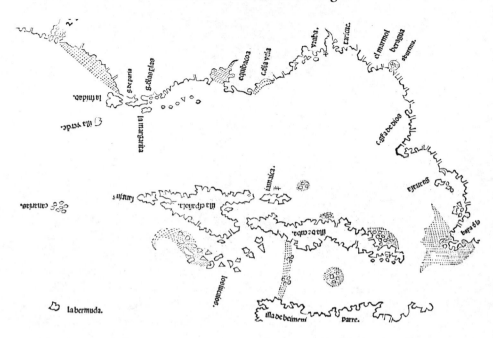

Figure 15.1. Martyr's 1511 map of Bermuda (courtesy Lilly Library, Indiana University, Bloomington, Indiana).

for English readers, well into the early 17th century. By 1593, sixteen years before the Summers incident, when Henry May was wrecked "upon the isle of Bermuda"—an account of which was printed in Hakluyt's 1598–1600 *Principall Navigations*[3]—the region was notorious in England. Two years later, in the popular account of Sir Walter Raleigh, it had acquired a reputation as a "perilous and fearful place," surrounded by "a hellish sea for thunder, lightning, and storms."[4]

Vaughan opines that such early Bermuda accounts are "irrelevant" to assessing the credibility of the standard thesis, and also attributes to us the belief that Hakluyt's 1600 account would have "preempted everything Shakespeare might have gleaned from Strachey's narrative."[5] Since Vaughan provides no footnote to this claim, we are at a loss to know whose view he purports to summarize. It is certainly not ours. He goes on to claim: "That explanation overlooks England's long-standing awareness of Bermuda's reputation, to which May's brief account of shipwreck as a result of the crew's negligence — no storm, many drowned, no conspiracies among the survivors—bears no resemblance to the *Tempest*."[6] On the contrary, the May account does contain references to conspiracies, as well as a mutiny and a storm.[7] More significantly, the account includes a rare description of a wreck allegedly caused by the drunkenness of sailors, which is why scholars such as Peter Moore[8] list it as among several very probable sources of Shakespeare's play.

Most troublesome is Vaughan's claim that the argument for May's possible influence on Shakespeare "overlooks England's longstanding awareness of Bermuda's reputation." This characteristically attributes to us the weakness of his own position; in fact it is the "standard thesis" that asks readers to "overlook England's long-standing awareness of Bermuda's reputation" as a fearful "isle of devils" by insisting that Shakespeare must have relied on Strachey or other accounts of the 1609 Gates shipwreck for this information. The practice of excluding earlier references to Bermuda — and earlier voyage narratives more generally — is endemic in *Tempest* scholarship and can be traced back to Malone's erroneous belief that the Bermudas were not known in England until the Gates voyage. On the contrary, as we have seen, long before the 1609 Gates misadventure, Bermuda had already become a familiar and terrifying locale throughout Europe.

Notwithstanding such errors, Malone succeeded in establishing the possible relevance of the Bermuda shipwreck literature to the *Tempest*, and his mistakes have cast a long shadow over all subsequent inquiry into the play's New World associations. Yet the very pamphlet that he designates as Shakespeare's *Tempest* source — Jourdain's *Discovery*— already in 1609 reports that

> the Islands of the Bermudas, *as every man knoweth that hath heard or read of them*, were never inhabited by any Christian or heathen people, but ever esteemed and reputed a most prodigious and enchanted place, affording nothing but gusts, storms, and foul weather, which made every navigator and mariner to avoid them as Scylla and Charybdis, or as they would shun the Devil himself; and no man was ever heard to make for the place but as, against their wills, they have by storms and dangerousness of the rocks, lying seven leagues into the sea suffered shipwreck.[9]

If it were true that the empirical evidence supported a link between Strachey and *The Tempest*, and if it had been certain that *Tempest* was not written until 1611 (or, as Furness surmised, 1613), then Malone's theory might possess the enduring relevance that Vaughan attributes to it. But Malone's analysis was flawed from the beginning by much more serious errors than mistaken assumptions about the history of knowledge of Bermuda. He demonstrated a faulty understanding of the play's plot when he surmised that Ariel's mention of the "Bermoothes"—a Spanish form of the word — identifies its scene of action. As Tristan Marshall and many others have subsequently noted, this borders on the impossible: "How does a voyage of the Duke of Naples from Tunis back to Naples in the Mediterranean end up several thousand miles off course?"[10]

On the contrary, it is obvious that the play's action takes place *anywhere but* the Bermudas. Indeed, Frank Kermode suggests that "Ariel, in mentioning the Bermudas, is merely *trying to emphasize how far away they were*,"[11] and Marshall concurs, seeing in the allusion "a contemporarily vivid point of reference to the Jacobean audience of the distance Ariel has traveled in the service of his master."[12] Not coincidentally, Eden's 1555 translation of Pygafetta's *A Briefe Declaration of the Vyage or Navigation made abowte the Worlde* confirms the aptness of these speculations, as we have noted, by defining the Bermudas as "the furthest of all the Islands that are found at this day in the world."[13]

By the mid–19th century the entire basis for Malone's theory of Jourdain's influence was already in serious doubt. This point cannot be overstressed: It was the influential skepticism of 19th century critics of Malone's theory such as Karl Elze and Joseph Hunter that would lead Furness and Luce to devise, as an alternative to Malone's theory, the modern "standard thesis" of *Reportory's* influence on Shakespeare. As early as 1839, for instance, Hunter wondered if

> There is anything beyond that similarity which must always exist when the subject is a storm at sea and the wreck of a vessel on the rocky shore of an island, whether the subject be repeated in a work of imagination, like *The Tempest,* or in such a pedestrian narrative as that of Jourdain. Mr. Malone has given the argument all the advantage it could derive from the artful aid of capitals and italics, but he seems to me to fail in showing coincidence in anything, except what has been common to all storms and all disastrous shipwrecks from the beginning of the world. For any critical or unusual circumstance, common to both, we look in vain....[14]

Elze (first English translation 1874) confirmed that much of what Malone conceived as unique to Jourdain could be found throughout the travel narratives of the era:

> The points of coincidence between Shakespeare and Jourdain enumerated by Malone are briefly as follows: of the whole fleet, with Shakespeare, only the king's ship is wrecked, just as in the expedition to Virginia, it was only the Admiral's ship that was driven out of its course and destroyed. This circumstance, however, necessarily proceeds from the story of the play, and is besides an event so likely to occur, that it did not require to be borrowed from Jourdain. Not only on Columbus's first voyage of discovery was the flag-ship separated from the others in a similar way, but also in Drake's voyage round the world (1577–1580) the same thing happened in the straits of Magellan, so that Drake had to sail on alone along the west coast of America.[15]

By the time of Furness' 1892 Variorum edition, Malone's original theory had been undermined beyond any reasonable hope of salvation, and Furness was obliged to concede that "the parallelisms which were to Malone so remarkable and so convincing in Jourdain's pamphlet, were either commonplace or non-existent."[16] Despite this admission, Furness set out to rescue the Bermuda theory. Having duly reviewed the evidence for the play's chronology, Furness rendered the already quoted verdict urging Shakespeare scholars to close ranks in support of a 1610–11 composition date and "henceforth be, in this regard, shut up in measureless content."[17]

Furness could not keep his own advice. Seven pages later, impelled to offer his own solution, he contradicts this injunction in favor of the majority and now places the play in 1613. His solution, moreover, is based on a double misconception. Like many from the mid–19th century until Ernest Law (1911)[18] established its authenticity to the satisfaction of most, Furness believed that the 1611–12 Revels manuscript which lists the 1 November 1611 *Tempest* production was a forgery.[19] To accommodate the new Strachey theory Furness surmised that *Reportory* might have been published as early as 1612, but still before the writing of the play:

> Malone ... was convinced that *The Tempest* was written in 1611. Therefore, of all the publications from which Shakespeare may be supposed to have drawn his materials, Malone could use those alone which preceded in date the year 1611. But if we postpone the date of the play to the only year in which we have positive evidence that it existed, viz: 1613, a larger and better account of Sir George Summers comes within our ken.[20]

Furness had *not even seen* the book in question: "Whether or not a pamphlet by Strachey dated 1612, wherof Malone gives merely the title (1821 XV: 390) is identical with that printed in Purchas, I do not know; the latter is the only one accessible to me."[21] In fact, the title given by Malone (XV: 390), *The Proceedings of the English Colonie in Virginia, from 1606 to the present year 1612, by W.S.*, is not by William Strachey, is not "identical" to *Reportory*,[22] and it does not mention the Bermuda shipwreck.

Mainstream Shakespearean scholarship has remained untroubled by this history of error, preferring instead to promulgate an account of the relationship between Shakespeare's play and the Bermuda narratives that is essentially fictional. Charles Mills Gayley's *Shakespeare and the Founders of American Liberty* (1917) and Robert Ralston Cawley's "Shakspere's Use of the Voyagers in *The Tempest*" (1926) went on to establish Strachey as the paramount *Tempest* source only by constructing an imaginary basis for Shakespeare's access to Strachey's unpublished manuscript. The erroneous premises of Malone and Furness were superseded by new errors of fact and more elaborate forms of specious reasoning, all aimed at preserving a Jacobean date for *The Tempest*. "No other account, written or printed before Hallowmas, 1611, or, for that matter, February 1613 [when the *Tempest* was again performed at the wedding of Elector Palatine Fredrick V and Elizabeth Stuart], save Strachey's confidential letter," Gayley confidently announced in 1917, "could have furnished Shake-speare not only with certain unique suggestions, but with the sequence of verbal details regarding the wreck, the Bermudas, and Virginia, discoverable in the *Tempest*."[23] Whether the Strachey document was, as Gayley states, the only plausible source of "verbal details regarding the wreck, the Bermudas, and Virginia"—or whether it could reasonably be considered even as a *possible* source for Shakespeare's play—is a question to be asked. In no other case has the putative source of a Shakespearean play exercised such a dominant role in establishing an alleged composition date.

Vaughan's *Shakespeare Quarterly* article not only omits this history of error, but seeks to build on it. Rather than citing for the purpose of critique our detailed *RES* analysis of the many reasons for supposing the implausibility of Strachey completing *Reportory* in Virginia, for example, he cites a third party source, quoting Lynne Kositsky's informal verbal remarks at a Concordia University debate.[24] In that summary, it is reported that "Kositsky pointed out that Strachey said he threw overboard trunks and chests to lighten the load and that it is hard to believe he would have retained enough paper to compose a letter of 24,000 words."[25]

Only by substituting that abbreviated "straw man" account for our actual published position could Vaughan reduce our multi-variable analysis to the *reductio ad absurdum* of whether or not there was enough paper in Virginia for Strachey to complete his 24,000-word manuscript. Our original *RES* case—which according to customary standards of scholarship ought to have constituted a position of record—listed the paper supply as merely one of several elements that made it implausible that *Reportory* could have been com-posed in Virginia:

> Circumstances in Jamestown during the weeks Strachey allegedly composed the letter could not have been worse. When the Bermuda survivors returned to Vir-ginia in May 1610, they had discovered a settlement burnt and in ruins (Wright 63–65, Major xxvi–xxvii). Under such circumstances, paper and books must both have been in limited supply. Yet, Strachey's letter, approximately 24,000 words in length, makes copious use of at least a dozen external sources, some mentioned by name, others silently appropriated.[26]

As is evident from all accounts, including Strachey's own, of the circum-stances in the Colony during the weeks in which Vaughan insists he completed the *Reportory* manuscript, the likelihood that paper was in short supply was only one of several challenges that Strachey would have faced in composing his document in Virginia. As the Secretary of the Colony at that time, Strachey would have been occupied by his official duties, which might well have included composing a short narrative like B, but seems unlikely to have included writing a 24,000-word "letter" to a "noble lady" that just coincidentally included much material requested months later by Richard Martin (see Chapter 16). After the Gates return voyage sailed, Strachey remained in Jamestown for many more months, not returning home to England until late 1611. When one adds to these circumstances the evidence of Strachey's own publication, with all its marks of being composed in leisure as a literary document making wide use of many of the same sources Strachey employed in writing *History of Travel*, the "standard thesis" of the document's completion in Virginia by 15 July 1610 grows ever less plausible.

16

Beyond a Reasonable Doubt

In December 1610, after the arrival of Gates' ship in London, Richard Martin, the London Secretary of the Virginia Company, wrote to Strachey, who had remained in Jamestown as the Colony Secretary, with specific questions about life in Virginia.[1] In our *RES* article, we noted that significant portions of Strachey's "letter" seem designed to answer these questions. Among other reasons, we suggested that this established a *terminus a quo* for *Reportory* long after 15 July 1610, when Gates left Virginia for London. In response, Alden Vaughan attributed to us the theory that *Reportory*, more or less in its entirety, "was Strachey's response to a (Dec. 1610) letter from Richard Martin ... requesting information about the Colony's ... characteristics," and concluded that such a theory is "implausible."[2] What we had actually written was this:

> Much of *Reportory—although not the parts about the storm or Bermuda—* appears to have been written in response to a 14 December 1610 letter to Strachey from Richard Martin, a leading shareholder and Secretary of the company ... Culliford says that Strachey's answer is "no longer preserved" (126), but by far the simplest and most elegant solution is that Strachey answered Martin in the manuscript later published as *Reportory*.[3]

Based on this analysis, we examined the Martin letter as one of several significant circumstantial elements in the case against the scenario that *Reportory* in (or near to) its *published* form had been transmitted from Jamestown to England in fall 1610. Among other elements contained in Strachey's document, such as the storm and shipwreck, life on Bermuda, and many pages of materials also contained in the 7 July 1610 De La Warr dispatch, *Reportory* supplies detailed answers to the questions posed in Martin's letter (Appendix C).

The fact that some of the *Reportory* content that appears to answer Martin's letter is duplicated in the 7 July De La Warr dispatch raises unresolved questions of priority and agency for both documents. That Strachey would make such a conflation, fusing parts of the De La Warr dispatch with his own words, should come as no surprise, even though Martin, as the Company's Secretary in London, would have seen some of the material before, because he had received De La Warr's official dispatch earlier that fall. Indeed this appears to have been Strachey's *modus operandi.* He was not shy about repeating what others had already said if he could find a place for it in his own work. He dedicated copies of *Travel*, largely a borrowing of the published texts of others, to three patrons who probably had already read many of the originals on which his compilation depended.[4] These were the Earl of Northumberland, who had "considerable interest in the voyages of colonization and exploration,"[5] Sir Allen Apsley, a nephew by marriage of Sir George Carew and member of the Virginia Council,[6] and Sir Francis Bacon, the Lord High Chancellor of England and member of the Virginia Company. Based on Vaughan's erroneous interpretation, we are confident of our original statement that the Martin letter suggests that Strachey, writing or revising in or around 1612, incorporated into *Reportory* elements of a response originally composed as a separate, much shorter document, answering Martin's queries. This conclusion is also supported by the fact that almost all of the portions of *Reportory* that answer to Martin are missing from the B manuscript.

Strachey was a literary packrat. His practice of keeping copies of everything he wrote or came across is evident in the copious use he made of such documentary sources in composing his own works. He appears to have kept a copy of the B draft on which *Reportory* depends. He must have kept a copy (or notes) of the De La Warr dispatch; as Colony Secretary, it would have been especially appropriate for him to do so. As *Travel* includes verbatim elements from Davies' manuscript "Relation of a Voyage,"[7] he must also have kept a copy of it and the multiple other *Travel* sources which Culliford has documented.[8]

Many of these items would likely have been gathered or copied while Strachey was still in Virginia. In fact, Strachey says himself in his dedication to the Earl of Northumberland that he keeps records, as he has made "the first Ca[r]tagraph or Draught, as [he has] had time to digest out of [his] journal or diary books."[9] It is worth noting Strachey's disingenuous claim that his sources for the volume were *his own* "journal or diary books" when the evidence proves that his primary source was Smith's already published *Map*, and that he drew on a number of other published or unpublished sources in constructing the work. Statements of such dubious reliability are common in Strachey's extant oeuvre.

If our analysis of the Martin letter's influence is correct, it confirms other evidence supporting a post–1610 *terminus a quo* for the finished *Reportory*.

Rather than engaging in thoughtful debate on this point, however, Vaughan misconstrues our position and responds to something we did not say. He concludes a string of misinterpretations of the case for *Reportory*'s dependence on the Martin letter by stating that it is "on such speculations that Stritmatter and Kositsky conclude that 'at the very least, Martin's nescience disproves the frequent assertion that the Strachey letter circulated widely in the court or Company during the winter of 1610–11.'"[10] As a finale, Vaughan attributes to us the belief that "the secretary of the Colony's report to the secretary of the Company was conveyed in a letter to an anonymous lady that dwells for three-quarters of its length on the Bermuda shipwreck and subsequent events about which Martin had not inquired."[11]

Vaughan asserts that "the court in which the manuscript circulated was not that of James I but the council of the Virginia Company of London,"[12] but does not say how this proposition squares with the fact that the document is addressed to a "noble lady." He misunderstands our clearly articulated position that *Reportory* is a palimpsest written over multiple other documents, including classical materials, earlier Iberian narratives, "storm set" descriptions, and significant parts of the De La Warr letter, the official dispatch to the Company. And the simplest explanation of the known facts — including the existence of Hume's B manuscript (see Chapter 11) — is that a copy of whatever went back to Martin, in response to the latter's questions, has been inserted into what is now known as *Reportory*.

Strachey's habits of composition and his history as a plagiarist, already discussed above, also bear on the question of how to interpret the relationship between *Reportory* and *Declaration*. *Reportory* shows definitive signs of intertextuality with *Declaration*, a work not published until after the autumn 1610 arrival in London of Gates' return voyage. For several reasons, in our *RES* article we judged these to be the result of Strachey copying from *Declaration* rather than the reverse. The attempt to counter this argument fell to Tom Reedy,[13] who undertook to show that the evidence is better explained by the premise that *Declaration* borrowed from *Reportory*:

> Stritmatter and Kositsky offer no explanation of how — if Strachey's narrative was not available — the author of *True Declaration* knew the date and latitude of the storm; that the location of the *Sea Venture*'s leak was unknown; the exact amount of water pumped and for how long; the exact dates of the Bermuda survivors' departure or their reception at Point Comfort; the difference in health of the colonists at Jamestown and the falls; the method of constructing of the colonists' houses — facts differing or absent from all the other known sources. The *True Declaration* author either took that information from Strachey or from one or more now missing sources that happened to parallel Strachey on every point. No evidence for any such hypothetical source exists.[14]

Two key issues are raised in Reedy's challenge. The first is whether it is plausible that one or more ancestors link the two documents. We think it is. The other is whether, regardless of a common ancestor, the two documents are directly connected to one another, and if so, which is the original. We agree with Reedy that they are directly linked, but his conclusion identifying *Declaration* as the debtor document is based on faulty reasoning. On the contrary, by a clear preponderance of the evidence, as we shall see, Strachey is copying from *Declaration*. Unfortunately, the powerful influence of an *a priori* assumption that *Reportory* had to have been transmitted to England on the 15 July Gates voyage has prevented scholars from recognizing the significance of this evidence.

Let us first consider the question of possible common sources for *Declaration* and *Reportory*, a possibility that Reedy rejects. There are several known possible common sources, any of which might have supplied elements that Reedy regards as definitive proof of *Declaration*'s direct reliance on *Reportory*. Instead of acknowledging the actual facts, Reedy argues from abstract first principles that "the multiplication of entities is neither necessary nor plausible."[15]

Abstractions such as "necessary" or "plausible" are irrelevant — it is *a fact* that a secret report, attributed to Captain Newport, was disclosed to the council when Newport returned to England with Gates in September 1610. Newport's report, although no longer extant, almost certainly contained many of the details — those concerning navigation, the storm, and the wreck at least — which Reedy obliges the *Declaration* author to obtain from *Reportory*. Reedy fails to mention this report, even though it contained critical information about the state of the Jamestown colony, as is evident from the surviving synopsis by Alonso De Velasco, the Spanish ambassador to the Jacobean Court (1610–13), who reported to King Philip III that Newport had

> secretly reported the misery suffered by those who remain there [Virginia] and said that if Lord de la Warca [Warre] who recently went there as Governor, had delayed three days longer, the island would have been abandoned by the 300 persons who had remained alive out of 700, who had been sent out. In order to encourage the merchants, at whose expense this expedition is undertaken, so that they may persevere in it, he has publicly given out great hopes, and thus they have formed several Companies by which men will be sent out in assistance, and they have determined, that at the end of January of the coming year, three ships shall sail, with men, women and ministers of their religion ... if Y[our] M[ajesty] were pleased to command that a few ships should be sent to that part of the world, which would drive out the few people that have remained there, and are so threatened by the Indians that they dare not leave the fort they have erected....[16]

Declaration also reports that De La Warr contributed "letters," the use of the plural word demonstrating that he submitted, in addition to his dispatch, at least one other report to the Company. Only two surviving documents fit the description of "letters" from De La Warr,[17] but there may have been more. The De La Warr dispatch, dated 7 July 1610 (a week before the 15 July date which appears in Strachey's *Reportory* text), is another obvious common source for *Declaration* and *Reportory,* and in fact shares extensive intertextuality with both. As the Colony's secretary and one of five signatories to this document (with De La Warr, Thomas Gates, Ferdinand Wainman and George Percy), Strachey may well have been one of the document's authors. His involvement however, if any, does not appear to have been significant. The dispatch, at least in the main, is written in the first person voice of De La Warr, and relates matters such as De La Warr's voyage to Virginia, to which Strachey was not a witness.

The author of *Declaration* acknowledges the use of such sources, explicitly "profess[ing] that he will relate nothing [concerning the colony] but what he hath from the secrets of the Judicial Council of Virginia, from the letters of Lord La Warre, from the mouth of Sir Thomas Gates."[18] These "secrets"[19] from the members of "The Judicial Council of Virginia"[20] could have included written reports from Gates (as well as the oral account specifically referenced in *Declaration*), Summers, Percy, or Wainman, in addition to that of Newport.[21] Newport's known report is especially significant because, as Captain, he is likely to have been the originator of specific nautical information such as the ships' bearings that found their way into both *B* and *Reportory*. Strachey himself attributes such detailed nautical information to Newport: "We had followed this course so long, as now we were within seven or eight days at the most, by Cap. Newport's reckoning, of making Cape Henry upon the coast of Virginia."[22]

Taking ship's bearings required the use of such specialized nautical tools as a compass, a cross-staff and an astrolabe. Only the captain or his navigator would have determined bearings using these instruments. Edward Maria Wingfield, in his report of the 1606 exploration of the James River, records that "Newport and Tyndall took observations for the latitude of the place, and notes for a 'draughte of our River.'"[23] There is no evidence that Strachey was able to conduct the specialized measurements required for determining latitude. Reedy, however, seems confident that neither Newport nor any of these colonial leaders were involved in producing oral or written reports attributable to "the judicial council." Instead, the attribution "the secrets of the Judicial Council" is to Reedy merely a circumlocution for the Colony's Secretary, William Strachey: "It is *certain beyond any reasonable doubt* that the information from the 'secrets of the Judicial Council of Virginia' used by the writer of *True Declaration* was that found in Strachey's letters."[24]

Reedy characterizes our treatment of the evidence on the topic of intertextuality as "cursory and flawed."[25] Coming from someone who purports to analyze the pertinent evidence for Strachey's possible sources while failing to mention Christopher Newport or his secret report, Eden's *Decades of the New World* (one of Strachey's acknowledged sources), or any of the texts utilized in constructing Strachey's "storm formula," such criticism is indeed ironic. While Reedy discourses with enthusiasm on our alleged lack of credibility, he fails to acknowledge such basic factual information as that the Strachey "letter"— as both he and Vaughan insist on calling it — is 24,000 words (almost a third the length of this book).[26] For context, the average length of the *actual* letters making the Atlantic crossing in the early days of Jamestown colonization was about 1200 words ($\frac{1}{20}$ the length of Strachey's document), and official dispatches seldom exceeded 4000 words.[27] Reedy accuses us of withholding from the reader that "the purported 'answers' [to Richard Martin's 14 December queries to Strachey] are present almost verbatim in the July 7 dispatch from De La Warre"[28] even though our table explicitly acknowledged that *two out of five* of the cited passages contain *some* parallel to the De LaWarr dispatch.

Reedy's use of the secondary literature is just as selective as his use of primary documents. He avoids any reference to the work of Strachey's biographer Culliford when discussing Strachey's reputation as a plagiarist. He ignores Harold Francis Watson's *The Sailor in English Drama* (1931), which established the importance of the concept of the "formula storm" in Strachey's narrative technique. He omits David Lindley's relevant opinion that "there is virtually nothing in the [Bermuda documents] which manifests the kind of unambiguous close verbal affinity" seen in such sources as Montaigne, Ovid, or Virgil."[29] Most surprisingly, Reedy fails to significantly address the all-important larger question raised by Lindley, of the strength of the evidence for Shakespeare's reliance on Strachey — without which Reedy's article would seem to be a fruitless exercise. Instead, he follows the familiar pattern of asserting that Shakespeare's reliance on Strachey is already beyond reasonable dispute.[30] Whatever his reasons, he is careful to hedge his conclusions, making only modest claims for Strachey's alleged influence on Shakespeare, asserting only that

> A close textual comparison between the letter, the published sources, and other contemporary documents ... demonstrate(s) the primacy of Strachey's letter and confirms its use as a source in the Virginia Company tract published in November 1610, therefore *preserving its accessibility* as a source for Shakespeare.[31]

Reedy's abstract consequently illustrates Fischer's "fallacy of possible proof," which "consists of an attempt to demonstrate that a factual statement is true or false by demonstrating *the possibility* of its truth or falsity."[32]

Swimming against the current of evidence is never easy, even when one claims to be "certain beyond a reasonable doubt," and both our critics frequently confuse what the reader must conclude for what they themselves believe. What they believe, all too often, can be reduced to the comforting dictum that everything of consequence about the topic upon which they are writing has already been said. They fail to recognize that advocates of the traditional Strachey story have not proven their case and are unlikely ever to be able to do so. Indeed, the *only* primary evidence that Strachey's manuscript went back to London on the 15 July voyage is that the narrative *appears* to break off at that point. By that reasoning, no historical work was written at any point after the last incident it records. This is why both Reedy and Vaughan spill so much ink trying to justify a much more modest standard of proof, arguing that because Strachey's manuscript was completed before the boat sailed, it must have been sent, and was therefore at least accessible to Shakespeare (Reedy) or must have been used by him (Vaughan). Thus, we find such unqualified challenges as Reedy's assertion that "there is no evidence that Strachey's letter was not sent to England in July 1610."[33] This classic argument from ignorance shifts the burden of proof onto skeptics of the Strachey "just so" story. However, it is not the skeptics' job to prove that Strachey's letter did not come back on the 15 July voyage, that it failed to reach Shakespeare, or that he did not use it in his play. On the contrary, it is Vaughan and Reedy's responsibility to show that these things did actually happen.

The effort to shift the burden of proof onto skeptics is a sign that the orthodox view is running out of arguments and must depend more and more on the most reliable of all fallacies, the appeal to authority. As Reedy says — offering only Vaughan and Vaughan's 1999 Arden edition for his reference — "For a century, most Shakespeare scholars have agreed that Shakespeare used [Strachey's letter] as a source for writing *The Tempest*."[34] Reedy need not have cited Vaughan. Hume puts the case more directly and with greater honesty when he says that "the Shakespeare connection ... is a non-issue. That the playwright took his theme from accounts of the wreck and salvation of Summers' company ... *cannot be doubted*."[35]

17

An Eyewitness?

As we have seen, advocates of the Strachey theory enjoy pointing out that Strachey was an "eyewitness" to the events of the Bermuda wreck, implying that for this reason we should trust his every word as embodying a kind of unique authenticity. The history of *Reportory*'s composition, however, shows that he was an eyewitness skilled at turning a fact into an entertaining fiction. The extent of Strachey's creative modifications becomes apparent when we consider the critical question of the intertextuality between *Reportory* and *Declaration*. As we have noted, much of Tom Reedy's *RES* article is devoted to proving that this is not a result of *Reportory* copying *Declaration* (which would in itself disprove the hypothesis of its July 1610 transmission to England). Instead, he argues, *Declaration* must have been copying from *Reportory*.

As we examine Reedy's modes of analysis, we soon find that matters he regards as having been conclusively proven are not, and that the methods he uses to draw inferences are often inconsistently applied. This is especially so when it comes to the essential task of determining the direction of influence between two related texts, where he often depends on arbitrary assumptions. An example is his belief that when comparing two texts with related content, the longer one must be the source.[1] Thus, according to him, our suggestion that Strachey copied from a passage in Smith describing Indian houses is in part proved "false" by the fact that "Strachey's ... description is much more detailed than those in Smith or *True Declaration*."[2]

Reedy rarely considers whether the evidence he presents can be interpreted in any other way. In fact, Strachey employed a well-documented habit of elaborating material borrowed from his sources by adding his own flourishes, sometimes padding the copied passages with extensive additional material, either from his own experience or from other sources. Even in the first book of *Travel*, although Strachey incorporates many passages from Smith's

Map of Virginia, Culliford observes that "he is able to add considerably to Smith's account from his own experience."[3] Numerous instances of Strachey's habit of padding his sources in this manner can be cited.[4]

Reedy also makes generous appeal to his own subjective evaluations of literary merit. He credits the author of *Declaration* with "perfecting" a figure of speech that, according to him, Strachey must have originated.[5] To Reedy the example supplies "almost incontrovertible textual evidence that the Virginia Company writer follows Strachey."[6] But, once again, Reedy's argument consists more of assumption than rational inference. Why wouldn't Strachey, borrowing the already "perfected" figure, convert an elegant expression into a wordier one? Anyone who has ever read a student paper composed by cutting and pasting selections from the internet knows that borrowers are quite capable not only of expanding but also of degrading the original. Reedy's argument, in other words, depends upon his assumptions — that Strachey was the original writer and that copyists inevitably improve what they borrow.

A remarkable feature of Reedy's procedure is his inconsistency about such matters of method. He is not shy about establishing rules when it suits his purposes, but is reluctant to observe them when it does not. In his very first table, "Location and date of [the] storm,"[7] he presents an argument for *Declaration*'s dependence on *Reportory* based on comparing the date and nautical coordinates of the storm in five different texts (B, Summers' Letter, *Reportory*, *Discovery* and *Declaration*). Discovering that the two Strachey texts generally agree more with *Declaration* than the others, Reedy classifies this as a proof of *Declaration*'s dependence on *Reportory*. However, a few pages later he claims that "a fixed distance, such as that between two Capes, cannot be a copied parallel, since it exists outside literary invention."[8] Whether it exists "outside of literary invention" or not, the fact is that the distance between two capes, as embedded in both texts, belongs to the pattern of intertextuality that reveals their connection. As many other "facts," such as the dates and nautical coordinates he used to make his case for *Reportory*'s alleged priority in his table a few pages earlier, would by this same reasoning "exist outside literary invention," it is difficult to see how Reedy can reconcile his argument with his own stated principles.

The more time one spends with Reedy's argument, the weaker it appears. In his second table[9] Reedy purports to show, on the basis of an alleged variant between B and *Reportory,* that "the authors of *True Declaration* used the letter later published in Purchas instead of the 'B' text."[10] His proof is that "only Strachey's [*Reportory*] includes the detail that the source of the leak could not be found."[11] The false dilemma of obliging the reader to choose between B *or Reportory* as *Declaration*'s source is bothersome, as it begs two questions:

whether the direction of influence may have run the other way, and whether there could have been a lost shared source. More directly, his argument is also based on an omission. Both the B and *Reportory* texts make quite clear (Table 17.1), in parallel language revealing *Reportory*'s close dependence on B, that the leak *was* discovered. Reedy's table[12] conveniently omits the relevant passage from *Reportory*.

Table 17.1. Parallel Passages from B and *Reportory* Describing Discovery of the Leak

B	Reportory
Many leaks were thus found; and hastily stopped; but the principle one could not be discovered. Though the pumps were kept constantly going, the water still rose; but from the quantities of bread brought up, the leak was conjectured to be in the bread room, where the carpenter made a search equally unsuccessfully as elsewhere. (70)	Many a weeping leak was this way found and hastily stopped, and at length one in the gunner room made up with I know not how many pieces of beef. But all was to no purpose; the leak (if it were but one) which drunk in our greatest seas and took in our destruction fastest could not then be found, nor ever was, by any labor, counsel, or search. The waters still increasing and the pumps going, which at length choked with bringing up whole and continual biscuit (and indeed all we had, ten thousand weight), it was conceived as most likely that the leak might be sprung in the bread room, whereupon the carpenter went down and ripped up all the room, but could not find it so. (9)
The leak was at length discovered in the hold on Tuesday morning, when our governor divided the whole people, being one hundred and forty men, besides women, into three portions... (71)	Our governor upon the Tuesday morning (at what time, by such who had been below in the hold, the leak was first discovered) had caused the whole company (about 140, besides women) to be equally divided into three parts... (10)

Declaration contradicts both Strachey accounts, describing the leak as "secret"—undiscovered. By Reedy's own logic, then, *Declaration* could not have been based on either the B or the *Reportory* accounts.

Reedy does acknowledge that Jourdain influenced *Declaration* in a number of obvious instances. A clear example of this may be seen in Table 17.2, in which both Jourdain and *Declaration* offer detailed accounts of shipwreck survivors carrying ashore "tack[l]ing" and provisions from the ship.

Table 17.2. Parallel Landing Passages in Jourdain, *Declaration*, and *Reportory*

Jourdain (October 1610)	Declaration (November 1610)	Reportory
We gained not only sufficient time, with the present help of our boat and skiff, safely to set and convey our men ashore (which were one hundred and fifty in number), but afterwards had time and leisure to save some good part of our goods and provision which the water had spoiled, with all the tacking of the ship and much of the iron about her. (107)	God continuing his mercy unto them, that with their longboats they transported to land before night all their company, men, women, and children to the number of one hundred and fifty. They carried to shore all the provision of unspent and unspoiled victuals, all their furniture and tackling of the ship. (10)	By the mercy of God unto us, making out our boats, we had ere night brought all our men, women, and children, about the number of one hundred and fifty safe unto the island. (16)

The central question here is not whether *Declaration* was influenced by Jourdain (Reedy agrees that it was), or whether there is intertextuality between *Declaration* and *Reportory* (Reedy agrees that there is). The debate is over the direction of influence between the two latter texts. The three-way comparison in Table 17.2 takes us directly to the heart of the matter. Jourdain (or a common source) has evidently influenced *Declaration*'s account in material ways, since both tell of the survivors carrying ashore provisions and usable remnants of the ship, while Strachey does not. On the other hand, it is equally evident (Table 17.3) that Strachey and *Declaration* share certain elements not visible in Jourdain.

For three primary reasons, Reedy is confident that in this (and every other) case *Declaration* is following *Reportory*, and not the reverse: (1) As we have seen, his misleading chronology places *Reportory*'s completion before the publication of *Declaration*; (2) Strachey was present at the event and the author of *Declaration* was not; and (3) there is no evidence for any possible alternative sources for the *Declaration* account. Before proceeding to a fuller analysis of these assumptions, it is worth considering why both *Declaration* and Jourdain

> ## Table 17.3. Detail of Landing Elements
> ## in *True Declaration* and *Reportory*
>
> **Declaration** *(November 1610)*
> *God continuing his mercy unto them ...* they transported to land before night all their company, men, women, and children to the number of one hundred and fifty. (10)
>
> **Reportory** *(published 1625)*
> *By the mercy of God unto us ...* we had ere night brought all our men, women, and children, about the number of one hundred and fifty. (16)

record the survivors carrying provisions and equipment ashore while Strachey does not. The reason is found in a striking disagreement between Strachey and every other known account of the wreck. According to Strachey, the material carried ashore in the other accounts had already been thrown overboard:

> We much unrigged our ship, threw overboard much luggage, many a trunk and chest (in which I suffered no mean loss), and staved many a butt of beer, hogsheads of oil, cider, wine, and vinegar, and heaved away all our ordnance on the starboard side, and now purposed to have cut down the main mast the more to lighten her.[13]

The discrepancy leaves the reader with a difficult choice. Which of the two accounts is correct, or is it possible that both express partial truths? The latter choice unfortunately seems obviated by Strachey's decision not to record the activity of carrying ashore the provisions when others do. Had he done so, it might have been possible to reason that the other accounts (both of which are much briefer than Strachey's) were merely deficient; while some provisions had been thrown overboard, others remained on board and were subsequently carried ashore. Strachey, however, effectively eliminates this basis for compromise, by choosing to omit all mention of the latter activity, apparently to preserve the credibility of his own highly dramatic account of the jettisoning of provisions in the storm. We are presented with two distinct accounts of what transpired and are forced to conclude that one of them has been altered for dramatic effect.

Nor is this the only case in which Strachey's account diverges markedly from that found in the other narratives in such a way as to raise the question of his reliability. His is the only version that records St. Elmo's fire, the possible splitting of the ship, and the "purposing" of cutting down the mainmast, as well as heaving ordnance, chests and other provisions overboard to lighten the ship. Taken together, these are very significant divergences, and the reader should wonder how they can be explained. Harold Francis Watson supplies an answer in his conclusion that Strachey used a literary "storm formula" throughout his account of the wreck.[14]

Watson goes on to note that "considerably over half the material in the *Reportory* [storm] ... conforms to this romantic tradition despite the fact that scarcely any other storm in the voyage narratives does so, not even the variation[s] of the same one."[15] David Lindley, citing Barbara Mowat, confirms Watson's view that Strachey's text is a literary invention, not a raw narrative based solely on experience: "Strachey's account of the storm is itself a variation on a standard set piece topic."[16] The extent of the influence of this "formula" storm on Strachey's narrative is evident in the large number of motifs brought together in his account that are absent from the other Bermuda pamphlets (Table 17.4).

Table 17.4. Storm Elements in Strachey Not Found in Other Bermuda Pamphlets

Reportory	Other Bermuda Pamphlets[17]
The sea touching the sky.	No.
The lightening of the ship by tossing provisions overboard.	No.
Sailors praying	No.
The probable splitting or breaking up of the ship.	No.
The probable overturning of the ship.	No.
The actual or "purposed" cutting down of the main mast.	No.
St. Elmo's Fire	No.

The literary sources of Strachey's "formula storm," which apparently influenced his vivid reconstruction of the real storm that stranded the *Sea Venture* survivors on Bermuda, have not been definitively identified, but plausible candidates include Erasmus' "Naufragium" (one of the most popular and influential of all early-modern literary storms), and Tomson's 1555 "Voyage into Nova Hispania," published by Hakluyt in 1600. A comparison of Tomson's account with the one found in *Reportory* reveals definite traces of his influence on Strachey's narrative (Table 17.5). It is here, for example, that Strachey may have obtained the idea of the lightening of the ship by tossing provisions overboard or the cue for the St. Elmo's fire narration.

Table 17.5. "Storm Formula" Parallels in Tomson Influenced Strachey's Construction of the *Reportory* Storm

Tomson in Hakluyt (1600)

For fear of sinking we threw and lightened into the sea all the goods we had or could come by; but that would not serve. Then we cut our main mast and threw all our ordnance into the sea. (344)

I do remember that in the great and boisterous storm of this foul weather, in the night, there came upon the top of our mainyard and mainmast, a certain little light, much like unto the light of a little candle which the Spaniards called the Querpo Santo, and said it was S. Elmo, whom they take to be the advocate of sailors. At the which site the Spaniards fell down upon their knees and worshipped it, praying God and St. Elmo to cease the torment and save them from the peril they were in ... this light continued aboard our ship about three hours, flying from mast to mast, & from top to top; and sometime it would be in two or three places at once. I informed myself of learned men afterwards what that light should be, and they said, that it was but a congelation of the wind and vapors of the sea, congealed with the extremity of the weather, which flying in the wind, many times doth chance to hit on the masts and shrouds of the ships that are at sea in foul weather. (Tomson 343–346)

Reportory *(f.p. 1625)*

We heaved all our ordnance on the starboard side, and had now purposed to have cut down the main mast the more to lighten her. (14)

Only upon the Thursday night Sir George Summers, being upon the watch, had an apparition of a little, round light, like a faint star, trembling and streaming along, with a sparkling blaze, half the height upon the mainmast and shooting sometimes from shroud to shroud, 'tempting to settle, as it were upon any of the four shrouds, and for three or four hours together, or rather more, half the night, it kept with us, running sometimes along the mainyard to the very end and then returning; at which Sir George Summers called diverse about him and showed them the same who observed it with much wonder and carefulness. But upon a sudden, toward the morning watch, they lost the sight of it and knew not what way it made.

The superstitious seaman make many constructions of this sea fire, which nevertheless is usual in storms, the same (it may be) which the Grecians were wont in the Mediterranean to call Castor and Pollux, of which if only one appeared without the other they took it for an evil sign of great tempest.[18] The Italians and such who lie open to the Adriatic and Tyrrhenian sea call it (a sacred body) *corpo sancto*; the Spaniards call it St. Elmo and have an authentic and miraculous legend for it. (12–13)

While recognition of Strachey's dependence on such sources for the construction of his storm does not directly resolve the question of whether *Reportory* or *Declaration* is the borrower, it does cast further doubt on Vaughan and Reedy's attempt to establish Strachey's narrative as the gold standard, unmediated "eyewitness" account of the Bermuda narratives. It also raises a pertinent question. If as Reedy maintains, *Declaration* is following *Reportory*, why does it fail to mention any of these highly dramatic circumstances, and instead relate a more prosaic version of the storm and wreck as presented in Jourdain and other surviving sources, without St. Elmo's fire, the tossing overboard of provisions and ordnance, the splitting of the boat, or desperate plans to cut down the mainmast? It also provides a revealing glimpse into Strachey's compositional process, one that supports the view of him as an active borrower of elements from other narratives. It casts a fresh light on the unexamined assumption shared by Reedy and Vaughan[19] that *Reportory* represents an unmediated "eyewitness" account that can be employed as the standard against which all other narratives of the Bermuda wreck should be measured. On the contrary, in composing *Reportory*, Strachey was calling on both his own memory and diverse written sources, in order to heighten the pathos and literary appeal of his narrative.

To maintain the position that *Declaration* was copying *Reportory*, Reedy must also deny the presence of intertextuality between *Reportory* and other texts published after the departure of Gates' 15 July return voyage. Chief among these is Smith's 1612 *Map of Virginia*. The difficulty of Reedy's position is well illustrated in the material given in Table 17.6, which compares passages extensively paralleled in *Reportory, History*, and Smith's *Map*. Culliford identifies the excerpt from *Travel* as one "quoted"[20] from Strachey's own *Reportory*. But, as we maintained in our original *RES* article, the common origin of both Strachey passages appears to be Smith's *Map*.

Examining all three documents, it is difficult to avoid concluding that Strachey, in each case, is borrowing from Smith. It is well known that Smith, who had first explored the Chesapeake region with George Percy in 1606–07,[21] *was* an eyewitness to the naming events described. Strachey was not. Percy himself supplies the earliest extant account of the naming:

> We rowed over to a point of Land, where we found a channel, and sounded six, eight, ten, or twelve fathom: which put us in good comfort. Therefore we named that point of Land, Cape Comfort. The nine and twentieth day we set up a Cross at Chesapeake Bay, and name[d] that place Cape Henry.[22]

Percy remained in Virginia, while Smith had already returned to England in October 1609, after Strachey had sailed from England but long before he

Table 17.6. After Stritmatter and Kositsky (2007)

Smith, 1612 Map	*Strachey,* History of Travel, *circa 1612*	*Strachey,* Reportory
There is but one entrance by sea into this country, and that is at the mouth of a very goodly Bay, the wideness whereof is near 18 or 20 miles. The cape on the South side is called Cape Henry in honor of our most noble Prince, The shew of the land there, is a white hilly sand like unto the Downs, and along the shores great plenty of Pines and Firs. The north cape is called Cape Charles in honor of our worthy Duke of York.	The Cape of this bay, on the south side, we call Cape Henry, in honor of that our most royal deceased prince, where the land shews white hilly sand, like unto the Downs, and all along the shore grow great plenty of pines and firs. (Major 28)	This is the famous Chesapeake Bay, which we have called (in honor of our young Prince) Cape Henry, over against which win the bay lieth another headland, which we called, in honor of our princely Duke of York, Cape Charles; and these lie northeast and by east and southwest and by west, and they may be distant each from the other in breadth seven leagues, between which the sea runs in as broad as between Queenborough and Leigh. Indeed it is a goodly bay and fairer one not easily to be found. (Wright 61)
Within is a country that may have the prerogative over the most pleasant places of Europe, Asia, Africa, or America.... This Bay lieth North and South... (Barbour 144)	The coast of south Virginian, from Cape Henry, lieth south and north, next hand some seven leagues, where there goeth in a river.... If we come in with the Chesapeake Bay open.... Our two capes, Cape Henry and Cape Charles, do lie no-east and by east, and so-west; and they be distant each from other in breadth (where the sea runs in between both lands, so making our Bay an only entrance into our country), as broad as may be between Queenborough and Leigh. (43–4)	

arrived in Jamestown in late May 1610.[23] Textual analysis supports the inference of historical context. Although each Strachey passage shares certain details with the other, each also reproduces language from Smith *not found in its counterpart*. Smith made a habit of noting on the title page of his Virginia works the names of collaborating writers (Figures 17.1–2); Strachey by contrast is known, even by his sympathetic biographer Culliford, for his habitual and well-documented practice of silently appropriating works written by others and presenting them as his own. His *Travel* is prefaced only by a perfunctory acknowledgment of having been "gathered and observed by those who went first thither,"[24] without mentioning by name a single one of the nine writers from which it borrows extensively and often verbatim.

Is it possible that Strachey could have seen a copy of Smith's *Map* before its 1612 publication? Some version of the *Map* was completed in manuscript as early as November 1608,[25] but there is no evidence that Strachey could have seen a copy before the extant version was published in 1612 by Joseph Barnes at the Oxford University Press. Strachey was not made Secretary of the Virginia Company until summer 1610, so he could not have had any official access to Smith or his work before that. Meanwhile, Smith left Virginia in 1609, on poor terms with the Virginia Company, so it is improbable that he would have left a copy of his valuable manuscript with them in Jamestown or in London, and in any case, they were not the publishers of it. Most significantly, Strachey's *Travel* reproduces a version of the Virginia map as published by Barnes in 1612. Based on these facts, the only way to extricate Strachey from the implication of having copied a work not likely available to him until 1612 would be to presume that Smith first borrowed from *Reportory* and then Strachey, writing *History of Travel*, copied from Smith.

Both Vaughan and Reedy are aware of the unacceptable implications of such a finding and do their best to counter our argument without reproducing it. Neither offers a fair summary of our case, and each pursues a different strategy in the attempt to avoid acknowledging its force. Vaughan focuses on the original triad of texts and assails us for mistaking evidence that he himself fails to understand:

> The authors sometimes miss the message in the very words they select for comparison. Although they position "True Reportory" after Strachey's *[History of Travel]* (1612), they fail to notice that while *[History of Travel]* says that Virginia's Cape Henry is named "in honor of that our most royal deceased prince," "True Reportory" reports the cape to have been named "in honor of our young Prince." Implicitly, Henry is still alive. The sequence of the texts is obviously not what Stritmatter and Kositsky imagine it to be.[26]

Vaughan's critique misrepresents our position. We did not designate *Travel* as a *Reportory* source, or claim that it was necessarily written *before* the latter text, only that

> many of the sources identified as influences on *History of Travel*, [i.e., *Virginia Britannia*] a book written in England between 1612 and 1618, also influenced *Reportory*, suggesting that this work or parts of it may likewise have been written in England, using the same 'reference library,' after July 1610."[27]

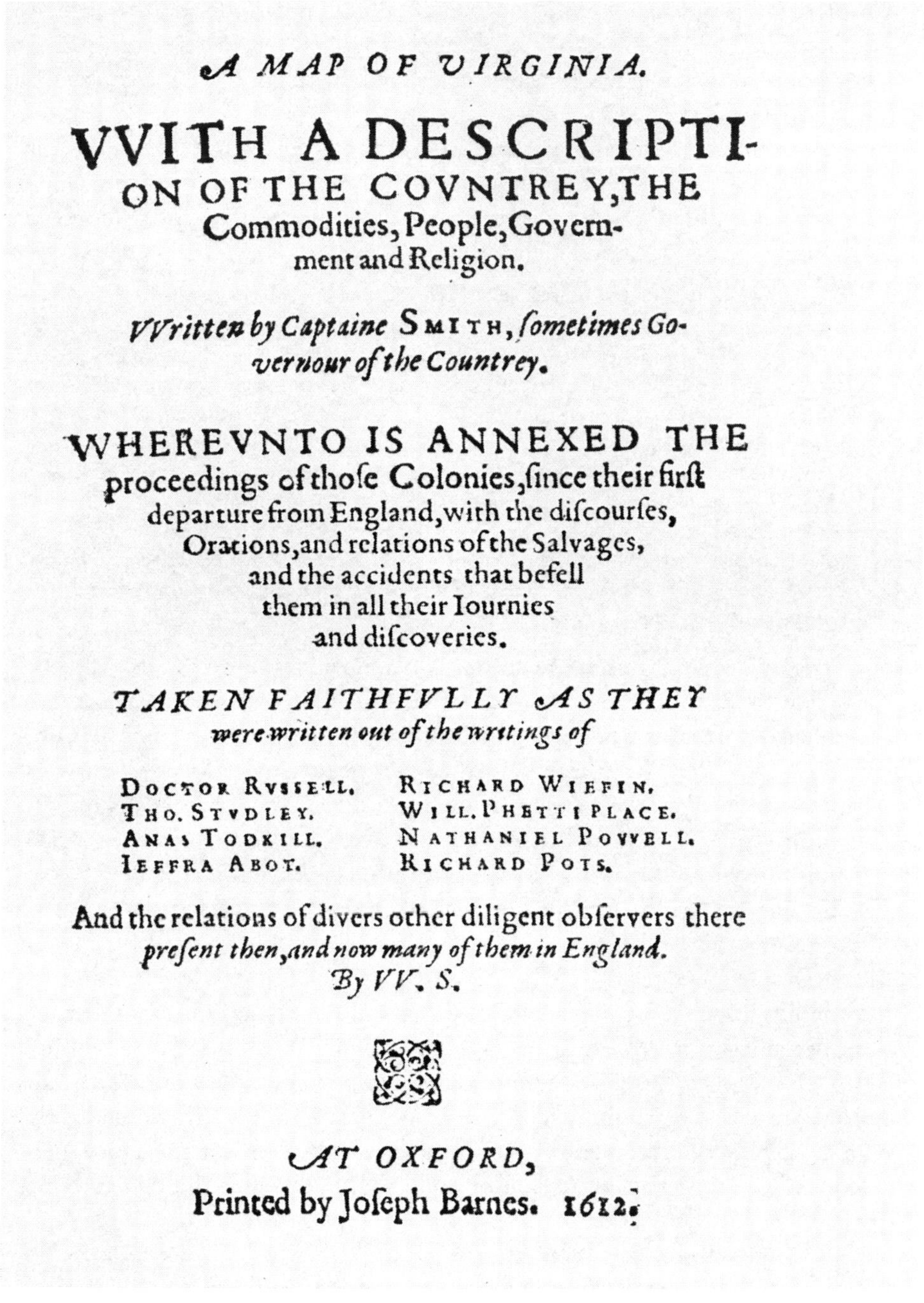

A MAP OF VIRGINIA.

VVITh A DESCRIPTI-
ON OF THE COVNTREY,THE
Commodities, People, Govern-
ment and Religion.

VVritten by Captaine S MI TH, *sometimes Go-*
vernour of the Countrey.

WHEREVNTO IS ANNEXED THE
proceedings of those Colonies, since their first
departure from England, with the discourses,
Orations, and relations of the Salvages,
and the accidents that befell
them in all their Iournies
and discoveries.

TAKEN FAITHFVLLY AS THEY
were written out of the writings of

DOCTOR RVSSELL.	RICHARD WIFFIN.
THO. STVDLEY.	WILL. PHETTI PLACE.
ANAS TODKILL.	NATHANIEL POVVELL.
IEFFRA ABOT.	RICHARD POTS.

And the relations of divers other diligent observers there
present then, and now many of them in England.
By VV. S.

AT OXFORD,
Printed by Joseph Barnes. 1612.

Figure 17.2. Smith's recognition of other writers on title page of *Map of V* (courtesy Wikimedia Commons).

Moreover, in the table to which Vaughan alludes, we made no inference as to the priority of one Strachey book over the other, but merely argued that the evidence unambiguously shows Strachey borrowing *from himself* as well as from Smith's *Map of Virginia* (1612).

Even more troubling, Vaughan's critique is based on a misconception that reveals a misinterpretation of the relevant historical documents.[28] Strachey's biographer Culliford clarifies that the language Vaughan erroneously supposes original to *Travel* was not added until much later:

> We do not know in what month in 1612 *A Map of Virginia* [by Smith] was published, but it must have been early in the year, since the fair copy of *The Historie of Travaile* was completed before November of that year, when Prince Henry died and his younger brother Charles became Prince of Wales. Strachey, quoting Smith tells us, "The Cape of this bay, on the south side, we call Cape Henry, in honor of our most Royal Prince.... The north foreland of this bay, which the Indians term Accowmack, we call Cape Charles, in honor of our Princely Duke of York." This is altered in the copy presented to Bacon in 1618 by the insertion of "deceased" before "Prince" and the changing of "Our Princely Duke of York" to "our now Prince, at that time Duke of York." These additions appear to have been made in 1617; hence all three copies of the manuscript must have been completed before the death of Henry.[29]

While Vaughan thus misrepresents our position and misunderstands the facts, Reedy summarizes our case more accurately but passes over the actual *evidence* in silence. His table (Table 17.7) eliminates *History* from the comparison, replacing it with *Declaration*, and then he tries to argue for *Declaration's* dependence on *Reportory*. Again he does not directly address our argument, in which the *three-way* parallelism between Smith and *both* of Strachey's texts reveals Strachey's borrowing. Reedy not only fails to address this evidence; he lists neither Smith's *Map* nor *Travel* among the documents worthy of consideration in his study.

Detailed analysis of Reedy's case further undermines confidence in its credibility (Table 17.7). The careful reader will notice that his argument for the dependence of *Declaration* on *Reportory* requires an ellipsis of twenty pages (pp. 61 to 81). The purpose of this ellipsis is to introduce the word "fort" into a *Reportory* passage that in itself does not contain the word. Why would Reedy go to such great lengths merely to capture a single word for this table? It is required to create the impression of a parallelism between the two excerpts where none in fact exists.

In the final analysis, Reedy's attempt to deny Strachey's dependence on Smith is unconvincing. Smith, *Reportory*, and the *Travel* excerpt Reedy has failed to include in his alternative table, are manifestly connected. The three documents have an identical purpose and structure as well as sharing common

Table 17.7. Tom Reedy's Alternative Version[30] of Stritmatter and Kositsky's (2007) Table 9.7, in Which Reedy Attempts to Show the Dependence of *Declaration* on *Reportory*

Smith's Map of Virginia, 1612	*"Reportory," (Strachey 'P'), 15 July, 1610*	*Declaration, 8 November, 1610*
There is but one entrance by sea into this country, and that is at the mouth of a very goodly bay, the wideness whereof is near 18 or 20 miles. The cape on the South side is called Cape Henry in honor of our most noble Prince. The show of the land there, is a white hilly sand like unto the Downs, and along the shores great plenty of pines and firs. The north Cape is called Cape Charles in honor of the worthy Duke of York. (Barbour 144)	This is the famous Chesapeake Bay, which we have called (in honor of our young Prince) Cape Henry, over against which within the Bay lieth another headland, which we called, in honor of our princely Duke of York, Cape Charles; and these lie northeast and by east and southwest and by west, and they may be distant each from the other in breadth seven leagues, between which the sea runs in as broad as between Queenborough and Leigh. Indeed it is a goodly bay and a fairer not easily to be found ... the fort is called, in honor of his Majesty's name, Jamestown. (Wright 61, 81)	The other comfort is the that Lord Governor has built two new forts (the one called Fort Henry and the other Fort Charles, in honor of our most noble prince and his hopeful brother) upon a pleasant hill and near a little rivulet, which we call Southampton River. (21)

words and phrases: they supply a general introduction to the topography of Chesapeake Bay. The excerpt from *Declaration* is of a different character, focusing only on the two forts, built some time after the naming of their respective capes. Ironically, the "fort" which Reedy retrieves from twenty pages later in *Reportory* to supply his connection to the *Declaration* passage is not even the right fort (Table 17.8).

Reedy is not content to argue that the *Declaration* passage derives from *Reportory*— a practical impossibility, as one describes capes and the other forts. He goes on to assert that there is insufficient parallelism between *Map* and

Table 17.8. Parallel Passages Regarding Cape/Fort Charles in Map, *Reportory*, and *Declaration*

Map	Reportory	Declaration
The north cape is called Cape Charles in honor of the worthy Duke of York. (144)	Which we have called, in honor of our princely Duke of York, Cape Charles ... (61) ... *the fort* is called, in honor of His Majesty's name, Jamestown... (81)	(The one called Fort Henry and the other Fort Charles, in honor of our most noble prince and his hopeful brother) (21)

Reportory to warrant a case for Strachey's reliance on Smith. To this end, he employs a curious "chop logic," which proceeds by isolating each element of the patterned relationships (see especially Tables 17.1, 17.10–11, 17.12) which connect *Reportory* to Smith, and argues that the only conceivably relevant connection between the two texts is the phrase "goodly bay." He concludes that "the slight verbal resemblances between Strachey and John Smith cannot be attributed to Strachey copying Smith."[31] Given this objective, Reedy's elimination from consideration of the corresponding Chesapeake Bay passage from Strachey's *Travel* is not accidental, for in this case (Table 17.9) there is no question of the existence of intertextuality.

Table 17.9. Chesapeake Bay Description Parallels in Smith's *Map* and Strachey's *Travel*

Smith	Travel
The cape on the South side is called Cape Henry in honor of our most noble Prince. The show of the land there, is a white hilly sand like unto the Downs, and along the shores great plenty of Pines and Firs. (Barbour 144)	The Cape of this bay, on the south side, we call Cape Henry, in honor of that our most royal deceased prince, where the land shows white hilly sand, like unto the Downs, and all along the shore grow great plenty of pines and firs. (Major 28)

The passages in themselves display an undeniable lexical and syntactical affinity, and Culliford agrees that Strachey copied from Smith.[32] As we noted in our original *RES* analysis, moreover, a similarly compelling intertexuality exists between the versions of this passage as reproduced by Strachey in *both* *Travel* and *Reportory* (Table 17.10).

Table 17.10. Intertextuality of Chesapeake Bay Descriptions in Strachey's *Reportory* and *Travel*

Reportory

This is the famous Chesapeake Bay, which we have called (in honor of our young Prince) Cape Henry, over against which within the Bay lyeth another headland, which we called, in honor of our princely Duke of York, Cape Charles; and these lie northeast and by east and southwest and by west, and they may be distant each from the other in breadth seven leagues, between which the sea runs in as broad as between Queenborough and Leigh. Indeed it is a goodly bay and fairer not easily to be found. (Wright 61)

Travel

If we come in with the Chesapeake Bay open ... our two capes, Cape Henry and Cape Charles, do lie no-east and by east, and so-west; and they be distant each from other in breadth (where the sea runs in between both lands, so making our Bay an only entrance into our country), as broad as may be between Queenborough and Leigh. (Major, 43–4)

From these considerations, we may proceed to a straightforward enumeration of the points directly connecting Strachey's *Reportory* to Smith's *Map* (Table 17.11). Smith refers to both Capes as named "in honor of" the two Stuart Princes. Strachey's version varies this by replacing Smith's "is called" with the (somewhat presumptuous) "we have called"—as if he were one of the origi-

Table 17.11. Five Points of Correspondence Between Smith and *Reportory*

Smith

1. The cape on the South side *is called Cape Henry in honor of our most noble Prince.*

2. The north Cape *is called Cape Charles in honor of the worthy Duke of York.*

3. The mouth of *a very goodly Bay*

4. The wideness whereof is near 18 or 20 miles

5. The white hilly sands like unto the downs

Reportory

1. The famous Chesapeake Bay, which *we have called (in honor of our young Prince) Cape Henry*

2. Within the Bay lyeth another headland, *which we called, in honor of our princely Duke of York, Cape Charles*

3. Indeed it is *a goodly bay*

4. In breadth seven leagues[33]

5. As broad as between Queenborough and Leigh

nators of the place names bestowed in 1607 by Percy and Smith.[34] Since we know that Strachey was not among those actually present, the small lie is worth noting as typical of his self-aggrandizing style. Despite the variation, the repetition of the verb "call" in an identical context already suggests a clear relationship between the two texts that is obscured in Reedy's analysis. Smith also calls the Chesapeake a "very goodly bay," and Strachey echoes by calling it "a goodly bay"—an echo Reedy tries to explain away by discoursing at length on the fact that the adjective "goodly" is an early-modern commonplace. As we have already noted, Reedy's commentary on the fact that both passages also estimate the width of the Chesapeake Bay's mouth—Smith using miles and Strachey leagues—further reveals the weakness of his methodology. Not many pages earlier Reedy compares storm dates and latitudes in five different texts in an attempt to establish that the author of *Declaration* must have been relying on Strachey. Apparently, the principle of facts that exist "outside of literary invention" applies only when expedient.

Most intriguingly, Smith describes a "show of the land" which contains "white hilly sand like unto the Downs." He refers to the downs of Kent, which as a geological formation are said to stretch all the way from the famed white cliffs of Dover to the "London and Surrey borders."[35] An almost identical passage (not included in Reedy's table) known, as we have seen, to be Strachey's borrowing from Smith, occurs also in *Travel* where "the land shows white hilly sand, like unto the Downs." *Travel* also includes a related passage, later in the book, duplicated in *Reportory* (Tables 17.7, 17.10), which focuses on the cardinal orientation of the Capes, and adds the illustrative comparison: "between which the sea runs in as broad as between Queenborough and Leigh."

Two conclusions may be drawn from this latter point of comparison. First, the language of Strachey's *Travel* version mediates between Smith's wording and that found in *Reportory*, including passages common to both. This provides further illustration of our original *RES* statement that unless Strachey is borrowing in both instances from Smith, Smith must have borrowed from Strachey's *Reportory* and then Strachey in *Travel* borrowed from Smith—a most unlikely circumstance. Second, and even more striking, Queenborough and Leigh stand on opposite sides of the Thames Estuary, Queenborough on the Kent side, within the region of the Downs. It is thus apparent that Strachey *in both of his versions* has taken a tip from Smith's reference to the downs and is searching for analogies to the Chesapeake geography from within the same English landscape in Kent. The names have been changed, but the location is the same.

The Chesapeake Bay description is not the only passage in which *Reportory*'s dependence on Smith is clearly demonstrable. In at least one critical instance both *Reportory* and *Declaration* make use of a document (or oral testimony) originating with George Percy or other early colonists, describing events prior to Strachey's arrival in Jamestown. The passage narrates Captain West's attempt to establish a camp at the James River Falls in 1609. Since neither authors of *Declaration* nor Strachey were in Virginia in 1609 during these events, it is evident that even if one writer borrowed from the other, the accounts in both *Reportory* and *Declaration* must be dependent on a previous source, such as a manuscript of George Percy's "Trewe Relacyon" (written 1612).[36]

Immediately following a table comparing the two accounts of this incident, Reedy announces that Strachey "includes details in the passage that he could not have gleaned from reading ... nor, being an eyewitness, did he need to."[37] As Strachey was not in Virginia during the described events, it is difficult to imagine a more serious error.

Reedy's handling of the comparison indicates the weakness of his position. His table on pp. 542–43, which attempts to prove *Declaration*'s dependence on *Reportory*, truncates the *Declaration* passage, obscuring several features of comparison. He strives to establish the priority of Strachey's text on the basis that "Strachey includes details ... that he could not have gleaned from reading *True Declaration*" or other sources. This may be so in the examples given, because Reedy has omitted half of the *Declaration* passage that corresponds to the remainder of the text he does supply from *Reportory*. When this passage is restored (Table 17.6), it is impossible to ascribe to Strachey significant detail not found in *Declaration*.

Further comparison allows us to conclude that the direction of influence is opposite that claimed by Reedy. Strachey and the author of *Declaration* both put the colonization of the falls to the same service: both texts contrast the unhealthy character of Jamestown with the salubrious geography of the falls and the country of the Nansemond natives. In developing this argument, both writers have interwoven their accounts with descriptive materials suggestive of Richard Eden's 1555 *Decades of the New World*. All three texts are debating the question of whether a settlement in a "marshy" region, believed to be conducive to disease, can be any basis for condemning the whole country. Thus, while they differ in emphasis and structure, and they describe different locations, all three exhibit a common logic: one cannot judge an entire country by one poorly situated colony. As Eden puts it, "Their habitation therefore in Dariena is pernicious and unwholesome only of *the particular nature of the place*" (emphasis supplied). It is apparent on close inspection that both *Declaration* and *Reportory* ultimately owe a debt to the Eden passage about Darien (Table 17.12).

Table 17.12. Three-way Comparison of Eden, *Declaration*, and *Reportory* Suggests That *Reportory* Borrows from *Declaration*, Not the Other Way Around

Eden, *1555*

For in many regions ... they find wholesome and temperate air, in such places where as the earth bringeth forth fair springs of water, or where wholesome rivers run by banks of pure earth without mud: but most especially where they inhabit the sides of the hills and not the valleys. But that the habitation which is on the banks of the river of Dariena is situate[d] in a deep valley and environed on every side with high hills.... Their habitation therefore in Dariena is pernicious and unwholesome only of the particular nature of the place.... The place is also contagious by the nature of the soil, by reason it is compassed about with muddy and stinking marshes. The infection whereof is not a little increased by the heat. The village itself is in a marsh, and in manner a standing puddle ... furthermore, where to ever they dig the ground the depth of a handful and a half there springeth out unwholesome and corrupt water of the

Declaration

No man ought to judge of any country by the fens and marshes (such as is the place where Jamestown stands) except we will condemn all England for the wilds and hundreds of Kent and Essex. In our particular, we have an infallible proof of the temper of the country, for of an hundred and odd which were seated at the Falls under the government of Captain Francis West, and of an hundred to the seaward on the south side of the river, (in the country of Nansemonds) under the charge of Captain John Martin, of all these two hundred there did not so much as one man miscarry. When in Jamestown at the same time and in the same months, one hundred sickened, and half the number died. The like experiment was long since in the regiment of Sir Ralph Lane, where, in the space of one whole year, not two of one hundred perished. Add unto this the discourse of philosophy; when in that country flesh will receive salt,

Reportory

True it is, I may not excuse this our fort, or Jamestown, as yet seated in somewhat an unwholesome and sickly air, by reason it is in a marish ground, low, flat to the river, and hath no fresh-water springs serving the town but what we drew from a well six or seven fathom deep fed by the brackish river oozing into it; from whence I verily believe the chief causes have proceeded of many diseases and sicknesses which have happened to our people, who are indeed strangely afflicted with fluxes and agues, and every particular season (by the relation of the old inhabitants) hath his particular infirmity too: all which, if it had been our fortunes to have seated upon some hill, accommodated with fresh springs and clear air, as do the natives of the country, we might have, I believe, well escaped. And some experience we have to persuade ourselves that it may be so, for of four hundred and odd men which were seated at the

Table 17.12. (cont.)

nature of the river.... Now therefore they consult on moving their habitation.... They had no respect to change the place although they were thus vexed by the contagion of the soil and heat of the sun, beside the corrupt water and infectious air by reason of venomous vapors... (121v–122)

They espied diverse islands replenished with sundry kinds of trees from which came fragrant savours of spices and sweet gums. (5) From the trees and herbs whereof when the morning dews began to rise, there proceeded many sweet savours. (29)

and continue unputrified (which it will not in the West Indies) when the most delicate of all flowers, grow there as familiarly, as in the fields of Portugal, where the woods are replenished with more sweet barks, and odors, then they are in the pleasantest places of Florida. How is it possible that such a virgin and temperate air, should work such contrary effects, but because our fort (that lyeth as a semi-island) is most part environed with an ebbing and flowing of salt water, the ooze of which sendeth forth an unwholesome & contagious vapour? (14)

Falls the last year when the fleet came in with fresh and young able spirits under the government of Captain Francis West, and of one hundred to the seawards (on the south side of our river), in the country of the Nansemonds under the charge of Captain John Martin, there did not so much as one man miscarry, and but very few, or none, fall sick. Whereas at Jamestown, the same time and the same months, one hundred sickened, and half the number died. Howbeit, as we condemn not Kent in England for a small town called Plumstead, continually assaulting the dwellers there (especially newcomers) with agues and fevers, no more let us lay scandal and imputation upon the country of Virginia because the little quarter wherein we are set down (unadvisedly so choosed) appears to be unwholesome and subject to many ill airs which accompany the like marish places. (Wright 82–83)

Analysis of the three passages (Table 17.13) shows beyond doubt that the direction of influence is from Eden, via *Declaration*, to Strachey. Strachey, in other words, *is* borrowing from *Declaration*.

Table 17.13. Detail of Three-Way Intertextuality Between Eden, *Declaration*, and *Reportory*, in Which *Declaration* Is at Several Points (see Esp. 1, 4, and 6) Closer to Eden Than *Reportory*

Eden	Declaration	Reportory
1. Wholesome and temperate air	1. Virgin and temperate air … a wholesome air	1. Clear air
2. Fair springs of water	2. Plenty of springs of fresh water (from another location in Declaration).	2. No fresh-water springs; fresh springs
3. Their habitation therefore in Dariena is pernicious and unwholesome only of the particular nature of the place … furthermore, where to ever they dig the ground the depth of a handful and a half there springeth out unwholesome and corrupt water of the nature of the river.	3. Because our fort (that lyeth as a semi-island) is most part environed with an ebbing and flowing of salt water, the ooze of which sendeth forth an unwholesome & contagious vapour...	3. I may not excuse this our fort, or Jamestown, as yet seated in some-what an unwholesome and sickly air.
4. No Parallel	4. The ooze (See above)	4. fed by the brackish river oozing into it
5. Unwholesome.... The contagion of the soil and heat of the sun, beside the corrupt water and infectious air by reason of venomous vapors	5. an unwholesome & contagious vapour	5. subject to many ill airs
6. They espied diverse islands replenished with sundry kinds of trees from which came fragrant savours of spices and sweet gums (5). From the trees and herbs whereof when the morning dews began to rise, there proceeded many sweet savours. (29)	6. As in the fields of Portugal, where the woods are replenished with more sweet barks, and odors, then they are in the pleasantest places of Florida.	6. DNA

Table 17.13. (cont.)		
7. Dariena [West Indies]	7. Kent, Essex, Jamestown, Florida, Portugal, West Indies	7. Kent, Jamestown, Virginia

To begin with, it is not difficult to see that *Declaration* is significantly closer to Eden than *Reportory* is. The author of *Declaration*—unlike Strachey—explicitly alludes to the "West Indies," "Portugal," and "Florida"—places named in Eden's book and consistent with the Iberian origins of his translations. The *Declaration* author formulates a contrasting response to Eden, advancing the generic advantages of Virginia, "where the woods are replenished with more sweet barks, and odors, than they are in the pleasantest places of Florida," and where unsalted meat does not putrefy, as it does in the West Indies. The deprecating comparison to the West Indies and the boast of the "sweet barks and odors" of Virginia, which excel those in Florida, show that the *Declaration* author is not merely copying from Eden, but is engaging an ideological battle with the Spanish interests represented in that book. In that regard he represents the official views of the Virginia Company and the cultural biases of England more generally.

Consistent with Strachey's willingness to criticize the Company's policies, his version is wholly disengaged from this international ideological debate. While the *Declaration* author is answering Eden directly, Strachey is not; yet he preserves language from *Declaration* that appears to have originated in Eden. This is only possible if *Reportory* is the last in a series of three texts.

Closer examination of the intriguing contrasts between the passage from *Declaration* and that from *Reportory* confirms that *Reportory* is the final document in the series. It will be noticed that both excerpts begin with a similar passage, but adopt very different points of view about its meaning. To the author of *Declaration*, "*no man ought to judge* of any country by its fens and Marshes (such as is the place where Jamestown stands)." Strachey, however, starts by stating that he "may not excuse" the choice of Jamestown as a location, because it is "seated in somewhat an unwholesome and sickly air." Just as *Declaration* is responding to Eden, one of these two texts is responding to the other. The further we dig, the more obvious it becomes that it is Strachey who is copying—and responding to—*Declaration*.

To start from their points of agreement, both Strachey and the author of *Declaration* ultimately agree with Eden that the whole should not be judged by its parts; just because Jamestown is sited in an unhealthy location is no reason to condemn all of Virginia as dangerous to the colonists' health. The two texts, however, arrive at this conclusion using different logic and following different paths. The *Declaration* author introduces it as part of his opening salvo that no one should judge a country by its marshes. As Strachey starts with a contrasting point of view, the comparison is of no service to him at the outset of his argument and appears instead in his conclusion, where, in his recapitulation, he comes round to the same position with which the *Declaration* passage began.

The least likely explanation for this is that *Declaration* is responding to Strachey, rather than Eden. As we have seen, several features of *Declaration* connect it directly to Eden, and could not have been transmitted via Strachey. What is more, these features are inflected to supply a response to their source text that would be irrelevant as a reply to Strachey, but makes perfect sense as an English nationalist response to Eden. Turning to Strachey, it is easy to imagine him setting out to counter the uncompromising official tone of *Declaration* and then realizing that the analogy to Kent would not serve this purpose. He is more interested in questioning than excusing the Company's decision to situate Jamestown in a marshy area. So he keeps the comparison to Kent in mind, and in his summation, when he wants to return to the idea with which *Declaration* had begun, he finally discovers a way to apply it.

The contrast in ideologies is also evident in the large block of text invented in each that has no parallel in the other. The *Declaration* author supplements the healthful and encouraging experience of Captain West at the falls with a discussion of the fact that salted meat will go unspoiled in Virginia but not the West Indies; Strachey instead relates the diseases Jamestown colonists acquired and argues that if the settlement had been located elsewhere they might have "escaped" these afflictions.

That these differences cannot easily be accounted for on the hypothesis that *Declaration* was copying Strachey becomes further evident when we compare their treatments of the episode of Captain West and his men at the James River falls. To the *Declaration* author the survival of the James River Company supplies "infallible proof" of the healthiness of the Virginia climate. Strachey is more reticent in his endorsement, offering only that we have "some experience ... to persuade ourselves that it may be so." The example again not only confirms the dependence of one text on another, but reveals the differing points of view each brings to a common topic. Most significantly, the *Reportory* James River passage contains a curious and consequential textual variant regarding the number of men in Captain West's company (Table 17.14). Strachey's text reads here "four hundred and odd," while in *Declaration* the number

> ## Table 17.14. Strachey, After Altering "an Hundred and Odd" to "Four Hundred and Odd," Made the Necessary Further Emendation of Dropping the Consequent Non-Sequitur, "of All These Two Hundred"
>
> | Declaration | Reportory |
> |---|---|
> | we have an infallible proof of the temper of the country, for of an hundred and odd which were seated at the Falls under the government of Captain Francis West, and of an hundred to the seaward on the south side of the river, (in the country of Nansemonds) *under the charge of Captain John Martin, of all these two hundred* there did not so much as one man miscarry. (14) | And some experience we have to persuade ourselves that it may be so, for of four hundred and odd men which were seated at the Falls the last year when the fleet came in with fresh and young able spirits under the government of Captain Francis West, and of one hundred to the seawards (on the south side of our river), in the country of the Nansemonds *under the charge of Captain John Martin, there did not so much as one man miscarry.* (83) |

is given as "an hundred and odd." That "an hundred and odd" is the more reliable number may be ascertained by cross-checking with Percy, who was not only present in Virginia at the time, but was also Assistant Governor of the Colony, and is probably the ultimate origin of both later versions. He gives the number as "one hundred and forty."[38]

Reedy seems to have realized an implication to this discrepancy that is unfavorable to his position: The evidence suggests that Strachey changed *Declaration*'s "an hundred and odd" to "four hundred and odd." If the *Declaration* author had relied upon Strachey, he should have reproduced Strachey's error. Unless some expedient can be devised, the fact that *Declaration* is closer to Percy while Strachey is the outlier means that Strachey must, once again, be placed at the far end of any hypothetical provenance chain. To solve the problem Reedy argues that "four hundred and odd" is a compositor's misreading of an original variant in Strachey's manuscript, which he reconstructs as "some hundred and odd." According to Reedy, "the compositor misread the initial English long 's' as an 'f' and interpreted the medial minims as 'ur.'"[39]

This conjecture, though clever, is incorrect, as closer comparative analysis of the two passages reveals. In both passages the men stationed at the falls are bracketed with another hundred, "to the seaward" in the "country of the Nansemonds." Both groups of men, in both versions, are under the charge of Captain John Martin, and in *Declaration* the total number of men under

Martin's charge is explicitly given as "two hundred." This calculation, however, is omitted in Strachey's text.

Although the omission is not consistent with Reedy's theory of compositorial error, it is consistent with the theory that Strachey himself altered "one hundred and odd" to "four hundred and odd," especially as he tends to enjoy exaggeration.[40] A full review of the circumstance shows why. Having made the error that Reedy attributes to him, why would a compositor pause over the logical contradiction introduced by the fact that 400 + 100 does not equal 200, and make the necessary emendation? Only an author (or editor) would concern himself with such a contradiction.[41] It would appear that Strachey trumped up the facts to emphasize his point about the absence of disease at the falls, but then was forced to amend the latter passage to preserve the logical coherence of his account. In doing so, he inadvertently left traces of his changes that exonerate his compositor from the error that Reedy imputes to him. In the transcript supplied in his *RES* article, Reedy acknowledges his own editorial activism in altering Strachey's printed text to "some hundred and odd." The modern transcript he prepared for the Virtual Jamestown website, on the other hand, changes the wording of Strachey's text without notice to the reader.[42] One can only hope that this is an oversight.

As we have seen, many reasons invalidate Reedy's claim that *Reportory* must have influenced the composition of *Declaration*. These include the existence of possible shared (but now lost) sources for *Reportory* and *Declaration* as well as several compelling details of textual comparison between the texts themselves. On the contrary, an examination of Reedy's methods warrants the conclusion that Strachey was copying *Declaration*. The likelihood of attributing everything, as Reedy does, to Strachey's seminal influence, becomes progressively more implausible as further relevant details are brought into focus. While it was less detailed and comprehensive than the present analysis, our original *RES* article arrived at the same conclusion: if Strachey copied from either Smith or *Declaration* in constructing *Reportory*, then the theory of *Reportory*'s July 1610 completion in Virginia is shattered.

18

A "Just So" Story

Perhaps the most creative element in Vaughan's defense of the "standard thesis" involves an imaginative (and imaginary) scenario invoked to explain the last days of Strachey's manuscript in Virginia before it left — as he believes — downriver on its way to England on Gates' return voyage. Throughout his narrative Vaughan is anxious to place Strachey's manuscript in Shakespeare's hands by any expedient means. To this end, nothing can be allowed to stand in the way of his belief that the narrative *must have* departed on the Gates ship. In truth of course Strachey himself was in no hurry to transmit his narrative because he had no idea that his future reputation would depend on the theory of his influence on *The Tempest*. The *Reportory* passage immediately preceding the concluding interpolation from *Declaration* describes the departure of Sir Thomas Gates on this return voyage:

> And the fifteenth day of July, in the "Blessing," Captain Adams brought [the king of Warraskoyak, Sasenticum, one of his chief men, and his son Kainta] to Point Comfort, where at that time (as well to take his leave of the lieutenant general, Sir Thomas Gates, now bound for England, as to dispatch the ships) the lord governor and captain general had pitched his tent at Algernon Fort. The king's son, Kainta, the lord governor and captain general hath sent now into England until the ships arrive here again the next spring, dismissing the old werowance and the other with all terms of kindness and friendship, promising further designs to be effected by him, to which he hath bound himself by divers savage ceremonies and admirations.[1]

According to Vaughan, the phrase "now bound for England" means that the ships were anchored at Point Comfort but "ready to cross Chesapeake Bay and enter the Atlantic as soon as winds and tide permit."[2] During the interim, they were able to "take on whatever small cargo went down the river that day, *almost certainly* including several letters besides Strachey's."[3]

This scenario, which Vaughan argues not with factual evidence but with definitions, is at best implausible. To begin with, both "now" and "bound

185

for" are ambiguous. They can either mean — as Vaughan prefers — that a ship is waiting to leave, *or* that it has already left port. "Bound for" can even mean that a ship is in mid-ocean as many examples from the period attest.[4] Even the *Tempest* uses the word in a way that evidently contradicts Vaughan's creative interpretation:

> And for the rest o' th' fleet
> (Which I dispers'd), they have all met again,
> And are upon the Mediterranean float
> *Bound* sadly home *for* Naples... [1.2.232–37]

In a pattern we have noticed over and again in both Reedy and Vaughan's critiques of our work, Vaughan's definition of "now,"[5] misleadingly, omits all *OED* definitions except for the one that supports his case, effectively depriving the reader of the opportunity to consider for him or herself which definitions are most pertinent to the passage.[6] Omission of relevant *OED* definitions is, however, only one of several flaws in Vaughan's argument which, collectively, completely undermine it. Even more interesting is the final sentence describing the sailing of Gates' fleet: "The king's son, Kainta, the Lord Governor and Captain General, *hath sent now* into England until the ships arrive here again the next spring."[7] Based on comparative evidence, the most natural interpretation is that the passage was written after the mid–July 1610 sailing of the fleet. The writer seems to have been either still in America (with his unfinished manuscript), or possibly back in England positioning himself as still in America for the edification of an actual or imagined noble patron; in either case, the usage "hath sent" places the action squarely in the past.[8] Strachey, himself, writing of what one must assume is the July 15 departure (as there is no mention anywhere of other ships going to England in July), uses a similar construction to indicate past action:

> The ninth of July (1610), [Gates] prepared his forces, and early in the morning set upon a town of [the Indians], some four miles from Algernon Fort, called Kecoughtan, and had soon taken it without loss or hurt of any of his men. The governor and his women fled (the young King Powhatan's son not being there), but left his poor baggage and treasure to the spoil of our soldiers; which was only a few baskets of old wheat and some other of peas and beans, a little tobacco, and some few women's girdles of silk, of the grass silk, not without art and much neatness finely wrought; of which *I have sent* divers into England (being at the taking of the town), and *would have sent* Your Ladyship some of them *had* they been a present so worthy.[9]

It is noteworthy that Vaughan (together with Reedy), while purporting to disprove the part of our argument that relies on internal sign to date the completion of *Reportory* after the July 15 sailing, cannot bring himself to mention this passage, let alone be concerned to rebut its reasonable, straight-forward implications. He is wise to avoid it, since in itself it supplies com-pelling grounds for rejecting the traditional scenario that Strachey's document as later published by Purchas returned to England on the July 1610 Gates voy-age. Strachey's "would have sent" is in the conditional perfect tense; when added to the perfect "have sent," it confirms unambiguously that the described events are both past and completed; the ships have already sailed, and Strachey is excusing himself, after the fact, for not having sent any of the girdles to the "noble lady."

In place of such textual analysis, which in myriad ways undermines his assumptions, Vaughan proceeds by constructing an elaborate imaginative nar-ration: "Officials at Point Comfort," we are informed, "communicated [during this period] intermittently with Jamestown by small vessel."[10] Vaughan asserts that Strachey completed his missive on July 15 at Jamestown, "perhaps early in the day," and that "several letters besides Strachey's" were "almost certainly"[11] transmitted on the same boat while the ships were waiting at Point Comfort for the right sailing conditions. The qualification "early in the day" reveals that Vaughan is not entirely ignoring the physical realities of navigation on the James River; he is trying to create time in his scenario for the transmission of the document. The attempt fails because Vaughan's scenario is impossible. The trip of over forty miles from Jamestown to Point Comfort, upriver or downriver, would likely have taken around two days (See Figure 18.1).[12] Vaughan's scenario is, however, necessary to justify the conviction that Stra-chey sent the manuscript downriver from Jamestown to the departing ship.

Vaughan is also confident about Strachey's physical location, placing him without qualification in Jamestown on July 15, with Gates and De La Warr downriver at Point Comfort. But how could Strachey from Jamestown have known when the ships, which in Vaughan's scenario were waiting for ideal conditions, actually departed? Such empirical evidence as we have suggests that Strachey was already with either Gates or De La Warr at Point Comfort when the ships were preparing to depart. In *Reportory*, Strachey places himself four miles from Algernon Fort, near to the mouth of the James River and Point Comfort (about two days by boat from Jamestown) on July 9.[13] As the Colony's secretary, moreover, he seems more likely to have been with De La Warr at Point Comfort during the critical period immediately prior to the sailing of the ships than upriver in Jamestown.

Nothing in Vaughan's scenario has even a slight anchorage in fact. He has not demonstrated that Strachey was in Jamestown, that the "letter" was finished, or that it was transmitted by water from Jamestown to the ship, yet now it has become a historical fact that several other letters have "almost certainly" joined the *Reportory* manuscript on its wholly hypothetical down-river voyage. Once again, the convenient phrase, "almost certainly," covers a multitude of errors, transmuting conjecture into fact by ignoring physical reality. One wonders if, after taking note of the tide and the weather, the helmsman was obliged to delay for another two days for Strachey's very important document and entourage of ghostly letters to wend their way to Point Comfort.

One may also wonder why Vaughan goes to such lengths to invent a scenario in which Strachey's document (as later published in Purchas) was transmitted downriver from Jamestown to Point Comfort at the last minute before the Gates ships departed on or about July 15. In part the scenario is an expedient to counter the straightforward, intuitively satisfying, proposition that a version of B, not *Reportory*, returned to England on Gates' voyage.[14] Another answer, however, is that Vaughan is anxious to reconcile a troubling anomaly in Strachey's new world narratives that endangers the "standard thesis." At issue is an anecdote, recounted in both *Reportory* and *Travel* but in different versions, about an Indian boy who Strachey claims was being sent to England on the Gates voyage. In *Reportory* the son of the local chief Sasenticum, Kainta, leaves for England on one of the departing ships, probably The Blessing. In *Travel*, however, the native son — now named Tangoit and with a different father, Tackonekintaco — does not go to England, but is substituted for a nephew who is imprisoned on the ship the *Delawarr*, but escapes.

These differing versions pose problems for Vaughan, even though he is confident that both refer to the same event "because it happened in 1610 at Point Comfort just before Newport left for England with Gates."[15] Vaughan's scenario of the ships transporting *Reportory* downriver at the last minute while Strachey remained in Jamestown is constructed partly to solve the riddle of why Strachey would present the same episode in significantly different versions. While still in Jamestown, in other words, Strachey was misinformed, but by the time he wrote *Travel*, he knew the real story. This scenario has a double attraction for Vaughan. It not only obviates the need to question Strachey's reliability as a historical witness but also allows Vaughan to convert the discrepancy into an attempted *coup de grace* to our view that *Reportory* was not placed in its final form until after Strachey had returned to England:

> Strachey *must have* learned the first of these details after he put his letter aboard the Blessing or the Hercules and *he may not have heard the whole story until the ships were on the Atlantic and de La Warre was back at Jamestown.* Had Strachey had the opportunity, he would, *of course,* have corrected his account of the negotiations with Powhatan....[16]

Vaughan may be uncompromising in 2008 that the *Travel* version must be the correct one, but as recently as 2006 he was far less certain:

Perhaps a third Powhatan visitor [to England] was Kainta, son of a local chief, captured by the English during the intermittent hostilities and — again, according to Strachey — "sent now [c. July 1610] into England, until the ships arrive here again the next Spring." But Kainta may not have left Chesapeake Bay. Strachey's subsequent account of the Chief's son [in *Travel*] relates that the English accepted a substitute hostage, who soon escaped. There is not further evidence.[17]

Vaughan's admission that "there is no further evidence"[18] is his way of acknowledging that the sole source of this dramatic anecdote, in either version, is William Strachey. It appears nowhere else in the Bermuda narratives; nor could we find any account in England of the arrival of such a hostage in 1610. It is difficult to avoid the impression that Vaughan has prematurely foreclosed the critical question of Strachey's reliability. As we have seen, Strachey makes a habit of embroidering his narratives with dramatic episodes that seem to have little to do with actual events as recorded by other eyewitnesses, but instead appear to have been imported from other texts. In this case, there is for starters the discrepancy in names. Strachey disagrees with himself about the name of the Captain who transported the Indians to Point Comfort. In *Reportory* it is Adams, and in *Travel* Newport.[19] There is also a discrepancy in the names of the native father and son involved in the episode. Vaughan hastens to assure readers that this discrepancy is irrelevant, since natives often had more than one name: "The names of two Indians, but not their identities, are different."[20] However, authorities on early Virginia history contradict Vaughan's assertion: According to Lyon Gardiner Tyler, Sasenticum and Tackonekintaco were *not* the same person, Sasenticum being a minor Werowance of village of Mathomank on Burwell's Bay.[21] John Bennett Boddie agrees (using the same language), adding that Tackonekintaco was the Werowance of Karraskoyak (Warraskoyak).[22] These two sites, both located on the western bank of the James downriver from Jamestown,[23] are clearly marked on Smith's map as different villages (Figure 18.1).

Perhaps the most damaging contradiction in Vaughan's account is, however, also the most obvious: if Strachey was not at Point Comfort to begin with, how would he have known that a native youth — by any name — had been taken prisoner? Since Mathomank was downriver from Jamestown, the ship carrying the Werowance, his son, and "one of his chief men" could not have passed by it on its way to Port Comfort. In Strachey's account, the captives arrived at Point Comfort on July 15, the same day that, according to Vaughan, Strachey completed his manuscript[24] and sent it down river — on a voyage that, as we have seen, would have required two days.[25] Obviously, this scenario does not work.

Finally, it deserves to be noted that Vaughan's theory requires the Virginia

Figure 18.1. Detail of Smith's map (courtesy Library of Congress Kraus Collection).

Colony secretary to have sent back on the Gates' voyage back to England an account of "Kainta" that everyone on board the ship would have known to be false. If, as Vaughan also assures us, Strachey was laboring to ingratiate himself with the leadership of the Virginia Company, this hardly seems like an effective strategy.

Such compounded problems suggest that there may be another explanation for the varying versions of Strachey's account than Vaughan's brittle scenario, which not only invokes contradictions he does not acknowledge, but uses the *assumption* of Strachey's reliability as a historical narrator to underwrite a scenario that otherwise suffers from its own damaging contradictions. In considering this alternative, it may be worth recalling Vaughan's own admission that although "Strachey related many events he had witnessed

... he also borrowed freely, unashamedly, and often without specific attribution."[26] In this case, it looks as though both versions of his account may actually represent Strachey's creative rearrangement, to suit his own purposes, of two previous episodes that, *according to several other independent sources*, actually took place not in 1610, but in 1608 and 1609. It would even appear that the discrepancies between Strachey's two versions result, not from the circumstances recounted in Vaughan's "just so" story, but from Strachey's habitual copying.

A spring 1608 dispatch to Spain by Spanish ambassador Don Pedro De Zuniga chronicles an episode in which Powhatan exchanged a young Indian, Namontack, said to be a son of the chief but more likely his servant, for an English youth named Thomas Savage. Namontack was put aboard Newport's ship in early 1608 and taken to England, from whence he later returned. These events survive in several slightly differing accounts,[27] including one by John Smith. Table 18.1 compares Strachey's account with Smith's:

Table 18.1. Comparison of *Proceedings* with Strachey's *Reportory* (1610–12)

Smith	Strachey
With many pretty Discourses to renew their old acquaintance, this great King [Powhatan] and our Captain spent the time, till the ebb left our Barge aground. Then renewing their feasts with feats, dancing and singing, and such like mirth, we quartered that night with Powhatan. The next day Newport came ashore and received as much content as those people could give him: a boy named Thomas Savage was then given unto Powhatan, whom Newport called his son; for whom Powhatan gave him Namontack his trusty servant, and one of a shrewd, subtle capacity. Three or four days more we spent in feasting, dancing, and trading, wherein Powhatan carried himself so proudly, yet discreetly (in his Savage manner) as made us all admire his natural gifts, considering his education.[28] (216)	And the fifteenth day of July, in the "Blessing," Captain Adams [the king of Warraskoyak, Sasenticum, and his son Kainta] to Point Comfort, where at that time (as well to take his leave of the lieutenant general, Sir Thomas Gates, now bound for England, as to dispatch the ships) the lord governor and captain general had pitched his tent at Algernon Fort. The king's son, Kainta, the lord governor and captain general hath sent now into England until the ships arrive here again the next spring, dismissing the old werowance and the other with all terms of kindness and friendship, promising further designs to be effected by him, to which he hath bound himself by divers savage ceremonies and admirations. (94)

Another incident from around 1609, recorded by George Percy in his
True Relation, might have inspired Strachey's *Travel* version, in which the
native boy escapes the fate of being brought to England by jumping ship and
possibly drowning. Compare the two passages.

Table 18.2. Comparison of Percy's Account (1609) of the Escaped Native Boy with Strachey's (1612)

Percy's True Relation *(1609–1612)*	*Strachey's* History of Travel *(1612)*
Captain Martin did appoint with half of our men to take the Island ... Martin seized the king's son and one other Indian and brought them bound unto the Island where I was, when a ship boy, taking up a pistol accidentally, not meaning any harm, the pistol suddenly fired and shot the Savage prisoner into the breast. And thereupon what with his passion and fear he broke the cords asunder where with he was tied and did swim over unto the main with his wound bleeding.[29] (263)	The imposture nephew, privy beforehand to the falsehood of the old man, watching his opportunity, leapt overboard one night (being kept in the Delawarr); and to be more sure of him at that time, fettered both legs together, and a sea gown upon him, yet he adventured to get clear by swimming, and either to recover the south shore, or to sink in the attempt. Which of either was his fortune we know not, only (if he miscarried) we never found his body nor gown... (58)

Although there is no final proof that either of these incidents was the
inspiration for Strachey's accounts in *Reportory* and *Travel,* it is interesting to
note the similarities. It should also be remembered that it is to Strachey, and
Strachey alone, that we owe record of an Indian boy (by any name) on the
verge of being transported to England on Gates' boat, whereas the 1608
"Namontack" anecdote is mentioned by several independent sources, and so
definitely appears to be factual. In his dedication of *Travel* to the Earl of
Northumberland, moreover, Strachey admits that he has borrowed material
from Percy, "your noble brother (from whose commentaries and observations
I must freely confess I have collected these passages and knowledges) out of
his free and honorable love for me."[30]

If these were the only such discrepancies in Strachey's narratives, we
would be inclined to ignore them. However, we have also seen that Strachey's
is the only contemporaneous account of the Bermuda wreck that includes reference to St. Elmo's Fire, the decision to cut down the main mast, the throwing
overboard of all the luggage, and the possible splitting of the ship, not to
mention that his account reflects the known imprint of a conventional "storm

formula."[31] Based on this fact pattern, the reader may be forgiven for concluding that Vaughan is at least right about one thing. Strachey "borrowed freely and unashamedly" from other sources — including both John Smith and George Percy — in order to enhance the literary appeal of his narratives. He frequently did so, moreover, at the expense of historical accuracy.

Vaughan's elaborate narrative, on the other hand, seems to be a necessary adjunct to the "standard thesis." It serves the critical rhetorical function of not only enabling, but conveniently *requiring* the manuscript of *Reportory* to have been returned to London on the summer 1610 crossing, in time for Shakespeare to consult it and write a play before the November 1, 1611, *Tempest* production. Through such a method Rudyard Kipling recounted how the leopard got its spots. The difference is that Kipling knew his was a fanciful tale; he did not pretend to be engaging in scholarly inquiry or debate.

19

The Myth of
Strachey's Influence

To Shakespearean traditionalists such as Alden Vaughan and Tom Reedy, Strachey's *True Reportory* is like the handkerchief in *Othello*. They don't consider where it came from or how it happened to be found, but they are confident that they know what it means. Only two pages into Vaughan's article, it is already "*almost certain* that two or more manuscript versions of Strachey's letter circulated within the Company and, presumably, among some of its friends"[1] shortly after Gates arrived in London. Throughout his entertaining story, Vaughan keeps upping the ante: By the conclusion of his narrative it has become a "*virtual certainty* that Strachey's letter reached London in September 1610" and an "*overwhelming probability*" that at least two copies circulated widely among company officials and their friends."[2] One of the earliest beneficiaries, of course, was Richard Hakluyt, who, we are assured, "had immediate access" to Strachey's manuscript[3]; another was the author of *Declaration*, presumably revising his work for publication, who likewise "*almost certainly* had a copy of Strachey's letter on hand as he wrote the Company's apologia."[4] Variations on the phrase "almost certain" constitute one of Vaughan's favorite expressions. He readily employs it as a substitute for actual evidence, to bolster a critical point in a scenario that is wholly lacking in independent verification, and is sometimes impossible.

Indeed, a reader soon learns that the "facts" that underwrite the validity of Vaughan's narrative are, like those employed to describe how Strachey's "letter" found its way downriver from Jamestown to Point Comfort on 15 July 1610, either incapable of demonstration or downright erroneous. According to Vaughan, "*Reportory* [in manuscript form] must have been widely read, often aloud," and "we can only surmise about the form in which Shakespeare encountered it."[5] But the statements that *Reportory* was widely circulated, was "often read aloud" or was read at all, or even that it was completed in time to be Shakespeare's chief *Tempest* source, are no more than surmise, unsupported by any evidence.

The fact that no manuscript copy of *Reportory* survives does not inspire confidence in Vaughan's belief that it circulated widely outside of the immediate Strachey-Hakluyt circle,[6] but there are other troubles with Vaughan's scenario as well. By his own count,[7] as many as eight other versions of the Bermuda shipwreck eventually circulated in Jacobean England. With that in mind, it is striking how little *Reportory* agrees in many essentials with other primary accounts of the Bermuda wreck. Vaughan acknowledges that published works such as Jourdain's exercised a manifest influence on such secondary accounts as Hughes' 1615 *Letter Sent into England from the Summer Islands*.[8] Given these circumstances, one must wonder why none of the other contemporaneous accounts follow Strachey's idiosyncratic version of the storm or mention the noteworthy occurrence of St. Elmo's fire.

Ironically, then, the weakest link in Vaughan's argument—notwithstanding its frequent repetition in the *Tempest* literature and widespread acceptance—is the notion that Strachey's narrative is provably foundational for *The Tempest*. Vaughan assures us of the "virtual certainty" that Strachey's manuscript made it to England in time to be edited and revised by Hakluyt and then somehow passed off to Shakespeare during the winter of 1610–11. But what use did Shakespeare make of this gift? Unless there is independent evidence "from sign" for Strachey's influence—unambiguous, parallel phraseology or distinctive shared ideas found in both texts and no other—Vaughan's convoluted argument that Shakespeare could have seen *Reportory* is pointless. If such independent evidence really existed, we would know that Shakespeare somehow saw the document, and could willingly suspend disbelief as to how it happened.

The plausibility of Vaughan's narrative therefore depends, ultimately, on the assumption that Strachey's influence on the play is beyond dispute. "Most readers of *The Tempest*," he assures us, "have found its congruities with the close at hand 'True Reportory' too numerous and too vivid to be coincidental"[9]; and "the abundant thematic and verbal parallels" between the play and *Reportory* "have persuaded generations of readers that Shakespeare borrowed liberally from Strachey's dramatic narrative."[10] Consequently, "it is beyond the scope of this essay to trace every resonance of Strachey's letter in Shakespeare's play."[11] Instead, like Hume, Vaughan falls back on the tradition that "the Shakespeare connection ... is a non-issue. That the playwright took his theme from accounts of the wreck and salvation of Summers' company ... *cannot be doubted*."[12] But, while Vaughan and Hume agree that Strachey's influence on Shakespeare is beyond doubt, and that both versions of the Strachey manuscript reached England by 1610, they disagree about which of them Shakespeare read. Indeed, Hume throws a monkey wrench into the traditional view of Shakespeare's dependence on a manuscript version of *Reportory* by insisting that B is as plausible a Shakespearean source as Strachey's published version:

> Although there is no unequivocal proof that Shakespeare used Strachey's account whereon to build his play, *there is equal likelihood* that it was the "B" rather than the [*Reportory*] text that provided the bard with his inspiration.[13]

Vaughan disagrees, and cites three reasons for adhering to the traditional view that *Reportory* must have been Shakespeare's source. These include Strachey's "brief reference to Queen Dido,"[14] and his "description of Governor Gates' gentle treatment of Indians in Virginia until he was 'startled' by the murder of a colonist"[15] (which Vaughan identifies "as a parallel, perhaps, to Prospero's handling of Caliban before he abused Miranda").[16] Most important, however, is that "close comparison of the *Tempest*'s storm with the two versions of Strachey's letter shows *a higher frequency* of overlap with the text of 1625."[17] This final statement appears without a footnote and is a classic example of what David Hackett Fischer terms the "fallacy of statistical nonsense," or the use of "statistical mumbo jumbo" which is "in context, literally meaningless."[18]

The disagreement between Vaughan and Hume illustrates the subjective character of the standards traditionally used for evaluating *Tempest* sources, which implicitly endorse the use of such empty phrases as "higher frequency of overlap" without requiring any justification. An absence of analytical standards has plagued the case for the influence of the Bermuda documents on Shakespeare since its earliest phases when Sylvester Jourdain — not B or *Reportory*— was claimed to be the vector of influence. While we ultimately concur with Vaughan's negative verdict on the plausibility of B's influence, his arguments in favor of *Reportory* are hardly more convincing. The association between Aeneas and the New World was a commonplace idiom (found, among other sources, in Eden's *Decades*— see Chapter 2); likewise, as we have seen, the theme of conflict between native and colonist is repeated in various New World accounts.

In other words, even if one were to concede the possibility that some version of the *Reportory* manuscript made it to Shakespeare's hands in time to spark his imagination, we must ask whether there is a case to be made for the actual influence of *Reportory* on *Tempest*. Ironically, it is far weaker than its advocates are willing to admit. To substantiate this claim for a "higher frequency of overlap," Vaughan refers readers to "three lengthy assessments"— Morton Luce's 1901 "Parallel Passages" appended to the Arden *Tempest*, Robert Ralston Cawley's 1926 *PMLA* survey,[19] and David Kathman's 1996 internet list.[20] Some fallacies of the latter have already been noted in Chapter 2. More generally, the skeptical reader must ask how well any of these studies have actually documented evidence "from sign" that can connect *The Tempest*, in particular and idiosyncratic detail, to Strachey's narrative.[21] Do they even consider alternative sources that could have furnished Shakespeare with details allegedly derived from Strachey?

Vaughan fails to address these questions. Instead, after assuring us that his three authorities have already demonstrated the point beyond reasonable doubt, he proceeds to compile his own "supplemental" list of alleged "thematic parallels"—claiming, for example, that in both texts "the island refuge is bountiful but troubled by storm and rife with danger from its other denizens."[22] One is at a loss to understand what "other denizens" of Bermuda threatened the English survivors in Strachey's narrative, as the islands were uninhabited when they arrived. Likewise, Vaughan inaccurately asserts that in both texts "everyone aboard miraculously survives, while the remainder of both fleets sail safely toward their destinations."[23] He has apparently forgotten that, in Strachey's narrative, another ship of the Third Supply also failed to arrive in Jamestown and was presumed lost.[24]

Vaughan prefers to avoid specific linguistic comparisons and rests his case instead on these types of vague "thematic parallels." "In both texts," he asserts, "conspiracies among the shipwrecked Europeans threaten the lives of the leaders and the islands' tranquility."[25] But our analysis of the influence of Richard Eden's *De Orbe Novo* (see Chapters 2 through 4) shows the same pattern, narrating numerous conspiratorial plots of conquistadors and natives in the New World.

Vaughan also finds it significant that in both *Reportory* and *Tempest* ships were separated from the mother fleet. He fails to understand that the separation of ships in a fleet during a storm was a frequent occurrence, and was therefore a commonplace of voyager literature. More specifically, as earlier noted, this argument has been anachronistic since 1874, when Elze, pointing out the flaws in Malone's theory of Jourdain's influence, noted that both Columbus and Drake experienced a similar division of their fleets.[26]

Although Shakespeare could thus in theory have drawn from any one of several accounts of such a circumstance, close comparison with the language of the same Pygafetta account from which he took the idea of "spritely" St. Elmo's fire, as we have seen, verifies that the real source of this *Tempest* motif is not Strachey, but Eden. (Table 19.1):

Table 19.1. Pygafetta in Eden and *Tempest* 1.2.232.–35

Eden

... by reason whereof, they so wandered out of their course and were *dispersed in sunder*, that they in manner dispaired to *meet again*. But as God willed, *the seas and tempest being quieted*, they came safely to their determined course... (217v)

Tempest

and for the rest o' th' fleet
(Which I dispers'd), they *have all met again*,
And are upon the Mediterranean float
Bound sadly home for Naples...
(1.2.232–35)

The thematic "parallels" which Vaughan attributes to Strachey are likewise either based on misconceptions or are more aptly supplied by alternative sources, especially Eden.[27] Based on such considerations, we had already concluded in 2005 that

> The evidence for Shakespeare's alleged reliance on Strachey's Bermuda narrative can no longer be accepted as substantive. In nearly every case cited the earlier sources or Shakespeare himself supply as good or better examples of intertextuality.[28] The possibility that Shakespeare relied instead, primarily, on some combination of the noted sources — Eden and either Ariosto or Erasmus — all available to him much earlier than 1611 — can no longer be dismissed.[29]

Postscript:
Something Rich and Strange

Oscar Wilde once said that history does not repeat itself, but historians do. Among the most striking findings of our study has been to discover how predictably, and with what scant justification, the myth of Strachey's influence on *The Tempest* has been repeated, purely or substantially on the basis of argument from authority. Over and again it was claimed that this influence has "already been proven" and therefore requires no demonstration. Scholarship accordingly consisted not only of repeating that answer with renewed conviction in every passing generation, but insuring that no one deviated from it and that those who insisted on rational demonstration were marginalized and disciplined.

Thus, in the process of writing the essays which eventually transmogrified into some chapters of the present book, we found that it was impossible to present evidence contradicting the "standard thesis" at either the World Shakespeare Congress or the Shakespeare Association of America. After we were invited to present at both conferences, organizers rescinded their invitations and then engaged in a protracted email correspondence that made it clear that their constituencies (at least in their opinion) were not interested in new research on the sources of *The Tempest*. They already knew the answer. Asking them to question it appeared to be tantamount to challenging the value of the laborious process of the advanced training required to enter the guild of Shakespeare professionals.

This confidence in the "Strachey solution" began early, before the thorough professionalization of Shakespearean studies that took place during the 20th century. Gayley was certain by 1917 that we had "already sufficient evidence that [Shakespeare] knew his Strachey from first page to last."[1] For this reason, asserted Gayley, it was unnecessary to consider the sources of the play's character names. As we have seen, this was an expedient omission: the names in the play are most likely derived from Richard Eden's 1555 travelogue, where even Gayley admits they occur.[2] Ironically, the likely origins of the names in Eden had been well established in the literature more than twenty five years before, and it had been known since 1778 that the most significant of all these names, Setebos, originated in Eden and/or Willes. But instead of considering the implications of this tradition, Gayley assures the reader that the question is irrelevant, since Strachey is already known to be Shakespeare's source. This illogical circumlocution not only masked the problem of proof, but also set forth a kind of template that later scholars imitated. Maintaining the Strachey myth required an extensive process of the exclusion of contrary evidence of all kinds. Over decades, editions of the play progressively deleted reference to the evidence originally assembled in Furness' 1892 survey, which had contradicted the idea of Strachey's influence by suggesting a significantly earlier date for the play.

Throughout this book we have striven to adopt a more flexible posture toward the knowledge of the past, preserving what seems valuable and declining to omit conceivably relevant data without cause or notice. We have accordingly subjected past opinion to critical cross-examination, and wherever alleged facts or inferences seemed doubtful we have offered alternatives. By the same token, we have discovered many opportunities to re-synthesize the insights of our predecessors, and wherever possible we have noted how ideas elaborated in our book were foreshadowed by their scholarship. We were especially impressed by the prominent role accorded to Eden as a *Tempest* source in studies by H.H. Furness, Frank Kermode, and Charles Frey. E.K. Chambers, in insisting on preserving the possible significance of *Die Schöne Sidea*'s intertextuality with *The Tempest,* even though its implications ran contrary to his own conclusions, effectively endorsed a commitment to the provisional nature of all authentic scholarship. Likewise, our inquiry was greatly enriched by the work of scholars of early-modern liturgical drama such as R. Christopher Hassel, Grace Hall, and François Laroque, who inspired and lent substance to our close reading of the play's Shrovetide symbolism. This discovery of the merits of prior scholarship even extends to some whom we otherwise have been obliged to criticize. Thus, while the book contains many criticisms of Alden Vaughan's 2008 *Shakespeare Quarterly* response to our work, we found much of value in Vaughan and Vaughan's 1999 Arden edition of the *Tempest,* especially their astute observation of the peripatetic pattern of the play's action — which as we noted corresponds to the play's structural conceit of an island labyrinth, an integral element of our argument for its Shrovetide design and symbolism.

Above all, we have found that honest scholarship means always being willing to reconsider a problem from first principles after clearing away what Francis Bacon called "the idols of the theatre." In this case, suspending the assumptions of the "already proven" was a fruitful exercise: not only did we uncover a cornucopia of new evidence linking *The Tempest* to Eden's travel narratives and confirming the play's earlier existence, but stumbled — with the assistance of Richard Malim — onto an inquiry that eventually revealed the play's fascinating and hitherto entirely unsuspected Shrovetide ambience.

Inevitably this discovery process involved controversy, and among the most potentially controversial choices of the book was our decision to include a detailed response to the criticisms of the arguments of our original *Review of English Studies* article, the rough draft of our present argument that Strachey's *Reportory* in the form published in 1625 seems not to have been completed until 1612. Having been denied the opportunity to present our findings at two professional conferences, the two journals in which Alden Vaughan and Tom Reedy published their critiques also denied us a right of reply. We labored many hours over the chapters that respond to Reedy and Vaughan, reviewing the data and wrestling with every textual or historical enigma we encountered.

To this task we brought two very different skill sets and experience. One of us was adept at cross-examining allegedly historical narratives for plausibility; she was not only quick to spot subtle connections between two or more ostensibly unconnected texts but skilled at puncturing a purportedly historical scenario that violated the axioms of navigation and the evidence of the history of transportation. The other was more experienced at putting together ideas in an academic context and anticipating some of the possible obstacles to further research. Together we undertook a highly technical inquiry aimed at determining, among other things, the correct order of three documents — *Declaration, Map, and Reportory*— each belonging to a previously undetermined sequence of influence.

In some cases, reconstructing such a problem might be easy. In this one, it proved challenging. Yet the more we revisited the problem, the more certain we became of our conclusion. All the evidence pointed in the same direction. When William Strachey was writing about the diseases at Jamestown and the number of men at the falls, he showed himself to be a poor student of history, altering facts in ways that others knew were not true. There were not four hundred men at the falls. There were only a hundred and odd. Likewise, meticulous comparison of accounts of Smith's *Map* with *Reportory* and *Travel* ultimately revealed compelling evidence of Strachey's dependence on Smith's version. Such evidence clearly supported the conclusion that Strachey's manuscript was completed subsequent to the appearance of both *Declaration* and Smith's *Map*.

Concluding our study affords the opportunity to reflect on some paradoxes of the research journey. Although our *RES* article elicited a dramatic response, a subsequent 2009 publication in *Critical Survey*, in which we detailed the impressive evidence supporting the significance of Eden as a major *Tempest* source, has been largely passed over in silence by the Shakespearean mainstream[3] for over three years, despite the fact that its implications are at least as damaging to the "standard thesis" of Strachey's influence on the play as our first article. By any reasonable standard we demonstrated a level and profundity of Eden's influence on *The Tempest* that is far greater than that claimed for any other potential "New World" source.

Of course, the responses to our book will be as varied as opinions about Shakespeare — and that is how it should be, for although one can be forced in school to read anything, even the "stubborn bear, authority" cannot crush the independent spirit of inquiry once it has learned to read for its own sake. From such a perspective we may have the freedom to appreciate once more how deeply remarkable a work of art *The Tempest* is. Apprehending the Shrovetide context of the play's genesis reveals significance in many otherwise obscure passages of the sort which pose enigmas to editors. Yet *The Tempest* so closely matches other English Shrovetide plays and masques, such as Townshend's *Tempe Restor'd* or Chapman's *Memorable Maske*, that it will require a serious effort for scholars to continue to deny its correct placement as a dramatic manifestation of the liturgical struggle between Carnival and Lent that has been such a favorite topic of European visual artists.

Although we made little of it in our book, this would mean that the latest possible first production of the play would have to be assigned to spring, not autumn, 1611. In itself this indication of an earlier composition date would have taken us nowhere if we had not also had the advantage of realizing how thoroughly an earlier *Tempest* date is confirmed by analysis of the dramatic literature of the early Jacobean period — to the point that we can now reliably ascertain that the play had been written and was starting to become known at least by 1603. As Penny McCarthy had already emphasized in 2005, there is no reason to assume that plays were written shortly before their earliest appearance in the historical record, and careful reading "between the lines" of contemporaneous literary allusions reveals that many plays were known long before their ostensible dates of composition in the orthodox chronology.

If understanding of this point gains reception within *Tempest* studies, then one may readily predict a significant re-investment of scholarly resources.

This is so because one reason for the continued controversial nature of *Tempest* chronology is the special role this play has assumed in discussions over the so-called "Shakespeare authorship question." Regrettably, inquiry into the identity of a man who is arguably the world's most enduring classic dramatist is taboo within professional Shakespearean studies. The attitude of the leadership of the Shakespeare industry is aptly summarized by Gail Kern Paster, editor of the Folger Library's *Shakespeare Quarterly* and former Director of the Library, in her 1999 contribution to an authorship debate sponsored by *Harpers* magazine:

> For well-schooled professionals ... the authorship question ranks as bardolatry inverted, bardolatry for paranoids, with one object of false worship (Shakespeare) replaced by another (Marlowe, Bacon, Edward de Vere). To ask me about the authorship question, as I've remarked on more than one occasion, is like asking a paleontologist to debate a creationist's account of the fossil record.... For much worse than professional disclaimers of interest in Shakespeare's life is the ugly social denial at the heart of the Oxfordian pursuit ... a ferociously snobbish and ultimately anachronistic celebration of birthright privilege.[4]

Traditionalists such as Paster argue that the case made for the Earl of Oxford's authorship of the plays is impossible because the proposed author died before several so-called "Jacobean" plays were written. David Kathman expresses this view, in his "Dating *The Tempest*," an internet essay widely cited by adherents to the traditional view of authorship:

> One of the biggest problems for [the Oxfordian] theory is *The Tempest*, which can be dated with virtual certainty as having been written between late 1610 and mid-to-late 1611, six to seven years after the death of the Earl of Oxford in 1604.

It seems likely that, partly in response to the present study, we will soon be reading a new round of revisionist scholarship assuring us of the definitively Jacobean dates of several other plays, especially *Timon of Athens, Lear, Winter's Tale, Pericles, Henry VIII,* and *Macbeth*. This would follow from the simple premise that the Shakespeare industry seems destined to continue for the foreseeable future to promote conformity to the traditional view of authorship as the prerequisite to membership in the community of scholars.

Of course, *The Tempest* is not the only play traditionally dated after 1604 — while the claim of some that the standard chronology places a full third of the plays after 1604 is suspect as exaggeration, it is correct that mainstream scholarship traditionally locates the composition of several plays (exactly how many varies) after the death of Queen Elizabeth in 1603, with *The Tempest* and *Henry VIII* bringing up the rear in 1611 and 1613.[5] But *The Tempest*, as Kathman indicates, *is* the play which scholars have traditionally been most definitive in assigning a late composition to, and it *is* the play most often mentioned as a "silver bullet" against the Oxfordians. In case after case, Strachey's alleged influence has been the linchpin in this argument; *The Tempest*, in other words, is the only Shakespearean play for which a Jacobean date has been established primarily by claims of its supposed dependence on a post–1604 source.

If scholars become aware of the faulty reasoning on which a late *Tempest* depends they may start to wonder why the orthodox view has been mistaken for so many decades, and to consider the possibility that all of the so-called Jacobean plays were actually written by 1604. Certainly there is no shortage of hints that the standard chronology has been systematically biased by biographical assumptions; E.K. Chambers, in the most influential study of the chronology ever written, admits as much. As Peter Moore[6] has shown, almost all sources for Shakespearean plays[7] predate 1604. Of the five post–1604 alleged sources,[8] Strachey's *Reportory* is by far the most significant, and is the only one often cited and insisted upon in both scholarly and popular literature.

Evidence for the late dates of other plays is far more circumstantial. More recently, *Dating Shakespeare's Plays: A Critical Review of the Evidence,* edited by Kevin Gilvary, comprehensively reviews the chronology of the entire canon from an independent perspective. William S. Niederkorn[9] calls Gilvary's study "a most informative and useful book on a subject at the center of the Shakespeare labyrinth" and speculates that due to its comprehensive review of evidence often omitted from more conventional studies, it has "a reasonable chance of becoming a standard reference work," one that will be supplemented with further details but never superseded.

The path forward for the orthodox view of authorship appears increasingly like Dante's wood.[10] The deepening perplexities invoked by a rigid adherence to orthodox assumptions in Shakespearean studies are still evident in the most recent scholarly publications on *The Tempest*. Dan Brayton's March 2010 article in the *Forum for Modern Language Studies,* updating Alec Falconer's influential 1964 monograph, *Shakespeare and the Sea,* illustrates clearly the orthodox dilemma by first asserting, and then denying, that the *Tempest* author's detailed knowledge of seamanship is so precise as to have required nautical experience. Summarizing Falconer's view, Brayton notes that

> The accuracy of Shakespeare's nautical vocabulary and the precision of his descriptions of such nautical manoeuvres [as those in *Tempest* 1.1] raise inevitable — and ultimately unfathomable — biographical questions which can only be answered by speculation about what the young poet from Stratford might have been doing in his twenties. Surely the young player must have gone to sea. That Shakespeare, on coming to London to take up his new career as a dramatist, brought with him knowledge of the sea and navy can be seen in his earliest plays.[11]

Such views, on the other hand, Brayton assures us, are now passé under the regime of New Historicism:

> London was the early modern centre of English shipping. In much the same way that he absorbed and employed the language of falconry, forestry, jousting, law and the court, Shakespeare could, one imagines, have assimilated the language of mariners at the Mermaid Tavern.[12]

While one certainly *could* imagine this, we wonder whether it is good scholarship to continue to insist that the magical ambience of the "Mermaid Tavern" supplies sufficient real world basis for the Bard's "myriad minded" artistry. Still further, one may doubt that the Mermaid Tavern theory has much to offer those interested in traditional textual interpretation, insofar as it employs elements of authentic historical context or the biographies of real authors to wring meaning from a text. On the contrary, far from reassuring independent readers, such expressions of piety may raise rational doubts about the uses to which trends in literary theory are put by adherents of a traditional bard.

For their part, the Oxfordians have affectionately dubbed the bard's watering hole "The Tavern of Universal Knowledge." While we cannot disprove the theory that the playwright absorbed his understanding of such arcane subjects as the principles of English equity law,[13] the most current Elizabethan scholarship on medicine and astronomy,[14] Latin and Greek drama in their original languages,[15] or even the behavior and vocabulary of sailors in a storm at sea from his drinking colleagues, we are confident that the reflexive argument that Oxford cannot have been the author because he died before *The Tempest* was written is rapidly becoming obsolete. In its wake will hopefully come a renewed appreciation for the durability and credibility of rational doubts about the legitimacy of the c[...]

of the many," wrote W. H. Furness (fa[...]

"who has never been able to bring [...]

planetary space of the plays. Are th[...]

incongruous?"[16]

The Tempest is a transcendent li[...]

to survive all the misapprehension t[...]

scholars can throw at it. Like Shrove[...]

Feast." Transferring it to its proper pl[...]

and within the historical framework [...]

drama, is only to invoke another of t[...]

sprightly Ariel sings:

> Nothing of [it] [...]
> But doth suffer [...]
> Into something [...]

Appendices

A. Table of David Kathman's Alleged Storm Scene Influences with Antecedent Passages in Shakespeare

Motifs allegedly derived from Strachey were known to and used by Shakespeare years or decades before *Tempest* (After Stritmatter and Kositsky 2005):

"Parallels" between Reportory *and* Tempest *storm, after David Kathman's "Dating the* Tempest*"*	*Other Shakespeare plays with similar language or themes*
1. The *Sea Venture* was one of a fleet of nine ships which set out in 1609 to strengthen the English colony in Virginia; it carried Gates, the newly appointed Governor of Virginia, and his entourage. A storm separated the *Sea Venture* from the other ships, and the rest of the fleet continued on safely to Virginia, assuming that Gates had drowned. Tempest description: *And for the rest o' th' fleet* *(Which I dispers'd), they have all met again,* *And are upon the Mediterranean float* *Bound sadly home for Naples,* *Supposing that they saw the King's ship wrack'd,* *And his great person perish.* (1.2.232–37)	*Elze writes: Not only on Columbus's first voyage of discovery was the flagship separated from the others in a similar way, but also in Drake's voyage round the world (1577–1580) the same thing happened in the Straits of Magellan, so that Drake had to sail on alone along the west coast of America. (11)* *This very common pattern, found in several other narratives of the time, occurs, for example, in Tomson in Hakluyt (1600). There were eight ships in the fleet. They were on a voyage when a wind came up followed by a tempest, and "eight ships that were together were so dispersed that [they] could not see one another." Eventually the ships managed to find one another and sail away, but Tomson's ship was lost.*

"Parallels" between Reportory *and* Tempest *storm, after David Kathman's "Dating the* Tempest*"*	*Other Shakespeare plays with similar language or themes*
	Our sever'd navy too *Have knit again,* and fleet, threatening most sea-like. *Antony and Cleopatra.* *(3.13.205–206)*
2. Strachey describes the storm as "roaring" and "beat[ing] all light from heaven; which like an hell of darkness turned black upon us.... The sea swelled above the clouds, which gave battle unto heaven" (6–7). In *The Tempest*, Miranda describes the waters as being in a "roar," and says that "The sky it seems would pour down stinking pitch, / But that the Sea, mounting to th' welkins cheek, / Dashes the fire out." (1.2.1–5)	*Parallel phraseology is ubiquitous in Shakespeare, starting as early as* Titus Andronicus*, written more than sixteen years before Strachey's narrative:* If the winds rage, doth not *the sea wax mad, Threatening the welkin* with his big-swoln face? And wilt thou have a reason for this coil? *Titus Andronicus* (3.1.224) I have seen *The ambitious ocean swell and rage and foam,* To be exalted with the threatening clouds: But never till to-night, never till now, Did I go through a *tempest dropping fire.* Either there is a *civil strife* in heaven, Or else the world, too saucy with the gods, Incenses them to send destruction. *Julius Caesar* (1.3.6–7) *I never saw The heavens so dim by day.* A savage clamor! Well may I get aboard! This is the chase: I am gone for ever. *Winter's Tale* (3.3.60–63) I have seen two such sights, by sea and by land! but I am *not to say it is a sea, for it is now the sky: betwixt the firmament and it you cannot thrust a bodkin's point ... now the ship boring the moon with her main-mast,* and anon swallowed with yeast and froth, as you'd thrust a cork into a hogshead. *Winter's Tale* (3.3.88–91) The **sea**, with such a storm as his bare head In *hell-black night* endured,

"Parallels" between Reportory *and* Tempest *storm, after David Kathman's "Dating the* Tempest*"*	*Other Shakespeare plays with similar language or themes*
	would have buoy'd up, *And quench'd the stelled fires...* *King Lear* (3.7. 67)
3. Strachey says that "Our clamors drowned in the winds, and the winds in thunder. Prayers might well be in the heart and lips, but drowned in the outcries of the officers" (7); in the play the boatswain says, "A plague upon this howling; they are louder than the weather, or our office" (1.1.36–7), and a few lines later the mariners cry, "To prayers! To prayers!" (1.1.51).	*Again the concept Kathman would derive from Strachey was used by Shakespeare at least by 1599, the traditional date for Henry V:* humbly *pray them* to admit the excuse... Behold, the English beach Pales in the *flood with men, with wives, and boys,/ Whose shouts and claps out-voice the deep-mouth'd sea...* *Henry V*, prologue to Act 5. *(9–11)* *how the poor souls roared, and the sea mocked them*; and how the poor gentleman roared and the bear mocked him, both roaring louder than *the sea or weather.* *Winter's Tale* (3.3.104–105)
4. Strachey tells how "in the beginning of the storm we had received likewise a mighty leak" (8); Gonzalo says the ship in the play is "as leaky as an unstanched wench" (1.1.47–48).	*Shakespeare did not require Strachey to instruct him that ships sometimes leaked:* *Leak'd is our bark* *Timon of Athens* (4.2.23) *Her boat hath a leak* *King Lear* (3.6.17) *Or that "leaky" could be a metaphor:* Antony. Sir, sir, thou'rt *so leaky* *Antony and Cleopatra* (3.11.80)
5. Strachey says that "there was not a moment in which the sudden splitting, or instant oversetting of the Ship was not expected" (8); the mariners in the play cry, "We split, we split!" (1.1.61).	*Or that ships "split":* That the ship Should house him safe is *wreck'd and split* *Pericles, Prologue to Act 2 (31–32)*

"Parallels" between Reportory *and* Tempest *storm, after David Kathman's "Dating the* Tempest*"*	*Other Shakespeare plays with similar language or themes*

	Assure yourself, after *our ship did split...*
	          Twelfth Night (1.2.9)
	
	Whiles, in his moan, the ship *splits* on the rock...
	          3 Henry VI (5.4.10)

6. Strachey tells how "we ... had now purposed to have cut down the Main Mast" (12); the boatswain in the play cries, "Down with the topmast!" (1.1.34).	*Or that masts were blown overboard or taken down:* What though *the mast* be now blown overboard, The cable broke, the holding-anchor lost, And half our sailors swallow'd in the flood? *3 Henry VI* (5.4.3–5)

7. Strachey tells how the sailors "threw over-board much luggage ... and staved many a butt of beer, Hogsheads of oil, cider, wine, and vinegar, and heaved away all our ordnance on the starboard side" (12). Stephano says that "I escap'd upon a butt of sack which the sailors heav'd o'erboard" (2.2.121–22), and later tells Caliban to "bear this away where my hogshead of wine is" (4.1.250–51); both Caliban (4.1.231) and Alonso (5.1.299) call the stolen apparel "luggage."	In Strachey, the "luggage" is thrown overboard, and many of the casks are "staved"—pierced so that the drink ran out and into the sea. In *Tempest*, Stephano survives drowning by floating ashore on a full hogshead of wine, which he later consumes with the revelers. Although we would never cite these discrepancies as evidence that Shakespeare could not have relied on an account such as Strachey's, it is obvious that the critical lexical items on which the comparison depends were part of his vocabulary long before *Tempest* was written:
	
	Come, bring your *luggage* nobly on your back
	          1 Henry IV (5.4.160)
	
	I must stay with the lackeys, with *the luggage* of our camp
	          Henry V (4. 4.69–70)
	
	Kill the poys and *the luggage...*
	          Henry V (4.7.1)
	
	Overboard:

"Parallels" between Reportory *and* Tempest *storm, after David Kathman's "Dating the* Tempest*"*	*Other Shakespeare plays with similar language or themes*
	What though the mast be now blown *overboard*, The cable broke, the holding-anchor lost, And half our sailors swallow'd in the flood? *3 Henry VI* (5.4.3–5) I threw her *overboard* with these very arms. *Pericles* (5.3.21)
8. Strachey says that "who was most armed, and best prepared, was not a little shaken" (6); Prospero asks, "Who was so firm, so constant, that this coil / Would not infect his reason?" (1.2.207–08).	*Both the grammatical construction and the language is original to Shakespeare, repeated many times, not an imitation of Strachey:* Or *who is he so fond* will be the tomb Of his self-love, to stop posterity? (Sonnet 3) *What is your substance*, whereof are you made, That millions of strange shadows on you tend? (Sonnet 53) *Moreover, Shakespeare had also spontaneously linked them to the idea of a human "coil," in response to a terrifying storm, decades before conceiving* Tempest: *If there were reason for these miseries*, Then into limits could I bind my woes: When heaven doth weep, doth not the earth o'erflow? If the winds rage, doth not the sea wax mad, Threatening the welkin with his big-swoln face? And *wilt thou have a reason for this coil?* *Titus Andronicus* (3.1.220–225)
9. Strachey says that "Our Governor was ... both by his speech and	*Kathman seems unaware that the phrase "play the men" occurs in the*

"Parallels" between Reportory *and* Tempest *storm, after David Kathman's "Dating the* Tempest*"*	*Other Shakespeare plays with similar language or themes*
authority heartening every man unto his labor" (10); as soon as he appears, King Alonso says, "Good boatswain, have care. Where's the Master? Play the men"	*Bible (Gen. and most Tudor trans., 2 Sam. 13.28; Gen. only, 1 Sam. 4.9; 2 Sam. 1.12, AV only), as well as being well attested in Shakespeare's earlier works:*
	When they shall hear how we have **play'd the men.** *1 King Henry the Sixth* (1.1.17)
10. Strachey: "Sir George Summers ... had an apparition of a little round light, like a faint Star, trembling, and streaming along with a sparkling blaze, half the height upon the Main Mast, and shooting sometimes from Shroud to Shroud, tempting to settle as it were upon any of the four Shrouds ... running sometimes along the Main-yard to the very end, and then returning ... but upon a sudden, towards the morning watch, they lost the sight of it, and knew not which way it made.... Could it have served us now miraculously to have taken our height by, it might have strucken amazement" (11–12).	*The account of St. Elmo's fire as part of the Bermuda tempest is unique to Strachey, which has provoked the suspicion that the event represents Strachey's literary embroidery, borrowed from one of a large number of precedent sources, which include Eden, Erasmus, Ariosto, De Ulloa, and Tomson.*
Ariel. I boarded the King's ship; now on the beak, Now in the waist, the deck, in every cabin, I flam'd amazement. Sometimes I'ld divide, And burn in many places; on the topmast, The yards and boresprit, would I flame distinctly, Then meet and join. Jove's lightning, the precursors O' th' dreadful thunder-claps, more momentary And sight-outrunning were not (1.2.196–203)	*Although this is the only one of Kathman's examples of storm motifs supposedly derived from the Bermuda literature for which there is no obvious precedent in Shakespeare, examples from Lear and Julius Caesar may prove an interesting point of reference:*
	The sea, with such a storm as his bare head In hell-black night endured, would have buoy'd up, And *quench'd the stelled* fires... *King Lear* (3.7.65–67)
	A tempest dropping fire... Julius Caesar (1.3.10)
11. Jourdain says that "all our men, being utterly spent, tired, and disabled for longer labor, were even resolved, without any hope of their	*To Kathman it is significant that both Shakespeare and Jourdain mention "hatches." The discrepancies between the two versions are, however, omitted*

"Parallels" between Reportory *and* Tempest *storm, after David Kathman's "Dating the* Tempest*"*	*Other Shakespeare plays with similar language or themes*

lives, to shut up the hatches" (4–5) and "were fallen asleep in corners" (6); Ariel describes "The mariners all under hatches stowed, / Who, with a charm joined to their suff'red labor / I have left asleep" (1.2.230–32).
 	
Strachey mentions "hatches" four times (10, 10, 13, 25); Shakespeare in Act 5 again mentions "the mariners asleep / Under the hatches" (5.98–99), and the boatswain says, "We were dead of sleep, / And (how we know not) all clapp'd under hatches" (5.230–31).
	from Kathman's essay: in Shakespeare the sailors fall asleep in the hold, i.e. under the hatches, but in Jourdain the water is so deep in the holds that they had given up hope of bailing it out, and wanted to shut the hatches up and stay above them. In Jourdain's text, moreover, the motif of sailors falling asleep in corners has absolutely nothing to do with the shutting of the hatches. Kathman has spliced together two unrelated passages in order to create a stronger impression of intertextuality.
	
	In any case, Shakespeare had been writing about hatches for at least twelve years before Tempest:
	
	If he come *under my hatches,* I'll never to sea again.
	    Merry Wives of Windsor (2.1.19)
	
	And, in my company, my brother Gloucester; Who from my cabin tempted me to walk Upon the *hatches*: thence we looked toward England As we paced along Upon the giddy footing of the *hatches*, Methought that Gloucester stumbled; and, in falling, Struck me, that thought to stay him, overboard, Into the tumbling billows of the main.
	    Richard III (1.4.9–18)
	
	I stood upon the *hatches* in the storm...
	    2 Henry VI (3.2.104)
	
	Sir, we have a chest beneath the *hatches*, caulked and bitumed ready.
	    Pericles (3.1.75–76)

12. Jourdain says that the sailors "drunk one to the other, taking their last leave one of the other" (5); in the play the boatswain says, "What, must	*Kathman finds it significant that both Jourdain and Shakespeare mention sailors who had been drinking, but it is obvious that the cliché had occurred to*

"Parallels" between Reportory and Tempest storm, after David Kathman's "Dating the Tempest"	*Other Shakespeare plays with similar language or themes*
our mouths be cold?" (1.1.52), after which Antonio complains, "We are merely cheated of our lives by drunkards" (1.1.56), and Sebastian says "Let's take our leave of him" (1.1.64).	*Shakespeare long before Jourdain was written:* Lives *like a drunken sailor on a mast* ready with every nod to tumble down/Into the fatal bowels of the deep. *Richard III* (3.5.103–105) *There is no mention in Jourdain (or Strachey) of the critical* Tempest *element that the negligence of the drinking sailors resulted in loss of life. For a parallel to this passage, we must turn to the earliest account of Henry May's Bermuda shipwreck in 1593.* It was his fortune to have his ship cast away, upon the north-west part of the isle *of Bermuda*... The pilots ... certified the captain that they were out of all danger; so *they demanded of him their wine of height, the which they had... After they had their wine, careless of their charge which they took in hand, being as it were drunken, through their negligence a number of good men were cast away (Foster 28).*
13. Strachey says that "death is accompanied at no time, nor place with circumstances so un-capable of particularities of goodness and inward comforts, as at Sea" (6); Gonzalo says, "Now would I give a thousand furlongs of sea for an acre of barren ground, long heath, brown furze, any thing. The wills above be done! But I would fain die a dry death" (1.1.65–68).	*Surprisingly, Kathman does not notice that the idea of a nautical voyager preferring or being destined to a "dry death" occurs conspicuously in* Two Gentlemen of Verona, *a play written many years before* Tempest: Go, go, be gone, *to save your ship from wreck*, Which cannot perish having thee aboard, *Being destined to a drier death on shore.* Two Gentlemen of Verona (1.1.139–141)
14. Strachey tells how "we were enforced to run [the ship] ashore, as near the land as we could, which brought us within three quarters of a	My name, Pericles; My education been in arts and arms; Who, looking for adventures in the world,

"Parallels" between Reportory and Tempest *storm, after David Kathman's "Dating the* Tempest*"*	Other Shakespeare plays with similar language or themes
mile of shore" (13); Jourdain adds that the ship "fell in between two rocks, where she was fast lodged and locked, for further budging" (7). Ariel in *The Tempest*, after confirming for Prospero that the ship was "nigh shore" (1.2.216) says, "Safely in harbor / Is the King's ship, in the deep nook" (1.2.226–27).	Was by the rough seas reft of ships and men, And after *shipwreck driven upon this shore.* *Pericles* (2.3.87–91) Whiles, in his moan, *the ship splits on the rock,* Which industry and courage might have saved? *3 Henry VI* (5.4.10–11)

B. Plot and Theme Parallels Between Die Schöne Sidea *and* The Tempest

Die Schöne Sidea	The Tempest
Ludolff, a magician-prince with a white staff, has "lost his princedom" to the usurping Leudegast and now rules a tiny forest plot with no citizens except his daughter, Sidea.	Prospero, a magician-Duke with a staff, has lost his dukedom to his usurping brother Antonio and now rules a desolate island with no citizens except his daughter and the native Caliban.
Ludolff keeps a spirit "devil," Runcival, who gathers intelligence and does his bidding.	Prospero keeps Ariel, a spirit, who gathers intelligence and does his bidding.
When the young prince Englbrecht, son to the usurper, comes to court Sidea, Ludolff bewitches him and enslaves him to "carry wood for my daughter."	When the young Ferdinand is shipwrecked on the island by Prospero's magic, he falls in love with Prospero's daughter Miranda and is bewitched by Prospero who requires him to carry wood as a test of Miranda's love.
When Englbrecht's servant Squire tries to draw his sword, Ludolff bewitches him.	When Ferdinand tries to draw his sword against Prospero, Prospero bewitches him.
Leudegast mourns his son, believing him dead, but then rejoices and "cannot express [his] joy" at the sight of his son alive.	Ferdinand's father King Alonso of Naples, mourns the apparent drowning of his son, but rejoices to find him alive.
Ludolff declares that if the young prince is to keep his daughter, "he	The love between Miranda and Ferdinand unites the Prospero to his old

Die Schöne Sidea	The Tempest
must bring me again into the grace and favor of his old father."	nemesis Alonso and brings about the happy reconciliation of two formerly competing dynasties.
Englbrecht, who has meanwhile plighted his troth to Julia as well as Sidea, begs release from his engagement to Julia, marries Sidea, and Ludolff is restored to his estates and imminence.	Ferdinand and Miranda are betrothed in marriage and Alonso promises Prospero the restoration of the Dukedom of Milan.

C. Comparison of Richard Martin's December 1610 Requests for Information with Passages from True Reportory

Martin letter	Reportory
The nature and quality of the soil & how it is like to serve you without help from hence	What England may boast of, having the fair hand of husbandry to manure and dress it, God and nature have favourably bestowed upon this country; and as it hath given unto it, both by situation, height, and soil, all those (past hopes) assurances which follow our well-planted native country and others lying under the same influence, if as ours, the country and soil might be improved and drawn forth, so hath it endowed it, as is most certain, with many more, which England fetcheth far unto her from elsewhere. Large fields we have, as prospects of the same, and not far from our palisade. Besides, we have thousands of goodly vines in every hedge and bosk, running along the ground, which yield a plentiful grape in their kind. Let me appeal, then, to knowledge, if these natural vines were planted, dressed, and ordered by skillful vignerons, whether we might not make a perfect grape and fruitful vintage in short time. And we have made trial of our own English seeds, kitchen herbs, and roots and find

Martin letter	**Reportory**
	them to prosper as speedily as in England (Wright 68). [Much of this also in De La Warr's dispatch].
The manners of the people	Not excusing likewise the form of government of some error, which was not powerful enough among so heady a multitude, especially, as those who arrived here in the supply sent last year with us, with whom the better authority and government, now changed into an absolute command, came along and had been as happily established, had it pleased God that we with them had reached our wished harbor. Unto such calamity can sloth, riot, and vanity bring the most settled and plentiful estate. Indeed (right noble Lady) no story can remember unto us more woes and anguishes than these people, thus governed, have both suffered and pulled upon their own heads. (65–66) [and other similar passages]
How the Barbarians are content with your being there	For besides that the Indians were of themselves poor, they were forbidden likewise (by their subtle king Powhatan) at all to trade with us; and not only so, but to endanger and assault any boat upon the river or straggler out of the fort by land, by which (not long before our arrival) our people had a large boat cut off and divers of our men killed, even within command of our blockhouse; as, likewise, they shot two of our people to death after we had been four or five days come in. And yet would they dare then to enter our ports and truck with us (as they counterfeited underhand) when, indeed, they came but as spies to discover our strength, trucking with us upon such hard conditions that our governor might well see their subtlety and therefore neither could well

Martin letter	Reportory
	endure nor would continue it. (71) [and further passages]
But especially how our own people do brook their obedience how they endure labor, whether willingly or upon constraint	Only let me truly acknowledge, they are not an hundred or two of debauched hands dropped forth by year after year, with penury and leisure, ill-provided for before they come and worse to be governed before they are here — men of such distempered bodies and infected minds who no examples daily before their eyes, either of goodness or punishment, can deter from their habitual impieties or terrify from a shameful death — that must be the carpenters and workmen in this so glorious a building [All the foregoing De la Warr] ... I will acknowledge, dear Lady, I have such propenseness already towards the unity and general endeavours. How contentedly do such as labour with us go forth when men of rank and quality assist and set on their labor! I have seen it, and I protest it, I have heard the inferior people with alacrity of spirit profess that they should never refuse to do their best in the practice of their sciences and knowledges when such worthy and noble gentlemen go in and out before them, and not only so but, as the occasion shall be offered, no less help them with their hand than defend them with the sword. (68–69) [And many other like passages]
How they live in the exercise of religion, whether out of conscience or for fashion	[The repaired chapel] is so cast as it be very light within, and the lord governor and captain general doth cause it to be kept passing sweet and trimmed up with diverse flowers, with a sexton belonging to it. And in it every Sunday we have sermons twice a day, and every Thursday a sermon, having true preachers, which take their weekly turns; and every

Martin letter	**Reportory**
	morning, at the ringing of a bell about ten of the clock, each man addresseth himself to prayers, and so at four of the clock before supper (80). [And further passages]

Chapter Notes

Foreword

1. F. Brittain, *Arthur Quiller-Couch: A biographical study of Q* (New York: Macmillan, 1948), 87.
2. Sir Arthur Quiller-Couch, *Shakespeare's Workmanship* (Cambridge: Cambridge University Press, 1951), 244.
3. Quiller-Couch, *Shakespeare's Workmanship*, 245.
4. *Shakespeare's Workmanship*, 251.
5. *Shakespeare's Workmanship*.
6. *Shakespeare's Workmanship*, 252.
7. *Shakespeare's Workmanship*, 253.
8. Samuel Johnson and George Stevens, ed., *The Plays of William Shakespeare* (London: C. Bathurst et al., 1778), I:270.
9. Peter Martin, *Edmond Malone, Shakespearean scholar* (Cambridge: Cambridge University Press, 1995), 34.
10. Martin.
11. Sir Arthur Quiller-Couch and John Dover Wilson, ed., *The Tempest* (New York: Macmillan, 1921), xviii.
12. Quiller-Couch and Wilson, xxvi.
13. Quiller-Couch and Wilson, xxii.
14. Quiller-Couch, *Shakespeare's Workmanship*, 267.
15. Joseph Hunter, *New Illustrations of the Life, Studies, and Writings of Shakespeare* (London: J.B. Nichols, 1845), I:123.
16. Quiller-Couch, *Shakespeare's Workmanship*, 271.
17. Edmond Malone, *An Account of the Incidents, from Which the Title and Part of the Story of Shakespeare's* Tempest *Were Derived; and Its True Date Ascertained* (London: C. and R. Baldwin, 1808), 10.
18. Malone, *Account*, 23.

Introduction

1. Email to R. Stritmatter, 7/28/05.
2. Vaughan, Alden. "William Strachey's 'True Reportory' and Shakespeare: A Closer Look at the Evidence," *Shakespeare Quarterly*, 59 (3): 245–273. The quote is from the source cite in FN 1.

3. Wylie, John. "New and Old Worlds: *The Tempest* and Early Colonial Discourse," *Social & Cultural Geography*, 1:1 (2000), 54. The list that follows is representative, although very far from comprehensive.
4. Wilson-Okumura, David Scott. "Virgilian Models of Colonization in Shakespeare's *Tempest*," *ELH* 70 (2003), 716.
5. Neil, Michael. "'Noises, Sounds, and Sweet Airs': The Burden of Shakespeare's *Tempest*" *Shakespeare Quarterly*, 59 (2008), 36–59; fn 25, 46.
6. Vaughan, 273.
7. Vaughan, 273.
8. Reedy, Tom. "Dating William Strachey's 'True Reportory of the Wracke and Redemption of Sir Thomas Gates': A Comparative Textual Study" *Review of English Studies* 61 (251), winter 2010, 529.

Chapter 1

1. Stritmatter, Roger and Lynne Kositsky. "Shakespeare and the Voyagers Revisited," *Review of English Studies,* 58: 236 (Spring 2007), 447.
2. Registered Nov. 8, 1610, by Sir Thomas Smith, Sir Maurice Buckley, Sir George Coffin, and Richard Martin, Secretary to the Virginia Council in London. The authorship has been variously assigned to Edwin Sandys and Francis Bacon.
3. Watson, Harold Francis. *The Sailor in English Fiction and Drama,* 1550–1800. New York: Columbia University Press, 1931, 76–77.
4. Hume, Ivor Noël. "William Strachey's Unrecorded First Draft of His Sea Venture Saga," *Avalon Chronicles*, VI (2001), 57. Hereafter, following the convention established by Hume, we shall refer to this transcript as "B."
5. Although full exploration of this idea falls outside the scope of this book, it is also possible that the B manuscript actually represents a derivative but greatly abbreviated transcript of the Strachey account as published by Purchas. Although we regard this as the less plausible explanation for the origin of the manuscript, we cannot rule it out on present evidence. For the purpose of this book,

we follow Hume's view that B is the transcript of a text antedating *Reportory* as printed by Purchas.

6. A paragraph evidently added in a subsequent redaction supplies a synoptic history of the Bermudas up until the 18th century.

7. Wright, Louis B. (ed). *A Voyage to Virginia in 1609: Two Narratives: Strachey's "True Reportory" and Jourdain's Discovery of the Bermudas.* Charlottesville: University Press of Virginia, 1964, 7.

8. Culliford, S.G. *William Strachey, 1572–1621.* Charlottesville: University Press of Virginia, 1965, 61–96.

9. "Captain John Smith." Humanities Web.org. Web. Accessed 1/11/11. A plausible alternative author is Captain Christopher Newport, who is mentioned once in *Reportory* but not at all in B. We have been unable to verify whether Newport, who of course had extensive shipping experience before being among the Bermuda survivors, had been to the Levant before 1610.

10. Strachey, William. *For The colony in Virginea Britannia. Lawes divine, morall and martiall, &c.* London: J. Stansby for Walter Burre, 1612. 5; emphasis added. Virtual Jamestown. Web. Accessed 12/1/11. ESTC citation # S111283.

11. Hamor, Raphe. *A true Discourse of the Present Estate of Virginia, and the successe of the affaires there till the 18 of June, 1614. Together with a relation of the severall English Townes and forts, the assured hopes of that countrie and the peace concluded with the Indians.* The Christening of *Powhatans* daughter *and her mariage with an English-man.* London, 1614. Virtual Jamestown. Web. Accessed 4/1/2010. ESTC citation # S105997. Our emphasis. Given this evidence, Hamor, like Christopher Newport, must be put on the list of possible authors of B. However, such informal stylistic study as is available to us does not encourage the likelihood of this theory. Nor were we able to find any evidence for Hamor's experience in the Levant before 1610.

12. Wright, xvii.

Chapter 2

1. Lindley, David. *The Tempest. The New Cambridge Shakespeare.* Cambridge: University Press, 2002, 25.

2. Kathman, David. "Dating *The Tempest,*" Shakespeare Authorship.com, Shakespeareauthorship.com/ tempest.html. Accessed 6/18/12.

3. For a thorough critique of Kathman's claims, see Stritmatter and Kositsky 2005, "Dating *The Tempest*: A Note on the Undocumented Influence of Erasmus' "Naufragium" and Richard Eden's 1555 *Decades of the New World.*" The Shakespeare Fellowship. Web.

4. Kathman, "Dating," n.p.

5. Gen. and most Tudor trans., 2 Sam. 13.28; Gen. only, 1 Sam. 4.9; 2 Sam. 1.12, AV only.

6. *The Compact Edition of the Oxford English Dictionary: Complete Text Reproduced Micrographically,* (Oxford: University Press, 1971)1007 (II:252).

7. Ironically, Strachey uses the word only as a noun ("glut of water"), which makes it a separate lexical entry and not, strictly speaking, the same word as that used in *Tempest.*

8. Cawley, Robert Ralston. "Shakspere's Use of the Voyagers in *The Tempest,*" *PMLA* 42:3 (Sept, 1926), 695–96, 699.

9. We'll have no Cupid *hoodwink'd* with a scarf (*R&J,* 1.4.1); and the disorder's such/As war were *hoodwink'd.* (*Cymb.* 5.2.15–16) And, *hoodwink'd* as thou art, will lead thee on/To gather from thee (*All's Well* 4.1.76–77).

10. Fischer, David Hackett. *Historians' Fallacies: Toward a Logic of Historical Thought* (Harper & Row, 1970), 116.

11. The word occurs only once in *Reportory,* which was Strachey's first major work, but also occurs once in *History of Travel* (1612). Only two poems by Strachey survive, and of all the "parallels" to Shakespeare that Kathman reports, only two "mild" parallels exist, in Strachey's "Upon Sejanus": cedar, thunder, lightning.

12. All quotations are from Eden, Rycharde, *The Decades of the Newe Worlde or West India by Pietro Martire d'Anghiera (f. 1555).* Readex Microprint. 1966.

13. Willes, R. *The history of Travayle in the West and East Indies. Done into Englyshe by R. Eden. Newly set in order, augmented, and finished by R. Willes.* London: R. Jugge, 1577. ESTC Citation # S122069.

14. Frey, Charles. "*Tempest* and New World," *SQ,* 30 (1979), 29–41. 29, fn. 2. Frey relates the history of this significant footnote in the history of Shakespearean scholarship: "What scholar first connected Shakespeare's 'Setebos' to the Patagonians remains a mystery. Richard Farmer cites Eden in correspondent's notes to the Johnson-Steevens editions of *The Tempest* (2nd ed., 1778) but mentions others who made the connection of Setebos and Patagonia through sources (non–Elizabethan) other than Eden. Farmer does not mention Setebos in his famous *Essay on the Learning of Shakespeare*" (Cambridge, 1767).

15. Unless otherwise noted, *Tempest* references are to the 1999 Arden edition, Virginia Mason Vaughan and Alden T. Vaughan, *The Tempest.* London: Thomson Learning, 1999.

16. Furness, who is followed by nearly every other commentator in identifying the 1577 book as the source of "Setebos" as well as the other shared motifs, was apparently unaware that the passages also occurred earlier in the 1555 edition of Eden's work. Almost every subsequent critic who has mentioned Eden alludes only to the second edition, no doubt partly because of the chronological implications of admitting the existence of an influential *Tempest* source of such an early date.

17. Furness, Horace Howard. *The Variorum Tempest,* Philadelphia, 1892, 77; Eden, 218v. Like "Castor and Pollux," the names "Saint Helen," "Saint Nicholas," and "Saint Clare" are alternative traditional names for St. Elmo's Fire.

18. Kermode, Frank. *The Arden Shakespeare: The Tempest.* London: Methuen, 1954, 1983, Xxviii.

19. Kermode, xxxii–xxxiii.

20. Smith, Hallet, *Shakespeare's Romances: A Study of Some Ways of the Imagination*. San Marino: Huntington Library, 1972, 140.

21. Frey, 31.

22. Vaughan, Virginia Mason and Alden T. *The Arden Shakespeare: The Tempest*. London: Thomson Learning, 1999, 40: our emphasis.

23. Trudeau-Clayton, Margaret. *Jonson, Shakespeare, and Early Modern Virgil*. Cambridge: University Press, 1998.

24. Brinton, A.C. "The Ships of Columbus in Brant's Virgil," *Art and Archeology* 26 (1928): 83–86; 94.

25. Mortimer, Ruth. "Vergil in the Light of the Sixteenth Century: Selected illustrations," *Vergil at 2000: Commemorative Essays on the Poet and His Influence*. Ed. John D. Bernard, *AMS Ars Poetica 3*. New York: AMS, 1986, 159–184; 160.

26. Wilson-Okumura, 709, 711.

27. Wilson-Okumura, 711.

28. Strachey: "As Vergil writeth Aeneas did, arriving in the region of Italy called Latium, upon the banks of the River Tiber" (Wright, 78). Compare Eden, clearly Strachey's source: "As is read in the beginning of the Romans ... Eneas of Troy arrived in the region of Italy called Latium, upon the banks of the river of Tyber" (124v). It may be worth noticing that as he so often does, Strachey here inflates his own authority by making it sound as if his source is Virgil, when the evidence manifestly shows that he went no further than Eden to discover his precedent.

29. This immensely popular and widely influential book appeared in numerous 16th century editions, including the critical (for our purposes) 1587 Parisian issue dedicated to the "*illustri et magannimo viro Gualtero Ralegho*" under the title *De Orbe Novo Petri Martyris Anglerii mediolanensis, protonotarii et Caroli quinti Senatoris, decades octo, diligente temporum observatione et utilissimis annotationibus illustratæ, suoque nitore restitæ labore et industria Richardi Hakluyti Oxoniensis, Angli*. As an apprentice work of the most important of all chroniclers of early modern English voyages Richard Hakluyt, dedicated to the most important explorer of the 1580's Sir Walter Raleigh and reproducing all eight decades as compared to Eden's three, the edition illustrates the central role that Martyr's work continued to exercise over the imagination of English explorers long after the 1555 and 1577 English editions. For a useful if possibly not exhaustive bibliography, see MacNutt, Francis Augustus. *De Orbe Novo, Volume 1 (of 2) The Eight Decades of Peter Martyr D'Anghera, translated from the Latin with Notes and Introduction*. In two volumes. *Project Gutenburg e-text*. Web. Accessed 20/5/2005.

30. MacNutt, 28–29.

31. MacNutt, I: Note 5.

32. Attempts to link Strachey to *Tempest* via his reference to Aeneas and Dido ironically overlook the fact that Strachey's "digression" about Aeneas is an almost verbatim copy of Eden.

33. See the jocular exchange (2.1.70–105) between Gonzalo, Antonio, and Antonio, with its iterated references to Carthage and Dido.

34. Conceived as a series of letters to Martyr's friend and patron Ascanio Sforza, brother to Ludovico Sforza, Duke of Milan (MacNutt 8), and afterwards also written to Cardinal Lodovike of Aragon, nephew of Ferdinand II of Aragon and III of Naples, Martyr's work was dedicated to Charles V. It swiftly became an early European classic, going through numerous imprints and translations, including that prepared and first published in 1555 by Richard Eden, a close friend and confidante of Sir Thomas Smith.

35. Parks, George Bruner. *Richard Hackluyt and the English Voyagers*, American Geographical Society, 1928, 56.

36. Parks, 21.

37. Parks, 23.

38. Gayley, Charles M. *Shakespeare and the Founders of American Liberty*, Cawley, "Voyagers," and Kathman, "Dating."

39. Cited in Furness 1892, 343. Since Halliwell, scholars have acknowledged the probable influence on Shakespeare of Thomas's *Historye of Italye* (1561), which narrates the rise and fall of Prospero Adorno, Lieutenant to the Duke of Milan. By the assistance of Ferdinando, King of Naples, Adorno was made Duke "absolutely" (Furness 343) over Milan but later deposed by Antony Adorno. See J.G. Waller, "The Prospero of the *Tempest*," *Gentleman's Magazine* 40 (July 1853), 122–127. Google books. Web.

40. Francesco, like Shakespeare's Prospero, was involved in magic, although as a inquisitor against those suspected of practicing the art rather than a magician himself (see Hunter, 110) as well as the dedicatee of Girolamo Visconti's famous treatise on witchcraft *Magistri Hyeronimi Vicecomitis Lamiarum* (1490).

41. Shakespeare might also have encountered the internecine quarrels of the Sforza dynasty in Geoffrey Fenton's popular translation of Guiccardini's *Historia d' Italia* (1579, 1599, 1617). The topic became a popular subject in drama, with three plays based on Ludovico Sforza's life before Massinger's 1623 *Duke of Millaine*.

42. It is difficult to overstate the historical importance of the dispute between Ludovico and his nephew Gian and his Aragonese backers for control of Milan. Ludovico's invitation for French intervention set loose the "Italian wars" and Charles VIII's brief conquest of Naples after he entered Italy in 1494.

43. "Fer. Yes, faith, and all his lords; the Duke of Milan,/And his brave son being twain" (1.2.436–7).

44. Furness, citing Malone, 4–5.

45. Gayley, 65.

46. Kathman, "Dating."

47. Cawley, "Voyagers."

48. The passage is also echoed in the Ovid passage that inspires Prospero's spell in 4.1: "ye Elves of Hills, *of Brookes*, of Woods alone,/Of standing

Lakes, and of the Night" (7.265–66). See Rouse, *Golding's Ovid*.

49. Bate, Jonathan. *Shakespeare and Ovid*. Oxford: Clarendon Press, 1993. Barkan, Leonard, *The Gods Made Flesh: Metamorphosis & the Pursuit of Paganism*. New Haven: Yale University Press, 1986.

50. Some *Tempest* "natural history" may also suggest Shakespeare's awareness of the early Virginia reports and narratives, Gosnold's 1602 voyage to Cuttyhunk (Archer 1602) May's December 1593 shipwreck in the Bermudas, Fletcher's unpublished notebooks from Drake's 1577–80 circumnavigation of the globe, or one of the narratives of Robert Dudley's 1594–95 voyage to the West Indies. But we can find nothing of substance allegedly reproduced from Strachey that is not already present in Eden or these earlier sources. See Archer, Gabriel, "The relations of Captain Gosnold's Voyage to the North part of Virginia" (1602). Electronic text reprinted by Virtual Jamestown. Web. Accessed 20 May 2005; May, Sir Henry, "A briefe note of a voyage to the East Indies, begun the 10 of April 1591," in *The Voyages of Sir James Lancaster to Brazil and the East Indies 1591–1603*. London: The Hackluyt Society, 1940: 22–30. May's account contains numerous elements that might have influenced *The Tempest*: a ship "taken with an extreme tempest or huricano" (22); a company which "began to be in a mutiny" and "conspired to take away the Frenchman's pinnace" (26); and especially sailors who "after they had their wine, careless of their charge which they took in hand, being as it were drunken, through their negligence a number of good men were cast away" (28). The latter is by far the closest parallel we have seen in early modern travel literature to Antonio's complaint that "we are merely cheated of our lives by drunkards (1.1.56). The possible influence of unpublished Fletcher materials, which include the name "Setebos," is discussed by Charles Frey, "Tempest and Old World." George F. Warner, *The Voyages of Robert Dudley, Afterwards Styled Earl of Warwick and Leicester and Duke of Northumberland to the West Indies, 1594–95, Narrated by Capt. Wyatt, by Himself, and by Abram Kendall, Master*. Nendeln/Liechtenstein: 1967 Kraus reprint of the 1899 Hakluyt Society Edition.

51. "*In the meane time the wood was cutting* (sic) and the barrells filling..." (15v). "They found the woods, entered into them, and *felled the high and precious trees*, whiche were to that day, untouched" (23).

52. Viz., "The place is also contagious by the nature of the soil, by reason it is compassed about with muddy and stinking marshes, *the infection* wherof is not a little encreased by *the heat*" (121v). Cf. *Cal*. All the *infections* that the *sun* sucks up From bogs, fens, flats, on Prosper fall, and make him By inch-meal a disease! (2.2.4–6)

53. "They deputed to that labour a multitude of bought servants, which *searching the veins of metals* in diverse places, and *piercing the earth* diverse ways ... brought forth great plenty of gold and silver." (biii)

54. C.f. "Though this island seem to be desert Uninhabitable, and almost inaccessible.... It must needs be of subtle, tender, and delicate temperance" (2.1.35–43).

55. Stephano's "cellar is in a rock by th'/sea-side where my wine is hid" (2.2.131–32).

56. Q reads "scamels," but this is often thought to be a corruption of *Seamewes*, a word found in Strachey and often said to be derived from it.

57. Ariel leads Trinculo and Stephano through "Tooth'd briers, sharp furzes, pricking goss, and thorns" into "th' filthy-mantled pool" (4.1.180–82).

Chapter 3

1. *The Tempest* motif of sleep doubtless has multiple sources of inspiration, among them, as Anne Pasternak Slater has argued, Isaiah XXIX. See her "Variations within a Source: From Isaiah XXIX to *The Tempest*," *Shakespeare Survey* 25 (1972), 125–135.

2. See Marshall, Tristan. "*The Tempest* and the British Imperium in 1611," *The Historical Journal*, 41:2 (Jun. 1998), 375–400. A 1622 attack on Jamestown by Powhatan's forces killed 347 colonists.

3. *A True Declaration of the Estate of the Colonie in Virginia. With a confutation of such scandalaous reports as have tended to the disgrace of so worthy an enterprise. Published by advise and direction of the Councell of Virginia*: London, Printed for William Barret, and are to be sold at the blacke Beare in Pauls Church-yard. 1610. On-line edition published by Virtual Jamestown. Web, 30.

4. Marshall, 383.

5. "**Pros.** I did say so,/When *first I raised the tempest*" (5.1.5–6).

6. In a recent analysis, David McInnis ("Old World Sources for Ariel in *The Tempest*," *Notes and Queries* 2008 55(2):208–213; doi:10.1093/notesj/gjn040) points out that the 1553 edition of Munster's *Cosmography* — translated, by none other than Richard Eden — recounts an experience of "ventriloquizing spirits" that comes very close to Ariel's unearthly music: "you shall heare in the ayre, the sound of Tabers and other instruments, to putte the Travellers in feare" (McInnis 212). We agree that this is strikingly close to *Tempest* 3.1.136–37 and must certainly have been among the sources that Shakespeare recalled.

7. The locus classicus of tale tales of travelers was of course, for Elizabethans, John Mandeville's 14th century travelogue, *The Travels of Sir John Mandeville*, which seems definitely to have influenced the idea of Gonzalo's speech that, as the proverb would have it, "A traveler may lie with authority" (Dent, R.W., *Shakespeare's Proverbial Language* (Berkeley, 1981), T476).

8. On Montaigne's New World sources more generally, see Stelio Cro, *The Noble Savage: Allegory of Freedom* (Ontario, CA: Wilfrid Laurier University Press), 14.

9. The literary archetype of this familiar topos

of a lost "golden world" is Ovid (book I), but it seems clear that Montaigne was also influenced by Oviedo's treatment of the theme when he wrote "On Cannibals."

10. As Leo Salingar (217) has noted, the *Tempest* passage also strongly recalls even the very earliest English colonial report, Arthur Barlowe's first voyage made to the coasts of America, published in 1584 (and reprinted by Hakluyt in 1589), in which Virginia is reported as a land in which "the earth bringeth forth all things in abundance as in the first creation, without toil or labour." No doubt Barlowe's account is influenced by Ovideo, but the Oviedo passage contains elements that seem to be unique in their connections to Shakespeare's play. For Barlowe, see Wright, Louis, ed., *The Elizabethan's America: A Collection of Early Reports by Englishmen in the New World*, Cambridge: Harvard University Press, 1965, 103–114.

11. *As You Like It*'s Arden, recalling Eden's America, is both a "golden world" (1.1) and a "desert inaccessible" (2.2). Othello's tale of "portance in my Travellers historie, wherein of antars vast and deserts idle, rough quarries, rocks, hills, whose head touch heaven ... and of the Canibals that each others eat, the anthropophagi, and men whose heads grew beneath their shoulders" (1.3.163–68) is as reminiscent in its own way of Eden, who uses the word "anthropophagi" as well as "canibal," as it is of Pliny or Mandeville. Anon, "Shakespeare's *The Merchant of Venice*," *The Explicator* 37 (1979), also detects the possible influence of Eden in *Merchant of Venice, Lear,* and *Troilus and Cressida.* Shakespeare's use of the term "Huricano," a Native American word introduced into England by Eden's book, in both *Lear* (3.2.2) and *Troilus and Cressida* (5.2.193), further testifies to the impression the text left on him. Cf. other miscellaneous parallels, cumulatively impressive: *Lear*: "you fen-sucked fogs, drawn by the powerful sun" (2.4.162); Eden 122v–123; *Antony and Cleopatra*: "Our sever'd navy too/ have knit again, and fleet, threatening most sealike" (3.13.206); Eden 217 verso; *Winter's Tale*: "the climate's delicate, the air most sweet,/fertile the isle" (3.1.1–2) Eden: "one day allured by the pleasantness of the place, and sweet savours which breathed from the land to the ships, they went aland" (30v). *MND*: "I'll follow you, I'll lead you about around through bog, through bush, through brake, through briar" (3.1.98–99); Eden 99v, 33v–34.

12. MacNutt, 26.

13. MacNutt, 40.

14. "The Viewers and the Viewed," *The Cultures and History of the Americas: The Jay I. Kislak Collection at the Library of Congress*, 8. Web. Accessed 11/26/2005.

15. Kerr, Robert. *A General History and Collection of Voyages and Travels, Arranged in Systematic Order.* Edinburgh: William Blackwood, 1824, 193; our emphasis. The work is extant in two early Italian publications: Columbus, Ferdinand. *Historie de S.D. Fernando Colombo nelle quali s'ha particolare e vera relazione della vita e de' fatti dell' Ammiraglio D.*

Christoforo Colombo suo Padre... 1571; Ulloa, De, Alonso, *Historia Dell Almirante don Cristobal Colon.* Venice, 1571. The Ovidian parallel is striking: "**Medea.** I have compelled streames to run backward to their spring/By charmes I make the calme Seas rough, and make ye rough seas plain" (7.197f). *Shakespeare's Ovid: Being Arthur Golding's Translation of the Metamorphoses.* London: De La More Press, 1904.

16. Mtt. 5.44: "But I say to you, love your enemies, bless those who curse you, do good to those who hate you, and pray for those who spitefully use you and persecute you." And, less familiarly but more aptly, Ecclesiasticus 28.1–5: See Stritmatter, Roger, "Ecclesiasticus 28.2–5: A Biblical Source for Ariel's Doctrine of Mercy," *Notes and Queries* 2009 56 (1):67–70; doi:10.1093/notesj/gjn252.

17. Gillies, 154.

18. See the discussion in Gillies, 151.

19. Gillies, 154.

Chapter 4

1. Neil, Michael. "Noises, Sounds, and Sweet airs": The Burden of Shakespeare's *Tempest*" *SQ,* 59: 1 (Spring 2008), 46, n. 25.

2. Vaughan, 272.

3. Vaughan, 272.

4. See Furness 324, citing Hunter.

5. Vaughan, 272.

6. Cawley, "Voyagers," fn 23. It is evident that Cawley has not closely compared Eden's text with Shakespeare's imaginative conception of the phenomenon, or he would have seen the evident connection between the two texts in this as well as many other places.

7. Cawley, 696, fn. 24.

8. Eden, Richard. *The Decades of the Newe Worlde or West India by Pietro Martire d' Anghiera* (f. 1555). Readex Microprint. 1966.

9. Pygafetta's references in Eden to Saint Helen, Saint Nicholas, and Saint Clare (St. Elmo's Fire):

For there appeared in their ships certain flames of fire burning very clear, which they call Saint Helen and Saint Nicholas. These appeared as though they had been upon the masts of the ships, in such clearness that they took away their sight.... I have here thought good to say somewhat of these strange fires which some ignorant folks think to be spirits or such other fantasies wheras they are but natural things proceeding of natural causes....

Of the kind of true fire, is the fire ball or star commonly called Saint Helen which is sometime(s) seen about the masts of ships and is a token of drowning (217v–218).

Here were they in great danger by tempest. But as soon as the three fires called saint Helen, saint Nicholas, and saint Clare, appeared upon the cables of the ships, suddenly the tempest and fury of the winds ceased (218v).

As they were entering into the port, there arose a boisterous and dark tempest which ceased as soon as the fires of the three saints (wherof we have spoken before) appeared upon the cables (228).

10. Ariel's speech is particularly evocative of the motion of St. Elmo's fire as it appears in Erasmus: "A ball of fire, which ... is to the shipmen a most fearful signe of hard success ... by and by the fiery globe sliding downe by the ropes ... rolled it self along the brims of the ship, and falling from thence down into the middle rooms..." (Gr-v).

11. We are unable to document this idea in any of the other sources of the St. Elmo's fire motif.

12. "Methinks he hath no *drowning mark* upon him."

13. Gayley, 54, 56–58.

14. Cawley, "Voyagers."

15. Kathman, "Dating."

16. Mowat, Barbara. "Knowing I Loved My Books: Reading the *Tempest* Intertextually," in Hulme and Sherman, eds., 27–36.

17. Wright, 13.

18. Mowat cites Eden's 1584 translation of Cortez' *Arte of Navigation*, which refers to "the bright and shining exhalations that appear in the tempests, whiche the Mariners call Santelmo, or Corpus sancti" (pt. 2, cha Xx, 51v–52).

19. *Amazement* is used 3X in the play; *wonder* 7X; *wondrous* 2X.

20. Pagden, A. *European Encounters with the New World*. New Haven, CT: Yale University Press, 1993, 24.

21. Greenblatt, Stephen, *Possessions*, 14, 54; our emphasis.

22. We are especially indebted on this score to John Wylie's perceptive analysis (59–60) of the relevance of these analytic categories. In *The Tempest*, "known and rehearsed paradisiacal motifs are transformed by the presence of radical 'otherness' into a deliberately unresolved 'wonder'" (60). Wylie, John, *New and Old Worlds: The Tempest and early colonial discourse Social & Cultural Geography*, 1:1 (2000), 45–63.

23. In the 1555 Eden this last example occurs on the page immediately following one of Pygafetta's descriptions of St. Elmo's fire (219).

24. Walter, James. "From *Tempest* to Epilogue: Augustine's Allegory in Shakespeare's Drama," *PMLA* 98:1 (Jan. 1983), 60–76, 62.

Chapter 5

1. Malim, Richard. "The Spanish Maze." In *Great Oxford: Essays on the Life and Work of Edward de Vere*. Richard Malim, ed. London: Parapress, 2004.

2. Bodleian Malone ms. 29, f. 69v.

3. Chambers, *Elizabethan Stage,* IV: 171–72.

4. The document records performances of plays by four authors only (and two untitled and unattributed masques) — Jonson, Chapman, Heywood, and Shakespeare. One play is recorded with neither title nor author, but only one, the *Spanish Maze*, remains without attribution. Two of the thirteen plays are by Jonson, one is by Heywood and one by Chapman; the remaining seven plays are by Shakespeare.

5. During the 16th century reign of Charles V, on the grounds of Alcazar in Seville, was constructed a "Spanish maze" which acquired an international reputation. The possible connection between it and *The Tempest* has yet to be thoroughly investigated. Charles V was the grandson of Ferdinand II of Aragon, also King of Naples.

6. Cunningham, Peter. *Extracts from the Accounts of the Revels at Court in the Reigns of Queen Elizabeth and King James I*. The Shakespeare Society, 1842, 203–04.

7. The practice was apparently not uncommon. In addition to the two variants evident in Malone ms. 29, Shakespearean examples include *Twelfth Night*, or *What You Will*; *All Is True*, an alternative title for *Henry VIII*; *Love's Labour's Won*, mentioned by Francis Meres in 1598 as a play by Shakespeare, and often identified as either *All's Well that End's Well* or *Much Ado about Nothing*. The 1612–13 Chambers' accounts list *Much Ado* under the title "Benedicte and Betteris," (as well, in the preceding entry, as *"Much adoe aboute Nothing,"* not to mention — apparently — *I Henry IV* as "Hotspur" and *II Henry IV* as "Sir John ffalstaffe" (Chambers, *Elizabethan*, II: 180).

8. On the 1611 performance, see Chambers, *William Shakespeare*, II, 342. The 1613 production, in honor of the marriage of Princess Elizabeth Stuart to the Elector Palatine, was also almost certainly at Whitehall.

9. Vaughan and Vaughan, 7–9; Lindley, 4.

10. Chambers, E.K. *William Shakespeare: A Study of Facts and Problems*. Oxford: Clarendon Press, 1930, II: 330; Cunningham, *Extracts*, 203–5. The online resource, *Calculation of the Ecclesiastical Calendar*, calculates that Shrove Sunday 1605 fell on Feb. 20, which would mean the performance date of Spanish Maze was Feb. 21; the Chamber accounts, however, list the date as Feb 11. Compensating for the ten day difference brought about by the shift to New Style dating reconciles these two dates.

11. Chambers, *William Shakespeare*, II: 330; Chambers, *Elizabethan Stage*, IV: 172.

12. Brosch, Mauritz. "Papal Policy" chapter XXII in *The Cambridge Modern History, vol. IV, The Thirty Years War*. Web. Accessed January 17, 2007. Actually, Spain's dominance was punctuated by periods of French control, and Spanish and French interests vied over some time for administration of the cities, with Spain mostly holding the upper hand.

13. The protagonist Mucedorus, Prince of Valencia, pursues Amadine, the daughter of the king of Aragon. The play appeared in 17 quartos between 1598 and the restoration, making it by this measure the most popular English play of Stuart England. It was written circa 1590, but not published until the year of Phillip II's death.

14. The full title was *The Comical History of Alphonsus, King of Aragon*. It was written circa 1592, but not published until the year after Phillip's death.

15. The play's Spanish associations are well

known. The term "Moor" referred to Berber or Arab immigrants from North Africa to Spain.

16. Erne, Lucas. *Shakespeare as a Literary Dramatist.* (Cambridge: University Press, 2003), 50.

17. Tillyard, E.M.W. "The Tragic Pattern: *The Tempest*," in Robert Langbaum, *The Tempest*. New York: Penguin Group, 1964, 1987, 119–127, 155

18. Langbaum, *Tempest*, xxii.

19. Greg, Walter W. *Pastoral Poetry and Pastoral Drama: A Literary Inquiry, with Special Reference to the Pre-Restoration Stage in England.* London: A.H. Bullen, 1906, 271. Google Books. Web. Accessed 1/10/11.

20. Cf., of course, Polonius in *Hamlet*, unwittingly parodying generic classifications: "The best actors in the world, either for tragedy, comedy, history, pastoral, pastoral-comical, historical-pastoral, tragical-historical, tragical-comical-historical-pastoral, scene individable, or poem unlimited: Seneca cannot be too heavy, nor Plautus too light" (2.2. 405–410).

21. Lindley, 31.

22. Crashaw, William. *A sermon preached in London before the right honorable the Lord Lavvarre, Lord Gouernour and Captaine Generall of Virginea, and others of his Maiesties Counsell for that kingdome, and the rest of the aduenturers in that plantation. At the said Lord Generall his leaue taking of England his natiue countrey, and departure for Virginea, Febr. 21. 1609. By W. Crashaw Bachelar of Diuinitie, and preacher at the Temple.* London: W. Hall for William Welby, 1610, H3v–H4r. ESTC citation # S109071.

23. Cedric Clive Brown in *his Patronage, Politics, and Literary Traditions in England, 1558–1658,* appreciates the cultural abyss that separated the players from the adventurers: "The Virginia Company itself needed to attract as colonists not parasitic gentry looking for an easy life exploiting cheap land and labour, the types represented in the drama by Sir Petronel Flash in *Eastward Ho,* or perhaps by Antonio and Sebastian in *The Tempest,* but skilled craftsmen and farmers. To reach this highly motivated but unbookish audience required the development of a plain style, of which Hakluyt's voyages and the company's various reports and propaganda by Crashaw and others set a model" (154). Google Books. Web.

24. *True Declaration,* 11.

25. Kathman, "Dating."

26. Mowat, Barbara A. "*The Tempest*: A Modern Perspective," in Barbara A. Mowat and Paul Werstine. *The New Folger Shakespeare: The Tempest.* New York: Washington Square Press, 1994, 196.

Chapter 6

1. Hassel, R. Chris. *Renaissance Drama and the English Church Year.* Lincoln: University of Nebraska Press, 1979, 1.

2. Hassel, 3.

3. Hassel, 2.

4. See, for instance, in addition to Hassel (1979); François Laroque, *Shakespeare's Festive World: Eliz-*

abethan Seasonal Entertainment and the Professional Stage. Cambridge: University Press, 1991; Steve Sohmer, "12 of June 1599: Opening Day at Shakespeare's Globe," *Early Modern Literary Studies* 3.1 (1997): 1.1–46. Web. Molly Carter, "Who is Jack a Lent? Personifications of Shrovetide and Lent in 16th and 17 th Century England," presented at the International Ethnological Conference on the Ritual Year, March 20–24, 2004. Web. Accessed 6/15/2006; Juliet Dusinberre, "Pancakes and a Date for *As You Like It.*" *The Shakespeare Quarterly.* 54: 4 (2004), 371–405; and Steve Roth, "Hamlet as the Christmas Prince: Certain Speculations on *Hamlet,* the Calendar, Revels, and Misrule." *Early Modern Literary Studies* 7.3 (January, 2002): 5.1–89. Web.

5. Shriving was an intrinsically reciprocal religious rite, meaning to hear or receive confession *and* to give or receive absolution.

6. As Stephen Roth notes, "Shrovetide was intimately related to rebellion — both in fact and in 'act.'"

7. Hutton, Ronald. *The Stations of the Sun: A History of the Ritual Year in Britain* (Oxford: University Press, 1997), 151.

8. Hassel, 118.

9. Neogeorg, Thomas. *The Popish Kingdome, or reigne of Antichrist, by T. Naogeorgus, englyshed by B. Googe.* London: H. Denham for R. Watkins, 1570. ESTC Citation # S109280, 03v.

10. Neogeorg , Plr. That these excesses did not disappear with the advent of Protestantism is witnessed by many accounts, among them, Henri Misson de Valbourg's 1698 eyewitness account of the Carnival atmosphere of London on Shrove Tuesday, quoted by Laroque: "I have sometimes met in the streets of London a woman carrying a figure of straw ... preceded by a drum, and followed by a mob, making a most grating noise with tongs, gridirons, frying-pans and saucepan" (100).

11. "German Baroque Literature." Web. Accessed 6/6/2006.

12. Chambers, E.K. *The Elizabethan Stage.* Oxford: Clarendon Press, 1923 (in four volumes), I, 265.

13. Hassel, 122.

14. Herford, C.H. and Evelyn Simpson (eds). *Ben Jonson.* Oxford: Clarendon Press, 1941 (in eleven volumes), VII, 663.

15. Chambers, *Elizabethan Stage,* 46.

16. Chambers, *Elizabethan Stage,* E44.

17. Chambers, *Elizabethan Stage,* 45.

18. "German Baroque Literature." Web. Accessed 6/6/2006.

19. Hassel, 114.

20. See Roth, "Christmas Prince."

21. Kifer, Divra Rowland. "*A Staple of News*: Jonson's Festive Comedy," *Studies in English Literary,* 1500–1900, 12:2, *Elizabethan and Jacobean Drama* (spring, 1972), 329–344.

22. Kernan, Alvin. *Shakespeare, the King's Playwright.* New Haven: Yale University Press, 1995; Hassel, 116–118.

23. Dusinberre, Juliet. "*Pancakes and a Date for*

As You Like It," The Shakespeare Quarterly. 54: 4 (2004), 371–405. *Merchant of Venice*, in particular, has received frequent attention for its Shrovetide associations, in part because it was performed twice during Shrovetide, 1605. Kernan (70) suggests that *Merchant's* masquing episodes were recognized by the royal audience as dramatic representations of Shrovetide revelry. In *Merchant* "the imperfect blending of this paradoxical [Lenten] half of the Shrovetide perspective among the Christian and romantic characters of the play" becomes the factor "that separates them from all of Shakespeare's other major comic characters and ... invites the ironic perspective to coexist with the romantic one" (Hassel 117).

24. Chambers, *Elizabethan Stage*, 4, 100.
25. Laroque, 203.
26. Hassel, 112.
27. Hassel, 112.
28. "Banns of Marriage," *Catholic Encyclopedia Online*; Cressy, David. "The Seasonality of Marriage in Old and New England," *Journal of Interdisciplinary Studies*, 16:1 (Summer 1985), 1.
29. Wickham, Glynne. *Early English Stages. Volume Three: Plays and Their Makers to 1576.* London: Routledge and Kegan Paul, 1981, 24.
30. Bentley, Gerald Eades. *Jacobean and Caroline Stage: Plays and Playwrights.* In Seven Volumes. Oxford: University Press, 1956, 1.
31. Bentley, 2.
32. Grace Hall, *The Tempest as Mystery Play: Uncovering Religious Sources of Shakespeare's Most Spiritual Play,* 1999. Jefferson, NC: McFarland, 29.
33. Hassel, 170.
34. Hall, 31.
35. Hall, 30–31.
36. See discussion, infra., chapter 10.
37. Neogeorgus, *Popish Kingdome,* Pir, emphasis supplied.
38. Lent was the special time for the highly effective "plenary indulgence," by which the penitent received "remission of the entire temporal punishment due to *sin* so that no further expiation is required in *Purgatory*" (*New Advent*, "Indulgences," Web. Consulted 2/13/2012).
39. Laroque, 203.
40. The Christian liturgical association between the maze and Lent endures, and modern contemplative works, both Protestant and Catholic, still stress it: "The journeys of Lent and of life are seldom straight roads; usually they are like complicated mazes or labyrinths. While we often can feel lost along the complex twisting patterns of the labyrinth path, traveling the maze of the Way is the greatest of all adventures." Edward Hays, *The Labyrinth Cross of Lent* [Ave Maria Press, 1994], as excerpted at www.homilies.com.
41. Hall, 58.
42. The modern practice is to distinguish sharply between mazes and labyrinths, but this distinction is anachronistic for the early modern period, as Chiasson (reviewing Doob) clarifies: "Doob underscores the discrepancy between the 'multicursal'

labyrinth of the literary tradition, with its numerous points of choice between two of more paths that may lead nowhere, and the 'unicursal' model of the visual arts, a single winding path that leads inevitably to the center, without any internal choices. Since this distinction goes virtually unnoticed by classical and medieval writers, Doob proposes an inclusive pre–Renaissance model ... that defines the maze as a complex artistic structure with a circuitous design that may imprison or enlighten the maze-walker as it prevents or controls access to the good or evil that lies at its center" (84).

43. Matthews, W.H. *Mazes and Labyrinths: Their History and Development.* New York: Dover, 1970 reprint of 1922 original, 66–68. Doob (1990) argues that this is a late and misleading interpretation, but this is irrelevant to our argument, in which the distinction between the maze and the labyrinth plays no significant role.
44. Mathews, 64; Adair Fischer, *Mazes and Labyrinths,* Buckinghamshire: Shire Publications, 2004, 8.
45. See "Labyrinth," which agrees in stressing the devotional nature of the labyrinth: "labyrinths were supposed to have originated in a symbolical allusion to the Holy City, and certain prayers and devotions doubtless accompanied the perambulation of their intricate mazes." *The Original Catholic Encyclopedia.* Web. Accessed 2/13/2012.
46. "Sixth Week." In critical respects the Christian labyrinth of the Middle Ages appears to prefigure the Stations of the Cross. Although the Stations were not established until later, both practices were traditional at Lent. The fourteen labyrs of the medieval labyrinth are replicated in the fourteen Stations of the Cross. Like walking the labyrinth, visiting the Stations of the Cross came to replace the Easter pilgrimage to Palestine for Christians unable to undertake the hazards and hardships of the actual journey (Catholic Bishops 1; Matthews 66–68). Indulgences are also closely associated with the Stations, which had originated as "special stopping-places with indulgences attached" and later became formalized. *Catholic Encyclopedia,* "Way of the Cross," Web.
47. Mowat, Barbara. "*The Tempest,* A Modern Perspective," in *The Tempest,* Barbara Mowat and Paul Werstine, eds., New York: Washington Square Press, 1994; 196 (emphasis supplied) David Lindley's New Cambridge edition illustrates the significance of the maze metaphor in the play with an emblem from Francis Quarles (Figure 6.1).
48. Herford and Simpson, VIII: 488,11. 255–57.
49. Herford and Simpson, VIII: 488,11. 261–62.
50. Hassel, 132.
51. Hassel, 129.
52. Vaughan and Vaughan, 17: emphasis supplied.
53. In 1350, Higden, Monk of Chester, wrote "Rosamund was the fair daughter of Walter, Lord Clifford, concubine of Henry II, and poisoned by Queen Eleanor, AD 1177. Henry made for her a house of wonderful working, so that no man or

woman might come to her, but he that was instructed by the king, or such as were right secret with him touching the matter. This house after some was named Labyrinthus, and was wrought like upon a knot in a garden called a maze. But the queen came to her by a clue of a thread, and so dealt with her that she lived not long after." Percy, Thomas. *Reliques of Ancient English Poetry.* London: George Routledge, 1857, 251.
Cf *Tempest*:
And peg thee in his *knotty* entrails till (1.2.347)
If thou dost break her virgin *knot* before (4.1.17)
54. These terms apparently refer to the straight (forthrights) and curved (meanders) elements of the traditional Church labyrinth. Their use in this context underscores the vitality of the maze as *Tempest* metaphor.
55. Eden, 43. In the preface to his 1555 translation of Martyr, Eden glosses the New World project with a typological precedent from Isaiah 66: "Of them that shall be saved, I will send some to the gentiles in the sea, into Aphrike and Libia, Italie, and Grecia, and into the Islands a far of, to them that have not heard of me, and have not seen my glory" (civ).
56. Lindley, 210 (OED Chalk v 4c).
57. Vaughan and Vaughan, 17.
58. The early modern connotations of the Prospero's word for the island's illusions, *subtleties* ("you do but taste some subtleties of the island"), are both more intellectual and more morally ambiguous than currently, and are specifically applied, for instance, in Jerome Cardano's *De Subtilate,* to the use of mechanical contrivances for the purpose of creating illusions, consistent with OED 4. "...a cunning or crafty scheme, an artifice, dodge" (3132).
59. In the early modern lexicon the negative polarity of *amazement* predominated, as in OED 1. "Causing distraction, consternation, confusion, dismay; stupefying, terrifying, dreadful."
60. Walter, James. "From Tempest to Epilogue: Augustine's Allegory in Shakespeare's Drama," *PMLA* 98.1 (1983), 62.
61. Aercke, Kristiaan P. "An Odd Angle of the Isle": Teaching the Courtly Art of *The Tempest*," in *Approaches to Teaching Shakespeare's The Tempest and Other Late Romances.* Maurice Hunt, ed. New York: Modern Language Association, 2001, 149.

Chapter 7

1. Gilman, Ernest. "'All Eyes': Prospero's Inverted Masque," *Renaissance Quarterly* 33:2 (Summer 1980), 228.
2. Neogeorgus, 04r.
3. Laroque, 98.
4. Demaray, John G. *Shakespeare and the Spectacles of Strangeness: The Tempest and the Transformation of Renaissance Theatrical Forms.* Pittsburgh: Duquesne University Press, 1998, 7.
5. Chapman, George. *The memorable maske of the two honorable houses or Innes of Court; the Middle Temple, and Lyncolns Inne. As it was performed before the King, at White-Hall on Shrove Munday at night;*

being the 15 of February. 1613. Lond: G. Eld, 1613. ESTC Citation # S107695, A2.
6. Chapman, *Memorable Mask,* Av.
7. Townsend, Aurelian. *Tempe Restord. A Masque Presented by the Queen and Fourteen Ladies, to the King's Majesty at Whitehall, on Shrove-Tuesday, 1631.* London: Printed by A.M. for Robert Allet and George Baker, ESTC Citation # S118499, 1631, Bi r.
8. Schelling, Felix E. *Elizabethan Drama, 1558–1642.* New York: Houghton Mifflin, 1908, 97.
9. Barber, C.L. *Shakespeare's Festive Comedy.* Princeton, NJ: University Press, 1959, 129 n. 9.
10. See, for example, H.D. Gray, "*Some Indications That The Tempest Was Revised,*" *Studies in Philology,* 18:2 (1921), 129–40. Currently this theory seems to be particularly popular among the purveyors of online for-sale essays marketed for students.
11. Rose, Mark. *Shakespearean Design,* Cambridge: Harvard University Press, 1974, 173.
12. Rose, 173
13. Vadevieso, Sofía Muñoz. "'He Hourly Humanizes': Transformations and Appropriations of Shakespeare's Caliban," *Sederi* VII (1996), 293–296.
14. Alonso's loss may be seen to prefigure the loss of the son of God at Easter.
15. *II Henry IV* 5.3.12. The association is an early modern commonplace. The prologue to *Staple of News,* a play apparently written for Shrovetide, emphasizes the connection between the festival and "merrymaking": "*I am Mirth, the Daughter of Christmas, and Spirit of* Shrovetide. They say, is merry when Gossips meet; *I hope your Play will be a merry one!*" (Herford and Simpson VI: 279, emphasis original).
16. A literary type most familiar to scholars through *Conflictus veris et Hiemis,* attributed to the 8th century Englishman Alcuin.
17. Søndergaard, Lief & Thomas Pettitt, "*The Flyting of Yule and Lent*: A Medieval Swedish Shrovetide Interlude," in *The Dramatic tradition of the Middle Ages,* Clifford Davidson, ed. Brooklyn: AMS, 2005, 297–307.
18. Campbell, A. "A Debate between Shrovetide and Lent," *Bulletin Du Conge, Archivum Latinitatis Medii Aevi.* Leiden: Brill, 1977, 115–123.
19. Hutton, in 157–59, includes an extensive discussion of the practice.
20. Wagner, Leopold. "Secular Observances" in *Manners, Customs, and Observances.* 1894. Web.
21. See Hutton, 59–60, 164–65, 187, 387. *The Enlightenment World.* New York: Routledge, 2004, eds. Martin Fitzpatrick, Peter Jones, et al., who describes Shrovetide as "an occasion for lent-crocking, that is, soliciting *festive doles* from householders, as well as for cock-fighting and cock-shying" (405; our emphasis).
22. *OED,* sv n2 2.
23. The Saturday before Shrove Tuesday, named after the practice of consuming as many eggs as possible before the prohibitions of Lent.
24. Bellinger, Martha Fletcher. "Moralities, Farces and Interludes of the Middle Ages," in *A*

Short History of the Drama. New York: Henry Holt, 1927, 138–44.

25. "At Shrovetide, but especially at Shrove Tuesday, everyone must dance, if the flax, the vegetables and the corn are to thrive." Frazer, Sir James. *The Golden Bough: A Study in Magic and Religion*, VIII (London: Macmillan, 1912), 326.

26. Herford and Simpson, VII, 263.

27. "'Tis well thou art not fish; if thou hadst, thou hadst been poor John. Draw thy tool; here comes two of the house of the Montagues" (*Romeo and Juliet* 1.1.19).

28. At Shrovetide households customarily used up all their rich foodstuffs, including eggs, fat, and cream, in one last Rabelaisian fling. After Lent began, together with these rich foods, meat was proscribed.

29. See, for example, John Donne's 3 March, 1619 Whitehall sermon: "since the woe in this Text is not S. John wo? His iterated, his multiplied wo, *Vae, vae, vae habitantibus terram*, a woe of desolation upon the whole world." (Potter, George R. and Evelyn M. Simpson, eds. *The Sermons of John Donne. In Ten Volumes*. Berkeley and Los Angeles: University of California, 1955, II, 349.

30. Is this reference to a survival of the very ancient "Crane Dance," also known as the "Troy Dance," which since pre-Platonic days had been closely associated with the labyrinth and its Trojan roots? See Matthews, 158–62.

31. Neogeorgus, 04r.

32. Townsend, Bi r.

33. Carew, Thomas. *Coelum Brittanicum. A Masque at White-Hall in the Banquetting-House on Shrove-Tuesdeay Night, the 18th of February, 1633*. London: Printed for Thomas Walkley, 1634, Cir.

34. Hassel, 132.

35. The peacock (4.1.74) would have signified immortality and Christ in the resurrection, the dove (4.1.94) the holy ghost, especially in representations of the baptism of Christ; and the lion, implicit in Ariel's name, Jesus himself.

36. Incidentally, the passage suggests that Queen Elizabeth was alive when this play was written: her association with the Phoenix is too well known to require detailed exposition. As early as 1574 medallions were struck bearing her image on one side and the phoenix on the other, and in 1575 she sat for the "Phoenix portrait" by Nicholas Hilliard wearing one. Jonson's *Chloridia*, a 1630 Shrovetide masque, also features Juno and Iris as prominent characters (Herford and Simpson VII: 758–60).

37. Impelluso, Lucia. *Nature and Its Symbols.* translated by Stephen Sartarelli. The J. Paul Getty Museum: Los Angeles, 2004, 368, 372.

38. "Aberdeen Bestiary," MythFolklore.net. Web. Accessed 6/16/2006.

39. In Shakespeare's pagan pretext, the myth of Theseus in the labyrinth, a monster plays a critical role. Not surprisingly, several species of monster including "dewlapped bulls" and "men whose heads stood in their breasts" (3.3.45–47) — together suggesting the emblem of the Minotaur — assume a role in the play's cosmic landscape.

40. Laroque, 104.

41. Caliban has recently been identified by Greenblatt and others as a personification of the European "wild man," a figure closely associated with Shrovetide festivities. In England the Green Man's official day of celebration was St. George's Day, 23 April, but one of his early appearances in the opening days of spring fell on Shrovetide.

42. It has sometimes mistakenly been supposed that the symbolism of Christ as ἰχθύσ a commonplace of ancient symbolism, did not survive into the Renaissance. The iconographic evidence (Figure 16.4), however, proves the durability and continuity of the symbolic association (see Impelluso 344–45).

43. Those inclined to doubt the playwright's capacity for such a sacrilegious meditation may wish to recall Hamlet's dictum that even "a King may go a progress through the guts of a beggar" (4.3.30–31).

44. As early as Frobisher's 1570s expeditions in search of the Northwest Passage, natives were being brought back to England as objects of display. For an engaging analysis, see Greenblatt, Stephen, *Marvelous Possessions: The Wonder of the New World*. Oxford: Clarendon Press, 1991, esp. "Kidnapping Language" (86–118) and "The Go-Between" (119–151).

45. In one of Shakespeare's ultimate ironies, it is the Europeans, rather than the "sauvage" Caliban, who cannot refrain from imagining other humans as food.

46. "Tempest," *Online Etymology Dictionary.* Web. Accessed 1/15/11.

47. John 17:1: "These words spake Jesus, and lifted up his eyes to heaven, and said, Father, *the hour is come*; glorify thy Son, that thy Son also may glorify thee." The phrase is a refrain in the New Testament, viz: Mark 14 .41: "And he came the third time, and said unto them, sleep henceforth, and take your rest: it is enough: *the hour is come*: behold, the Son of man is delivered into the hands of sinners." John 7:30: "Then they sought to take him: but no man laid hands on him, because *his hour was not yet come*." John 8:20: "These words spake Jesus in the treasury, as he taught in the temple: and no man laid hands on him; for *his hour was not yet come*." John 13:1: "Now before the feast of the passover, when Jesus knew that *his hour was come* that he should depart out of this world unto the Father, having loved his own which were in the world, he loved them unto the end." All Biblical quotations are from the 1599 Genevan.

48. Hall, 161–62.

49. As Driver (366) notes, there are definite further indications that the unity of time has not been observed in the play, for instance Ferdinand's remark "'Tis fresh morning with me when you are by at night" (3.1.34–45), which makes no sense if their acquaintance is less than a day old.

50. Unless otherwise specified, quotations are from the Geneva Bible, modern spelling text.

51. "Lent," *Catholic Encyclopedia*. Web. Accessed 1/10/11.
52. Hall, 162.
53. "Sext," *Catholic Encyclopedia*. Web. Accessed 1/10/11. Matt: "Now from the sixth hour was there darkness over all the land, unto the ninth hour."
54. Gash, Antony. "Shakespeare, Carnival and the Sacred: *The Winter's Tale* and *Measure for Measure*," in Knowles, 177.
55. Cf. the peculiar debate over Tunis as a resurrection of Carthage (2.1.76–86).
56. Baptism of new Christians was customary at Lent, a theme particularly evident in the comic fate of the revelers, whom Ariel describes the revelers as so "red hot with drinking" that they are transformed at the sound of his tabor into "unbacked colts" — a popular emblem of lust — which he leaves "dancing up to th' chins" (4.1.171; 176; 183) in the mire. This submersion in the pool parodies the play's shipwreck scene, and the Christian sacrament of baptism, a practice mocked in popular rituals of Shrovetide:

Some others bear upon a staff their fellows
  horsed high,
And carry them unto some pond, or running
  river nigh,
That what so of their foolish feast, doth in
  them yet remain,
May underneath the flood be plunged, and
  wash't away again.
                              (Neogeorgus P1r)

57. See, e.g. Chetwood, W.R. *The Life and Writings of Ben Jonson*. Dublin, 1756; 1970.
58. Hassel, 112.
59. Hassel, 113.
60. Since the 19th century the phrase "leaving not a *racke* behind" — as the folio spells *racke* — has provoked copious controversy. The Furness Variorum reprints five pages (212–17) of commentary on it. The word has sometimes been interpreted as meaning a "rack of cloud," but Malone first proposed an echo of "shipwreck." In a Shrovetide context, the latter reading — with the extended meaning of "stage equipment" — assumes a particularly potent semantic force as again emphasizing the imminent theatrical prohibitions of Lent.
61. The idea of the high priest, a mediator between God and man who, like Prospero experiences the frailties of the flesh ("One of their kind, that relish all as sharply,/Passion as they..." (5.1.23) yet is free from sin, is critical to the doctrines of Lent. *The Catechism of the Catholic Church* states, "For we have not a high priest who is unable to sympathize with our weaknesses, but one who in every respect has been tested as we are, yet without sinning" [Heb. 4:15]. By the solemn forty days of Lent the Church unites herself each year to the mystery of Jesus in the desert" (Catechism 540).
62. Laroque, 203.
63. Hassel, 126.

Chapter 8

1. But c.f. *Midsummer Night's Dream*: "**Puck.** I'll put a girdle round about the earth/In forty minutes" (2.1.178–79).
2. While we believe this passage in context clearly alludes, as Kermode and Marshall among others suggest, to the Bermuda Islands, we also find plausible the theory first advanced by Richard Roe and supported by Paul Hemenway Altrocchi that the line may invoke a pun on the notorious red light and brewery district of London by the same name (See "Bermoothes: An Intriguing Enigma," *Shakespeare Matters*, 5:3 (Spring 2006), 10–14). This part of the city could comically be said to be "still-vexed," i.e. vexed by distilleries, and from here Ariel could logically fetch "dew," i.e. liquor.
3. Both Frank Kermode and Tristan Marshall understand that this comment of Oviedo's furnishes the epistemic context for Shakespeare's reference: "Ariel, in mentioning the Bermudas, is merely *trying to emphasize how far away they were*" (Kermode 192); "a contemporarily vivid point of reference to the Jacobean audience of the *distance* Ariel has Traveled in the service of his master" (Marshall).
4. Argier: 1.2.308; 313.
5. Tunis: 2.1.79; 271; 2.1.68; 70; 78; 92; 281; 286; 5.1.237.
6. Carthage: 2.1.78; 79; 80; 81.
7. Milan: 1.2.64; 69; 126; 146; 509; 511; 2.1.107; 131; 309; 322; 3.3.85; 5.1.91; 113; 170; 216; 233; 350.
8. Naples: 1.2.129; 141; 273; 504; 524; 2.1.107; 131; 269; 272; 282; 323; 504; 2.1.505; 285; 289; 2.2.74; 3.3.25; 5.1.166; 234; 347.
9. Lindley, 45.
10. Skura, Meredith Anne. "Discourse and the Individual: The Case of Colonialism in 'The Tempest,'" *Shakespeare Quarterly* 40:1, Spring 1989: 42–69, 47.
11. Leo Salingar, "The New World in *The Tempest*," in *Travel and Drama in Shakespeare's Time*, Jean Pierre Maquerlot and Michèle Vellems, eds., Cambridge: University Press, 1996, 203.
12. Fuchs, Barbara. "Conquering Islands: Contextualizing *The Tempest*," *Shakespeare Quarterly* 48.1, Spring 1997: 45–62, 46.
13. Wilson-Okumura, 709.
14. Given the latter's relevance to the play's setting, it is unsurprising that a number of studies over the years, most thoroughly Donna Hamilton's 1990 *Virgil and The Tempest: The Politics of Imitation* (Ohio State University, 1990) have been devoted to exploring the play's many and significant Virgilian associations.
15. Gillies, 48.
16. Gillies, 49.
17. Gillies, 49.
18. According to Paul K. Davis, Lepanto "stopped Turkey's expansion into the Mediterranean, thus maintaining western dominance, and confidence grew in the west that Turks, previously unstoppable, could be beaten." *100 Decisive Battles: From*

Ancient Times to the Present. Oxford: University Press, 2001, 194.

19. One recent book, Richard Roe's *The Shakespeare Guide to Italy* (New York: Harper Perennial, 2011), identifies Caliban's island as Vulcano, a tiny volcanic island similar in some respects to Lampedusa, but located to the North of Sicily very near to the tip of the boot of the Italian coastline. While Roe makes some interesting arguments, we believe Hunter's original case for Lampedusa, as augmented in our analysis in this chapter, is more convincing. Vulcano may possess some of the *physical* characteristics of Caliban's island, but it lacks the mytho-geographical associations which contribute such richly ironic undertones to Shakespeare's play. Roe's reasons concerning geology, topography, flora, and fauna could apply to many islands. On the other hand, his attempts to secure the theory on the grounds of the play's alleged descriptions of a specifically volcanic nature are unconvincing. Miranda's "the sky, it seems, would pour down stinking pitch" (1.1.3) may be the sole exception. Regrettably, Roe mentions neither Hunter nor the alternative theory of Lampedusa as a *Tempest* locale. Pantelleria, which lies more directly northward, had been continuously inhabited since Neolithic times, therefore also makes a poor substitute for Lampedusa, as well as lacking its literary associations.

20. Wilson, Richard. "Voyage to Tunis: New History and the Old World of *the Tempest*," *ELH* 64: 2 (1997), 333–357, 209.

21. Wilson, 355.

22. But see the work of Oxfordian W. Ron Hess, *An Iron-fisted Romantic in England's Most Perilous Times* (Lincoln, NE, 2002, Writers Club Press, Vol. 1), 72, for an independent discussion of suitability of Lampedusa as a Tempest locale. Today the island of ten square miles belongs geopolitically to Italy, but geographically is part of Africa; located along the shallow continental shelf extending from Tunisia, which never reaches a depth of more than 120 meters, and its flora and fauna are substantially North African in character.

23. Hunter, 17.

24. Smyth, 287.

25. Smyth, 285.

26. Smyth, 287.

27. Hunter, 24.

28. According to Stephen Runciman, *Turco Graecia* constitutes "notre source principale d'information sur le monde grec du 16-ème siècle," Cited in Jean Michel Cantacuzène, "Sur la trace des livres de Michel Cantacuzène 'Saitanoglou' Quatre ou cinq livres rares des 16ème et 17ème siècles," 45 (http://www.bcu-iasi.ro/biblos/biblos14/pag45.pdf).

29. Crusius, Martin. *Turco-Graecia*. Basil, 1584, "Noctes ibi spectris tumultuosae" (528).

30. *De rebus Siculis Decades duae* (Palermo, 1558).

31. Anon, cited in Hunter: "estre utile à ceux aui abordent dans l'isle, don'ils peuvent se server librement, en cas qu'ils en ayent besoin pour achever leur voyage, mais qu qui que ce soit ne peut prendre sans nécessité qu la punition suit de prés la crime,

puisqu'on peut sortir de l'isle jusqu'à ce quón ait fait restitution de ce qu'on a pris..." (34).

32. Crusius: "Aiunt qui non offerat, aut aliquid auferat, nec restituit, non posse ab insula abire" (528). Our translation.

33. Although Hunter drew attention to the facts of this Lampedusan tradition, he seemed unaware of the textual implications of his own findings.

34. "Vestes" (Crusius) or "des habits" (Anon).

35. On the theme of clothing in the *Tempest*, see also, especially, 1.2.217–219; 2.1.60–72; 103–105; 273–74; and, of course, the "frippery" scene itself, 4.1–220–254.

36. "Vestuto et collapso castello," Hunter, 23.

37. Muir, 52.

38. Cairncross, Andrew S. "Shakespeare and Ariosto: *Much Ado About Nothing, King Lear,* and *Othello*," *Renaissance Quarterly* 29:2 (Summer 1976), 178–182, 182.

39. Gillespie, Stuart. *Shakespeare's Books: A Dictionary of Shakespeare's Sources*. London: Athlone Press, 2001, 27.

40. Ludovico Sforza is referenced at least five times in *Orlando Furioso*, including 13.62–3; 33.31; 40.41; 42.91; 46.94.

41. Reynolds, Barbara (ed.) *Orlando Furioso, Translated with an Introduction by Barbara Reynolds*. In two volumes. London: Penguis, 1973. VI: 30. All translations and line references are from the Reynolds edition.

42. Sometimes he thought to swim the stormy main,

> By stretch of arms the distant shore to gain
> Thrice he the sword assay'd, and thrice the flood;
> But Juno, mov'd with pity, both withstood.
> And thrice repress'd his rage; strong gales supplied,
> And push'd the vessel o'er the swelling tide.

(*Aeneid*, book X, Dryden's translation)

43. Canto 41 also contains a possible source for the *Tempest* imagery of "water with berries in it" (1.2.334) in the hermit's diet of "pure water, fruit or berries from a tree" (41.58.5).

44. Furness, 274.

Chapter 9

1. Smith, Hallett. *Shakespeare's Romances: A Study of Some Ways of the Imagination*. San Marino: Huntington Library, 1972, 2.

2. See chapter 2 and, especially, chapter 10.

3. There is, for example, neither performance history of nor extant reference to *Timon of Athens, Coriolanus*, or *All's Well That End's Well* until their folio publication in 1623, but no one doubts that these plays were written at least fifteen years before surfacing in the folio.

4. Chambers, *William Shakespeare*, I: 269.

5. Chambers, 492, emphasis ours.

6. Chambers, 493.

7. Chambers, 245.

8. Muir, 280. It should be noted that Muir's skepticism on this point did not, unfortunately,

lead him to contest the premise of Shakespeare's access to the Bermuda pamphlets.

9. Gurr, Andrew. "The *Tempest*'s tempest at Blackfriars," *Shakespeare Survey*, 41 (1989), 91–102.

10. McCarthy, Penny. "Some *Quises* and *Quems*: Shakespeare's true Debt to Nashe," in *New Studies in the Shakespearean Heroine. The Shakespeare Yearbook*, 14 (2004): 175–192.

11. McCarthy, 176.

12. McCarthy, 176.

13. Kathman, "Dating."

14. Adams, Stephen. *The Best and Worst Country in the World: Perspectives on the Early Virginia Landscape*, Charlottesville: University Press, 2001, 92.

15. Furness, *Tempest*, 306. Interestingly, Furness made no effort to reconcile this statement with his previous claim that the play had not been written until 1612, as if a mere two years made no difference in the plausibility of either scenario.

16. McCarthy, 175.

17. Kirk, Florence Ada. *The Faithful Shepherdess by John Fletcher: A Critical Edition*, New York: Garland, 1980.

18. Herford, C.H. and Evelyn Simpson. *Ben Jonson*. Oxford: Clarendon Press, 1950, II: 229.

19. Kirk, vi–x.

20. Furness, 350.

21. Furness, 350.

22. Rouse, W.H.D. *Shakespeare's Ovid Being Arthur Golding's Translation of Metamorphoses*. London, 1961, 142.

23. "Beaumont and Fletcher," G.C. Macaulay. *The Cambridge History of English and American Literature*. Vol. 6. Web.

24. Co-written with Phillip Massinger and first published 1647.

25. "Some Political and Social Aspects of the Later Elizabethan Period and Earlier Stewart Period," *Cambridge History of English and American Literature*, volume 5. Web.

26. Campbell, Oscar James and Edward G. Quinn, *The Reader's Encyclopedia of Shakespeare*. New York: Thomas Y. Crowell, 1966, 51.

27. Brennecke, Ernst. *Shakespeare in Germany, 1590–1700*. Chicago: University of Chicago Press, 1964, 220.

28. Such a scenario, while wholly lacking substantive support, has frequently been endorsed. Chambers' view is typical: "use of a common source is a more plausible explanation than borrowing on either hand" (I: 439). "But," Chambers concedes, "it has not been found" (I: 493).

29. Goddard, Harold. *The Meaning of Shakespeare*, Chicago: University Press, 1960, II, 287.

30. Cohn, Albert. *Shakespeare in Germany in the sixteenth and seventeenth centuries: An account of English actors in Germany and the Netherlands and of the plays performed by them during the same period*. London: Asher, 1865, LXIX.

31. Cohn, LXX.

32. Brennecke, 3.

33. Brennecke, 9.

34. Cohn, LXXVI.

35. Cohn, LXIV.

36. Cohn, LXIV.

37. Cohn, LXIV. Italics supplied.

38. Furness, 324.

39. Furness, 284.

40. Cited in Furness, 284.

41. McCarthy (citing Tobin): "The author who has a particular history or person as his subject, and is tied to using appropriate signs for that subject, ought to be seen as the originator. The one who is free to invent, yet has the same phrases as the 'tied' author, will be the echo" (178).

42. "As th' Ocean flowes, and ebbes, states rise and fall" (d1r); "When a strange terrour troubled all the host:/The multitudes did murmure in all parts:/ *They did resemble ships with tempests toste*" (i3v).

43. "More happie he whome a poore cottage shroudes/Against *the tempest* of the threatning hev'n" (c4v); "Make all my voyage through the world a sport;/That tossed with *a tempest of despight*/I now might perishe entering at my port...." (d2r); "Nowe toss'd with stormes in th'Ocean of dispaire,/By ruine only I attend relief,/Threatned above with pitchie cloudes of care,/Threatened below with swelling gulfes of greefe" (E1v); "The skilfull Pilote when he feares a storme,/To save the ship will cast out precious things" (g2r); "such glorious gorgeous showes doe serve for nought:/All cannot calme *the tempest of the thought*" (k2r).

44. McCarthy, 182.

45. Potter, Lois. "The Swan Theatre and Shakespeare's Contemporaries: the 2002 Season," *SQ* 54:1 (Spring 2003), 87–96, 90.

46. Horwich, Richard. "*Hamlet* and *Eastward Ho*," *SEL* 11 (1971):223–33. A recent survey of current scholarship (Egan et al., *Year's Work in English Studies, 2001* (80), 236–301) agrees that *Eastward Ho* "contains multiple parodies of *Hamlet*" (256). Potter, 90.

47. Compare, e.g., "**Fals.** Will your lordship lend me a lend a thousand pounds? **CJ.** Not a penny, you are too impatient to bear crosses (1.1.68–70) with "**Quick.** Sweet Touchstone, will you lend me two shillings **Touch.** Not a penny. **Quick.** Not a penny? I have friends, and I have acquaintance; I will piss at thy shop posts, and throw rotten eggs at thy sign. *Work upon that now!*" (2.1.138–43); **Pet.** Ay me, we are undone forever. Hast any money about thee? **Sea.** Not a penny, by Heaven! **Pet.** Not a penny betwixt us, and cast ashore in France!" (IV.1.45–48).

48. See Hillman, Richard. "Returning to One's Vomit: An Intertextual Tour of *Eastward Ho*'s Isle of Dogs," *Notes and Queries*, Dec. 2006, 508–514.

49. We survey the significant and largely still underappreciated intertextuality between *Eastward Ho* and the Shakespearean plays in our unpublished essay, "The Pattern of Parody in *Eastward Ho* ... and a New Date for *King Lear*."

50. CF Ovid, *Metamorphoses, aurea aestas*, I.89.

51. The early Spanish travel narratives are of course filled with alluring tales of abundant new world gold; to their disappointment, the English colonizers soon discovered that most of the east

coast of North America was barren of the commodity. As Herford and Simpson (IX: 643) observe, the proximate source of the reference is to the "chamber-pots and close-stools of gold" of More's *Utopia* (25–35).

52. The scene is Chapman's, according to Herford Simpson IX, 643.

53. The proximate and obvious reference, of course, is to the New Scots who came south with James and filled many state roles in the new Jacobean government.

54. Herford and Simpson, IX, 644–45.

55. Cf., "We are merely cheated of our lives by drunkards" (1.1.65)

56. Frank Kermode agrees: "Ariel, in mentioning the Bermudas, is merely *trying to emphasize how far away they were*" (*The Age of Shakespeare.* New York: Modern Library, 2003, 192–93, our emphasis).

57. Eden, Richard. *The Decades of the Newe Worlde or West India by Pietro Martire d'Anghiera* (f. 1555). Readex Microprint. 1966, 203v.

58. "Order for the Administration of the Lord's Supper," *Liturgies and Occasional Forms of Prayer Set forth in the Reign of Queen Elizabeth.* Edited for the Parker Society, the Rev. William Keatinge Clay, Cambridge: University Press, 1847, 188.

59. Andrew Gurr, while not regarding Quicksilver as a parody of Ariel (since he adheres to a more traditional chronology), does see a significant connection between the two characters. See his "The *Tempest*'s tempest at Blackfriars," *Shakespeare Survey* 41 (1988), 91–102, and "Industrious Ariel and Idle Caliban," in Maquerlot and Vellems, eds. Gurr describes Ariel as a "winged Mercury ... the antithesis of *Eastward Ho's!* get rich quick Quicksilver" (203).

60. Emphasis supplied. Petronel and his wife Gertrude, Touchstone's daughter, also echo the *Tempest* denouement:

> **Pet.** Dear Lady-wife, forgive me. **Gert.** As heartely, as I would be forgiven....
> (5.5.161–62)

The existence of common scriptural and liturgical precedents cannot entirely remove the impression of an intentional echo of Prospero's "as you from crimes would pardon'd be,/Let your indulgence set me free" (epi.).

61. "Our ship,/which but three glasses since we gave out split" (5.1.223). The nautical "glass" of the day measured time in units of a half hour.

62. This is also a spoof of *Hamlet*: "Good-night, *ladies*; good-night, sweet *ladies*" (4.5.72–73).

63. Since the incendiary 1597 satire named after the location, the Isle of Dogs had become a *cause célèbre* of literary parody and an emblem of the "unspeakable" literary crimes of satirists. The play was vigorously suppressed, and no copy has survived.

64. Kathman, "Dating."

65. And, we believe, *Lear.* See Stritmatter and Kositsky, "The Pattern of Parody," fn 49.

66. To this day the phrase "front of house" is a technical term in theatre referring to the area in which the audience sits as distinct from backstage parts of the theatre.

67. McCarthy identifies this *Lenten Stuffe* passage as a distinct reference to *The Tempest:* "One can hardly shut down one's reception of Shakespearean parody when the ... paragraph ends 'shee dreamed that Leander and Shee were playing at checkestone with pearles in the bottom of the sea' (3.197, G2v)" (183–84). As we have seen, McCarthy's argument for the play's early influence on Nashe represents only a tiny fraction of the evidence for a much earlier *Tempest* date.

68. Two of Jonson's early masques involve maritime themes that implicate the possible influence of *The Tempest*; in *The Masque of Blackness* (1605) "an artificiall sea is seene to shoote foorth it selfe abroad the roome as if it flowed to ye lande," and Oceanus, "his head, and bearde gray" and "gyrlanded wth Sea-grasse" (Herford and Simpson VII: 195), is a major figure. Jonson's next court masque, *The Masque of Beauty* (1608) features an "island floating on a calm water" (Barnet in Langabum 218).

69. Elizabeth's association with the Phoenix is too well known to require detailed exposition. As early as 1574 medallions were struck bearing her image on one side and the phoenix on the other, and in 1575 she sat for a "Phoenix *portrait*" by Nicholas Hilliard wearing one of these medallions.

Chapter 10

1. Stritmatter, Roger and Lynne Kositsky, "Voyagers."

2. Vaughan, Alden. "Evidence."

3. Reedy, Tom, "Dating."

4. Vaughan seems unwilling to concede either our rationality or good faith. He introduces us to readers of the *Shakespeare Quarterly* as "the prominent anti–Stratfordians" who have "launched an unparalleled attack ... on Strachey and his letter" (245). As this quotation illustrates, Vaughan's lack of objectivity is conspicuous in the prejudicial verbs used to summarize our discourse: Not only do we "attack"; we also "charge"; "label"; "misrepresent" and "berate," and all in the same paragraph! (245). These terms, we submit, are more indicative of Professor Vaughan's state of mind than they are descriptive of the actual tone and manner of our article. We did not "launch an unparalleled attack" on anything; we did invite readers to critically consider the unexamined "assumptions" — to again use Vaughan's own revealing word — bolstering the standard thesis of Strachey's influence on *The Tempest*.

5. Malone, Edmond. *Account of the Incidents from Which the Title and Part of the Story of Shakespeare's Tempest Were Derived: And Its True Date Ascertained,* 1808.

6. Vaughan, 245.

7. Vaughan, 267.

8. Elze, Karl. "The Date of *The Tempest*" in Essays *on Shakespeare.* Translated with the author's sanction by Dora L. Schmitz. London: Macmillan, 1874.

9. Muir, Kenneth. *The Sources of Shakespeare's Plays*, New Haven, Ct.: Yale University Press, 1977, 280.

10. Gurr, Andrew. "The *Tempest*'s Tempest at Blackfriars," *Shakespeare Survey* 41, 91–102. In personal communication with the authors (11/28/05), Gurr confirms his belief that *Tempest* may be dated too early for Strachey to have been a source, even assuming a traditional scenario like Vaughan's.

11. Shaksper discussion group, 03/20/01. Italics original. Web. Accessed 2/7/09.

12. Lindley, 31.

13. McCarthy, Penny. "Some *Quises* and *Quems*: Shakespeare's True Debt to Nashe," in *New Studies in the Shakespearean Heroine. The Shakespeare Yearbook,* 14 (2004), 176.

14. Thus, in progressive sciences such as archaeology, where technological advances and robust research programs continue to recover additional data, the dates of sequences such as the earliest human habitation of the Americas, continue to be revised backward.

15. Moreover, absence of evidence is not evidence of absence. Some plays may not have been produced until long after their dates of composition or completion.

16. Bawcutt, N.W. "New Revels Documents of Sir George Buc and Sir Henry," *Review of English Studies* 35:139 (1984), 316–331. Surely this remarkable anecdote reveals, if any does, that something is amiss with the traditional assumptions of English theatrical history.

17. Vaughan, 245.

18. Vaughan, 245.

19. Vaughan, 245.

20. Morton Luce, ed. *The Tempest.* London: Methuen & Co., 1902, summarizes: Malone's list "excludes the most important of all these contemporary documents, viz. Strachey's *Reportory* or *Letter*" (149). Instead of basing his case on Strachey, as Vaughan incorrectly implies, Malone's alleged verbal parallels (30–34) are based (primarily) on Jourdain and (secondarily) *Declaration*.

21. Vaughan, 273.

22. Furness, Horace Howard. *The Tempest: A New Variorum Edition Shakespeare*. New York: Dover. 1964 reprint of 1892 ed., 312–13.

23. Vaughan, 245.

24. Stritmatter and Kositsky, 448 fn. 2. See our more detailed discussion in Chapter 7.

25. Furness, 313.

26. Gayley, Charles Mills. *Shakespeare and the Founders of Liberty in America,* New York, Macmillan, 1917, 48. This concession is remarkable given Gayley's corresponding confidence in Strachey's role in shaping *The Tempest*, and further illustrates the stark divide between Malone's actual belief and the "standard thesis" of Strachey's influence as articulated by Vaughan.

27. Luce, xiii.

28. Luce, xiv. Strachey's early oeuvre, before he set off for Virginia, consists of only two extant poems, both at best mediocre. He was by no means a significant poet.

29. Stritmatter and Kositsky, 450.

30. Or Hakluyt. See discussion, Chapter 18.

31. Luce, 152; 154.

32. Luce, 152.

33. Harl. 7009, fol. 58.

34. Portions of the De La Warr letter were incorporated into *True Declaration*, registered November 1610.

35. It might be argued that Luce's omission merely results from less strict standards of documentation employed in early 20th century scholarship, but this theory is contradicted by Luce's fastidious attention to bibliographical detail for the other texts in question (which differs only from wholly modern conventions by not listing STC numbers, which did not exist in 1902). His omission of the Purchas date is all the more conspicuous by contrast.

36. Luce, 154; emphasis added.

37. Luce, 154.

38. Luce, 154.

Chapter 11

1. Vaughan, 257.

2. Vaughan, 257.

3. Vaughan, 258.

4. Hume, 59–61.

5. Hume, 63.

6. Culliford, 182–83.

7. Culliford, 182.

8. See William S. Powell. "Books in the Virginia Colony Before 1624." *William and Mary Quarterly* 3:5 (1948), 177–84.

9. Vaughan, 258.

10. Vaughan, 273

11. Does the fact that B, unlike *Reportory*, has no identifiable addressee resolve the longstanding enigma about whether Strachey's text was written to the Company or to a noble lady? It seems plausible that a copy of the B version, whether written for the Company or for a more private purpose in Virginia, was later expanded and amended in England, first by Strachey and then again by Purchas (and/or Hakluyt) to assume the form eventually published by Purchas in 1625.

12. Watson, Harold Francis. *The Sailor in English Fiction and Drama*, 1550–1800. New York: Columbia University Press, 1931, 76–77.

13. Strachey, *Lawes,* 5.

14. Vaughan, 258.

15. Hume, 85.

16. *Reportory* gives the date as May 23 (Wright 63), but some other sources say May 24.

17. Hume, 19–20

18. Hume, 84–85.

19. Hume, 85.

Chapter 12

1. Vaughan, 251.

2. *Pilgrims* 3.31.2 (A3v).

3. *Pilgrims*, 4.10.1950.

4. *Pilgrims*, 4.10.1950. Italics supplied.

5. *The Historie of Lopez Vaza Portugall (taken by Captaine Withrington at the River of Plate, Anno 1586, with this Discourse about him) touching American places, discoveries, and occurentes; abridged.* In Purchas, 1432–1448.

6. *Pilgrims*, 4.1432. Italics added. We are indebted to Tom Reedy for these and following examples of Purchas' and Hakluyt's contrasting editorial styles.

7. Vaughan, 249.

8. Vaughan, 267, fn. 55.

9. Reedy, 535.

10. Personal communication, 1/09.

11. There are only five instances of the usage in *Principal Navigations*, once in the 1589 "To the Favourable Reader" (A4v) twice in the 1599 "Epistle Dedicatorie to Sir Robert Cecil" (A3v, A4v), and twice in an introduction on 1.53–54). Hakluyt doesn't use the expression when inserting material from other sources.

12. Tom Reedy (personal communication) calculates that there are 43 total occurrences of such uses in *PP* (discounting the usage in Strachey); of those 43, 3 are in titles, 10 in marginal notes. Of the remaining 30, only 8 are clearly authorial (comparing *PP* with available original sources), and one is impossible to determine. Of the 22 clearly by Purchas, 9 do not refer to inserted material. Omitting Strachey, there are 11 examples of Purchas using the word as it is used in *Reportory*.

13. Parks, 181–82. Italics supplied.

14. Parks, ibid, 229.

15. Vaughan, 251; italics ours. A marginal note reads: "The particulars are here omitted. They contained a preface and 21 articles for piety, loyalty, and polity convenient to the colony" (PP 4.17.49).

16. *The Hakluyt Handbook* D.B. Quinn, ed. Volume I. 1974.

17. Steele, 83.

18. *A large relation of the Port Ricco Voiage; written, as is reported, by that learned man and reverend Divine Doctor Egamblie, his Lordship's Chaplaine and Attendant in that expedition, very much abbreviated.* In Purchas, 1155–1197.

19. *Pilgrims*, 4.1154.

20. Vaughan, 256.

21. Ignoring these problems, including the contrast between Hakluyt's editorial conservatism and Purchas' corresponding activism, Vaughan even claims that it is "obvious" that the *Declaration* extract was added by Hakluyt "in the fall of 1610." Actually, there is scant basis for claiming that this scenario is even plausible, let alone asserting that it is "obvious"; even if Vaughan could establish (he cannot) that the excerpt was *added by* Hakluyt, it would not prove *when* Hakluyt received the document or *when* the alteration was made. Vaughan asserts (267) that that the language of the *Repertory* passage "evokes recent events ... rather than over a decade of hindsight" (251). Setting aside the hy-

perbole of "over a decade of hindsight," we disagree. "I have here inserted" does sound like a recent action, but the remainder of the statement has no such air of immediacy and instead seems to recall events not only past but already completed.

22. *Pilgrims*, 4.1432. Italics added. We are indebted to Tom Reedy for these and following examples of Purchas's and Hakluyt's contrasting editorial styles.

23. Culliford, 179.

24. Culliford, 178.

Chapter 13

1. The Shakespearean plays are a case in point; some seventeen appeared for the first time in print in the 1623 Folio, although all were written, even by conservative estimate, thirteen or more years earlier. Of the seventeen, there is no explicit mention in any document of at least three — *Timon of Athens, Coriolanus,* and *All's Well That Ends Well*— before their publication in the folio.

2. Vaughan, 254.

3. Vaughan, 255.

4. Reedy, 550.

5. W.C. *A Plaine Description of the Barmudas, Now Called Sommer Ilands. With the manner of their discoverie Anno 1609, by the shipwrack and admirable deliverance of Sir Thomas Gates, and Sir George Sommers, wherein are truly set forth the commodities and profits of that Rich, Pleasant, and Healthfull Countrie. With An Addition, or more ample relation of divers other remarkable matters concerning those Ilands since then experienced, lately sent from thence by one of the Colonie now there resident.* William Welby, London, 1613. ESTC citation # S109447. This is a reprint, with supplemental materials, of Jourdain's *Discovery* (1610). Conversion to TEI.2-conformant markup: Jennifer S. Muter, Virginia Center for Digital History, Virginia Center for Digital History, Charlottesville, Virginia.

6. ESTC # S121921, *Good nevves from Virginia. Sent to the Counsell and Company of Virginia, resident in England. From Alexander Whitaker, the minister of Henrico in Virginia. Wherein also is a narration of the present state of that countrey, and our colonies there. Perused and published by direction from that Counsell. And a preface prefixed of some matters touching that plantation, very requisite to be made knowne (London: Felix Kyngston for William Welby, 1613).* While the work is sometimes attributed to William Crashaw, the STC indicates that the author is Alexander Whitaker.

7. Reedy, 551.

8. Hamor, *True Discourse.*

9. Wright, 64.

10. *The New Life of Virginea: Declaring the former successe and present estate of that plantation Being the Second part of Nova Britannia.* London: Felix Kingston for William Welby, 1612. Virtual Jamestown. Accessed 14/1/11. ESTC citation # S122143.

11. *New Life.* Our emphasis. Accessed 14/1/11.

12. Wright, 95–97.

13. Vaughan cites the introduction of *Declaration* to illustrate his point about "palliation," but as this passage is *not* excerpted in *Reportory,* and the actual excerpt from *Declaration* fails to provide the slightest indication of palliative intent or function (except perhaps arguing that the man who ate his wife did so even though there was plenty of available food), this argument is dubious. If the purpose was to use *Declaration* to palliate, why weren't the "palliatives" applied?

14. Vaughan, 256.

15. Vaughan, 256.

16. See Wright, 114–15.

17. Vaughan, 255–56.

18. Vaughan, 256.

19. Craven, Wesley Frank. 1997. *The Virginia Company of London, 1606–1624.* Jamestown 350th Anniversary Historical Booklet #5. Baltimore, MD: Genealogical, 34.

20. Wright, 109.

21. Malone, 22. Jourdain was printed in London by John Windet for Roger Barnes. Neither of them was the Company's official printer.

22. As we have already noted, the second (1613) edition, published by Company printer William Welby, was authorized.

23. Vaughan, 255.

24. As *Declaration* summarizes the circumstances: "Cast up this reckoning together: want of government, store of idleness, their expectations frustrated by the traitors, their market spoiled by the Mariners, our nets broken, the deer chased, our boats lost, our hogs killed, our trade with the Indians forbidden, some of our men fled, some murdered, and most by drinking the brackish water of James fort weakened, and endangered famine and sickness by all these means increased, here at home the monies came in so slowly, that the Lo. Laware could not be dispatched, till the Colony was worn and spent with difficulties: Above all, having neither Ruler, nor Preacher, they neither feared God nor man, which provoked the wrath of the Lord of Hosts, and pulled down his judgments upon them. *Discite Justitiam moniti*" (Wright 99–100).

25. Vaughan, 257. One dimension of Strachey's narrative that may be unique to him, and which might plausibly have occasioned *Reportory*'s suppression, is his detailed account of "conspiracies" among the Bermuda survivors which led to an execution. On the other hand, accounts of similar tragedies had already been published by Hakluyt.

26. Vaughan, 255.

Chapter 14

1. Reedy, 546.

2. MacNutt, Book Seven (Web, n.p.). For an extended discussion of this case, see Antonelli Gerbi (trans. Jeremy Moyle), *Nature in the New World: From Christopher Columbus to Gonzalo Ferdinández de Ovideo* (Pittsburgh, PA: University of Pittsburgh Press, 2010), 75. That such sentiments were more widespread than is often recognized is suggested by

similar well-known complaints by Ben Jonson, in his "On Poet-Ape" sonnet about the playwriting plagiarist,

that would be thought our chief,
Whose works are e'en the frippery of wit,
From brokage is become so bold a thief,
As we, the robb'd, leave rage, and pity it.
From locks of wool, or shreds from the whole
   piece ? (Herford and Simpson, VIII: 44–45)

Less well known, but no less significant, are Jonson's lines on "Proule the plagiarist," in which he relates that he

will not show
A Line unto thee, till the World it know;
Or that I'have by two good sufficient Men,
To be the wealthy Witness of my Pen.
(Herford and Simpson, VIII: 54)

3. Vaughan, 269.

4. Vaughan, 269, fn. 62.

5. Even these critics of Strachey's practices have routinely failed to give equal attention to *Reportory,* which has instead been largely exempted from scrutiny due to the pervasive influence of, and need to perpetuate, the "standard thesis."

6. "Norumbega and Its English Explorers," (1884), in J. Winsor (ed.), *Narrative and Critical History of America.* Vol. 3. Boston: Houghton, Mifflin, online at the Davistown Museum.

7. "Norumbega," in Winsor 3: 192.

8. Culliford, 182–83.

9. Culliford, 165.

10. Culliford, 149–50.

11. Vaughan, 269.

12. Vaughan, 268; emphasis added.

13. Vaughan, 268.

14. Stritmatter and Kositsky, 453–59.

15. Vaughan, 269, fn. 62.

16. Or Willes 1577 reissue.

17. Major, R.H., ed. *The Historie of Travaile into Virginia Britannia expressing the cosmographie and comodities of the country, together with the manners and customes of the people. By William Strachey.* London: Printed for the Hakluyt Society, 1849.

18. Culliford summarizes this period of Strachey's life: "Having returned to England and knowing that the Virginia Company thought well of his work in the colony, again he was to be disappointed. Although he remained friendly with members of the Virginia Company, and was a shareholder until his death, he did not serve the Company again, and the remaining years of his life were to be spent in obscurity, and if not in poverty, at least in reduced circumstances" (130).... "He was later to observe, somewhat bitterly, that 'the fashion of the world is to deal with us a[s] Pilate did with Christ, put a goodly superscription upon us, first in treating us with honor and much ostentation of glory, as Pilate upon Christ ... and afterward he caused him to be crucified'" (129).

Chapter 15

1. Malone, Edmond. *Account of the Incidents*

from which the Title and Part of the Story of Shakespeare's Tempest Were Derived: And Its True Date Ascertained. London: 1808.

2. Malone, cited in Furness 274.

3. *The Principal Navigations, Voyages, Traffiques & Discoveries of the English Nation by Richard Hakluyt*. In twelve volumes. Glasgow: James MacLehose, 1903–5.

4. Whitehead Neil L., ed. *The discoverie of the large, rich and bewtiful empyre of Guiana By Sir Walter Raleigh*. Manchester: University Press, 1997, 96.

5. Vaughan, 260.

6. Vaughan, 260.

7. May, Henry. "A Briefe Note of a Voyage to the *East Indies...*," in Hakluyt, *Principal Navigations*, 3.571–74, MacLehose ed. In May's account these events occurred before, rather than after, the wreck.

8. For May's narrative, see Sir William Foster, *The Voyages of Sir James Lancaster to Brazil and the East Indies, 1591–1603* (London: Printed for the Hakluyt Society), xi–xix, 22–30. The episode is also discussed at length in Kenneth R. Andrews, *English Privateering Voyages to the West Indies, 1588–1595* (Cambridge: University Press, 1959), 284–294. On the case for May's influence on *The Tempest*, see Ruth Loyd Miller, ed. *Shakespeare Identified* (Kennikat Press, 1975), vol. 2, 446–57. No complete analysis of the verbal parallels has been enumerated. As later published in Hakluyt's *Principal Navigations*, May's account declares that the sailors, "after they had their wine, careless of their charge which they took in hand, being as it were drunken, through their negligence a number of good men were cast away" (Foster 22), which is closer to Antonio's "we are merely cheated of our lives by drunkards" (1.1.55) than anything else from the voyager literature we have seen. The account also declares that "our ship did split," which may be echoed in Gonzalo's "we split, we split, we split!" (1.1.62).

9. Wright, 108. Our emphasis.

10. Marshall, Tristan. "*The Tempest* and the British Imperium in 1611," *The Historical Journal*, 41:2 (June 1998), 375–400; 380.

11. Kermode, Frank. *The Tempest*. London: Methuen, 1958, 92–93.

12. Marshall, 380, emphasis original.

13. Eden, 203v.

14. Hunter, 34.

15. Elze, 10–11.

16. Furness, 313.

17. Furness, 306.

18. Law, Ernest. *Some Supposed Shakespeare Forgeries*. London: G. Bell, 1911.

19. Furness, 280; for a useful review see Chambers, *Elizabethan Stage*, 1923 IV, 136–141.

20. Furness, 312.

21. Furness, 313.

22. Reprinted in Barbour, II:191–289. Barbour (195) designates the work a collaboration prepared under the editorship of William Symonds.

23. Gayley, 53.

24. Schumann, Howard. "Concordia Proposes Shakespeare Authorship Studies Center," *Shakespeare Matters* 5:3 (2006), 1, 26–31.

25. Schumann, Howard, 28.

26. Stritmatter and Kositsky, 451, fn. 8.

Chapter 16

1. Culliford, 123–25.

2. Vaughan, 267.

3. Stritmatter and Kositsky, 452. Italics added. Our appendix A (466–67) listed the actual passages in *Reportory* that answer Martin's questions, so there can be no real question of our claiming, as Vaughan implies, that the entire document was written in reply to Martin.

4. See Culliford 165–84 for a comprehensive list of the sources Strachey used, very often verbatim, to write *Travel*.

5. Culliford, 130–31.

6. Culliford, 131.

7. Culliford, 182–83.

8. Culliford, 181–82.

9. Quoted in Culliford, 130.

10. Vaughan, 267.

11. Vaughan, 267.

12. Vaughan, 261.

13. Reedy, Tom. "Dating William Strachey's 'A true Reportory of the Wracke and Redemption of Sir Thomas Gates': A Comparative Textual Study," *Review of English Studies*. Published online January 16, 2010. doi:10.1093/res/hgp107.

14. Reedy, 552.

15. Reedy, 552.

16. From a translated copy of Velasco's letter to Philip III, September 1610. Brown, Alexander. *The Genesis of the United States. A narrative of the movement in England, 1605–1616, which resulted in the plantation of North America by Englishmen, disclosing the contest between England and Spain for the possession of the soil now occupied by the United States of America; set forth through a series of historical manuscripts now first printed together with a reissue of rare contemporaneous tracts, accompanied by bibliographical memoranda, notes, and brief biographies. Collected, arranged, and edited by Alexander Brown*. 2 vols. New York: Houghton Mifflin and Co., 1964 (reprint of 1890 Russell & Russell edition), I: 418–9. It is reasonable to surmise that Velasco would focus on those portions of Newport's report that would concern Phillip III. Velasco's larger purpose is to identify an opportunity for Spanish interests resulting from the imminent collapse of the Jamestown Colony, which represented a serious threat to Spanish dominance in the region.

17. The two surviving De La Warr documents are his official dispatch, Harl. 7009.58, and a letter to Lord Salisbury, received September 1610. The former is available in Major, *Travel; Jamestown Narratives: Eyewitness Accounts of the Virginia Colony (The First Decade: 1607–1617)*, Champlain, VA: Roundhouse, 1998, Edward Wright Haile, ed., reprints the Salisbury letter, 467.

18. *A true Declaration of the Estate of the Colonie in Virginia. Published by advise and direction of the Councell of Virginia: London, Printed for William Barret, and are to be sold at the blacke Beare in Pauls Church-yard.* 1610. On-line edition published by Virtual Jamestown. Web. "Page 3." Accessed 2/28/09. ESTC citation #S122265.

19. They were so secret in fact, that for the most part we do not know who wrote them or what they wrote.

20. We interpret "The Judicial Council of Virginia" to be De La Warr's newly constituted Council in Virginia, rather than the Company Council still in London, because only the members of the Council in Virginia would have the information necessary for fashioning *True Declaration*.

21. See Wright 85–86 for a complete list. Strachey, as secretary to the colony council, is on it, one of many.

22. Wright, 4.

23. Brown, Alexander, *Genesis,* 29.

24. Reedy, 552. Our emphasis.

25. Reedy, 531.

26. Instead of a word-count, Reedy gives the pages on which *Reportory* appears on in Purchas — 1734–1758. For those unfamiliar with *Pilgrim*'s folio-sized pages, this might appear to be a very short narrative, but in fact there are almost 1000 words per page.

27. Of the twenty-six letters reproduced in Haile's *Jamestown Narratives* the longest, excepting the official De La Warr Dispatch of 7 July, is around 1400 words.

28. Reedy, 546. It is worth quoting *in extenso* Reedy's astonishing statement on this topic: "The problem of how these answers — supposedly written in response to a month's later request — are present in De La Warr's dispatch is not addressed by Stritmatter and Kositsky, but they insist that the passages were written later than the 15 July 1610 Strachey letter, even though they themselves acknowledge that the purported 'answers' are present almost verbatim in the 7 July dispatch from De La Warr a fact that is not disclosed to the reader" (546). Reedy cannot seem to make up his mind in this sentence whether Stritmatter and Kositsky "themselves acknowledge that the purported 'answers' are present" or whether this "fact"—as he calls it—"is not disclosed to the reader." Perhaps the problem lies in Mr. Reedy's own failure to "disclose to the reader" *either* the facts or what we actually wrote about them. The existence of some elements from the De La Warr dispatch later reproduced by Strachey in *Reportory* to answer Martin's question is not a mystery. Indeed, it seems likely that Martin's questions were themselves written in response to the De La Warr letter, received a few weeks earlier, by way of requesting further detail from Strachey. Whatever the exact transmission, however, it is not difficult to understand how some passages subsequently could have found their way into *Reportory*. Having already in his possession a document approximating the B text, Strachey

supplemented this manuscript with answers to Martin's questions, some from the De La Warr dispatch, some drawn on other sources (i.e., Jourdain and *Declaration*), and some of his own devising.

29. Lindley, 31.

30. Reedy, 530.

31. Reedy, 259. Our emphasis.

32. Fischer, 53. Our emphasis. Fisher continues: "Valid empirical proof requires not merely the establishment of possibility, but an estimate of probability. Moreover, it demands a balanced estimate of probabilities pro and con"—something one will search in vain for in either Vaughan or Reedy's defense of the "standard thesis."

33. Reedy, 552.

34. Reedy, 529.

35. Hume, "First Draft," 63. Our emphasis.

Chapter 17

1. This contradicts the fact that in copying B Strachey added 18,000 words.

2. Reedy, 547.

3. Culliford, 150.

4.

Comparison of Hakluyt and *Travel* (after Culliford, 173)

Hakluyt	*Travel*
Therefore it is to be supposed that he and his people inhabited part of those countries: for it appeareth by Francis Lopez de Gomara that in Acuzamil and other places the people honored the cross. Whereby it may be gathered that Christians had been there before the coming of the Spaniards. (Hack, VII, 134)	And late observations taken in these times may confirm the probability hereof, as first in Acuzamil (so in writing Francis Lopez de Gomara) the natives when they first found, had their crosses in their chapels, and in dedicated groves, by woods, springs, and fountains, which they did honor and fall down before thereto saying their usual prayers, which must make illustration that Christians had been there before the coming of the Spaniard. (5–6)

5. Shown at top of page 239.

6. Reedy, 539.

7. Reedy, 536

8. Reedy, 548.

9. Reedy, 536.

10. Reedy, 537.

11. Reedy, 537.

12. Reedy, "Description of the Leak," 536, and subsequent discussion, 537.

13. Wright, 13–14.

Comparison of passages from B, *Reportory,* **and** *True Declaration,* **after Reedy**		

To Reedy "it is very doubtful Strachey would have marred [the antimetabole] had he been copying *True Declaration*" (539).

B	*Reportory*	*Declaration*
How willing they were to make the greatest exertions, though almost drowning amidst them. (71)	How mutually willing they were yet by labor to keep each other from drowning, albeit each one drowned whilst he labored. (10)	Those which labored to keep others from drowning were half-drowned themselves in laboring. (252)

14. Watson, 76.
15. Watson, 76.
16. Lindley, 31.
17. Jourdain, *Declaration*, and R. Riche, *Newes from Virginia: The lost flocke triumphant. With the happy arriuall of that famous and worthy knight Sr. Thomas Gates: and the well reputed & valiant captaine Mr. Christopher Newporte, and others, into England. With the maner of their distresse in the Iland of Deuils (otherwise called Bermoothawes) where they remayned 42. weekes, & builded two pynaces, in which they returned into Virginia. By R. Rich, Gent. one of the voyage. London: Printed by Edw: Allde, and are to be solde by Iohn Wright at Christ-Church dore, 1610.* ESTC citation # S122506
18. This distinction between the single (ill-omened) and double (propitious) forms of the phenomena also links Strachey's account to Pliny, who relates of St. Elmo that "two of these lights forebode good weather and a prosperous voyage, and extinguish one that appears single and with a threatening aspect. This the sailors call Helen, but the two they call Castor and Pollux" (Cited in Swainson, Charles, *A handbook of weather folk-lore: being a collection of proverbial sayings*. Edinburgh: William Blackwood and sons, 1878, 194).
19. Vaughan, 245
20. Culliford, 188 fn. 101.
21. Percy, George. *Observations gathered out of a Discourse of the Plantation of the Southerne Colonie in Virginia by the English, 1606.* Virtual Jamestown. Web. Accessed 4/1/2010.
22. Percy. Accessed 4/1/2010.
23. Wright, 63.
24. Major, iii.
25. Arber, Edward. *Travels and Works of captain John Smith, President of Virginia, and Admiral of New England 1580–1631*, edited by Edward Arber, a New Edition, with a Biographical and Critical Introduction, by A.G. Bradley. Edinburgh, 1910. New York: Burt Franklin, II Volumes, I: 42.
26. Vaughan, 269.
27. Stritmatter and Kositsky, 454.
28. Among other problems, Vaughan seems to

have ignored the fact that our bibliography makes clear that our text was the one edited by Major, to which Strachey made emendations in around 1617 to account for the death of Prince Henry.
29. Culliford, 188 our emphasis.
30. Reedy, 548.
31. Reedy, 531.
32. Culliford, 149–150.
33. Seven leagues equals approximately 21 miles.
34. Percy, *Observations*, Virtual Jamestown. Accessed 10/1/11.
35. "Grassland-Kent Downs," BBC. Web. Accessed 10/1/11.
36. "A Trewe Relacyon of the Predeinges and Ocurrentes of Momente wch have hapned in Virginia from the Tyme Sr Thomas GATES was shippwrackte upon the BERMUDES ano 1609 untill my depture outt of the Country wch was in ano Dñi 1612." This unpublished letter to Percy's brother is reproduced in *Tyler's Quarterly Historical and Genealogical Magazine*, III:4, edited by Lyon Gardiner Tyler, (Richmond: Virginia Historical Pageant, 1922) as well as on Virtual Jamestown.
37. Reedy, 543.
38. Percy, "Relacyon," Virtual Jamestown, 263.
39. Reedy, 543, fn. 36.
40. See fn. 4 above for a passage in Strachey enlarges the word "cross" into "crosses in their chapels, and in dedicated groves, in gardens, by woods, springs, and fountains." Culliford makes clear that Strachey's "expansion is drawn *from his own imagination*" (174; italics supplied).
41. As we have seen, Strachey followed the same *modus operandi* when he heightened the pathos of his narrative by having *Sea Venture* passengers and crew throw their luggage overboard in the storm and consequently had to omit all reference, preserved in other accounts, to them carrying ashore the same luggage after running aground.
42. Consulted 12/27/11 and 6/26/12.

Chapter 18

1. Wright, 94.
2. Vaughan, 263. Reedy concurs with Vaughan, inventing a scenario in which "in modern terminology, De La Warr has just now ordered the King's son to be conveyed to England" (550).
3. Vaughan, 263, our emphasis.
4. Raleigh, Sir Walter. *Discovery of Guiana*, Part III, 1595: "Those canoas that were taken were loaded with bread, and were *bound for* Margarita in the West Indies, which those Indians, called Arwacas, proposed to carry thither for exchange..." Hakluyt: "It fell out that the Toby, which was *bound for* Constantinople, had made such good speed, and gotten such good weather, that she first of all the rest came back to the appointed place of Zante, and not forgetting the former conclusion, did there cast anchor, attending the arrival of the

rest of the fleet" (*Voyagers' Tales from the Collections of Richard Hakluyt* ([1900]). Web. Accessed 2/38/09.

5. After selectively presenting 2a ("In the time directly following the present; immediately, forthwith"), and ignoring the contrary definitions that contradict his theory, Vaughan claims that "Strachey *clearly means* that the ships will sail 'forthwith'" (263 fn 48; our emphasis).

6. The others are "1. a) At the present time or moment; b) in extended use; under the present circumstances; in view of what has happened... 3. In the time directly preceding the present moment." *The Compact Edition of the Oxford English Dictionary: Complete Text Reproduced Micrographically.* Oxford: University Press, 1971, 1951.

7. Wright, 94, our italics. In modern English this would be phrased, "The Lord Governor and Captain General (i.e., De La Warr) has sent the King's son Kainta into England."

8. As several examples from the *KJV* illustrate: John 5.37: And the Father himself, which *hath sent* me, *hath borne* witness of me; I Kings 1.44: And the king *hath sent* with him Zadok the priest, and Nathan the prophet; John 5.23: He that honoreth not the Son honoreth not the Father which *hath sent him.*

9. Wright, 89. Our emphasis.

10. Vaughan, 263.

11. Vaughan, 265.

12. Travel times upriver and downriver in the tidal estuary of the James appear to have been comparable, at about 2–3 days each way. Examples are given in *The Voyage of Captaine Samuell Argall, From Jamestown in Virginia to Seek the Isle of Bermuda ... Begun the 19th of June 1610* and in *PP.* The former reports that "Sir George Summers ... set sail from Jamestown in Virginia the 19th of June, 1610. The two and twentieth at noon we came to an anchor at Cape Henry [somewhat further than Point Comfort] to take more ballast" (*PP,* 4:1758). A comparable estimate is from *Reportory:* "When we got into [Point Comfort], which was the one-and-twentieth of May, being Monday about noon; where riding before an Indian town called Kecoughtan, a mighty storm of thunder, lightning and rain gave us a shrewd and fearful welcome. From hence *in two days* (only by the help of tides, no wind stirring), we plied it sadly up the river, and the three-and-twentieth of May we cast anchor before Jamestown" (Wright 63).

13. Wright, 89.

14. Or perhaps no version at all.

15. Vaughan, 266.

16. Vaughan, 265; our emphasis.

17. Vaughan, Alden. *Transatlantic Encounters American Indians in Britain, 1500–1776.* Cambridge: University Press, 2006, 51.

18. Vaughan, *Transatlantic,* 51.

19. For Adams, Wright, 94; for Newport, Major, 58.

20. Vaughan, 266.

21. Tyler, Lyon Gardiner. *The Cradle of the Republic: Jamestown and James River,* Volume 1, Wil-

low Bend, Westminster, Maryland (2001), 12. Originally published 1900.

22. Boddie, John Bennett. *Seventeenth Century Isle of Wight County, Virginia: A history of the County of Isle of Wight, Virginia, during the seventeenth century, including abstracts of the county records,* Volume 1, Heritage Books, Westminster, Maryland, 1980, 2–3 (Reprint of 1935 original). Although we find the material concerning Sasenticum and Kainta (Kaintu) intriguing, we are bound to say that we have not yet found a primary source to confirm Tyler and Boddie's statements. But neither have we found a primary source that justifies Vaughan's unqualified and undemonstrated assertion that Tackonekintaco and Sasenticum were the same person. The discrepancy in the names of villages, however, tips the balance in favor of the view that Sasenticum and Tackonekintaco were different individuals.

23. According to the *Isle of Wight Historical Review*'s entry on the Warraskoyak, Jamestown lay "twenty miles to the north-east" of the territory. UKOnline. Web. Accessed 17/1/11.

24. Wright, 94.

25. Vaughan, 263, 265.

26. Vaughan, 269. Emphasis ours.

27. In addition to De Zuniga and Smith, Francis Maguel, the Spanish envoy to Virginia, recorded the incident in a July 1610 to the Spanish Council of State: "The Emperor [Powhatan] sent one of his sons to England, where they treated him well and returned him once more to his own country, from which the said Emperor and his people derived great contentment thro' the account which he gave of the kind reception and treatment he received in England" (Brown, *Genesis,* I:396).

28. *The Proceedings of the English Colony in Virginia,* in Barbour, Philip L., *The Complete Works of John Smith,* I: 191–279. This is a collaborative work edited by William Symonds. In composing *Travel,* Strachey borrowed almost verbatim from *Proceedings,* at a location in the text very near to the one recounting this passage, to describe how native women do most of the work.

29. Percy, *True Relation.*

30. Strachey, William. *The Historie of Travell into Virginia Britania (1612),* ed. Louis B. Wright and Virginia Freund. London: Hakluyt Society, 1953, 4. So it is not implausible to suggest that Percy is the originator of Strachey's *Travel* anecdote about the Indian boy who escaped from the De La Warr.

31. Watson, 76.

Chapter 19

1. Vaughan, 256. Our emphasis.

2. Vaughan, 273. Our emphasis.

3. Vaughan, 254.

4. Vaughan, 268. Our emphasis.

5. Vaughan, 271.

6. This might readily be contrasted, for example, with the three extant copies of *Travel,* a manuscript

that Strachey obviously lavished attention on and did circulate widely.

7. Vaughan, 271.

8. Vaughan, 270–71.

9. Vaughan, 272.

10. Vaughan, 272.

11. Vaughan, 271.

12. Hume, 63. Our emphasis.

13. Hume, 61.

14. Vaughan, 259.

15. Vaughan, 259. Our emphasis.

16. Vaughan, 259.

17. Vaughan, 259.

18. Fischer, 116.

19. Cawley, R.R, "Voyagers."

20. Kathman, David, "Dating."

21. While Vaughan accepts at face value the inflated conclusions of Luce, Cawley and Kathman, and "generally agrees" that the "verbal parallels between the Bermuda pamphlets and *Tempest*" are real and compelling evidence for intertextuality, he also places special emphasis on the claim that "the importance of ... thematic parallels" and more generally even "the impact on English public opinion of the events of 1609–10," which he accuses us of "overlooking or outright denying" (271).

22. Vaughan, 273.

23. Vaughan, 273.

24. A pinnace, which the Sea Venture had been towing before the storm, was also lost (Wright, 4, 62).

25. Vaughan, 273.

26. Elze, 11.

27. Although the influence of such literary works as *The Aeneid* or Erasmus' "Naufragium,"/"The Shipwreck," and *Orlando Furious* should not be overlooked. On The *Aeneid* see Donna B. Hamilton, *Virgil and the Tempest: The Politics of Imitation*. Columbus, Ohio: Ohio State University Press: 1990); for *Orlando Furioso*, Hunter, the Rev. Joseph. *A Disquisition on the Scene, Origin, Date, etc. etc. of Shakespeare's Tempest* (London: C. Whittingham, 1839). We discuss the influence of Erasmus in "Pale as Death: The Fictionalizing Influence of Erasmus's *Naufragium* on the Renaissance Travel Narrative," *Discovering Shakespeare: A Festschrift in Honor of Isabel Holden).* Each of these sources is far more intimately connected to the themes of Shakespeare's play than any of the Bermuda pamphlets.

28. Had we the opportunity to amend this statement, we would omit the word "nearly." There is no case we have seen in which sources other than Strachey do not provide a more solid basis for influence.

29. Lynne Kositsky and Roger Stritmatter, "Dating *The Tempest*: A Note on the Undocumented Influence of Erasmus" "Naufragium" and Richard Eden's 1555 *Decades of the New World*. Shakespeare Fellowship. Web. 6/25/05. Accessed 2/7/09. For further details of the deficiencies of Kathman's case, which are representative of Luce, Gayley, and Cawley, see this online study.

Postscript

1. Gayley, 65.

2. Gayley, 62.

3. The only response of which we are aware is Gabriel Egan's prejudicial account in the 2009 *Years Work in English Studies*, available online at Gabriel Egan.com. Egan devotes considerable effort in this review to uncritically summarizing Vaughan's *SQ* critique. He regards our *RES* article as "comprehensively invalidated in [Vaughan's] expert study." Egan also dismisses our *Critical Study* article as a "repetition of [the] groundless claim that *The Tempest* is not dependent on the Strachey Letter report of the shipwreck of the *Sea Venture*," and states that Kositsky and Stritmatter's "whole argument depends on the reader sharing [their] conviction that long-acknowledged tenuous links [between *Tempest* and Eden] are actually strong ones." The implication that the extent and complexity of Shakespeare's indebtedness to Eden was "long-acknowledged" in prior scholarship is incorrect. Although our article built on the work of Furness, Kermode, and Frey, among others, it also brought forward dozens of corroborative passages that were previously unknown to *Tempest* scholarship. If Egan had read Vaughan carefully he would have realized that Vaughan asks his readers to believe in the impossible. Strachey's 24,000 word "letter" could not have travelled from Jamestown to Pt. Comfort in a single day. As we have noted, all the historical data suggests that the trip — one way only — required two days to complete. Nor could Strachey, whom Vaughan locates in Jamestown "early in the day," have known to include events of July 15 that occurred (conservatively) 32 miles downriver at Pt. Comfort, in a missive completed and launched from Jamestown on the same day. This problem is compounded by Vaughan's speculation that Strachey himself remained in Jamestown (263–266) while receiving incorrect intelligence from Pt. Comfort of events alleged to have transpired on the same day.

4. Paster, Gail Kern. "The Sweet Swan," *Harpers*, April 1999, 38.

5. Interestingly, however, the original *Pelican Shakespeare* (1969), certainly among the top scholarly editions of the plays, edited by Alfred Harbage, included two sets of dates for the plays. One set was the majority opinion date, and the other was the range of uncertainty. For example, most scholars assigned a date of 1608 for *Coriolanus*, but Harbage admits that the play migh be dated as early as 1598. Strikingly, Harbage lists only two plays with ranges of uncertainty ruling out a pre-1604 composition date. These are *The Tempest* and *Henry VIII*.

6. Moore, Peter R. "The Dates of Shakespeare's Plays," *Shakespeare Newsletter*, Fall 1991. Reprinted by the Shakespeare Oxford Society. Web.

7. As listed in Geoffrey Bullough's classic *Narrative and Dramatic Sources of Shakespeare*. London: Routledge and Kegan Paul, 1966. In eight volumes.

8. The five post–1604 alleged sources included in Bullough's work are Camden's *Remaines* (1605), Daniel's *Arcadia Reformed* (1605), Jourdain's *Discovery of the Bermudas* (1610) Strachey's *True [Reportory]* (1625), and Speed's *History of Great Britain* (1611). According to Moore, the only one of these that Muir designates as a "certain source" is Speed's 1611 work, used in a part of *Henry VIII* that Muir and most other authorities attribute to John Fletcher.

9. Niederkorn, William S. "The Shakespeare Chronology Recalibrated," *The Brooklyn Rail*, April 2011. Web. Accessed 7/6/12.

10. "In the middle of the journey of our life, I came to myself, in a dark wood, where the direct way was lost" (Canto I.1).

11. Brayton, Dan. "Sounding the Deep: Shakespeare and the Sea Revisited," *Forum for Modern Language Studies,* 46:2, March 10, 2010, 189–206, 196.

12. Brayton, 196.

13. See Regnier, Thomas, "Could Shakespeare Think Like a Lawyer? How Inheritance Law Issues in *Hamlet* May Shed Light on the Authorship Question," *University of Miami Law Review*, 57 (2003): 377–428; "Teaching Shakespeare and the Law," *Shakespeare Matters* 6:1 (Fall 2006), 1, 11–13. Another fine scholar, who has brought the 19th and 20th century literature of the topic up to date as of 2001, is Mark Andre Alexander. See his "Shakespeare's Knowledge of Law: A Journey through the History of the Arguments," *The Oxfordian* IV

(2001), 51–119. This essay is also available online in the "Virtual Classroom" of the Shakespeare Fellowship.

14. See Guthrie, W.G., "The Astronomy of Shakespeare," *Irish Astronomical Journal*, 6(6), 201–210; Usher, Peter, "Shakespeare's Support for the New Astronomy," *The Oxfordian* V (2002), 132–146; Davis, Frank M., "Shakespeare's Medical Knowledge: How Did He Acquire It, *The Oxfordian* III (2000), 45–48; Showerman, Earl, "Shakespeare's Medical Knowledge: Reflections from the ER," *Shakespeare Matters* 11:3 (Summer 2012), 1, 18–25.

15. The field has been ably surveyed in recent years by Earl Showerman, among many others. See Showerman's "Shakespeare's Many Much Ado's: *Alcestis*, Hercules and *Love's Labour's Wonne*," reprinted in *Shakespeare Criticism 141* (Gale, Cengage Learning, 2012). Originally published in *Brief Chronicles,* I (2009), 109–154; "*Timon of Athens*: Shakespeare's Sophoclean Tragedy," *The Oxfordian* Vol XI (2009), 205–234; "Look down and see what Death is doing": Gods and Greeks in *The Winter's Tale,*" *The Oxfordian*, X (2007), 55–74; "*Orestes* and *Hamlet*: from Myth to Masterpiece," *The Oxfordian*, VII (2004), 89–114. See also Werth, Andrew, "Shakespeare's 'Lesse Greeke,'" *The Oxfordian*, V (2002), 11–29.

16. Cited in Reed, Edwin. *Noteworthy Opinions, Pro and Con: Bacon vs. Shakespere*. Boston: Coburn, 1905, 9.

Bibliography

Alexander, Mark André. "Shakespeare's Knowledge at Law: A Journey Through the Arguments," *Oxfordian* IV (2001), 51–119.

Alexander, William. *The Tragedie of Darius*. Edinburgh, 1603. New York: Da Capo Press, 1971. STC 349.

A True Declaration of the Estate of the Colony in Virginia, with a Confutation of such Scandalous Reports that have tended to the disgrace of so worthy an enterprise. Not in STC.

Acosta José de. *Historia natural y moral de las Indias*. Sevilla: Casa de Iuan de Leon, 1590.

Adams, Charles Francis. *Chapters of Erie, and Other Essays*. New York: A.M. Kelley, 1967. Reprint of 1871 edition.

Aercke, Kristiaan P. "An Odd Angle of the Isle": Teaching the Courtly Art of *The Tempest*," in *Approaches to Teaching Shakespeare's The Tempest and other Late Romances*. Maurice Hunt, ed. New York: Modern Language Association, 2001, 146–152.

Anonymous. *Nouvelle Relation du Voyage et Description exact de l'Isle de Malthe, &c*. Paris, 1679.

Arber, Edward. *Travels and Works of captain John Smith, President of Virginia, and Admiral of New England 1580–1631*, edited by Edward Arber, a New Edition, with a Biographical and Critical Introduction, by A.G. Bradley. Edinburgh, 1910. New York: Burt Franklin, II Volumes.

Archer, Gabriel. "The relations of Captain Gosnold's Voyage to the North part of Virginia" (1602). Electronic text reprinted by Virtual Jamestown. Accessed 20 May 2005. Not in STC.

Ariosto, Lodovico (Baker, Stewart A., and A. Bartlett Giamatti, eds.). *Orlando Furioso,* *Translated by William Stewart Rose*. New York: Bobbs Merrill, 1968.

Bartels, Emily C. *Spectacles of Strangeness: Imperialism, Alienation, and Marlowe*. Philadelphia: University of Pennsylvania Press, 1993.

Bate, Jonathan. *Shakespeare and Ovid*. Oxford: The Clarendon Press, 1993.

"Beaumont and Fletcher," *The Cambridge History of English and American Literature*. Vol. 6. http://www.bartleby.com/216/05 07.html.

Beecher, Donald, Massimo Ciavolella, and Roberto Fedi, eds. *Ariosto Today: Contemporary Perspectives*. Toronto: University of Toronto Press, 2003.

Bellinger, Martha Fletcher. "Moralities, Farces and Interludes of the Middle Ages," in *A Short History of the Drama*. New York: Henry Holt, 1927. 138–44.

Bentley, Gerald Eades *Jacobean and Caroline Stage: Plays and Playwrights*. In Seven Volumes. Oxford: University Press, 1956.

Boas, Fredrick S. *The Arden Shakespeare: The Tempest*. Boston: Heath, n.d.

Bolza, Dott G.B. *Manuale Ariostesco*. Venezia: H.F. & M. Münster, 1866.

Bono, Barbara. Literary Transvaluation: from Vergilean Epic to Shakespearean Tragicomedy. Berkeley: University of California Press, 1984.

Braudel, Fernand. *The Mediterranean and the Mediterranean World in the Age of Philip II*. Berkeley: University of California Press, 1996.

Breight, Curt. "'Treason Doth Never Prosper': *The Tempest* and the Discourse of Treason," *Shakespeare Quarterly* 41:1 (Spring, 1990), 1–28.

Brennecke, Ernst. *Shakespeare in Germany, 1590–1700*. Chicago: University Press, 1964.

Brinton, A.C. "The Ships of Columbus in Brant's Virgil," *Art and Archaeology* 26 (1928), 83–86.

Brockbank, Phillip. *The Tempest*: Conventions in Art and Empire," in *Later Shakespeare*, ed. John Russell Brown and Bernard Harris. London, 1966, 184–201.

Brosch, Mauritz. "Papal Policy" chapter XXII in *The Cambridge Modern History, vol. IV, The Thirty Years War*. Accessed at http://www.uni-mannheim.de/mateo/camenaref/cmh/cmh423.html. January 17, 2007.

Brotton, Jerry. "'This Tunis, Sir, was Carthage': Contesting Colonialism in *The Tempest*," in *Post-Colonial Shakespeares*, ed. Ania Loomba and Martin Orkin. London: Routledge, 1998, 23–42.

Bullough, Geoffrey. *Narrative and Dramatic Sources of Shakespeare*. Volume VIII. London: Routledge and Kegan Paul, 1975.

Cairncross, Andrew S. Shakespeare and Ariosto: *Much Ado About Nothing, King Lear, and Othello*. *Renaissance Quarterly* 29:2 (Summer 1976), 178–182.

Carroll, Clare. *Orlando Furioso: A Stoic Comedy*. Tempe, AZ: Medieval and Renaissance Texts and Studies, 1997.

Carroll, Linda. "Fools of the Dukes of Ferrara: Dosso, Ruzante, and Changing Este Alliances," *Modern Language Notes*, 118 (2003) 60–84.

Cawley, R.R. "Shakespeare's Use of the Voyagers in *The Tempest*," *PMLA* XLI (1926), 688–726.

_____. *Unpathed Waters: Studies in the Influence of the Voyagers in Elizabethan Literature*. Princeton, NJ: University Press, 1940.

_____. *The Voyagers in Elizabethan Drama*. Boston, 1938.

Chalmers, George. *Another Account of the Incidents from which ... Shakespeare's Tempest was Derived*. 1815.

Chambers, E.K. *The Elizabethan Stage*. Oxford: Clarendon Press, 1923. Four volumes.

_____. *William Shakespeare: A Study of Facts and Problems*. Two volumes. Oxford: Clarendon Press, 1930.

Chew, Samuel C. *The Crescent and the Rose: Islam and England During the Renaissance*. New York: Oxford, 1937.

Ciornescu, Alejandro. *Primera Biographia De Cristóbal Colón*. Ferdinando Colon y Bartolomé y las Casas. Aula de Cultura de Tenerife, 1960

Clarke, B.R. "The Virginia Company and The Tempest," *J. Drama Studies* (July 2011).

Cline, Howard F. Guide to Ethnohistorical Sources. Part 2: Handbook of Middle American Indians.

Cohn, Albert. *Shakespeare in Germany in the sixteenth and seventeenth centuries: An account of English actors in Germany and the Netherlands and of the plays* performed by them during the same period. London: Asher, 1865.

Columbus, Ferdinand. *Historie de S.D. Fernando Colombo nelle quali s'ha particolare e vera relazione della vita e de' fatti dell'Ammiraglio D. Christoforo Colombo su Padre*. 1571.

Craig, Hardin. "Shakespeare and Wilson's *Arte of Rhetorique*, An Inquiry Into the Criteria for Determining Sources," *Studies in Philology* 28:4 (October 1931), 618–630.

Cressy, David. *Bonfires and Bells: National Memory and the Protestant Calendar in Elizabethan and Stuart England*. London: Weidenfeld and Nicolson, 1989.

Crusius, Martin. *Turco-Graecia*. Basil, 1584.

Culliford, S.G. *William Strachey, 1572–1621*. Charlottesville, VA: 1965.

Cunningham, Peter. Extracts from the Accounts of the Revels at Court in the Reigns of Queen Elizabeth and King James I. The Shakespeare Society. 1842.

Dauverd, Celine. *The Mediterranean: A Cultural Landscape*. Los Angeles: University of California Press, 1999.

De Costa, the Rev. Benjamin F. "Norumbega and Its English Explorers" (1884), in Winsor, Justin, Ed. *Narrative and Critical History of America*. Vol 3. Boston, MA: Houghton, Mifflin, online at The Davistown Museum. http://www.davistownmuseum.org/InfoNorumbegaDeCosta.html.

De La Warr, Lord (Thomas West). *The Relation of the Right Honourable the Lord De-La-Warre, Lord Governour and Captaine Generall of the Colonie, planted in Virginea*. London, 1611. http://etext.lib.virginia.edu/etcbin/jamestown-browse?id=J1034

Demaray, John G. *Shakespeare and the Spectacles of Strangeness: The Tempest and the Transformation of Renaissance Theatrical Forms*. Pittsburgh: Duquesne University Press, 1998.

Dover Wilson, John. "The Meaning of *The Tempest*," the Robert Spence Watson Memorial Lecture for 1936, delivered before the Literary and Philosophical Society of Newcastle-upon-Tyne, on October 5, 1936.

Dusinberre, Juliet. "Pancakes and a Date for *As You Like It*." *The Shakespeare Quarterly*. 54: 4 (2004), 371–405.

Eden, Richard. *History of Trauayle / in the / VVest and East Indies, and other / countreys lying eyther way, / towardes the fruitfull and ryche / Moluccaes. / As / Moscouia, Persia, Arabia, Syria, Ægypte, / Ethiopia, Guinea, China in Cathayo, / and Giapan: VVith a discourse of / the Northwest pas / sage. / In the hande of our Lorde be all the corners of / the earth. / Psal. 94*. Imprinted at London by Richard Iugge: 1577.

Eden, Rycharde. *The Decades of the Newe Worlde or West India by Pietro Martire d'Anghiera (f.p. 1555)*. Readex Microprint. 1966.

Elton, Charles Isaac. *William Shakespeare: His Family and Friends*. London: John Murray, 1904.

Elze, Karl. "The Date of the Tempest" in *Essays on Shakespeare*. Translated with the Author's Sanction by Dora L. Schmitz. London: Macmillan, 1874.

English-America: The Voyages, Vessels, People & Places (nd) http://english-america.com/places/val61.html. Accessed June 23, 2005.

Erasmus, Desiderius. "Naufragium." Bibliotecha Latina. from *Desiderii Erasmi Roterodami Colloquia Familiaria et Encomium Moriae Ad Optimorum Librorum Fidem Diligenter Emendata Cum Succintum Diffiiciliorum Explanationum*. Tomus 1. Lipsiae: Sumptibus et Typis Caroli Tauchnitii, 1829.

_____. "The Shipwreck." The Online Library of Liberty. Classics in the History of Liberty. From *The Colloquies* (1518) Volume I. November 23, 2004. Accessed 20 May 2005. Based on *The Colloquies of Erasmus*. Translated by Nathan Bailey. Edited with Notes, by the Rev. E. Johnson, M.A. (London: Reeves and Turner, 1878). 2 Volumes.

Farmer, Richard. *Essay on the Learning of Shakespeare*. Cambridge: 1767.

Fazellus, Thomas. Le due deche dell'Historia di Sicilia. Palermo, 1628.

Foster, Sir William ed. "A briefe note of a voyage to the East Indies, begun the 10 of April 1591 ... by Henry May, who, in his returne homeward by the West Indies, suffred shipwracke upon the isle of Bermuda..." in *The Voyages of Sir James Lancaster to Brazil and the East Indies 1591–1603*. London: Hakluyt Society. 1940.

Frey, Charles H. "*The Tempest* and the New World," *SQ*, 30 (1979), 29–41.

Fuchs, Barbara. "Conquering Islands: Contextualizing *The Tempest*," *Shakespeare Quarterly* 48.1, Spring 1997: 45–62.

Furness, Horace Howard. *The Tempest: A New Variorum Edition Shakespeare*. New York: Dover. 1964 reprint of 1892 ed.

Gayley, C.M. *Shakespeare and the Founders of Liberty in America*. 1917.

Gillespie, Stuart. *Shakespeare's Books: A Dictionary of Shakespeare's Sources*. London: The Athlone Press, 2001.

Gillies, John. *Shakespeare and the Geography of Difference*. Cambridge: University Press, 1994.

_____. "Shakespeare's Virginia Masque," *ELH* 53:4 (1986), 673–707.

Gilvary, Kevin. *Dating Shakespeare's Plays: A Critical Review of the Evidence*. Tunbridge Wells, Kent: Parapress, 2010.

Gray, H.D. "The Sources of *The Tempest*," *MLN* (1920), xxxv, 321.

Greenblatt, Stephen. *Marvelous Possessions: The Wonder of the New World*. Oxford: Clarendon Press, 1991.

Grey, Zachary. *Critical, Historical and Explanatory Notes on Shakespeare*. London: Printed for the Author and sold by Richard Manby, on Ludgate-Hill, 1754. AMS Reprint 1973.

Greg, Walter W. Pastoral Poetry and Pastoral Drama: A Literary Inquiry, with Special Reference to the Pre-Restoration Stage in England. London: A.H. Bullen, 1906.

Griffin, Robert. *Ludovico Ariosto*. New York: Twayne.

Guiccardini, Francesco. *The History of Italy* (f.p., London, 1561). Princeton: University Press, 1984.

Gurr, Andrew. "The *Tempest*'s tempest at Blackfriars," *Sh. Sur.*, 41 (1989), 91–102.

Hakluyt, Richard. *The Principle Navigations, Voyages, Traffiques & Discoveries of the English Nation*. London, 1589.

Hall, Grace. *"The Tempest" as Mystery Play: Uncovering Religious Sources of Shakespeare's Most Spiritual Work*. Jefferson, NC: McFarland, 1999.

Hamilton, Donna B. *Virgil and The Tempest: The Politics of Imitation*. Columbus: Ohio State University Press, 1990.

Hamor, Raphe. *A True Discourse of the Present Estate of Virginia, and the successe of the affaires there till the 18 of June, 1614*. London: John Beale for William Welby, 1615.

Hariot, Thomas. *A brief and true report of the new found land of Virginia, Directed to the adventurers, favourers, and welwishers for the*

Planting There. London: R. Robinson, 1588. Reprinted by *Virtual Jamestown.* Accessed 20 May 2005. STC #12785. 1995): 1–10.

Hassel, Chris R. *Renaissance Drama and the English Church Year.* Lincoln: University of Nebraska Press, 1979.

Hays, Edward. *The Labyrinth Cross of Lent.* Notre Dame, IN: Ave Maria Press, 1994.

Hazlitt, W. Carew. *Faiths and Folklore: A Dictionary.* 2 vols. London: Reeves and Turner, 1905.

Herford, C.H., Percy Herford, and Evelyn Simpson (eds). *Ben Jonson.* Oxford: Clarendon Press, 1941. In eleven volumes.

Hopkins, Lisa. "'Absolute Milan': Two Types of Colonialism in *The Tempest,*" *Journal of Anglo-Italian Studies 4* (1995), 1–10.

_____. "Orlando and the Golden World: The Old World and the New in *As You Like It*" *Early Modern Literary Studies* 8.2 (September, 2002): 2.1–21 http://purl.oclc.org/emls/08-2/hopkgold.htm.

Horwich, Richard. "*Hamlet* and Eastward Ho," *Studies in English Literature, 1500–1900.* 11:2, Elizabethan and Jacobean Drama, Spring 1971, 223–33.

Hulme, Peter, and Tim Youngs. *The Cambridge Companion to Travel Writing.* Cambridge: University Press, 2002. Introduction online.

_____, and William Sherman. *The Tempest and Its Travels.* Philadelphia: University of Pennsylvania Press, 2000.

Hunter, the Rev. Joseph F.S.A. *A Disquisition on the Scene, Origin, Date, etc. of Shakespeare's Tempest. In a Letter to Benjamin Heywood Bright, Esq.* London: C. Whittingham, 1839.

Impelluso, Lucia. *Nature and Its Symbols.* Translated by Stephen Sartarelli. Los Angeles: J. Paul Getty Museum, 2004.

"Indulgences." *Catholic Encyclopedia. New Advent.* Web. Accessed January 14, 2006.

Javitch, Daniel. "Proclaiming a Classic: The Canonization of *Orlando Furioso,*" *Comparative Literature,* Vol. 44, No. 4 (Autumn, 1992), pp. 430–432.

Jourdain, Sylvester. *A Discovery of the Barmudas,* otherwise called the Ile of Divels. London: J. Windet, sold to R. Barnes, 1610. (Reg. Oct 13, 1610). Reprinted in Wright 1964. STC #14816.

Kathman, David. "Dating *the Tempest.*" n.d. *The Shakespeare Authorship Page.* http://shakespeareauthorship.com/tempest.htm. Last accessed May 24, 2005.

Kermode, Frank. *The Arden Shakespeare: The Tempest.* London: Methuen. 1954, 1983.

Kernan, Alvin. *Shakespeare, the King's Playwright.* New Haven: Yale University Press, 1995.

Kerr, Robert. *A General History and Collection of Voyages and Travels, Arranged in Systematic Order.* Edinburgh: William Blackwood, 1824.

King, Russell, Paolo De Mas, and J. Mansvelt-Beck. *Geography, Environment and Development in the Mediterranean.* Portland: Sussex Academic Press, 2001.

Kingsbury, Susan Myra. *The Records of the Virginia Company of London,* edited by Susan Myra Kingsbury. In three volumes. Washington: United States Government Printing Office, 1933.

Kinney, Arthur. "Revisiting *The Tempest,*" *Modern Philology,* 93 (1995), 161–77.

Kislak Collection at the Library of Congress. www.kislakfoundation.org/pdf/CR01.pdf. Accessed November 26, 2005.

Knapp, Jeffrey. *An Empire Nowhere: England, America, and Literature from Utopia to The Tempest.* Berkeley: University of California Press, 1992.

"Labyrinth," *Catholic Encyclopedia. New Advent.* Web. Accessed January 14, 2006.

Langbaum, Robert. *Signet Classic: The Tempest.* New York: Penguin Group, 1964, 1987.

Laroque, François. "A Comparative Calendar of Folk Customs and Festivities in Elizabethan England." *Cahiers Élisabéthains* 8 (October 1975), 5–13.

_____. *Shakespeare's Festive World: Elizabethan Seasonal Entertainment and the Professional Stage.* Cambridge: Cambridge University Press, 1991.

Lindley, David. Court Masques: Jacobean and Caroline Entertainments, *1604–1640.* Oxford: Clarendon Press, 1995.

_____. *The Tempest. The New Cambridge Shakespeare.* Cambridge: University Press, 2002.

Looney, John Thomas. *"Shakespeare" Identified in Edward de Vere, 17th Earl of Oxford.* London: Cecil Palmer, 1920.

Luce, Morton. *The Arden Shakespeare: The Tempest.* London: Methuen, 1902.

Major, R.H., ed. *The Historie of travaile into Virginia Britannia expressing the cosmographie and comodies of the country, together with the manners and customes of the people.* By William Strachey. London: Printed for the Hackluyt Society, 1849.

Malim, Richard. "The Spanish Maze," in *Great Oxford. Essays on the Life and Work of Edward de Vere, Seventeenth Earl of Oxford, 1550–1604.* London: Parapress, 2004: 284–288. Foreword by Sir Derek Jacobi. General Editor, Richard Malim.

Malone, Edmond. *Account of the Incidents from which The Title and Part of the Story of Shakespeare's Tempest Were derived: and its True Date Ascertained, 1808.*

_____. "An Attempt to Ascertain the Order in which the Plays of Shakespeare Were Written" (1778).

_____. "An Attempt to Ascertain the Order in which the Plays of Shakespeare Were Written" (1790).

_____. "An Attempt to Ascertain the Order in which the Plays of Shakespeare Were Written" (1821).

Marshall, Tristan. "*The Tempest* and the British Imperium in 1611," The Historical Journal, 41:2 (Jun. 1998), 375–400.

Martyr, Peter. *De Orbe Novo Petri Martyris Anglerii mediolanensis, protonotarii et Caroli quinti Senatoris, decades octo, diligente temporum observatione et utilissimis annotationibus illustratæ, suoque nitore restitæ labore et industria Richardi Hakluyti Oxoniensis, Arngli,* Parisiis apud Guillemum Auvray, 1587.

Marx, Stephen. *Shakespeare and the Bible.* Oxford: University Press, 2000.

Matthews, W.H. *Mazes and Labyrinths: Their History and Development.* New York: Dover, 1970 reprint of 1922 original.

May, Sir Henry. "A briefe note of a voyage to the East Indies, begun the 10 of April 1591," in *The Voyages of Sir James Lancaster to Brazil and the East Indies 1591–1603.* London: The Hackluyt Society, 1940: 22–30.

McCarthy, Penny. "Some *Quises* and a *Quem*: Shakespeare's True Debt to Nashe," in *New Studies in the Shakespearean Heroine. The Shakespeare Yearbook,* vol. 14. Edited by Douglas Brooks. 2004: 175–192.

McKerrow, Robert. *Works of Thomas Nashe.* London: Sidgewick and Jackson, 1905–1908. In five volumes.

McNutt, Francis Augustus. *De Orbe Novo, Volume 1 (of 2) The Eight Decades of Peter Martyr D'Anghera, Translated from the Latin with Notes and Introduction.* In two volumes. Project Gutenburg e-text. Release Date: May 24, 2004 [EBook #12425]. Accessed 20 May 2005.

Miller, Ruth Loyd. "On Dating *The Tempest,*" *The Shakespeare Newsletter.* XL: 1, #205 (Spring, 1990), 12.

Moore, Peter R. "The Dates of Shakespeare's Plays," *The Shakespeare Newsletter.* Fall 1991, 40.

_____. "The Tempest and the Bermuda Shipwreck of 1609," *The Shakespeare Oxford Society Newsletter,* 32:3 (Summer 1996), 6.

Mortimer, Ruth. "Vergil in the Light of the Sixteenth Century: Selected Illustrations." *Vergil at 2000: Commemorative Essays on the Poet and His Influence.* Ed. John D. Bernard, AMS Ars Poetica 3. New York: AMS, 1986, 159–184.

Muir, Kenneth. *Shakespeare's Sources: Comedies and Tragedies.* London: Methuen, 1957.

_____. *The Sources of Shakespeare's Plays.* London: Methuen, 1977.

Murphy, Patrick. *The Tempest: Critical Essays.* Garland, 2001.

Naogeorgus, Thomas. *The popish kingdome, or reigne of Antichrist.* London: Henrie Denham and Richard Watkins, 1570.

Nosworthy, J.M. "The Narrative Sources of *The Tempest,*" *Review of English Studies,* 24 (1948), 281–94.

Orgel, Stephen. *The Oxford Shakespeare: The Tempest.* Oxford: Clarendon Press, 1987.

Pagden, A. *European Encounters with the New World.* New Haven, CT: Yale University Press, 1993.

Poynting, Sarah, et al. "Renaissance Drama: Excluding Shakespeare." In *Years Work in English Studies.* 82 (2003): 385–408.

Quiller-Couch, Arthur. *The New Shakespeare: The Tempest.* Cambridge: The Syndics of the Cambridge University Press, 1969.

Raleigh, Walter Alexander. "The English Voyages of the Sixteenth Century," in Hakluyt, 1598–1600 12 (Glasgow, 1903–5), 10–11.

Rea, J.D. "A Source for the A Storm in *The Tempest,*" *Modern Philology,* XVII, 279–86.

Reynolds, Barbara. *Orlando Furioso: A Romantic Epic by Ludovico Ariosto.* Translated with an Introduction by Barbara Reynolds. In Two Books. London: Penguin Books, 1977.

"Review of New Publications," *Gentleman's Magazine* XIII (168) January to June 1840, 49–54.

Riche, R. *News from Virginia of the Happy Ariuall of that famous & worthy knight Sir Thomas Gates and well reputed and valiant Captaine Newport in to England.* STC gives subtitle: *The Lost Flock Triumphant.* London: E. Aldee, solde by J. Wright. STC #23350. 22 stanzas.

Roth, Steve. "Hamlet as The Christmas Prince: Certain Speculations on *Hamlet*, the Calendar, Revels, and Misrule." *Early Modern Literary Studies* 7.3 (January, 2002): 5.1–89 http://www.shu.ac.uk/emls/07-3/2RothHam.htm.

Rubiés, Joan-Pau. "Travel Writing and Humanistic Culture: A Blunted Impact," http://www.usc.edu/dept/LAS/history/emsi/papers/Rubies.pdf.

Sammut, Alfonso. *La Fortuna Dell'Ariosto Nell'Inghilterra Elisabettiana*. Milano: Editrice Vita e Pensiero, 1921.

Sandwich, Earl of. *Voyage Round the Mediterranean*. 1799.

Saward, Jeff. "The Center of the Labyrinth," *Labrynthos*. http://www.labyrinthos.net/centre.htm. Accessed January 14, 2006.

Shackford, Martha Hale. "Shakespeare and Green's *Orlando Furioso*," *Modern Language Notes*, 39:1 (Jan., 1924), 54–56.

Shapiro, Marianne. *The Poetics of Ariosto*. Detroit: Wayne State University, 1988.

Skura, Meredith Anne. "Discourse and the Individual: The Case of Colonialism in 'The Tempest,'" *Shakespeare Quarterly* 40:1 (Spring 1989), 42–69.

Slater, Anne Pasternak. Variations within a Source: From Isaiah XXIX to *The Tempest*," *Shakespeare Survey* 25 (1972), 125–135.

Slights, William. A Source for *The Tempest* and the Context of the *Discorsi*," *Shakespeare Quarterly*, 36:1 (Spring, 1985), 68–70.

Smith, Hallet. *Shakespeare's Romances: A Study of Some Ways of the Imagination*. San Marino: Huntington Library, 1972.

_____. *Twentieth Century Interpretations of the Tempest: A Collection of Critical Essays*. Englewood Cliffs, NJ: Prentice Hall, 1969.

Smyth, Captain W.H. *Memoir Descriptive of the Resources of Sicily and Its Islands*. London: J. Murray, 1824.

Sohmer, Steve. "12 of June 1599: Opening Day at Shakespeare's Globe," *Early Modern Literary Studies* 3.1 (1997): 1.1–46. Web.

"Some Political and Social Aspects of the Later Elizabethan Period and Earlier Stewart Period," *Cambridge History of English and American Literature*, volume 5. Web.

Southall, James P.C. "Links in a Chain," *The Virginia Magazine of History and Biography*, 41:4 (October 1943), 383–86.

Still, Colin. *Shakespeare's Mystery Play: A Study of the Tempest*. London: Cecil Palmer, 1921.

Stoll, J. Edgar. "The Tempest," *PMLA* 47:3 (Sept. 1932), 699–726.

Strachey, William. *For The colony in Virginea Britannia. Lawes divine, morall and martiall, &c*. London: J. Stansby for Walter Burre, 1612. Virtual Jamestown. Web.

_____. *The True Reportory of the Wracke and Redemption of Sir Thomas Gates* (f.p. 1625).

Stritmatter, Roger, and Lynne Kositsky. "A Movable Feast: *The Tempest* as Shrovetide Revelry," *The Shakespeare Yearbook* (Volume XVII), 365–404.

_____. A Note on the Undocumented Influence of Erasmus' "Naufragium" and Richard Eden's 1555 *Decades of the New World* on Shakespeare's *Tempest*." *6/2/05 The Shakespeare Fellowship Online*. Web. Accessed 4/107.

_____. "How Shakespeare Got His *Tempest*: Another "Just So" Story," *Brief Chronicles I* (2009), 205–266, print edition.

_____. "O Brave New Worlde: *The Tempest* and Peter Martyr's *De Orbe Novo*," *Critical Survey* 21:2 (Summer 2009), 7–42.

_____. "Pale as Death: The Fictionalizing Influence of Erasmus' 'Naufragium' on the Renaissance Travel Narrative, Festschrift in honor of Isabel Holden, fall 2008, Concordia University, 141–51.

_____. "Shakespeare and the Voyagers Revisited," *Review of English Studies* (September 2007), 447–472.

_____. The Spanish Maze and the Date of The Tempest." *The Oxfordian* X (2007), 1–11.

Takaki, Ronald T. *Iron Cages: Race and Culture in 19th Century America*. New York: Random House, 1979.

Thompson, Craig R. "The shipwreck." Translation of Erasmus Desiderius. London: Thomson Learning, 1999.

Tilley, M.P. "On the Name 'Seignor Prospero,'" *Modern Language Notes*, 26:6 (June XXXX).

Tillyard, E.M.W. "The Tragic Pattern: *The Tempest*," in Robert Langbaum, *The Tempest*. New York: New American Library, 1964. 119–127.

Tomson, Robert. "The Voyage of Robert Tomson, Marchant, into Nova Hispania in the yeere 1555. with divers observations concerning the state of the Countrey: and certaine accidents touching himselfe," in Hakluyt, Richard. *The Principal Navigations Voyages Traffiques & Discoveries of the English Nation*, 338–347. Volume IX. Glasgow: James MacLehose, 1904.

Trudeau-Clayton, Margaret. *Jonson, Shakespeare, and Early Modern Virgil.* Cambridge: University Press, 1998.

Tyler, Lyon Gardiner [ed]. *Narratives of Early Virginia, 1606–1625.* New York: Barnes and Noble, 1959 reprint of Charles Scribner's 1907 edition.

Ulloa, De Alonso. *Historia Dell Almirante don Cristobal Colon.* Venice, 1571.

Vaughan, Alden. "William Strachey's 'True Reportory' and Shakespeare: a Closer Look at the Evidence," *Shakespeare Quarterly Fall 2008,* 245–73.

Vaughan, Virginia Mason, and Alden T. *The Tempest.* London: The Arden Shakespeare.

Walter, James. "From Tempest to Epilogue: Augustine's Allegory in Shakespeare's Drama," *PMLA* 98:1 (Jan. 1983), 60–76.

Warner, George F. *The Voyage of Robert Dudley, Afterwards Styled Earl of Warwick and Leicester and Duke of Northumberland to the West Indies, 1594–95, Narrated by Capt. Wyatt, by Himself, and by Abram Kendall, Master.* Nendeln/Liechtenstein: 1967 Kraus reprint of the 1899 Hakluyt Society Edition.

Watson, Harold Francis. *The Sailor in English Fiction and Drama.* New York: AMS Press, 1966. Originally published 1931.

White, John. The fourth Voyage made to Virginia with three ships, in the yere 1587. Wherein was transported the second Colonie. Virtual Jamestown. Accessed 20 May 2005. Not in STC.

Willes, R. *The history of travayle in the West and East Indies.* Done into Englyshe by R. Eden. Newly set in order, augmented, and finished by R. Willes. London: R. Jugge, 1577. STC # 649.

Wilson, David. *Caliban: The Missing Link.* London: Macmillan, 1973.

Wilson, Richard. *Secret Shakespeare: Studies in Theatre, Religion, and Resistance.* Manchester, UK: University Press, 2004.

_____. "Voyage to Tunis: New History and the Old World of *The Tempest*," *ELH* 64: 2 (1997), 333–357.

Wilson-Okamura, David Scott. "Virgilian Models of Colonization in Shakespeare's Tempest," *ELH* 70 (2003), 709–737.

Wiltenburg, Robert. "*The Aeneid* in *The Tempest*," *Shakespeare Survey Volume 39: Shakespeare on Film and Television.* Ed. Stanley Wells. Cambridge University Press, 1987. Cambridge Collections Online. Cambridge University Press. 21

Woodward, Hobson. *Brave Vessel: The True Tale of the Castaways Who Rescued Jamestown and Inspired Shakespeare's The Tempest.* New York: Viking, 2009.

Wright, Louis B. *The Elizabethan's America: A Collection of Early Reports by Englishmen in the New World.* Cambridge, MA: Harvard University Press, 1965.

_____. *The True Reportory of the Wracke and Redemption of Sir Thomas Gates* (f.p. 1625). By William Strachey. Charlottesville: University Press of Virginia, 1964.

Wylie, John. "New and Old Worlds: *The Tempest* and Early Colonial Discourse," *Social & Cultural Geography,* 1:1 (2000), 45–63.

Index